Lord Randolph Churchill

AND

Rudyard Kipling

WINSTON CHURCHILL
AND
EMERY REVES

CORRESPONDENCE
1937–1964

edited with an introduction and notes by
Martin Gilbert

University of Texas Press
AUSTIN

Frontispiece: Emery Reves and Winston Churchill at Le Bourget airport, Paris, 1938.

Publication of this book was supported by a grant from the Sid Richardson Foundation.

The paper in this publication meets the minimum requirements of
American National Standard for Information Sciences—Permanence of Paper for
Printed Library Materials, ANSI Z39.48-1984.

LIBRARY OF CONGRESS CATALOGING-IN-PUBLICATION DATA

Churchill, Winston, 1871–1965.
Winston Churchill and Emery Reves : correspondence, 1937–1964 /
edited with an introduction and notes by Martin Gilbert.
p.   cm.
Includes index.
ISBN 0-292-71201-4 (cloth : alk. paper)
1. Churchill, Winston, 1871–1965—Correspondence.   2. Prime
ministers—Great Britain—Correspondence.   3. Literary agents—
Europe—Correspondence.   4. Reves, Emery, 1904–   —Correspondence.
I. Reves, Emery, 1904–   .   II. Gilbert, Martin, 1936–   .
III. Title.
DA566.9.C5A4   1997
941.084'092—dc21   97-14310

CONTENTS

ACKNOWLEDGMENTS

I am grateful above all to Wendy Reves, who made the preparation of this volume possible. Her determination to see this volume published has been an inspiration and a spur. It was at her request that I began work more than a decade ago on a comprehensive collection of the Reves-Churchill correspondence, the completion of which has been possible only through her generosity. She has also given essential support to the seven-volume set of Churchill's War Papers, the first two volumes of which, *At the Admiralty* (September 1939 to May 1940) and *Never Surrender* (May to December 1940), were published in 1993 and 1995 respectively. In this way, Wendy Reves has continued her husband's ideals and work in making Churchill's writings, and his thought, better known in the world.

In seeing this edition of the Churchill-Reves correspondence through to publication, my thanks are due to the University of Texas Press, and especially to Joanna Hitchcock, director of the press, and Sherry Solomon and Tayron Tolley Cutter, her assistants. Permission to quote from Churchill's letters was given by the Churchill Trust, through Anthea Morton-Saner, of the literary agents Curtis Brown. The Churchill Archives Centre, Churchill College, Cambridge, has provided me with a great deal of material and answered my many queries: I would like to thank especially Correlli Barnett, Keeper, and Moira MacKay, Search Room Assistant.

All the letters and documents published here are from the Churchill Papers, with the exception of a few documents and extracts, whose source is given on the page. The letters from Churchill to Reves in the Churchill Papers are carbon copies; they therefore lack, for the most part, the salutation, the signature, and the address from which they were sent.

No one preparing a book on Churchill's writings can fail to obtain crucial information from Frederick Woods's *A Bibliography of the Works of Sir Winston Churchill, KG, OM, CH,* a work which, since its first publication in 1963 (a year after I began my own Churchill researches) has been a constant companion. The encouragement of Richard Langworth, President of the Churchill Center, Washington, D.C., and President of the International Churchill Society of the United States, has, as always, meant a great deal to me.

Several friends, colleagues, and strangers have kindly, and patiently, answered my queries. I am particularly grateful to Larry Arnn and Julie Kessler of the Claremont Institute, California; Mrs. J. D. Broome, Administrator, Chartwell; Michael Cook, University Archivist, University of Liverpool; Sir William Deakin; the late Denis Kelly; Shiela Sokolow Grant; Lady Solti; Anthony Montague Browne; and David Sclater, Economics Division, Bank of England. I have also benefited from the suggestions of Professor Bernard Wasserstein. In the final editorial stage, I benefited considerably from the copy-editing skills of Lorraine Atherton and from the advice and scrutiny of Ronald I. Cohen.

In addition to my own notes of conversations with Emery Reves and our correspondence, I drew on his interview with Roger Berthoud ("The Idealist Who Sold Churchill to the World," *Times* [London], 7 September 1981) and on material in *The Wendy and Emery Reves Collection,* edited by Robert V. Rozelle (Dallas Museum of Art, 1985). My daughter Natalie undertook the scrutiny of Churchill's engagement cards. The burden of the secretarial work and many other enquiries was undertaken by Kay Thomson.

Editor's Note: Except where typist's errors were clearly involved, I have retained the sometimes eccentric spellings and punctuation used by Reves and his correspondents.

WINSTON CHURCHILL
AND EMERY REVES

Emery Reves and Winston Churchill in Paris, October 1938.

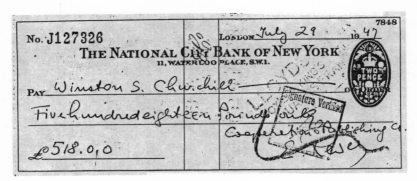

A check dated 29 July, 1947, made out by Emery Reves to Winston Churchill.

Wendy and Emery Reves at La Pausa, South of France.

Ad.Telegr.: Cooperation, Paris

Téléphone: Balzac 57-00

Cooperation

Service de Presse pour le Rapprochement International
Press-Service for International Understanding
Presse-Dienst für Internationale Verständigung

AIRMAIL
EXPRESS

Paris (8:)
33, Champs-Elysées

Prague
July 21, 1937.

Dear Mr. Churchill,

A British statesman suggested me
to write an article on Palestine. I should
like to make the acceptance of this
proposal dependant from the subject
of your next article. I should be most
grateful, therefore, if you would kindly
inform my office in Paris by a short
telegram, whether your next article will
be on Palestine or not.

Personally, I think that both, the Far East
situation, and the Spanish problem would
be more interesting.

As far as I can see from the first reports
your last article has been very well
published on the Continent. I shall give
you full information in about a week.

Yours very sincerely,

The Rt. Hon.
Winston Churchill, P.C., M.P.
11, Morpeth Mansions
Westminster, S.W.1.

R.C.SEINE 280.932 B

Letter from Emery Reves to Winston Churchill

28 March 1952.

Dear Mr. Reves,

Thank you for your letter of February 22.   I
have amended the three points about Volume VI which you
would like to tell the various publishers, and I have no
objection to your using them as follows :-

    1.   That Volume VI is already in a very
advanced state.

    2.   That the last Volume of the work will be
published.   It is however too early yet to say
when the exact date of publication will be.

    3.   That my Memoirs on the Second World War
will certainly be completed.

        In addition you will by now have received the
reply to your inquiry from Lord Camrose.

        Every good wish.

        Yours sincerely,

Winston S. Churchill

Mr. Emery Reves.

*Letter from Winston Churchill to Emery Reves, on 10 Downing Street notepaper
that carried a black border following the death of George VI.*

BRITISH NATIONALITY AND STATUS OF ALIENS ACT, 1914.

CERTIFICATE OF NATURALIZATION

Whereas Imre Revesz, known as Emery Reves

has applied to one of His Majesty's Principal Secretaries of State for a Certificate of Naturalization, alleging with respect to   him   self the particulars set out below, and has satisfied him that the conditions laid down in the above-mentioned Act for the grant of a Certificate of Naturalization are fulfilled in   his   case :

Now, therefore, in pursuance of the powers conferred on him by the said Act, the Secretary of State grants to the said

Imre Revesz, known as Emery Reves

this Certificate of Naturalization, and declares that upon taking the Oath of Allegiance within the time and in the manner required by the regulations made in that behalf he shall, subject to the provisions of the said Act, be entitled to all political and other rights powers and privileges, and be subject to all obligations duties and liabilities, to which a natural-born British subject is entitled or subject, and have to all intents and purposes the status of a natural-born British subject.

In witness whereof I have hereto subscribed my name this   24th day of

February, 1940.

HOME OFFICE,   *Under Secretary of State.*
LONDON.

PARTICULARS RELATING TO APPLICANT.

Full Name	Imre REVESZ, known as Emery REVES.
Address	12a, Lansdowne House, Berkeley Square, W.1.
Trade or occupation	Director.
Place and date of birth	Bacsfoldvar, Hungary, 16th February, 1904.
Nationality	Hungarian.
Single, Married, etc.	Single.
Name of wife or husband	---
Names and nationality of parents	Simon and Gisela REVESZ. Hungarian.

(For Oath
see overleaf.)

Emery Reves's Certificate of Naturalization

Oath of Allegiance.

I, *Emery Reves*

swear by Almighty God that I will be faithful and bear true allegiance to His Majesty,
King George the Sixth, His Heirs and Successors, according to law.

(Signature) *E. Reves*

Sworn and subscribed this 26ᵗʰ day of *February*, 19 4 0, before me,

(Signature) *Cecil Austin*

Justice of the Peace for

A Commissioner for Oaths.

Address { *8 Bolton Street*
London W.

Unless otherwise indicated hereon, if the Oath of Allegiance is not taken within one calendar month after the date of this Certificate, the Certificate shall not take effect.

Wt 3881   10 Bks/7/39   Wt & Sons Ltd   69b/66579/24

Emery Reves's Oath of Allegiance

Map 1. European cities in which Emery Reves placed Winston Churchill's articles.

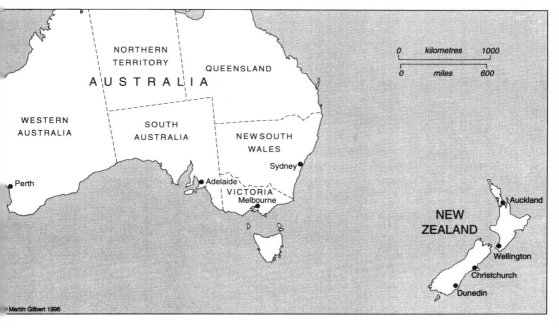

Map 2. Cities in Australia and New Zealand in which Emery Reves placed Winston Churchill's articles.

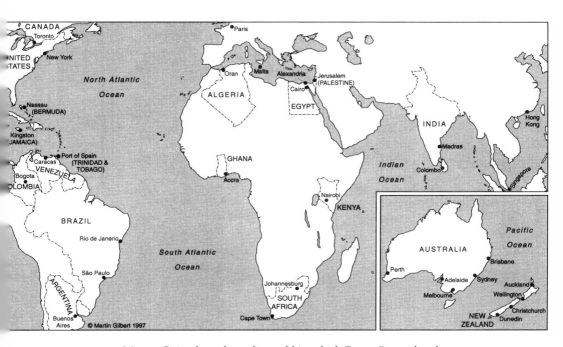

Map 3. Cities throughout the world in which Emery Reves placed Winston Churchill's articles.

INTRODUCTION

On 1 April 1933, the day of the German boycott of all Jewish shops and offices in Berlin, Nazi storm troopers entered an office in the capital to seize its contents and its owner. The office was a center for the distribution of newspaper articles upholding democracy. The troopers wrecked the office. Its owner was Emery Reves. "I had to flee from Germany in the clothes I stood in," he later wrote, "just saving my life." Reves was then twenty-nine years old.

Soon after leaving Berlin, Reves reopened his office in Paris. From there he syndicated to an ever-widening public throughout Europe the views of leading anti-Nazis and leading democratic statesmen. These included, by 1936, two future French Prime Ministers, Paul Reynaud and Léon Blum, and a future British Prime Minister, Clement Attlee. In 1937 Reves met Winston Churchill. Their collaboration began almost at once. Within six months, Reves was placing Churchill's newspaper and magazine articles throughout Europe and beyond. After the Second World War their collaboration continued, centered upon the publication of Churchill's war memoirs. After retiring from public life in 1955, Churchill was a frequent visitor to Reves's villa in the South of France, as the guest of Reves and his American companion, and future wife, Wendy Russell. While at La Pausa, Reves negotiated the foreign language editions of Churchill's last book, *A History of the English-Speaking Peoples.*

The Reves-Churchill correspondence contains the text of more than 200 letters and telegrams from Reves to Churchill between 1937 and 1963 and of about 130 letters and telegrams from Churchill to Reves. There are a further 60 or so communications from Reves's office to Churchill. I have also included at least 80 references to visits that Reves made to Churchill at Morpeth Mansions (before 1939), at Chartwell, and at Hyde Park Gate (from 1946).

Many years ago, when I first came across the correspondence between Reves and Churchill in the Churchill papers, I was curious to know how

Reves had come to be a central figure in the distribution of articles by so many prominent people, all seeking to uphold democratic values. On the last occasion that we met, in October 1980 in Montreux, he told me his life story. He was very ill and feared that his story would die with him if he did not tell it there and then.

Reves was born on 16 September 1904, a citizen of the Austro-Hungarian Empire, in Bacsfoldvar, a small village in Hungary, the only child of Simon and Gizela Revesz. His father, like many Jews in the villages of that region, was a wood supplier and grain merchant. Born Simon Rosenbaum, he had changed his name to Revesz in order to be allowed to do business with Hungarian officialdom. Shortly after his son's birth he moved to the town of Ujvidek, then in southern Hungary, later (as Novi Sad) a part of Yugoslavia. As a young boy, Reves revealed considerable talent as a pianist and was trained by his parents for concert performances. But he rebelled against this path and refused to pursue it. In 1914, with the outbreak of the First World War and the fighting on the nearby frontier with Serbia, the family left for Budapest. Reves was then ten years old. It was in Budapest that he received his schooling, but, he told me, "I had only one desire: to leave Hungary."

In 1922, when he was just eighteen, Reves moved from Budapest to Berlin, where he began to study economics at the university. "Then came the big inflation," he recalled. "My family wanted me to come back to Budapest. I tried to get to Oxford, but my two semesters in Berlin were not enough." He did manage to gain admission to the Sorbonne, where he enrolled in the law faculty. He studied in Paris for a semester but was looking for a university that would enable him to read for a doctorate. "I was in a bit of a hurry. My father was sick. He had lost everything in the war. He spent his last few pennies on my education."

The University of Zurich was willing to accept the work that Reves had done in Berlin and Paris as the basis for a doctorate in economics. While in Zurich he befriended two young men, both Hungarian-born like himself. One of them, John von Neumann, was later to become a pioneer of computer science at Princeton and to work on the atomic bomb at Los Alamos. A victim of cancer at the age of fifty-two, on his death bed he was given the Congressional Medal of Honor by President Eisenhower. The other, William Fellner, later a distinguished professor of economics at Berkeley and then Yale, was a member of President Nixon's Presidential Advisory Council on Economic Affairs. "We formed a little group in Zurich. We were together night and day while studying."

Reves, despite having refused to become a concert pianist as a child, retained his love of music. Not only did he have perfect pitch, but also it was said that he could whistle from memory the entire score of a Beethoven symphony. At the very moment that Reves was studying in Zurich, his twenty-two-year-old cousin, Georg Solti, was beginning his own career as a conductor, which was to culminate in his time as Musical Director of the Covent Garden Opera Company from 1961 and Music Director of the Chicago Symphony Orchestra from 1969. Solti was to receive a British knighthood in 1971.

In Zurich, Reves worked for his doctorate, which was on the economic theories of Walther Rathenau, a leading German-Jewish industrialist, philosopher, and Foreign Minister, who was murdered by right-wing extremists in 1922. The young student needed to earn money to pay for his studies and daily life. He began to work as a journalist, interviewing prominent figures in Zurich and writing articles about their views on current affairs. He discovered that he liked the work. "I never found it difficult to talk to famous people. And then I had a scoop. I located where Lenin had lived before the Russian revolution and talked to Lenin's landlord. It was 1924, only seven years after the revolution. I traced the place through the police."

In 1926 Reves was awarded his doctorate in economics. But journalism was now his métier. He began to publish regular articles, some in an intellectual newspaper in Budapest, in Hungarian, and some in Berlin, in German. Interviewing those with a dramatic story to tell, often based on the most recent political developments, became a feature of his success. "I interviewed Nitti, who had escaped from Mussolini's Italy; Rabindranath Tagore; Thomas Mann; Schnitzler: whoever came to Zurich, I caught them." Reves was also interested in the League of Nations and traveled to Geneva for the annual meetings of the League Council. There too he interviewed the politicians who arrived from all over the world.

While in Geneva, Reves was invited to a press lunch for the French Foreign Minister, Aristide Briand. "Briand made a speech in which he complained about the press, saying how the ministers who are meeting in Geneva quite often agree on the solution of problems, but when they go home it is like standing before a wall, the press judging everything only from a nationalistic point of view, and their people having no idea about the views of other nations." At that moment, Reves told me, "I got the idea that the world needs an organization that can arrange publication in the press of articles on world issues, articles by Englishmen and Germans in the French press, by Frenchmen and Germans in the English press, and so on."

Reves decided to set up just such an organization. The first person he approached was a leading British supporter of the League of Nations, Lord Robert Cecil, who was then one of Britain's representatives at the League. "He said that this was the most brilliant idea that he had ever heard." Thus encouraged, Reves went to see two leading Frenchmen who were then in Geneva, Senator Jouvenal and Louis Loucheur, "the king of electioneering and the richest man in France." Loucheur was then in charge of German reparations. "Jouvenal's reaction was, 'I do not understand why this organization does not yet exist.' Loucheur tapped his fingers on the table and asked me how much money I had. I said about fifty francs, and smiled. He said, 'This is an important problem. If you get French money, you could not do anything in England or Germany. If you get British money, you could not do anything in France. It must be financed by neutral money.'"

Reves had no money and could not find a patron. His father had died, and his family had returned to Ujvidek. Reves went to Germany, where for four years, following an introduction by Professor Georg Bernhard, he worked for an industrial corporation in Dresden, ghosting speeches for the head of the firm and writing promotional articles: "Four horrible years working as if I had no doctorate at all," he later recalled. Then, in 1930, at the age of twenty-six, he decided to start the organization whose purpose he had outlined to Jouvenal and Loucheur four years earlier. Opening a small office in Berlin, he asked Lord Robert Cecil, Loucheur, and Bernhard if they would each write a monthly article analyzing public events from their respective national points of view. They agreed. "I offered them a fee for their articles which was far superior to all my possessions. It started with an article by Lord Robert Cecil. I was able to publish it in six or seven papers in Europe and sent him all the money, which pleased him very much. So I had the first successful month. I was able to get money for these articles from several newspapers. After two to three months I had enough money to travel to Scandinavia. I made arrangements with newspapers there. Two months later I had enough money to go to Prague, Vienna, and Warsaw. In each place I signed contracts with newspapers. I also enlarged the number of my writers and signed up people like Painlevé, Jouvenal, Chancellor Wirth, and the German socialist leaders Breitscheid and Lobe." On his first visit to Britain, Reves signed up two leading socialists, Arthur Henderson and Hugh Dalton.

Not everyone understood Reves's method or motives when he embarked upon his venture. In a letter to Churchill nine years later (24 October 1939) he wrote, "When I started Cooperation in 1930, Dr. Beneš made inquiries as to whether I was a Hungarian revisionist, and the Hungarians were convinced that I was paid by the Czechs. Many democratic Germans at the time thought that I was an agent of the Quai d'Orsay, and in Paris they thought I was a Fascist propagandist. Senator Borah said in the lobby of the Senate in Washington in 1934 that I was an agent of the League of Nations and that my aim was to bring the United States into the League." For an isolationist American leader, this was worse than a crime, just as Dr. Beneš, then the Czech Foreign Minister, was suspicious of any Hungarian claims on his country. But Reves had no ulterior intentions, only the desire to promote mutual understanding by making the views of different countries known to their neighbors, as expressed by their most thoughtful and articulate spokesmen.

From his base in Berlin, Reves found more and more politicians and public figures willing to write monthly articles. He traveled to more and more cities in Europe and beyond to sign contracts not only with the leading newspapers in a dozen capital cities but with many provincial newspapers as well. "In this way," he told me, "all alone, and to my great luck, without any help, in about two years I was able to build up an organization that united about a hundred of the most important statesmen and political writers, including Austen Chamberlain, Bertrand Russell, Sir Herbert Samuel, Herriot, Flandin, Reynaud, Blum, Stresemann, Sforza, Azaña, Madariaga, and about four hundred newspapers in about seventy countries. Naturally the organization was rather profitable."

As Cooperation Press Service grew, Reves was able to guarantee that he could provide articles by prominent people on a daily basis. He sent these articles out from Berlin by telegram and radiogram. "I made an important arrangement in America with the *New York Herald Tribune* and through their syndication with thirty or forty leading United States newspapers from the Atlantic to the Pacific. I also went to Italy and negotiated with Count Ciano, Bottai, and some other Fascist leaders, including Gayda, the mouthpiece of Mussolini. They published several articles I sent them, and Gayda wrote several articles for me, with the approval of Mussolini."

Reves was determined to extend his catchment area for articles even across the border of the Soviet Union, then under Stalin's firm grip. "From Italy I went to Moscow, where I saw Bukharin, Radek, and Borodin, the head of *Moscow News,* the English-language newspaper. I went to Radek to his country dacha for lunch. It was a hot June day. As I was leaving in the car with his secretary he called out—he was standing there dressed all in white with his two enormous dogs—'And if you want anything from Stalin or Voroshilov, just send me a note.' I made very interesting arrangements in Moscow for a regular exchange of articles between the Russian and western press. Unfortunately, four months after my departure from Moscow, all the leaders with whom I negotiated were executed." Stalin's purges had put an end to one of Reves's imaginative schemes.

In January 1933 Hitler came to power in Germany. Two months later Reves was invited to the German Foreign Office by the head of the Press Department, Councillor Wolf, and shown "a pile of files about me." Wolf told Reves that the new authorities objected to what he was doing. "You are only publishing German democratic and socialist views, but never the German national point of view." Reves tried to explain that his organization's purpose was to publish exchanges of views, but the Councillor was not assuaged. "If you wish," Reves told him, "I can leave in twenty-four hours."

Ten days later, on 1 April 1933, the first manifestation of Nazi fury against the Jews was seen, and felt, in the streets of Berlin. Reves was an eyewitness. "Storm troopers took over the streets. They carried out what we call a pogrom. Shouting, yelling, beating, screaming, breaking windows. I wanted to see what was going on. I walked into the middle of the pogrom, fascinated that such a thing is possible in the twentieth century. All of a sudden I realized it was almost lunchtime. So I had the idea to telephone to my office, to say that I am far away and won't be back for lunch. My secretary answered. As she was on the phone she whispered, 'Herr Doctor, Herr Doctor, six storm troopers are here. They are asking for you. They are in the entrance waiting for you.' I told her to look out my passport and papers and come to a little pastry shop."

Reves then went, as on any normal day he might, to lunch at Kempinski's Hotel. From there he telephoned Councillor Wolf at the Foreign Ministry. "This has nothing to do with the government, this is the party," Wolf protested. "I can't do anything. The best thing for you to do is to go to the nearest police station and ask for protection." Reves knew exactly what such a journey would mean. "You had to sign a paper saying you would be taken voluntarily to a concentration camp." Such was the protection envisaged by the Nazi regime. That afternoon Reves met his secretary in the pastry shop, took his passport and personal papers, and went to the station. Afraid that he would be arrested by the Gestapo if he tried to board the train in the normal way, Reves walked to the end of the platform before the train came in and, as it slowly made its way into the station, jumped on board unseen by those who had begun to gather at the barrier. It was the night express to Paris. The following morning, when he was safely in Paris, the Gestapo raided his Berlin office and took all his papers away. He was never to see them again. On crossing the Belgian frontier he embraced the conductor and wept.

Reves opened a new office in Paris, working alone from his small one-room apartment, with a balcony that overlooked the Champs Elysées. He called it Cooperation Press Service. "It became a sort of routine for leading statesmen when they were out of office to write for me. I followed events, and whatever was newsworthy, I telephoned one of my hundred people and asked them for an article. The newspapers got a service which they needed: a news comment service."

From across the English Channel, Reves watched as Churchill began, in March 1936, a series of fortnightly articles on world affairs for the *Evening Standard*. Churchill was also publishing monthly articles on more general topics in *Collier's* magazine, and yet others in the *Sunday Chronicle*. Reves was determined to include Churchill among his prominent authors and used two of his best British contacts, the diplomat Sir Charles Mendl (see the document in this volume dated 29 January 1937) and the former Foreign Secretary Sir Austen Chamberlain (see 4 February 1937), to try to fix up a meeting during one of his visits to London.

"Why don't you have Winston? He's our best man," Austen Chamberlain had asked Reves. "He's already said no," Reves replied. On reaching London, Reves had sent Churchill details of his service and a draft contract. "I'm going to talk to him," Chamberlain promised. "I will see him at the House of Commons this afternoon. I will talk to him." On the following morning Churchill's secretary telephoned the hotel where Reves was staying. "Mr. Churchill would like to see you at Morpeth Mansions." The meeting was to take place that morning, 25 February 1937, at eleven-fifteen.

Churchill's flat was at the top of the mansion block. "I was going up the stairs," Reves later recalled. "All of a sudden I hear his voice. 'Is that you, Dr. Reves?' I cannot see him, but we began to talk, from one room to another. All of a sudden I hear his voice is nearing me. He appears in a doorway completely naked, drying himself with a towel." Bluntly, Reves told Churchill, "I don't think your articles are published widely enough." Churchill was not convinced. "He looked at me as if I were an impertinent young man. I showed him a folder of one article of Austen Chamberlain's newspaper clippings. He closes the folder, goes to the telephone. 'Get me Lord Beaverbrook.' Lord Beaverbrook is not in his office, but Mr. Robertson is there. Asks for a list and what each is paying 'and what I get every month.' I hear him say to Robertson, 'I've just seen that Austen Chamberlain's articles are much more widely distributed than mine.' Then he asks me, what are my conditions."

Reves and Churchill met again four days later, on 1 March 1937. Churchill was still not convinced that he needed to change his existing arrangements. "He said to me, 'I don't need you. Every article I write is published.' I asked him, 'Find out what you are making each month all over the world. I offer you fifty percent of the gross.' He was furious. 'I never pay more than ten percent to an agent.'" Reves persevered. "I wanted him at that moment, and told him, 'I guarantee you a minimum of double of what you are paid now.'" When Churchill asked Reves how he could do it, Reves replied, "I can." "Can you put this in writing?" Churchill asked. "Certainly," Reves replied.

Nothing came of these discussions. During his conversation with me at Montreux, Reves described, in vivid language, the sequel. "I wrote. No reply. Four or five months passed, and I am traveling in Scandinavia. I was just about to take the night boat from Stavanger to Bergen. I went to little places that the United Press or Reuters never dreamed of going to. They were all rich enough papers. I had arrived in Stavanger by air from Oslo. All of a sudden, as I walk from the plane, I heard the loudspeaker shouting my name. I go. There is a telephone message from Paris. Will you telephone Westerham 81 urgently. Churchill wants to talk to you. From Stavanger airport I telephoned Chartwell. 'Look here. Will you propose the contract? But only for three months. And only for Europe.'"

Reves continued on his journey. While on board ship between Bergen and Trondheim he wrote to Churchill (13 June 1937), setting out a detailed contract as Churchill had asked, in which Reves sought exclusive rights on all Churchill's newspaper articles outside Britain and the United States. Four days later Churchill accepted. By the time Reves reached Helsinki at the end of the month, their working relationship had begun. In a letter from Warsaw (12 July 1937), Reves pointed out that as the newspapers in the Baltic countries could not afford the sums demanded by the western news agencies for articles, these papers were "entirely at the mercy of German propaganda," the German agencies being willing to provide their articles virtually free of charge. Churchill agreed to accept the lower fees. By the third week of July, when Reves was in Prague, he was suggesting a topic on which Churchill might write (21 July 1937). Churchill did not agree to this, but he did agree to a further suggestion by Reves five months later (12 December 1937). Reves also encouraged Churchill to send him his nonpolitical articles, such as one on divorce (13 November 1937), which Reves then placed as widely as he could.

In order to get his articles to Reves quickly, Churchill would send them from Victoria Station by overnight boat train and even by air. In times of dramatic political developments, Churchill's secretary would dictate the article over the telephone to Reves's office in Paris. Politics sometimes intervened to prevent the publication of Churchill's articles in particular countries. "Budapest refuses even Christmas article," Reves telegraphed to Churchill (23 December 1937). "Considered too anti-Nazi."

Churchill's advocacy of the rearmament of the democracies and their united stand against the threat of Nazi Germany did not sit well with those in Britain who believed that an accommodation with Germany was still possible. As the leading public critic of Neville Chamberlain's policy of appeasement, Churchill was anathema to those who sought an accord with Germany. Even as Reves was placing Churchill's clarion calls for resistance to Nazi tyranny in newspapers throughout Europe, in London the editor of *The Times,* Geoffrey Dawson, wrote to a friend, "I should like to get going with the Germans. I simply cannot understand why they should apparently be so much annoyed with *The Times* at this moment. I spend my nights in taking out anything which I think will hurt their susceptibilities and in dropping in little things which are intended to soothe them." This was not Churchill's method; his articles were outspoken criticisms of German totalitarianism, militarization, and threats to other nations. In a conversation with me in November 1975, Reves recalled, "When I was in England the Foreign Office reproached me. The senior official there said I was doing a great disservice to England in disseminating Churchill's opinions. I should think it over. It was doing no good. His opinions were not those of England."

From the earliest days of their collaboration, Reves had made it possible, through his Cooperation Press Service, for Churchill's writings and, most important, his opinions to become far more widely known than ever before, and on a fortnightly basis. In the two and a half years before the outbreak of war, Reves later recalled of Churchill, "He was really in the political doghouse. Through my service he got on the front pages of the newspapers in twenty-five languages, with up to a fifteen, even twenty million total circulation." From his initial exclusive rights in Europe, Reves moved quickly to an even wider geographic area, the British Dominions (5 May 1938). He was also able to place Churchill's articles on a regular basis in two South American cities, Buenos Aires and Rio de Janeiro. Later in 1938 Churchill granted Reves "exclusive handling" of his articles in the United States (27 August 1938).

Among those who watched Reves at work was Churchill's literary assistant, Bill Deakin, who wrote to me about Reves while I was preparing this volume: "He was a genius. I was always fascinated by his technique—an intensive study of the world press leading to selling extracts e.g. to the Indonesian press for £10 then multiplied globally. He regarded himself not only as an agent, but a commentator on current events, and he did have an accurate knowledge of the public affairs of his generation—especially of central Europe. His character: he was not a bore but always a stimulating talker and quick to seize any opportunity."

During the Munich crisis, Reves asked Churchill to send him a message for circulation to all the European newspapers. This Churchill did (15 September 1938). When, a week later, Churchill flew to Paris to meet the French leaders, in the hope of stiffening their resolve to stand up to Hitler, it was Reves who went with him from the center of Paris to Le Bourget airport (22 September 1938). During the journey, as Reves later told me, Churchill remarked to him, "The articles I write are much more important than my speeches in parliament. The press print one or two short paragraphs from the speeches, and that is all." The articles appeared in full, at least every two weeks. Churchill's parliamentary speeches, often poorly reported, were in any case much less frequent.

Even as the Munich crisis intensified, Reves was vigilant in Churchill's interest, informing him that he had just secured another newspaper contract for Churchill's articles, this time in Hong Kong (17 September 1938). But the growing strength of Nazi Germany began to show itself in German pressure to prevent Churchill's articles from being published in several European countries. In informing Churchill of the first examples of this, Reves noted that "the terror is spreading all over Europe" (4 November 1938).

Like Churchill, Reves recognized the enormous importance of the United States at this critical time. In Britain and France the strength of proappeasement feeling after Munich was evident. Reves was convinced that there was a need to show "the strength and the solidarity of the great democratic nations," as he wrote to Churchill (1 November 1938), and he went on to explain what he had in mind: "Since years we have been passive and it seems really that the time has come to start an offensive. And I have the feeling that in view of the unfortunate situation in England and France such a renaissance could only be initiated in America."

Three months later, Reves was able to report a breakthrough with regard to the United States (10 February 1939): he was in New York and had secured a contract with the *New York Herald Tribune* to take, and to syndicate, Churchill's articles. Reves would arrange for these articles to be sent by shortwave radio from Holland, so that they would be as topical as in Europe. The first transmission began a month later, just before the German occupation of Prague. That week, Reves went down to Chartwell with one of the leaders of Czech democracy and came away with an article by Churchill that was a clarion call for the unity of the threatened nations of Europe, before it was too late.

In the early summer of 1939 the success of Hitler in establishing a protectorate in Bohemia and Moravia, without war, and the apparent, possibly imminent threat to countries beyond the former Czechoslovakia, led several European newspapers to refuse to take Churchill's articles. In a long memorandum, Reves set out the details of the pressures being applied, country by country, and submitted it to the British Foreign Office (31 May 1939), sending a copy to Churchill. This was the second time in a month that Reves had described the worsening situation with regard to the circulation of articles supporting democratic ideals and the independence of democratic states. After the first of these letters, Churchill wrote to him (8 May 1939), "I am indeed sorry to hear that the net is closing round our activities, through fear of Germany. Luckily, you have already called in the New World to redress the balance of the Old." This reference to the New World was to one of Reves's most remarkable prewar successes: an agreement whereby Churchill would make a series of broadcasts to the United States (20 June and 11 July 1939). The first was made on 8 August 1939. Churchill spoke for eight minutes, his words relayed from coast to coast. The coming of war less than four weeks later, on 3 September 1939, and Churchill's entry into the War Cabinet as First Lord of the Admiralty, meant that this first broadcast was also the last of what Reves had negotiated as a monthly series, and was a considerable scoop.

In his letters to Churchill, Reves revealed that he held the same concept of collective security as Churchill, and the same fear of the effect of further appeasement. In a report to Churchill (21 August 1939), as Hitler threatened Poland over Danzig, Reves gave the view of Hermann Rauschning, the former National Socialist head of the Danzig government, "that the German army cannot make war against England and France and Hitler knows that." Reves added, "So, should England be absolutely firm, probably nothing would happen in Danzig. But if there is the slightest interpretation possible as to the willingness of England to make war, they will undoubtedly attack Poland." Despite the Anglo-Polish Treaty signed four days later, Hitler remained convinced that the English whom he had seen at Munich would never stand firm. Fortified by his own pact with Stalin, on 1 September 1939 he gave the order for the German invasion of Poland. Such British hesitations as still remained were confronted by a burst of parliamentary opinion. During September 2, several leading members of Parliament turned to Churchill to save the country from a second Munich. On the following morning Britain declared war on Germany.

By any standard, what Reves accomplished between the summer of 1937 and September 1939 is impressive. Among the newspapers to which he had circulated Churchill's articles were those in Brussels, Copenhagen, Stockholm, Helsinki, Oslo, Warsaw, Cracow, Prague (in both Czech- and German-language newspapers), and Kaunas (in both Lithuanian and Yiddish). His Dutch outlets included ten provincial newspapers. Beyond Europe, he placed these same articles in cities as far afield as Rio de Janeiro, Buenos Aires, Cape Town, Accra, Perth, Sydney, Colombo, Singapore, Hong Kong, Nairobi, Cairo, and Jerusalem. On average, thirty newspapers reprinted the articles every two weeks: an annual total of 750 different outlets. This was a formidable achievement by Reves, and a remarkable gain for Churchill.

Churchill's first wartime Principal Private Secretary, Eric Seal, wrote after the war that the key to understanding Churchill was "Liberty: a devotion to, and determination to defend the concept of freedom of the individual, and the efforts of the State to uphold that individual's place of honour." Reves's ideal mirrored Churchill's. From the moment of their first meeting in 1937 he recognized Churchill's power to give effect to it both in his writings and in his political activities. Each of Churchill's articles which Reves placed before September 1939 in a European newspaper or beyond Europe was a call for the maintenance and supremacy of the rights of the individual and for the energetic defense of the democratic process, then under such massive attack.

With the coming of war and his return to the British Cabinet as First Lord of the Admiralty, Churchill had to cancel all further newspaper articles and to abandon the series of broadcasts to the United States that Reves had negotiated. The second of those broadcasts was to have been made on September 5. By then, Churchill was deep into his work at the Admiralty, with the German submarine danger and the need to transport British troops across the Channel to France dominating his waking hours. But he did not forget Reves, or neglect him.

Reves was then in Paris. After a few days, he later recalled, "I got a message from the British Embassy in Paris that Churchill would like to see me. I went over on an embassy plane. I gave him the lists of his most recently published articles and the cheque. 'Is that all?' he said. 'No, it takes months to get the distant money,' I replied. He said, 'You know, Chamberlain pays me much less than you did.'"

Four days after Britain's declaration of war, Churchill wrote to the Minister of Information, Lord Macmillan, suggesting that the Minister make contact with "a very remarkable man," Emery Reves (7 September 1939). Churchill added, "I am sure you could not possibly find anyone who would be such help in the Neutral Press, and I beg you to see him."

There was a rather dramatic setback for Reves, fortunately for him only temporary, when, after he had returned to Paris and was embarking on his second visit to London since the outbreak of war, the French security service alerted its British opposite number to the allegation that Reves was "a very suspect pro-Nazi" (21 October 1939). This was strenuously combated by Churchill, who, in a letter to the head of British Military Intelligence, insisted that far from being pro-Nazi, Reves was "an anti-Nazi propagandist" (22 October 1939).

Reves was emphatic in his own defense (24 October 1939). "I am a 100% individualist and hate with my whole heart any form of collective regime, under which I could not exist. I think my whole life and career is indisputable proof of that." Churchill's defense of Reves was accepted by the authorities. Nevertheless, in a bureaucratic oversight, Reves was detained at Heston airport and his papers confiscated. It was a horrible moment for Reves, who had escaped from the clutches of the Gestapo less than six years earlier. On his release from custody, Reves continued to London. He was then in the process of acquiring British nationality, his application supported by a formidable quartet of his former authors: Churchill, Anthony Eden, Attlee, and Samuel. "This will be a unique document in the files of the Home Office," remarked the official who received the application.

Reves began work at the Ministry of Information. In a long letter and memorandum to Churchill (31 January 1940), he set out what he felt was needed with regard to winning the neutrals to the Allied cause: "organisations and local movements inside each of these countries under the direction of prominent leaders of each nation" to carry out "a constant activity" for democratic values "in the press, in the cinema, on the radio, in pamphlets, in public meetings and on the most important field of all, private relations." Churchill recognized what Reves might do. "I can speak from personal experience of his altogether exceptional abilities and connections," he wrote to Lord Reith, the new Minister of Information (8 February 1940). To Cecil King, one of the leading newspaper proprietors, Churchill described Reves as "a most brilliant writer" who "holds our views very strongly." He was given a room in the ministry next to the owner of the *Daily Telegraph,* Churchill's friend Lord Camrose, who was also working for the ministry at that time.

In February 1940 Reves became a British subject, but his work at the ministry was not a success. "I completely failed at the Ministry of Information," he later recalled. "With the exception of Camrose, people just thought that I was nuts when I said that this Second World War proved that the League of Nations, and self-determination, and the right of each nation to its sovereign state—what did it mean? They had all suffered hell. National sovereignty is no protection whatsoever. We must integrate all the nation states into a higher legal order, and we must tell them now, this is what we are going to do when we win the war."

Churchill became Prime Minister on 10 May 1940. Reves was on the French Riviera when the German army invaded France. He was then working with the German industrialist Fritz Thyssen, helping him to finish his memoirs on Hitler's early career: Thyssen had been one of the main financial backers of the young Nazi Party. That day Reves sent Churchill a memorandum of his conversation with Thyssen, reporting Thyssen's view that Hitler "has perhaps the means of sustaining one 'battle of material' like that of the Somme during the last war, but no more."

With the German army advancing rapidly across northern France, Reves hurried to Paris, taking with him the Thyssen manuscript. On reaching the French capital he learned that the German army had broken through the French defenses and was advancing toward Paris itself. As German troops reached the outskirts of the city, he managed to buy a car with all the cash he could gather and drive southward. He was still carrying the Thyssen manuscript. But everything that he had built up since reaching Paris seven years earlier was lost, as it had been in Berlin in 1933. "When I fled from Paris in June 1940," he wrote to me in 1980, "my office and all my possessions were taken away by the Gestapo, and when I boarded a British destroyer in Bordeaux I was not allowed to take with me more than a toothbrush and pyjamas."

Reves did manage to carry the Thyssen manuscript with him on board ship. The destroyer sailed down the Gironde, where he was transferred to a cargo ship that took him to England. A few days later France capitulated. Reves returned to the Ministry of Information. He was determined to push his idea of a pooled or single sovereignty and to tell the nations of the world that this was what the future would hold for them. "Churchill said, 'No. We must wage war first, in order to win it.' I said that once you have won it is too late. Once it is quiet again, people will not want to change." Reves was dispirited by the lack of positive response to his ideas; he told me when we met at Montreux, "I saw that this doesn't work, among all the retired people—ambassadors—who had returned to Britain, and for whom they had to find jobs. They had not the slightest idea about what information was. They wanted to get rid of me. I bothered them too much."

Reves made one last effort, preparing a memorandum in which he argued "that we have got to have a political warfare machine and tell people what we want, where we are going. People didn't want to go back to what they had before. That had failed them." Reves sent his memorandum to five members of Churchill's government: Attlee, Eden, Lord Lloyd, Leo Amery, and the new Minister of Information, Alfred Duff Cooper. "I only got answers from Duff Cooper, who was in full agreement, and Lord Lloyd, who said it was vital." He hoped to send it to Churchill, but Duff Cooper told him, "It is impossible to talk to Winston about anything but war and weapons."

This was a time when a German invasion of Britain seemed imminent, and Britain's lack of resources to meet it was a daily anxiety for Churchill and those in charge of Britain's war policy. But Churchill did not ignore Reves, and shortly after the fall of France, at a time when Britain was being portrayed in the world as beaten, he wrote to Duff Cooper (30 June 1940), "I have long thought very highly of Mr. Reves' abilities in all that concerns propaganda and the handling of the neutral press."

Reves hoped to be asked by the British government to go to New York and help build up the British propaganda organization in both North and South America. His aim, he wrote to Churchill (10 July 1940), would be to convince those in the New World "that Hitler is directly menacing the American nations, and he will conquer them one by one, just as he conquered Europe." To this end he would seek to convince the people of the United States "that principles like 'neutrality,' 'isolation,' 'non-intervention,' 'defence of the national territory but no war abroad,' etc, etc—principles which also Great Britain has followed until she was plunged into war and which have also been the principles of some twenty European nations until they were conquered one by one—are principles of a lost world, which lead every nation to the abyss."

Reves received no official mandate for his plan, despite Churchill's hope, as expressed to Duff Cooper, "that you will not allow it to be weakened by official caution" (19 August 1940).

~

On the night of 16 September 1940, in a heavy German air raid on London, a bomb exploded on the terrace of Reves's apartment, less than three yards from where he was sitting. As he explained to Churchill (18 September 1940), he was fortunate not to be killed. He still hoped to be sent to the United States by the Ministry of Information, but his hope was not fulfilled, nor did Churchill agree to help him obtain a passage on the official flying boat service from Lisbon to New York (13 and 14 November 1940).

Reves was nevertheless determined to go to the United States and to do something effective once he was there. That Christmas Eve he left Britain for the United States, traveling first to Lisbon, where, with thousands of refugees, he, a British subject, waited for a boat to take him across the Atlantic. After two months he was successful, and on one of the very last passenger liners to leave Lisbon before the German submarine blockade became fully effective, he reached New York in February 1941. There, in an office in Rockefeller Plaza, he recreated his Paris system, finding multiple outlets for articles by those who had firsthand testimony of totalitarianism.

During 1941, Reves arranged for the publication of the Thyssen manuscript, which he had carried with him so diligently from France to Britain in June 1940. It was published as *I Paid Hitler*. He also published *Conversations with Hitler*, by Hermann Rauschning, and the memoirs of the Austrian anti-Nazi

Prince Ernst von Starhemberg, *Between Hitler and Mussolini.* The propaganda impact of these three works was considerable, and there was another aspect. "It was a very profitable running venture," Reves later recalled. "Almost all my books were chosen by the Book of the Month Club." In 1942 he published his own first book, *A Democratic Manifesto,* a manuscript copy of which he sent to Churchill (17 June 1942). "It was an unexpected success," being translated into more than a dozen languages. Reves then reworked the book as *The Anatomy of Peace,* which was published in 1945. It was an appeal for the abandonment of individual sovereignties and nation states in favor of world government.

The message of world government which both these books asserted was in contrast with Allied policy, as set out by Churchill and Roosevelt in the Atlantic Charter, calling for the establishment after the war of independent nation states based on self-determination. Indeed, in an advertisement placed in the *New York Times* in 1943, an article by Reves in the *American Mercury* was described, in bold capitals, as "THE FALLACY IN THE ATLANTIC CHARTER!" Reves was convinced that national sovereignties were the enemy of peace and the prescript for further wars.

"After the Atlantic Charter," Reves told me, "I really thought that our friendship was over, and when the war ended and the question of his memoirs came, I heard every publisher and every newspaper had made an offer, I didn't write."

During an interview in November 1945, Albert Einstein told an interviewer, Raymond Swing, that he himself did not have "the gift of explanation" but that he wanted "to commend someone" who did. This was "Emery Reves, whose book *The Anatomy of Peace* is intelligent, brief, clear, and, if I may use the abused term, dynamic on the topic of war and the need for world Government." In July 1946 Reves was in Chicago. "I was invited by a group of atomic scientists at the university, including [Edward] Teller, for a sort of seminar on the political problems created by the atomic bomb: How can we prevent an atomic war. Einstein had said that the answer to the atomic bomb was *The Anatomy of Peace.* After that, we couldn't print enough copies." Before Einstein's endorsement, made during the scientist's first published interview after the dropping of the atomic bomb on Hiroshima, the book had sold about 8,000 copies. Within six months of the endorsement it sold 180,000 copies in the United States and was subsequently translated into twenty-five languages, including, as Reves proudly told me, "Korean, Indonesian, Afrikaans, and three Indian dialects." Its eventual worldwide sales reached 800,000.

Reves was confident that he could do for Churchill's war memoirs what Einstein had done for *The Anatomy of Peace:* that the combination of Churchill's name and his own negotiating skills would be the perfect match. Yet still Reves held back. "He didn't need me. All he had to do was to choose one of four or five hundred offers. But several newspapers wrote to me, knowing my prewar connection. I sent the list to Churchill's secretary, telling her that here are the letters which I had received, without saying that I would like to do anything." In fact, on the day that he telegraphed to Churchill's secretary Kathleen Hill (26 July 1945), Reves also telegraphed to Churchill. He telegraphed again direct to Churchill five days later, twice on the same day. When Mrs. Hill replied that Churchill was "not making any plans for writing books or articles at present" (2 August 1945), Reves sent Churchill three more letters, as well as a copy of *The Anatomy of Peace,* and asked to see Churchill in London. His persistence was rewarded. After two more letters, and when all might have seemed lost, he reentered Churchill's orbit, negotiating, with Lord Camrose, the sale of Churchill's war memoirs in the United States. How this happened was a saga in itself: Reves subsequently gave two separate accounts of it. One, which he dictated to me in 1980, described how Churchill summoned him from Chicago to Miami (see 20 January 1946). The other, dictated to Randolph Churchill in 1966, charted the course of the subsequent talks and negotiations (see 21 and 26 January, 14 September, and 15 October 1946).

Starting in 1946 and continuing for almost a decade, Reves embarked on an intense and constructive exchange of ideas with Churchill, both on the monetary aspects of the war memoirs and on their contents. Reves became a frequent visitor to Churchill's homes in London and at Chartwell. On one of these visits, Churchill learned for the first time how much Reves's life had been scarred by the slaughter of almost all the members of his close family, including his mother. As Jews, some of his relations had been murdered after the Hungarian occupation of Yugoslavia in the spring of 1941. Others had been deported from Hungary to Auschwitz in the summer of 1944.

One of Churchill's research assistants at Chartwell, Denis Kelly, once recalled to me the grim look on Churchill's face as he described what Reves had told him of their terrible fate: his mother, his aunt, and his aunt's children had been driven out onto the ice of a tributary of the Danube and there, isolated and defenseless, had been killed when the ice was deliberately and systematically shelled and broken up. Reves dedicated his book *The Anatomy of Peace* to the memory of his mother, who, he wrote, "was atrociously and senselessly assassinated, like countless other innocent victims of the war whose martyrdom can only have meaning if we who survive learn how to prevent the tragedy of future wars."

Those who worked at Chartwell saw a great deal of Reves. His comments on Churchill's war memoirs were passed on to them for their scrutiny. Bill Deakin, the head of Churchill's research team, later wrote to me, "His services to Churchill were essentially an immense financial contribution as his agent for promoting the Memoirs." The immensity of that contribution was seen when Reves rejected a $1,400,000 offer for American serial and book rights; he was able to separate the two and acquire a further $250,000 for the American book rights. He also negotiated the outright sale of Churchill's foreign-language rights, for which the highest bidder was himself. He paid Churchill £80,000 ($400,000 in the money values of the 1990s) and proceeded to serialize them in twenty-seven newspapers: fourteen in Europe, nine in Latin America, one in the Philippines, one in Egypt, and two in Palestine (the Hebrew-language *Ha-aretz* and the English-language *Palestine Post*). He also secured book rights in eleven European countries, including Czechoslovakia and Greece. He sent these lists to Churchill (2 December 1947).

Reves not only sold the war memoirs, but he also made a considerable editorial input. Several of his letters contain detailed points and proposals, many of which Churchill accepted. Reves also objected to the mass of documentation which Churchill had included within the main body of the narrative (5 January 1948). Churchill was cast down by Reves's criticisms, so much so that his daughter Sarah hastened to reassure him. After initially telegraphing to Reves that he refused to change "the whole character" of the work with regard to the documents, Churchill eventually agreed to relegate some, though not all, of them to appendices.

Reves also criticized Churchill's title for the first volume, *The Downward Path,* which Reves felt "sounds somewhat discouraging" (7 January 1948). He suggested *Gathering Clouds, The Gathering Story,* or *The Brooding Storm.* Churchill found what proved to be a perfect compromise: *The Gathering Storm.* When the second volume was ready for publication in France, Reves sent Churchill the criticisms of several French generals who felt that their fighting spirit had been belittled by Churchill's English-language version and wanted changes. Reves commented laconically (23 February 1949): "It seems that your Memoirs have aroused the aggressive spirit of the French generals which was so sadly lacking in 1939. Perhaps it was a mistake not to publish this second volume at the beginning of the war."

Churchill had originally intended his war memoirs to be five volumes, and all the book and serial contracts had been made on that assumption. When he decided to write six volumes, Reves supported him, but the American serial publishers *Life* and the *New York Times* objected. Reves was active in ensuring that a sixth volume was published (23 March and 1 April 1949, and 3 November 1950). He himself paid Churchill a further £10,000 for the foreign-language rights of the final volume. The issue of the sixth volume proved complex and even vexatious, involving Reves in difficult negotiations (10 May and 30 May 1951). In securing the foreign rights of the war memoirs, Reves traveled throughout Europe. He sent Churchill a full report of his successes, and also some failures, including in Germany (2 August 1951).

Reves continued to send Churchill his points for each of the volumes throughout 1950, 1951, and 1952, when the war memoirs were completed and Churchill had returned to Downing Street as Prime Minister. In 1954, while still Prime Minister, Churchill received a letter from Reves about his next intended book, which they had discussed together, *A History of the English-Speaking Peoples* in four volumes (31 March 1954). Churchill had completed the work on this book at the time of the outbreak of war in 1939. Within eight months of receiving Reves's letter, Churchill asked him to handle all foreign-language book and serial rights, as he had done for the war memoirs. "It is a great pleasure to me," Churchill wrote to the owner of the English-language serialization rights (21 November 1954), "to feel that these books are translated into 26 languages and I am sure no one could have done it except Reves who buzzed around the world for nearly a year making contacts."

In April 1955 Churchill left Downing Street and retired from public life. His final literary work remained to be completed, and he assembled a team of researchers to help him, headed first by Bill Deakin and then by Alan Hodge. Within a month of Churchill's retirement, Reves was corresponding with him about the apparent unsuitability of "English-speaking peoples" in a title intended for European readers (20 May and 14 June 1955). In January 1956 Churchill went for the first time to the villa which Reves had just bought and restored in the South of France, La Pausa, above Roquebrune, where he was made welcome by Reves and his future wife, Wendy Russell. Here Churchill worked on his book, painted, and sought privacy. This was broken only once, to Reves's distress, by *Paris-Match* (20 November 1958). Life at La Pausa was idyllic. Churchill called the villa Pausaland and was to return there ten times, usually twice a year.

One of those who often accompanied Churchill to La Pausa, and who saw much of Reves in Churchill's last decade both there and in London, was Anthony Montague Browne, Churchill's Private Secretary and confidant. He later recalled, in conversation with me while I was preparing this introduction, that Reves could be "deeply cynical and suspicious of people" and that he liked to be alone with Churchill when business matters were being discussed. Among the proposals that Reves brought to Churchill was the publication of the official minutes he had exchanged with Anthony Eden during the Second World War. It would have made an impressive and no doubt commercially successful volume, and Eden was keen, but it seems that Churchill's trustees wanted to retain the Churchill side of the exchanges for his own future biographer. "The Trust, of course, gives full weight to any wishes I express," Churchill explained to Eden, "but nevertheless these papers are not my personal property." Reves was disappointed, but having secured the foreign-language rights of Churchill's war memoirs, he had the satisfaction, year after year, of seeing the volumes appear in many languages and in many editions: multivolume, single volume, paperback, and serial.

Montague Browne was also a witness to Churchill's relaxation at La Pausa. "Reves had been a child prodigy, a pianist, and had a remarkable knowledge of music," he recalled. "He introduced Winston to classical music. As a result of this, Winston became very fond of Brahms' First Symphony." Nor was Brahms the only composer to whose works Churchill was introduced at La Pausa. In a letter to his wife, Clementine, in February 1956, Churchill wrote, "My hosts are very artistic, they paint and collect. More than that, they delight in the various painters of Europe and I am having an education in art which is beneficial. Also they play Mozart and others on these multiplied gramophones."

While at La Pausa, Churchill completed *A History of the English-Speaking Peoples.* Reves's part in this can be seen in a letter that Churchill wrote to Alan Hodge. "Reves has given me back the amended text which I proposed of the Preface," Churchill wrote. "He has had lengthy telephonings with French, German, Italian and Scandinavian publishers, showing what they want for their editions." Reves also negotiated Spanish, Portuguese, Norwegian, and Hebrew editions.

Churchill was comfortable and cosseted at La Pausa. Emery and Wendy were diligent and enthusiastic hosts. They invited only those whom he wished to see, among them Konrad Adenauer and Paul Reynaud. Shortly before he died, Reves estimated—in an interview with the writer Roger Berthoud—that Churchill had spent a total of four hundred days at the villa. To me he had spoken of "more than a thousand meals" together. But something went wrong: several of Churchill's family members felt that Reves and Wendy were monopolizing him in his old age and that, as a result of the attractions of La Pausa, he was seeing less and less of his family and friends in England. On one occasion, at a luncheon honoring President Coty of France, Lady Churchill was upset that the President seemed to regard Wendy Russell rather than herself as the hostess. Eventually there was a breach. When, in the late summer of 1960, Churchill suggested a further visit, which would have been his eleventh within five years, Reves explained why he felt he could not ask him at that moment, expressing his distress in a long letter to Churchill (21 August 1960). After that, Churchill, then aged eighty-five, went elsewhere for his relaxation, even when he was in the South of France. But even after the breach he continued to see Reves and Wendy, as his engagement cards show. He even offered to be the Best Man at their wedding. Reves visited Chartwell only six months before Churchill died.

I first met Reves in 1965, shortly after Churchill's death, when he came to see Randolph Churchill, for whom I was then working, at Randolph's home in Suffolk. Within only a few minutes of meeting him, I was struck by his devotion not only to Churchill's literary sales and receipts, which he had so greatly enhanced, but also to Churchill's philosophy and to the need even in 1965 to make that philosophy as widely known as possible. I later had the chance of several long talks with Reves: at Randolph's funeral three years after our first meeting, at La Pausa in 1978, and at Montreux on Lake Geneva in 1980, a year before his death, when he spoke at length about his life and career.

In his library at La Pausa, Reves showed me the many foreign editions of Churchill's war memoirs, each of which he had negotiated. As someone who had lost so many family members as a result of wartime persecution, he had decided not to place the book with a German publisher. There was also the problem created by the refusal of the British and American occupation authorities in Germany to grant proper terms to authors. The German-language edition was therefore published in the Swiss capital, Bern, by Alfred Scherz. Reves also showed me with pride an array of foreign-language editions of the war memoirs, including the Swedish, Finnish, Japanese and Hebrew editions, two Portuguese editions (one from Portugal and one from Brazil), and three Spanish-language editions, two published in Barcelona (in 1954 and 1965) and a third in Buenos Aires (between 1948 and 1955). This latter publisher, Reves commented with resignation, had never paid, despite a lawsuit. He also showed me the equally impressive array of foreign-language editions of *A History of the English-Speaking Peoples.*

In addition to what he told me at our meetings, Reves also corresponded with me from 1969 to 1980 about his work for Churchill both before and after the war, and about his own life. He had a gift of storytelling and of vivid recollection. This book documents the part he played from 1937 in making Winston Churchill's articles, books, and ideas better known in Europe and beyond. I would like to dedicate it to his memory.

PART ONE

TAKING FIRST STEPS
1937

FORGING A PARTNERSHIP
1938

MOVING TOWARDS WAR
1939

TAKING FIRST STEPS

1937

Emery Reves[1] to Winston S. Churchill

18 February 1937

Batt's Hotel
Dover Street
London W.I.[2]

Dear Sir,

I have pleasure in sending you enclosed a letter of introduction from Sir Charles Mendl[3] of the Embassy in Paris, who has requested me to give you detailed information of an international organization called COOPERATION, which might interest you. I am also enclosing a letter from Sir Austen Chamberlain.[4]

I am staying for some days at Batt's Hotel, Dover Street, W.I., and should be most grateful if you would have the kindness to let me know whether you can receive me, and at what time this would be most convenient to you.

Thanking you in advance, I beg to remain

Yours very sincerely
I. Révész

1.   In 1939 Imre Révész changed his name to Emery Reves: it is in this form that I have headed, throughout this volume, each of the letters and documents sent by him or to him.

2.   Reves wrote this letter on his office note paper, headed "Cooperation Press Service, 33 Champs Elysées, Paris."

3.   Sir Charles Mendl, the Press Attaché at the British Embassy in Paris. Three years older than Churchill, he was educated, like Churchill, at Harrow.

4.   Sir Austen Chamberlain, a former Foreign Secretary (in the government in which Churchill was Chancellor of the Exchequer). He was Neville Chamberlain's half brother.

*I have exceptionally included the next two letters out of chronological se-
quence, as they were enclosed with Emery Reves's letter of 18 February and had
not therefore been seen by Churchill before he received that letter, which constituted their first communication.*

~

Sir Charles Mendl to Winston S. Churchill

29 January 1937   British Embassy
                                                                    Paris

My dear Winston,
      Would you receive Dr. Revesz who owns & runs an organization called
'Co-operation'.
      His organ publishes & pays well for articles of Statesmen in nearly all the
big newspapers of Europe & America. He covers 25 countries in Europe. He
lately published some articles of Sir A. Chamberlain in about 75 papers & I
believe that he might be a very useful channel for your excellent views. You
will find him a most interesting person, a Hungarian by birth who has lived
the last 10 years in Paris. He publishes articles of about 80 statesmen & his
organ wishes to create better international understanding by informing the
public of other countries the views held by the statesmen of the different
nations.
    · If you will receive him & listen to what he has to say I shall be grateful.
                                                                Yours ever,
                                                            Charles Mendl

P.S. Dr. Revesz says that for reference if you required then you could refer to
Sir A. Chamberlain, Lord Cecil[1] & Sir Herbert Samuel.[2]

      1.   Viscount Cecil of Chelwood (formerly Lord Robert Cecil), a leading supporter
of the League of Nations. In 1937 he was awarded the Nobel Peace Prize for his efforts
to promote international harmony.
      2.   Sir Herbert Samuel, a leading Liberal politician, who had been a member of
the pre-1914 Cabinet in which Churchill was First Lord of the Admiralty. Samuel was
created Viscount in 1937.

Sir Austen Chamberlain to Winston S. Churchill

4 February 1937   [1]

My dear Winston,
      Dr. Revesz, founder and director of 'Co-operation' would like very much
to make, if possible, arrangements with you for the publication of your articles on the continent of Europe, as he has done for those of mine published

in the Daily Telegraph. He has certainly given them a wide distribution and my relations with him have been very satisfactory. I venture, therefore, to give him this letter of introduction and to express the hope that you will receive him.

Yours sincerely,
Austen Chamberlain

    1.   Whenever the writer's address is not given at the top of a letter, or there is no salutation or signature at the bottom, the reader should assume that it was absent in the copy of the letter as seen by me (often a carbon copy in Churchill's papers). When such a document contains evidence of the place of composition, I have given it in brackets.

Emery Reves to Winston S. Churchill

[18 February 1937] [1]

COOPERATION PRESS SERVICE (DR. REVESZ)

"COOPERATION, Press Service" was founded in 1930. The creation of this organization was the result of long discussions between Statesmen and Newspaper Editors of various nationalities, who deplored the fact that public opinion in almost all countries was incapable of understanding the mentality and feelings of other nations—a fact that, above all, prevented the realisation of a better international understanding.

COOPERATION was founded on the idea that it was necessary to create an independent international organization to bring together the most important Statesmen and pressmen of all countries, as well as the most important newspapers of the whole world, in order to promote a regular exchange of views in the world press. The programme of COOPERATION excludes propaganda for any positive idea. This programme endeavours to clarify the most topical political and economic problems of international interest from the point of view of all the nations interested, and to give the public of all countries direct authoritative information as to the opinions held by other nations on current events.

After nine years' activity, COOPERATION became the channel for the publication of articles by some hundred political leaders of all nations who are perhaps the best known to-day. The list of contributors is, of course, not complete[:] COOPERATION's programme being to appeal at any time to those most competent to deal with special topical subjects. COOPERATION publishes 12–15 articles in a month, which appear regularly in the most important newspapers of some sixty countries. This success is due to the correspondence of COOPERATION'S programme with that of the big newspapers, which have always endeavoured to explain the major problems of international life in their columns by the ablest and most competent authorities.

COOPERATION has not operated in the United States up to now for two special reasons: 1) it was necessary to make the scheme perfectly working before approaching the press of the United States; 2) it was indispensable that articles which are topical features and comments on world events should be transmitted by cable or wireless beams.

Ever since the war, but particularly during the past year, the press of the United States has shown an increasing interest in international affairs. American press associations with foreign staffs have had vastly increased appropriations for their work. They have sent their best reporters abroad to see what was happening and to report to them by cable and radio: they have NOT engaged foreign experts to interpret the events of the day for them and to give their own views on the events and the policy of their own countries.

The American method has had great advantages. American correspondents have known exactly what the American public was interested in reading. But the method has also had its disadvantages. It is extremely difficult for foreign correspondents to explain exactly why a certain nation or a certain Government is pursuing a particular policy and thus to get to the root of events. It seems to be obvious that owing to the more and more complicated world situation the American method of news-gathering should be completed by a service of comments and views on foreign events by the most outstanding statesmen and journalists of the countries concerned.

COOPERATION, offering, as it does, the opinions of experts of all nationalities, may be said to possess a service well calculated to supplement American foreign news sources for newspapers in the United States. COOPERATION articles, frequently of a controversial nature, could, for example, be printed side by side with comments on the same subject written by a local expert of the city in which the articles appear. This method of presentation has been proved in all countries to stimulate controversy and the public interest.

COOPERATION proposes to initiate a bi- or tri-weekly cable or wireless service of topical comments on the major problems of international life, written by the greatest economic and political writers of the leading nations.

1.   This document was enclosed in Reves's letter to Churchill of 18 February 1937.

Emery Reves to Winston S. Churchill[1]

[18 February 1937]   33 Champs-Elysées,
                                                                        Paris

I confirm our agreement whereby COOPERATION has the exclusive rights of publication of all my newspaper articles all over the world. You have full authority for the exclusive handling of my articles in all countries including the United States of America.

1.   This draft agreement was drawn up for Churchill's signature and included with the first communication from Reves of 18 February 1937.

Winston S. Churchill: engagement cards [1]

25 February 1937   11 Morpeth Mansions
                                                               London

11.15   Dr. Revesz at flat.

1.   Churchill's secretaries entered his forthcoming engagements on monthly cards. A scrutiny of these cards, which are now at the Churchill Archive Centre, Churchill College, Cambridge, revealed that Churchill and Reves met in London or at Chartwell at least eighty-two times over a period of twenty-seven years.

Emery Reves to Winston S. Churchill

25 February 1937   Batt's Hotel
                                                            Dover Street
                                                          London W.1.

Dear Mr. Churchill,

I should like to thank you very sincerely for your kindness in receiving me this morning.

I have had a conversation with Mr. Robertson [1] this afternoon. His attitude was that should Cooperation come to an arrangement satisfactory to you, they would be glad to hand over to us their arrangements. Their existing arrangements are the following:

Paris-Soir	£9.9.0. [2]
Telegraaf, Amsterdam	£5.5.0.
Dagens Nyheter, Stockholm	£4.4.0.
Berlingske Tidende, Copenhagen	£4.9.0.

These arrangements we could, of course, take over and carry out by trying to improve their terms, which are, in my opinion, not very favourable. The agreement I would venture to propose would be identical with the agreement we have with Sir Austen Chamberlain, which is as follows:

Cooperation will have the exclusive rights of publication of all your articles of international interest, outside the British Empire and North America. You will be kind enough to let us have, at the earliest possible moment, a copy of all your articles, so that we should be able to arrange for translations, and, if possible, simultaneous publication in as many countries as possible.

Cooperation will remit to you as remuneration 60% of the gross proceeds received from all newspapers. We will cover our expenses, translations, telegrams, telephones, stereotyping, circulating, etc. out of the remaining 40%.

The 60% honorarium will be guaranteed to you with a minimum of £25 for each article. This guaranteed minimum will be remitted within three weeks following the publication of each article, and at the end of each Quarter an exact statement will be submitted.

This arrangement will be valid for a trial period until the end of 1937, and shall continue from year to year by mutual agreement.

I should be very much obliged to you if you would be kind enough to let me know whether you agree with the terms of this proposal. I am absolutely convinced that you will find the diffusion of your articles satisfactory.

I think that Sir Austen Chamberlain, Lord Cecil or Sir Herbert Samuel will be pleased to let you know their experiences of their collaboration with us.

I shall be in London until the end of this week, possible a few days longer, and am entirely at your disposal, should you wish to have some further information.

I beg to remain,

Yours very truly,
I. Révész

1.   William Harris Robertson was the Business Manager of the *Evening Standard*, Lord Beaverbrook's London evening newspaper, for which Churchill had been writing fortnightly articles since April 1936.

2.   In 1996 the equivalent of £9.9.0 (9 guineas) would be approximately £250 ($375). The sterling equivalent of £1 would be just over £25 ($37.50).

Emery Reves to Winston S. Churchill

[25 February 1937] [1]

CONTRIBUTORS OF 'COOPERATION'

Mr. Léon BLUM, Prime Minister of France

Mr. Edouard DALADIER, Former Prime Minister of France, War Minister of France

Mr. Albert SARRAUT, Former Prime Minister of France

Mr. PAUL-BONCOUR, Former Prime Minister of France

Mr. Pierre-Etienne FLANDIN, Former Prime Minister of France

Mr. Henry BERENGER, President of the Foreign Affairs Commission of the French Senate

Mr. GEORGES-BONNET, French Ambassador to Washington, Former Minister of Commerce of France

Mr. François de TESSAN, Under-Secretary of State of France

Mr. Pierre COT, Air Minister of France

Mr. Paul REYNAUD, Former Minister of France
Mr. Marcel RAY, Minister of France
Admiral LACAZE, Former Minister of the Navy of France
Mr. Guiseppe BOTTAI, Former Governor of Roma
Mr. E. ROSSONI, Minister of Agriculture of Italy
Mr. Virginio GAYDA, Editor of "Giornale d'Italia"
Comte SFORZA, Former Minister of Foreign Affairs of Italy
Mr. Guglielmo FERRERO, Professor at the Geneva University
Professor EINSTEIN
Mr. Thomas MANN
Professor Georg BERNHARD
Professor M. J. BONN of the London School of Economics
Mr. Edouard BENES, President of the Czechoslovakian Republic
Dr. Kamil KROFTA, Minister of Foreign Affairs of Czechoslovakia
Mr. N. TITULESCO, Former Minister for Foreign Affairs of Rumania
Mr. N. MATUSZEWSKI, Former Minister of Finance of Poland
Dr. Kurt SCHUSCHNIGG, Chancellor of Austria
Mr. de KANYA, Minister for Foreign Affairs of Hungary
Professor Elemer HANTOS, Former Secretary of State of Hungary
Mr. ULMANIS, Prime Minister of Latvia
Mr. V. MUNTERS, Foreign Minister of Latvia
Mr. LOZORAITIS, Minister for Foreign Affairs of Lithuania
Mr. SELJAMA, Minister for Foreign Affairs of Estonia
Mr. HANSSON, Prime Minister of Sweden
Mr. UNDEN, Delegate of Sweden to the League of Nations
Mr. MOWINCKEL, Former Prime Minister of Norway
Mr. KOHT, Foreign Minister of Norway
Mr. MUNCH, Minister for Foreign Affairs of Denmark
Mr. Alvarez del VAYO, Foreign Minister of Spain
Mr. Augusto BARCIA, Former Prime Minister of Spain
Mr. Alejandro LERROUX, Former Prime Minister of Spain
Mr. Angel Ossorio y GALLARDO, Ambassador of Spain in Brussels
Mr. Gil ROBLES, Former War Minister of Spain
Dr. Gregorio MARANON, Madrid
Mr. Salvador de MADARIAGA, Former Delegate of Spain to the League
  of Nations
Mr. Henry L. STIMSON, Former Minister for Foreign Affairs of the
  U.S.A.
Prof. Rexford G. TUGWELL, Under-Secretary of State for Agriculture of
  the U.S.A.
Mr. Owen D. YOUNG
Professor Raymond MOLEY
Mr. James P. WARBURG, Vice-President of the Bank of Manhattan
  Company

Colonel HOUSE
Dr. Nicholas Murray BUTLER
Professor James T. SHOTWELL
Mr. Nicholas ROOSEVELT
Mr. Norman DAVIS

Etc . . . Etc . . .[2]

1. This document was enclosed in Reves's letter to Churchill of 25 February 1937.
2. This was how the list, as sent to Churchill, ended.

Violet Pearman[1] *to Winston S. Churchill*

27 February 1937

Mr. Churchill,
    Dr. Revesz telephoned to say that he would be glad if you could give him a short interview either tomorrow or Monday as he has to go away on Tuesday.
    Tel No. Regent 1622.

1. Violet Pearman, Churchill's secretary since 1929. Her duties included Churchill's literary correspondence.

Winston S. Churchill: engagement cards

1 March 1937

    6.30 p.m.   Dr. Revesz.

Emery Reves to Winston S. Churchill

1 March 1937

Dear Mr. Churchill,
    I have pleasure in confirming our conversation of this afternoon as follows:
    1. COOPERATION will have the exclusive rights of publication of all your articles of international interest, outside the British Empire and North America.
    2. You will let us have in Paris, at your earliest possible convenience, three copies of all your articles, so that we should be able to arrange for translations and, if possible, simultaneous publication in all countries.
    3. The arrangements existing between you and continental newspapers will be taken over and carried out by COOPERATION. These newspapers are the following which now pay for each article:

Paris-Soir	£9.9.0.
Telegraaf, Amsterdam	£5.5.0.
Dagens Nyheter, Stockholm	£4.4.0.
Berlingske Tidende, Copenhagen	£4.9.0.

Needless to say we shall do our utmost to retain friendly relations with these newspapers. We shall try, however, after some time to improve the terms for the publication of your articles in France, Holland, Denmark and Sweden, but we shall give you information in advance of all possible changes, and nothing will be undertaken without your consent.

4. We shall collect the payments of these four newspapers which shall be remitted to you entirely without any deduction.

5. Concerning publication in other countries, 50% of the gross proceeds will be remitted to you as remuneration. All our expenses, such as travelling, telegrams, telephones, stereotyping, circulating, etc, will be covered out of the remaining 50%.

6. This arrangement will come into force in the middle of March.

Violet Pearman to Winston S. Churchill

3 March 1937
URGENT

Mr. Churchill,

To remind you to talk to Mr. Robertson about the foreign (small) articles about which Dr. Revesz spoke last night, so that they will not spoil the market for Cooperation's enquiries on the Continent.

Violet Pearman to Emery Reves

3 March 1937   11 Morpeth Mansions

Dear Dr. Revesz,

Mr. Churchill wishes me to thank you for your letter of the 1st. Owing to certain questions of a legal character which have been raised by Dr. Meyer,[1] nothing can be done immediately. It is probable that the remaining March article will have to be allocated upon the existing basis. Meanwhile Mr. Churchill will consider the position and will write to you again. He cannot give you at present any authorisation to deal for him, although perhaps this may be arranged at a later date.

Yours faithfully,
[Violet Pearman]
Private Secretary

1. A German émigré journalist who had been translating Churchill's articles for publication in Europe since the beginning of 1936.

Emery Reves to Winston S. Churchill

8 March 1937   Paris[1]

Dear Mr. Churchill,

I thank you very much for your letter of March 3rd, informing me that questions of a legal character have been raised by Dr. Meyer, and that it might be that your remaining March article will have to be allocated upon the old basis.

I have the intention to leave for a European trip about the middle of March, visiting some fifteen countries in North and Eastern Europe. I should very much like to use this opportunity to negotiate personally with all the important newspapers of these countries the publication of your articles.

I should be most grateful, therefore, if it would be possible for you to give me some further information before the middle of the month, so that I shall be able to fix my programme. Should no decision be possible, I should be quite prepared to postpone my trip a week or two, as I think this would be a most useful occasion for negotiations.

I beg to remain,

Yours very truly,
I. Révész

1.   In this book, the address on all letters from Reves to Churchill from Coopera-tion, Press Service for International Understanding, 33 Champs Elysées, Paris 8, has been abbreviated to "Paris."

Violet Pearman to Emery Reves

13 March 1937

Dear Dr. Revesz,

I am desired by Mr. Churchill to thank you for your letter of the 8th instant, and to say that the case of Dr. Meyer is raising a great deal of diffi-culty over here, and may possibly be the subject of a lawsuit. Meanwhile Mr. Churchill is not able to give you any information as to his future course.

Yours faithfully,
[Violet Pearman]
Private Secretary

Emery Reves to Winston S. Churchill

18 April 1937   Paris

Dear Mr. Churchill,

I am terribly sorry that circumstances have not yet allowed to start with our collaboration the terms of which we have discussed in February last. As I have told you, I wanted to leave on April 1st for a European tour, visiting 16 countries. The success of COOPERATION is entirely due to personal contacts. I shall see this time over 100 newspaper editors, to make contracts for the coming year, and I am absolutely sure that if I could negotiate by this occasion the publication of your articles, I could obtain most satisfactory results.

Hoping that it will be possible for you to settle the matter, I have postponed my trip, but now I have to leave, and that is why I ventured to telephone to you this morning. I was very happy to hear that you believe we might start in June, as I am really convinced that you will find COOPERATION a very useful channel for your views. I should like to give you some figures concerning the publication of Sir Austen Chamberlain's last articles:

| | published in | | fees obtained [French |
article	countries	newspapers	Frcs.]
England & Germany	16	22	8,150
Lord Grey (published in two parts)	14	16	16,700
German Colonies	18	20	9,700
Bülow & Chamberlain	18	21	8,850

So for 5 articles we have obtained fees amounting to 43,400—French Francs,[1] and they appeared in an average of 20 papers each. This result has been achieved outside Great Britain and North America.

We are publishing to-day the articles of almost all the important statesmen, but I feel sure that your articles could have a larger circulation than the articles of anybody else. And I feel equally sure that this circulation could be twice as large, if I could handle the matter personally during my next journey.

I should be most grateful, therefore, if you would kindly consider the possibility of an arrangement, which would start on June 1st, or at any later date, but which would give me authority for negotiations.

The best solution, of course, would be, if I could sign arrangements everywhere after May 1st. I would be quite prepared to pay Dr. Meyer an indemnity of £10.-.- for the coming month or two, if you think it useful.

I should be most obliged if you would kindly let me know your opinion about this suggestion, and would be glad to come over to London to discuss the matter any time you like during the week.

I beg to remain,
Yours very truly
I. Révész

---

1. In 1937, the sterling equivalent of 43,400 French francs was £320 (£8,500 in the money values of 1996).

Emery Reves to Winston S. Churchill

29 May 1937   Hôtel d'Angleterre
                                                          Copenhagen

Dear Mr. Churchill,

Last April, when I have telephoned to you from Paris, you were kind
enough to ask me to write to you in respect of the publication of your articles
in the International Press about the 1st of June.

I see in the newspapers that you are starting a new series of articles in the
NEWS OF THE WORLD, and wonder, whether circumstances would
allow you now to make a trial with COOPERATION.

You have certainly seen M. Flandin's [1] article in the Sunday Times, and Sir
Austen Chamberlain's last article in The Daily Telegraph, which was a great
international success.

I am writing this letter from Copenhagen, where I shall stay until Tuesday,
but if you will have the great kindness, to let inform my Paris office about the
situation, I shall receive your letter the next day, wherever I am.

Thanking you in advance, I beg to remain,

                                                   Yours most respectfully
                                                              I. Révész

1.   Pierre-Etienne Flandin, leader of the Right Center group of Deputies in the
French National Assembly from 1932. Prime Minister, November 1934–June 1935.
Minister for Foreign Affairs, January–June 1936. After his visit to Germany in 1937,
Léon Blum's government issued a communiqué declaring that he went as a private
individual only. Arrested by the Allies in North Africa, 1943. Tried by the French
government, 1946, but acquitted of the charge of collaboration with the Germans
(Randolph Churchill spoke in Flandin's defense at the trial, on his father's behalf).
Following the trial Flandin was declared ineligible for Parliament.

Winston S. Churchill to Emery Reves

31 May 1937

I am considering the whole of the question of the handling of my foreign
material with a strong desire that you should undertake it. I will write to you
again in the course of the next week.

Emery Reves to Winston S. Churchill

13 June 1937   On Board
                                                   Bergen–Trondheim

Dear Mr. Churchill,

I am writing this letter on a steamer between Bergen and Trondheim. As
you were kind enough to ask me by telephone, I am submitting you my pro-

posals regarding the publication of your articles in the international press by
COOPERATION.

COOPERATION shall have exclusive rights of publication of all your
newspaper-articles outside Great Britain and the United States of America.
I note that the collaboration should start on July 1st 1937. Regarding the
validity of our arrangement I am prepared to accept your conditions, would
suggest, however, that it should last for a trial period of six months. Should
neither party cancel it one month prior to its expiration, so it would go on
automatically from six month to six month.

You will be good enough to let us have copies of your articles as soon as
possible, and ask British and American papers to quote at the beginning or
at the end of the articles a Copyright line (like the Daily Telegraph did on
Sir Austen Chamberlain's articles) in order to prevent unauthorized reproductions, and to make possible publications abroad even some days later. It
would save time if you could always despatch to us 3 copies of the articles to
make the translations simultaneously.

Should one or the other article deal mainly with an English subject, which
might arise less interest in Continental countries so we shall consult you
regarding the advisability of an international diffusion of that article.

As to the remunerations, we have discussed two possibilities in
February last.

1) We shall take over the existing arrangements, and shall secure for you
60 per cent of the gross proceeds of all publications, guaranteeing this
amount with a minimum of £25.-.- per article. All expenses, translations, telegrams, telephones, diffusion, etc. will be on our charge.

2) We shall take over and carry out the existing arrangements, which are,
if I remember well, as follows:

a) Paris-Soir	about	£ 9.-.-
b) De Telegraaf	"	" 5.-.-
c) Berlingske Tidende	"	" 5.-.-
d) Dagens Nyheter	"	" 5.-.-

We would transmit to you the fees these four papers pay as arranged by the
Evening Standard (about £23–24.-.-) without any deduction. The surplus
we may achieve and payments received from other papers will be divided
between you and COOPERATION on the basis of 50/50.

I am quite prepared to accept the method you would prefer.

Regarding the payments, we usually remit the guaranteed amount at the
end of each month, and establish an exact statement quarterly. Should you
choose the second method, so I would suggest that we remit to you at the
end of each month an à conto payment of £50.-.- (or £25.-.- if there is only
one article) and the surplus quarterly. Should you like to get a detailed statement monthly, I could do that, but in that case you would get the informa-

tion concerning the publications in fragments, as it takes sometimes several weeks until I get reports from remote countries.

I think these are the questions we have to settle in advance. I would be most obliged if you would have the great kindness to let me know your agreement or your objections by telegram as soon as possible, as I am visiting at the moment 3–4 places weekly, and should like to discuss this matter personally even here in Scandinavia. Should you be able to send a telegram Tuesday (June 15th) not later than 4 p.m., so kindly address it to Hotel Bristol, Oslo. I shall leave by the night train for Stockholm Grand Hotel, where I shall stay from Wednesday morning certainly until Sunday next.

As soon as I receive your agreement in principle, I shall give instructions that written proposals shall be sent to all countries I am not visiting during this trip, so that as many arrangements as possible should be made before July.

I beg to remain,

Yours very truly,
I. Révész

Winston S. Churchill to Emery Reves: telegram

17 June 1937

Revesz Grand Hotel Stockholm
  Letter despatched Stockholm air mail 18th

Churchill

Winston S. Churchill to Emery Reves

17 June 1937

Dear Dr. Revesz,

I am willing in principle to confide to you the marketing of the Evening Standard articles and such other articles as I may from time to time specify outside the United States and the British Empire for a period of six months, subject to my contract with the Evening Standard remaining in force during this period.

I prefer in the first instance the arrangement whereby I receive the payments now in force from the four specified papers (including Paris Soir which is now 1500 fcs. an article) coupled with the 50% basis which you propose for the rest of the assigned area. I suggest that the option you offered me to revert to the 60-40 basis shall be open at the end of each quarter. The other arrangements you propose seem satisfactory.

Will you kindly have a contract made out on these lines and forward it to me in duplicate.

Emery Reves to Winston S. Churchill

20 June 1937   Grand Hotel
                                                           Stockholm

Dear Mr. Churchill,

Kindly find enclosed the contract in duplicate made out on the lines we agreed upon. I should be grateful if you would be good enough to send one copy of it to Paris, duly signed.

I must apologize for the poor English in which this contract is written, I have here no English stenographer to dictate. Should it be too bad, please, let it rewrite by your Secretary.

I have discussed the matter here with the Editor of DAGENS NY-HETER. He paid for your articles in the past two years 85.- Swedish Crowns (£4.6.-). We are going to sign a new contract from July 1st to-morrow, and he will pay 150.- Crowns per article, i.e. about 80% more than in the past. I hope you will find this first intervention satisfactory.

You would very much oblige me if you could let me know the approximate date by which we could expect your first article.

                                                    I beg to remain,
                                                    Yours very truly
                                                    I. Révész

P.S. I am staying in Stockholm certainly until Tuesday evening. During the following two days my address will be Hotel Societätshuset, Helsinki, Finland.

Emery Reves to Winston S. Churchill

20 June 1937

ARRANGEMENT
between The Rt. Hon. Winston Churchill, P.C., M.P., in London
and
COOPERATION Press Service for International Understanding, in Paris.

1. COOPERATION will have exclusive rights of publication of the articles Mr. Churchill is writing for the Evening Standard and for such other articles he may specify from time to time. These rights are exclusive for the whole world outside the British Empire and the United States of America.

2. Mr. Churchill will send to the Paris office of COOPERATION three copies of his articles as early and as quickly as possible.

3. In view of the fact that simultaneous publication in the international press requires about a week and in order to make possible a large diffusion even after the publication of the articles in the English press, Mr. Churchill will arrange that his articles shall be published in Great Britain and in

America with a Copyright-line and with the mention "Reproduction even partially strictly forbidden".

4. Should one or the other article deal mainly with a British subject which might arise less interest abroad, so COOPERATION might consult Mr. Churchill, whether this article should be offered in foreign countries.

5. COOPERATION will remit to Mr. Churchill the payments as arranged with four newspapers by the Evening Standard without any deduction. These arrangements are a) Paris Soir (1500 French Francs) b) Dagens Nyheter (£4.6.-) c) Berlingske Tidende (about £5.-.-) and De Telegraaf (about £5.-.-). The surplus COOPERATION may achieve, and all payments received from other newspapers will be divided between Mr. Churchill and COOPERATION on the basis of 50/50.

6. Mr. Churchill has the right to revert this method of payment to an arrangement whereby COOPERATION will remit to him 60% of all proceeds including the four papers mentioned. In this case COOPERATION will guarantee the 60% with a minimum of £25.-.- for each article published. This option shall be open at the end of each quarter.

7. COOPERATION will make an à conto payment on the basis of £25.-.- per article published at the end of each month. An exact statement will be established and the surplus remitted quarterly.

8. This arrangement comes into force on the 1st of July 1937 and will be valid for a trial period of six months. Should neither party cancel it at least one month prior to its expiration, so this arrangement will go on automatically from six months to six months.

Violet Pearman to Winston S. Churchill

23 June 1937

Mr. Churchill,

Mr. Robertson has asked you to look at one clause which the solicitor pointed out to him; it is the one in which you are bound to Dr. Revesz for 6 months. This he supposes would automatically be washed out if your contract with E.S. expired at a month's notice on either side—which he thought was very unlikely. But it is a point to note. There are one or two things which the solicitor wants to go into and Mr. Robertson will send the contract back here tomorrow.

V. Pearman

Winston S. Churchill to Emery Reves

23 June 1937

This contract is quite satisfactory to me, but it must be clearly understood that my contract with the Evening Standard is for six months, terminable at a month's notice at their option or at mine. If for any reason the series of articles in the Evening Standard comes to an end, your contract for the foreign marketing falls to the ground at the same time. This is of course obvious from the facts, but it should be made clear on this contract.

With regard to other articles, I hope to entrust the whole of the foreign marketing of anything I may release for publication abroad to you, as it is much better this foreign work should be handled from one source, and that you only should be dealing with the foreign newspapers. However this matter remains entirely at my discretion and there is no liability upon me to furnish you with any articles other than the Evening Standard series for a period of six months, should that continue so long.

I should not have thought it necessary to make these detailed stipulations which are implicit in the contract but for the trouble I have had with Dr. Meyer.

I have signed the contract as it stands and it will be sufficient if you write me a letter acknowledging it and stating your agreement with this letter.

Emery Reves to Winston S. Churchill

30 June 1937   Helsinki

Dear Mr. Churchill,

I have received copy of your covering letter you were kind enough to send to Paris together with the contract. I entirely agree with the terms of this letter.

I quite understand that after the troubles you have had, you wished to make these detailed stipulations. In all my arrangements I make it clear that should you be prevented to write newspaper articles (by taking an office or by any other reason) so COOPERATION has no obligation to submit such articles.

I am very glad to read in your letter that you believe it is better that the whole foreign work should be handled from one source. This is, indeed, the condition of a success. When newspapers receive articles from the same author by various sources simultaneously, this usually spoils the market. I hope therefore—without asking you any commitment—that you will entrust the whole of the foreign marketing of anything you may release for publication abroad to us. Needless to say, I am fully aware that you will only do so, if the result of our activity will be satisfactory to you.

I have just received a cutting of an important Flemish paper in Brussels HET LAATSTE NIEUWS, with an article from you, published under the Copyright of a Paris agency OPERA MUNDI. I am sending you enclosed this cutting, as I wonder whether you know about this publication, and whether you gave authorization to that agency. This is the type of publication which might make our negotiations difficult. I have made to the same paper a proposal regarding the regular publication of your articles. This proposal, in which I have asked a fee certainly 3–4 times higher than what they have paid for this article, has arrived in Brussels by a strange coincidence the same day when this publication took place. I am very much afraid that now the Editor will not even consider our proposition, believing that he will always get your articles cheaper, and without any contract.

Should you have given authorization to that publication, so there is, of course, nothing to do. But should this not be the case, so I think it is in our mutual interest to inform about it this newspaper, and to protest against it. The Editor of HET LAATSTE NIEUWS in Brussels is Mr. Stijns. Should you be in a position to write to him, so it would be most useful if you would mention that from July 1st COOPERATION has exclusive rights in handling your articles on the Continent.

You would very much oblige me if you would kindly let us know whether this publication in Brussels is all right, or whether you are undertaking something.

I beg to remain,
Yours very sincerely
I. Révész

Winston S. Churchill to Emery Reves

2 July 1937

Opera Mundi was authorised by Curtis Brown[1] on my behalf to market the first six of the series of twelve articles now appearing in the News of the World. The Flemish paper no doubt has one of them. I have asked Curtis Brown to bring this to an end as soon as these six articles have been finished, and if possible sooner. The second six I will entrust to you. They will appear in a month or two.

There are also some other articles which have been published in America and which, after some editing, I have allowed to be published in the Sunday Chronicle here.[2] These with further editing could be made available for you.

Meanwhile you are authorised by me to tell all the newspapers that you will have the sole negotiation of my continental business. This of course does not affect the basis of our contract in any way.

P.S. Pray keep me informed of any arrangements you make.

1.   Curtis Brown, a literary agency in London.
2.   Churchill's article "Soapbox Messiahs," published in *Collier's* on 20 June 1936, was reprinted in the *Sunday Chronicle* on 28 June 1936 as "Money for Nothing." His next article for *Collier's*, "Oldest and Richest," published on 11 July 1936, was reprinted in the *Sunday Chronicle* on 12 July 1936 as "Money-Grabber—but Money-Giver Too." It was about John D. Rockefeller.

Violet Pearman to Emery Reves

6 July 1937

Dear Dr. Revesz,

I am asked by Mr. Churchill to send herewith a list of the papers which have been publishing his articles. Those that have been publishing more or less regularly are marked with a cross.[1] Mr. Churchill will shortly be sending you the first article with you, which will be published here on the 9th instant.[2]

Yours faithfully,
[Violet Pearman]
Private Secretary

1. In Paris: *Paris-Soir* and *Pariser Tages Zeitung*. In Brussels, *Le Soir*. In Scandinavia, *Berlingske Tidende* (Copenhagen), *Tidens Tegn* (Oslo) and *Dagens Nyheter* (Stockholm). In Lithuania, *Zydu Balsas* (a Yiddish daily newspaper). In Vienna, *Neue Freie Presse*. In Switzerland, *Tages Anzeiger*. In Romania, *Le Moment* (Bucharest).
2. On 9 July 1937 the *Evening Standard* published Churchill's article "The Ebbing Tide of Socialism." Like most of his *Evening Standard* articles it was reprinted in his volume *Step by Step,* first published by Thornton Butterworth in June 1939.

Emery Reves to Winston S. Churchill

7 July 1937   Riga

Dear Mr. Churchill,

I hope your articles will be regularly published in the Baltic countries. Of course, the newspapers are very small and poor here, but nevertheless the total result will not be uninteresting.

You have certainly received my previous letter with the cutting of HET LAATSTE NIEUWS in Brussels. As I was afraid of, this paper has refused our proposal, saying that it was too expensive, etc . . . But on the 29th of June they have published a second article, and on the 2nd of July a third article by you, again Copyright Opera Mundi. I have also learned that in Bucarest the same articles are appearing, from the same source. It is most unfortunate that this incident happens just when we have opened negotiations with the newspapers. I wonder whether there is a possibility to stop these publications just now, as they are spoiling many possibilities.

I beg to remain,
Yours most respectfully
I. Révész

R. McMartin[1] *to Emery Reves*

8 July 1937   3 Regent Square
                                                    London W.C.1.

Dear Doctor Rewecz,

I was given your address by friends of both of us. Allow me to write to you to-day about Winston Churchill's series of articles, which I hear is being distributed by you.

As you presumably know, for 18 months the series has been distributed in about 20 countries by German emigre journalists on a percentage basis. A termination of the underlying agreement before the end of the series was not expected. Much tiresome introduction work was done for which the later articles of the series were to bring in the financial equivalent. The premature termination of the agreement will therefore be considered not only an adverse arrangement but also as unfair.

Now I am coming to the first concrete object of these lines. Definite agreements for a long period were made with a number of European newspapers, notably the Escher Tageblatt in Luxembourg, the Freie Presse in Vienna, the Lidove Noviny in Prague, the Neue Zuercher Zeitung in Zuerich, with positive acceptance of the "Evening Standard" as the control centre for the European rights from the 21st January. By these agreements, which have not yet run out, the papers were in some cases only authorised, but in others obliged, to publish the articles of the Churchill series at fixed prices. Non-fulfilment of the agreements will possibly cause complications with the papers, losses for these dealing with the articles and thereby even give rise to a further increase in existing tension and difficulties.

This undesirable development could certainly be avoided if your management would allow it, by supplying the said papers in the present way until their agreements run out. I should be grateful to you if you would consider this possibility.

Perhaps you would allow me to touch upon one more thing:

The facts accumulated here recall the point that some continental papers wish to publish the Churchill articles only on the day of their appearance in London. Transmitting the manuscripts to Paris and sending them on from there make it difficult or even entirely impossible when they come out as late as up to the present.

I wonder, therefore, if it would not be in your interest to undertake the distribution of the articles for certain papers and countries, following your directions and intentions, from here.

I can well believe that agreements were sought which would be advantageous for the distribution of the articles and for you, and which would allow a conciliatory settlement of the difficulties which, as mentioned above, have arisen.

The colleagues, who have lost what is for them a commercially significant job under present conditions, as your financially favourable offer was accepted, could continue their work.

Will you be kind enough to consider this suggestion and to let me know if it agrees with your intentions. If this is the case a telegram would suffice, and to-morrow's article at least would go to the above-mentioned papers in German.

I hardly need to emphasise that these searching lines should in no way have an influenced character, after an outlet from a painful situation.

In anticipation of your reply, I remain,

1.   R. McMartin, a literary agent, of 3 Regent Square, London W.C.1.

Emery Reves to R. McMartin

9 July 1937

Dear Mr. Martin,

Thank you for your letter of July 8. We should like to inform you that, according to the contract we have concluded with Mr. Churchill, we have acquired all rights for the publication of his articles.

R. Gayman[1] to Winston S. Churchill

9 July 1937   33 Champs-Elysées
                                              Paris

Dear Mr. Churchill,

We beg to acknowledge receipt of your letter of July 7th, with three copies of your first article under our new arrangement, which we shall publish on Continent in the course of the next week.

We beg to remain,
Yours faithfully,
R. Gayman

1.   Rachel Gayman, Secretary General of Cooperation. She began working for Reves, as his first employee, when he reached Paris in 1933. During the Second World War she was active in the French Resistance, for which she was decorated.

Cooperation to Winston S. Churchill

[9 July 1937][1]

ARREST OF BRITISH SOCIALISM[2]

Published by	Gross proceeds £	Mr. Churchill £	Cooperation £
Paris-Soir, Paris	11. 6. 0.	11. 6. 0.	———
Berlingske Tidende, Copenhagen	5. 0. 0.	5. 0. 0.	———
Dagens Nyheter, Stockholm	7.10. 0.	5.18. 0.	1.12. 0.
Tidens Tegn, Oslo	5. 0. 0.	2.10. 0.	2.10. 0.
Le Soir, Bruxelles	10. 0. 0.	5. 0. 0.	5. 0. 0.
Luxemburger Zeitung	1. 0. 0.	0.10. 0.	0.10. 0.
Helsingin Sanomat, Helsinki	3. 0. 0.	1.10. 0.	1.10. 0.
Briwa Zeme, Riga	2.10. 0.	1. 5. 0.	1. 5. 0.
Paevaleht, Tallinn	1. 0. 0.	0.10. 0.	0.10. 0.
Lietuvos Aidas, Kaunas	1.10. 0.	0.15. 0.	0.15. 0.
Lidove Noviny, Prague	2. 0. 0.	1. 0. 0.	1. 0. 0.
Neue Zuercher Zeitung, Zurich	4. 0. 0.	2. 0. 0.	2. 0. 0.
Neues Wiener Tagblatt, Vienna	2. 0. 0.	1. 0. 0.	1. 0. 0.
Kurjer Warszawski, Varsovie	10. 0. 0.	5. 0. 0.	5. 0. 0.
Pesti Hirlap, Budapest	5. 0. 0.	2.10. 0.	2.10. 0.
Politika, Belgrade	4. 0. 0.	2. 0. 0.	2. 0. 0.
Bourse Egyptienne, Cairo	2. 0. 0.	1. 0. 0.	1. 0. 0.
La Nacion, Buenos Aires	10. 0. 0.	5. 0. 0.	5. 0. 0.
O Estado de Sao Paulo	7. 0. 0.	3.10. 0.	3.10. 0.
Total	93.16. 0.	57. 4. 0.	36.12. 0.

1. This was the first account sent to Churchill from Cooperation. I have dated each of these accounts from the date of the publication of the article concerned. The total income to Churchill from this single article, £57. 4.0, was the equivalent in 1996 of £1,500.

2. Published in the *Evening Standard* as "The Ebbing Tide of Socialism."

Emery Reves to Winston S. Churchill

12 July 1937   Warsaw

Dear Mr. Churchill,

I have received a long letter from Dr. Mayer. The letter begins with a phrase that he feels it was unfair that your articles have been taken away from him. After this pleasant remark he wonders whether I could agree that he should continue to publish your articles in some 20 countries. He says that he has done great preliminary work since 1½ years without profit, and <u>now</u> he was expecting the financial reward . . . It is really childish. My secretary answered him that you have charged COOPERATION with the publication of your articles, and that we shall carry out this contract.

I have received a copy of your first article which is excellent, and which I hope it will be a great success. But I see already that we shall be always about a week behind the Evening Standard. It would be most important, therefore, that the Evening Standard should publish your articles with the Copyright-line "Copyright by EVENING STANDARD, on the Continent by COOPERATION. Reproduction even partially prohibited."

As I have told you in my last letter, I hope your articles will be well published in the Baltic countries. The situation in these countries is briefly the following: The newspapers are so small and poor that they can hardly pay 1 Pound for an article. That is the reason why no West-European organization touches them, and why these papers are entirely at the mercy of German propaganda. They get almost all their stuff from German agencies practically free of charge. I have visited those countries for the first time 4 years ago, without any result. My second trip was also negative. Now I went for the 4th time to that part of Europe, and we have excellent relations since last year. They are publishing almost all of our articles. We are working on subscription basis, so they are interested to publish as many articles as possible. I trust that our proceeds from these small countries will be 8–10 Pounds monthly.

I have received a cable from Buenos Aires, LA NACION has accepted my proposals. Six months contract, 10.- Pounds per article.

A similar contract for six months has been concluded with LE SOIR in Brussels. 10.- Pounds per article. (I hope that in about a month, when the recent publications in HET LAATSTE NIEUWS will be forgotten, I shall come to some arrangement also with a Flemish paper in Belgium.)

As you have told me I have signed an arrangement with BERLINGSKE TIDENDE in Copenhagen on the old basis: 5 Pounds per article.

But DE TELEGRAAF in Amsterdam refused even that. They say that they have paid 5 Pounds for your articles without any obligation, and should not like to raise this honorarium or to commit themselves in any way. This is one of the richest papers in Europe, and could easily pay twice as much. As soon as I am back in Paris, I shall go to Amsterdam, and if they maintain their rigid attitude, I think we must have the courage to renounce to that paper. There are many big newspapers in Holland. Of course, for the time being I am submitting your articles on the old basis.

I should be most obliged, if your Secretary would send me a list of the articles DE TELEGRAAF has published during the past 12 months. I should not like to insist upon a contract if de facto the articles are published. But on the other hand we should not admit that too many articles are dropped.

I do beg to kindly keep all information regarding our arrangements confidential.

Now I shall try to make some arrangements here in Poland, then in Prague, Budapest, Belgrade and Vienna.

Yours very sincerely
I. Révész

Emery Reves to Winston S. Churchill

21 July 1937   Prague
AIR MAIL EXPRESS

Dear Mr. Churchill,

A British statesman suggested me to write an article on Palestine. I should like to make the acceptance of this proposal dependent from the subject of your next article. I should be most grateful, therefore, if you would kindly inform my office in Paris by a short telegram, whether your next article will be on Palestine or not.

Personally, I think that both, the Far East situation, and the Spanish problem would be more interesting.

As far as I can see from the first reports your last article has been very well published on the continent. I shall give you full information in about a week.

Yours very sincerely,
I. Révész

Winston S. Churchill to Emery Reves: telegram

21 July 1937

Article this week deals with Palestine Zionist question. Should be of special interest. Please press it upon your clients. Do they object to 1,500 words or shall I cut to 1,100.

Churchill

Emery Reves to Winston S. Churchill: telegram

23 July 1937   Paris

Can publish long article.

Cooperation

Cooperation to Winston S. Churchill

[23 July 1937]

CAN PARTITION BRING PEACE TO PALESTINE [1]

Published by	Gross proceeds £	Mr. Churchill £	Cooperation £
Paris-Soir, Paris	11. 6. 0.	11. 6. 0.	———
Berlingske Tidende, Copenhagen	5. 0. 0.	5. 0. 0.	———
Der Telegraaf, Amsterdam	5. 0. 0.	5. 0. 0.	———
Dagens Nyheter, Stockholm	7.10. 0.	5.18. 0.	1.12. 0.
Pariser Tages Zeitung, Paris	1. 0. 0.	0.10. 0.	0.10. 0.
Le Soir, Bruxelles	10. 0. 0.	5. 0. 0.	5. 0. 0.
Luxemberger Zeitung, Luxemburg	1. 0. 0.	0.10. 0.	0.10. 0.
Tidens Tegn, Oslo	5. 0. 0.	2.10. 0.	2.10. 0.
Briwa Zeme, Riga	2.10. 0.	1. 5. 0.	1. 5. 0.
Paevaleht, Tallinn	1. 0. 0.	0.10. 0.	0.10. 0.
Lietuvos Aidas, Kaunas	1.10. 0.	0.15. 0.	0.15. 0.
Lidove Noviny, Prague	2. 0. 0.	1. 0. 0.	1. 0. 0.
Neue Zuercher Zeitung, Zurich	4. 0. 0.	2. 0. 0.	2. 0. 0.
Journal des Nations, Geneva	0.14. 0.	0. 7. 0.	0. 7. 0.
Neues Wiener Tagblatt, Vienna	2. 0. 0.	1. 0. 0.	1. 0. 0.
Pester Lloyd, Budapest	2. 0. 0.	1. 0. 0.	1. 0. 0.
Politika, Belgrade	4. 0. 0.	2. 0. 0.	2. 0. 0.
Bourse Egyptienne, Cairo	2. 0. 0.	1. 0. 0.	1. 0. 0.
La Nacion, Buenos Aires	10. 0. 0.	5. 0. 0.	5. 0. 0.
O Estado de Sao Paulo, Sao Paulo	probably published but no confirmation until now		
Total	77.10. 0.	51.11. 0.	25.19. 0.

1. Published in the *Evening Standard* on 23 July 1937 as "Partition Perils in Palestine."

Emery Reves to Winston S. Churchill: telegram

30 July 1937   Budapest

Biggest Hungarian newspaper accepted contract five pounds article stop Last minute signature refused because Operamundi offered today series your articles for two pounds Please stop immediately these publications spoiling all arrangements Kindly wire Hotel Hungaria to save situation Thanks.

Revesz

Winston S. Churchill to Emery Reves: telegram

30 July 1937

Point out Operamundi only entrusted with second serials six articles
whereas you are dealing with new and topical matter.

Churchill

Winston S. Churchill to Charles M. Ronsac[1]

30 July 1937

Dear Sir,

I have, after much consideration, decided to entrust all my Continental
business to Cooperation, and therefore I must ask you to discontinue the service you have hitherto rendered me in respect of some of my articles.

Thanking you for your past attention,
Believe me,

1.   Charles M. Ronsac, Proprietor of Opera Mundi, a leading French literary
agency.

Emery Reves to Winston S. Churchill

1 August 1937   Budapest

Dear Mr. Churchill,

I thank you very much for your telegram. The situation here is the
following:

I came to an agreement with the largest Hungarian newspaper on a basis
of £5.-.- per article. This is an unusually high fee in this country, and the only
reason why they have accepted it, was that I have secured exclusivity for them
in Hungarian language. The contract was ready, the Editor approved it, and
asked me to come back next morning, as he was obliged to get it signed also
by the financial director. Yesterday, when I arrived, he received me with an
ironic smile, what kind of exclusivity I can guarantee, they have just received
an offer from Opera Mundi, six articles for £2.-.-. I tried to explain that these
articles have been published already in the News of the World, whereas the
articles you are writing for us are topical and unpublished features. The answer of the Editor was that nobody reads in Hungary the News of the World,
the value of these articles is for their readers the same, and if they can get a
"Churchill article" for £2.-, he is not willing to pay for another "Churchill
article" £5.-. Besides, if they can get your articles by various sources, he is not
prepared to sign a contract, as we cannot really guarantee exclusivity.

So the contract was dropped, and the Palestine article, accepted on Thursday, has been turned down yesterday.

I quite understand this point of view, and after having lost 2 important newspapers on account of this second serializing by Opera Mundi, I do beg to kindly cancel these publications. If I remember well, you have authorized Curtis Brown with these publications several weeks ago, and you are entirely at your liberty to declare that today—5–6 weeks later—these articles are spoiling the publication of your new and topical articles. Should you suffer any financial loss by this, I am prepared to pay an indemnity, if you could arrange that Curtis Brown and Opera Mundi should inform by telegram all their agents in Europe to stop the circulation of these articles at once.

Should this not be possible, I am expecting most disagreeable conflicts with newspapers. Our success in the international press is due to the fact that since the existence of COOPERATION we have never had the slightest misunderstanding with any newspaper. Now it is for the first time that—from the point of view of the newspapers—we seem not to keep our engagements.

Indeed, the fact is that over a month after our contract entered into force, and we have signed exclusivity-contracts with various newspapers, dozens of small local agencies (in connection with Curtis Brown and Opera Mundi) are circulating your articles, not as second serials, but as original, unpublished articles, and are offering them for 20–40% of the fee I am endeavouring to obtain.

I do hope that you will not misunderstand me, and that you will be able to terminate this unpleasant situation which causes a great prejudice both for you and for COOPERATION.

Besides these incidents things are going very well. Your articles will be published in all the Danubian countries. Of course, the political situation will not allow to print all your articles here. Italo-German influence is stronger than ever, and though the great majority of the newspapers and of the public opinion is against that policy, government pressure is very strong.

I have received news that a French paper in Egypt, La Bourse Egyptienne, accepted a six months contract, for £2.- per article. We have also made an arrangement with a Brasilian paper, O Estado de Sao Paolo, for one article monthly, to start with. They will pay £7.- per article.

I am leaving for Vienna to-day, and hope to be back in Paris in about a week. As soon as I arrive, I shall let you have all information concerning the publication of your first two articles. Should you leave for holiday, I should be most obliged if you could let me know your address.

I beg to remain,
Yours very sincerely,
I. Révész

Winston S. Churchill to Emery Reves: telegram

3 August 1937

Curtis Brown say Operamundi no rights outside France am enquiring strictly and endeavouring wind up France soonest

Churchill

Emery Reves to Winston S. Churchill

4 August 1937   Baur au Lac
                                                                      Zurich

Dear Mr. Churchill,
  I have received copies of your letter and telegram concerning OPERA MUNDI, for which I thank you very much.
  As soon as I shall be back in Paris, I shall have to go to Brussels to arrange this matter with LE SOIR. You know that I have signed a contract with this paper on the basis of £10 per article. This morning I have received a letter from the Editor protesting against the publication of your articles by another Belgian newspaper under the Copyright of OPERA MUNDI. He says that the only reason why he has accepted to pay such a high fee was that he desired to have your exclusive collaboration. If other papers are publishing simultaneously your articles, so he is not interested in them.
  I shall certainly let you have a detailed statement concerning the publication of all of your articles. I only wish to prepare the first statement myself, and by therefore to kindly give me another few days. I shall be in Paris Monday morning.

I am,
Yours most respectfully
I. Révész

Violet Pearman to Emery Reves

5 August 1937   Chartwell

Dear Dr. Revesz,
  I am asked by Mr. Churchill to send you herewith two proofs of his article for the Evening Standard for next Friday.[1] The third copy is coming to you direct from the Evening Standard offices, as they did not send enough copies down here to me to enable me to send the correct number off to you.

Yours faithfully,
[Violet Pearman]
Private Secretary

1. Churchill's article "Anglo-Italian Friendship—How?" was published in the *Evening Standard* on 6 August 1937.

Cooperation to Winston S. Churchill

[6 August 1937]

ENGLAND AND ITALY

Published by	Gross proceeds £	Mr. Churchill £	Cooperation £
Paris-Soir, Paris	11. 6. 0.	11. 6. 0.	———
Berlingske Tidende, Copenhagen	5. 0. 0.	5. 0. 0.	———
Dagens Nyheter, Stockholm	7.10. 0.	5.18. 0.	1.12. 0.
Europe, Paris	2. 0. 0.	1. 0. 0.	1. 0. 0.
Le Soir, Bruxelles	10. 0. 0.	5. 0. 0.	5. 0. 0.
Pariser Tages Zeitung, Paris	0.16. 0.	0. 8. 0.	0. 8. 0.
Luxemburger Zeitung, Luxembourg	1. 0. 0.	0.10. 0.	0.10. 0.
Nieuwe Rotterdamsche Courant, Rotterdam	3. 0. 0.	1.10. 0.	1.10. 0.
Tidens Tegn, Oslo	5. 0. 0.	2.10. 0.	2.10. 0.
Dagsposten, Trondheim	1.10. 0.	0.15. 0.	0.15. 0.
Helsingin Sanomat, Helsinki	3. 0. 0.	1.10. 0.	1.10. 0.
Paevaleht, Tallinn	1. 0. 0.	0.10. 0.	0.10. 0.
Lidove Noviny, Prague	1.12. 0.	0.16. 0.	0.16. 0.
Prager Tagblatt, Prague	1.10. 0.	0.15. 0.	0.15. 0.
Tages Anzeiger, Zurich	4. 0. 0.	2. 0. 0.	2. 0. 0.
St. Galler Tagblatt, St. Gallen	1.10. 0.	0.15. 0.	0.15. 0.
Luzerner Tagblatt, Luzern	1.10. 0.	0.15. 0.	0.15. 0.
Journal des Nations, Geneva	0.14. 0.	0. 7. 0.	0. 7. 0.
Neues Wiener Tagblatt, Vienna	2. 0. 0.	1. 0. 0.	1. 0. 0.
Kurjer Warszawski, Varsovie (Fee still uncertain)	4. 0. 0.	2. 0. 0.	2. 0. 0.
Politika, Belgrade	4. 0. 0.	2. 0. 0.	2. 0. 0.
Bourse Egyptienne, Cairo	2. 0. 0.	1. 0. 0.	1. 0. 0.
La Nacion, Buenos Aires	10. 0. 0.	5. 0. 0.	5. 0. 0.
Total	83.18. 0.	52. 5. 0.	31.13. 0.

Winston S. Churchill to Emery Reves

6 August 1937

Dear Dr. Revesz,

I send you the enclosed letters from Curtis Brown which will show you the position in respect of Opera Mundi. They have these six articles only and have them only for France and Belgium. They will therefore no doubt be ready to cancel the arrangements they made with the Hungarian papers about which you have written me. I am however allowing them to finish this series of six articles in France where they have still to deal with the provincial press. I have also agreed to recognise the contract they had made in Belgium for the six articles. I am glad you are going to explain the situation to the Belgian newspaper and if necessary we might make some special offer to them as the contract they made was a good one. They might perhaps have the first two articles at half price. However I leave this to you.

I am most anxious to see the full account of the sales of the two articles you have handled.

I may be going on a tour of the Continent in the Autumn in which case I will get in touch with the papers or the proprietors of the papers who are taking my articles, and show them a civility.

Emery Reves to Winston S. Churchill

9 August 1937   Paris

Dear Mr. Churchill,

I just arrived in Paris and have found here your letter of August 6th, for which I have to thank you very much.

The series of articles diffused all over Europe by OPERA MUNDI has caused a real disaster. I have informed you already about some cases. Arriving in Paris I have found here a letter from a Polish newspaper with which I have made a verbal contract on the basis of £10.0.0. per article, denouncing this arrangement: (Translation from German) ". . . We cannot commit ourselves regarding the publication of the articles by Mr. Winston Churchill, as we have just received a proposition from a newspaper agency offering us a series of such articles for a fee 50 per cent less than you have suggested".

I am persuaded that, on account of this OPERA MUNDI incident, we have lost 50 per cent of the Continental business which I did hope to make. I feel sure that we can get back all these papers but we are definitely losing some months.

Arriving in Paris after an absence of two months and a half, I have found here a tremendous lot of work, and beg to give me another day or two. I shall certainly let you have a detailed statement regarding the publication of your first two articles latest on Wednesday. To-day, we are despatching your article on Italy.

Yours very faithfully,
I. Révész

Emery Reves to Winston S. Churchill: telegram

10 August 1937   Paris

If any possibility kindly stop Operamundi publications French provinces stop Could spoil great possibilities thanks.

Revesz

Emery Reves to Winston S. Churchill

10 August 1937   Paris

Dear Mr. Churchill,

Kindly find enclosed two statements regarding the publication of your first two articles.[1] These statements might suffer some alterations later. There might be some other publications, and the fees which have not been fixed in Pound sterling might be influenced by the fluctuations of the exchange rates.

I should be most obliged if it would be possible for you to allow me to send you the cheques directly. It has been a principle since the existence of COOPERATION that all payments received by us came from newspapers, and all the payments remitted by us have been sent directly to the authors of the articles. Needless to say I could make an exception and send the cheques to the EVENING STANDARD if you wish so. But the method of payment I imagine is a very simple one. I would let you have every month a cheque of £50.0.0. and at the end of each quarter the surplus.

I enclose a cheque of £100.0.0. for the first two articles, as your part for these two articles will be more than this amount.

I should be most obliged if you would kindly let me know your opinion about these statements, and if you would tell me whether you desire some other method.

I have sent you a telegram to-day asking you to be kind enough to stop the publication of your articles by Opera Mundi in the French provincial press. In the French provincial newspapers there are very great possibilities, and I firmly believe that we could make a very interesting combination for a regular publication of your articles. I think that the fee PARIS-SOIR pays to-day is not sufficient. My opinion is that sooner or later we shall have to discuss this matter with that paper, and if they refuse to pay higher remuneration or to renounce to their exclusive rights, we must have the courage to look for a better arrangement. It is evident that I shall not undertake anything before having had an opportunity to talk over the matter with you. It would be therefore a great mistake to spoil the French provincial market in allowing Opera Mundi to offer now your articles, if some times later we had to negotiate with the same papers. I am really convinced that these simultaneous activities are against your own interest, as it very much depreciates the value of your articles if Editors see that an agency is publishing your articles almost two months after we have informed them that COOPERATION is charged with the exclusive publication of your articles.

I beg to remain,
Yours most faithfully,
I. Révész

P.S. Should you like to see some cuttings of newspapers containing your articles, I shall be glad to let you have some.

1. "The Ebbing Tide of Socialism" (9 July 1937) and "Partition Perils in Palestine" (23 July 1937).

Violet Pearman to Emery Reves

19 August 1937

Dear Dr. Revesz,
    Herewith the three copies of Mr. Churchill's article this week,[1] with the final amendments and corrections, which have rather delayed my sending them to you. But it was important to have these final amendments absolutely correct before they were sent off to you, as you will quite understand.

Yours faithfully,
[Violet Pearman]
Private Secretary

1. Published in the *Evening Standard* on 20 August 1937 as "A Plain Word to the Nazis." It was circulated by Cooperation under the title "Anglo-German Relations."

Cooperation to Winston S. Churchill

20 August 1937   Paris

ANGLO-GERMAN RELATIONS

Published by	Gross proceeds £	Mr. Churchill £	Cooperation £
Paris-Soir, Paris	11. 6. 0.	11. 6. 0.	———
Berlingske Tidende, Copenhagen	5. 0. 0.	5. 0. 0.	———

Dagens Nyheter, Stockholm	7.10. 0.	5.18. 0.	1.12. 0.
Le Soir, Bruxelles	10. 0. 0.	5. 0. 0.	5. 0. 0.
Nieuwe Rotterdamsche Courant, Rotterdam	3. 0. 0.	1.10. 0.	1.10. 0.
Tidens Tegn, Oslo	5. 0. 0.	2.10. 0.	2.10. 0.
Dagsposten, Trondheim	1.10. 0.	0.15. 0.	0.15. 0.
Helsingin Sanomat, Helsinki	3. 0. 0.	1.10. 0.	1.10. 0.
Paevaleht, Tallinn	1. 0. 0.	0.10. 0.	0.10. 0.
Lietuvos Zinios, Kaunas	1. 0. 0.	0.10. 0.	0.10. 0.
Lidove Noviny, Prague	1.12. 0.	0.16. 0.	0.16. 0.
Neue Zuercher Zeitung, Zurich	4. 0. 0.	2. 0. 0.	2. 0. 0.
Journal des Nations, Geneva	0.14. 0.	0. 7. 0.	0. 7. 0.
Ujsag, Budapest	0.16. 0.	0. 8. 0.	0. 8. 0.
Kurjer Warszawski, Varsovie (Fee still uncertain)	4. 0. 0.	2. 0. 0.	2. 0. 0.
La Nacion, Buenos Aires	10. 0. 0.	5. 0. 0.	5. 0. 0.
Total	69. 8. 0.	45. 0. 0.	24. 8. 0.

Emery Reves to Winston S. Churchill

26 August 1937   Paris

Dear Mr. Churchill,

I shall arrive in London on Friday evening and shall telephone to you Saturday morning, hoping that you will be able to receive me either Saturday afternoon or on Sunday. I shall have to come back to Paris on Monday.

I beg to remain,
Yours very sincerely,
I. Révész

Winston S. Churchill: engagement cards

28 August 1937

Dr. Revesz to lunch.

Emery Reves to Winston S. Churchill

31 August 1937   Paris

Dear Mr. Churchill,

Returned to Paris, I should like to express my most sincere thanks for your kind invitation.

I have seen Mr. Robertson Monday morning, but when our conversation took place, he did not yet receive your letter. I discussed with him particularly the situation which arises in case the Evening Standard publishes your articles several days before the Continental newspapers can get them. I asked him to quote a more precise copyright line in order to prevent unauthorized reproductions abroad. But of course, the only solution of this problem would be if you could, at least from time to time, write your articles four, five days before their release date.

I am sending you a cutting of today's Het Laatste Nieuws, still publishing the Opera-Mundi series. This has been started in June and is still going on more than two months later. I wonder whether you could write to the Editor of this paper a few lines explaining that this is a second series of old articles, the publication of which today disturb very much your fresh and topical articles. So he either should stop these publications or go on with them in more frequent intervals in order to finish it as soon as possible.

I shall let you have a statement regarding the publication of your last two articles before the end of this week.

I should be particularly interested to undertake the publication of your articles in the United States. As I have told you, I should be prepared to go over to America later in the year, being sure that the market there is several times bigger than in Europe. I should be much obliged, therefore, if you would consider the possibility of giving me an option for some months.

I have told you already about the reaction in the German press of your last article. This publication seems to trouble them very seriously. You know that, at the moment, a great meeting of the Germans living abroad takes place at Stuttgart. Two days ago, the President of this Organization, Herr Bohle, as well as the Foreign Minister, Baron von Neurath, and Herr Rudolf Hess delivered speeches,[1] all three referring to your article and protesting against your accusations. It seems that the article was most useful.

Thanking you once again for the kindness with which you have received me in Chartwell,

I beg to remain,
Yours very sincerely,
I. Révész

1.   Ernst Bohle, British born of naturalized British parents, joined the Nazi Party in 1931, and from 1933 was head of the Organization of German Residents Abroad; in August 1937 he repudiated his British nationality. Konstantin von Neurath was German Foreign Minister. Rudolph Hess had been Deputy Leader of the Nazi Party under Hitler since 1933.

Violet Pearman to Emery Reves: telegram

1 September 1937

Despatched article today

Pearman

Winston S. Churchill to Emery Reves

2 September 1937

You kindly said you would give me figures to show that there was only a pound or two difference between one article and another in the alternating bases we have discussed. Assuming this is so there would be the advantage in choosing the 60/40 basis that you would be able to have the whole business of the translated articles entirely in your hands. I have no doubt you could make a better bargain for me particularly in France by utilising the provincial press. I have ascertained from Mr. Robertson that there are no commitments in the foreign sphere which would hamper your making new arrangements. At the same time I should like Paris-Soir to be treated with all courtesy. Will you therefore proceed on the basis of 60/40 over the whole translated matter after the present article upon the Far East crisis has been disposed of.[1] I should be much obliged if you would keep me informed of what you do, and perhaps you will let me know about Paris-Soir before action is actually taken.

I shall be glad to receive from you a list of the papers which have taken, at any time, my articles, and to know of any new ones added to them, so that I can see what parts of Europe they suit. Will you kindly send me this type-written, together with the prices they pay and the country to which they belong.

I have forwarded your complaint about Het Laatste Nieuws to Curtis Brown. I can do no more.

1. "China and Europe," published in the *Evening Standard* on 3 September 1937 as "The Wounded Dragon."

Cooperation to Winston S. Churchill

[3 September 1937]   Paris

CHINA AND EUROPE

Published by	Gross proceeds
Paris-Soir	£10. 8. 0.
Pariser Tages Zeitung, Paris	0.16. 0.
Le Soir, Bruxelles	10. 0. 0.
Luxemburger Zeitung, Luxembourg	1. 0. 0.
Algemeen Handelsblad, Amsterdam	2.10. 0.
Nieuwe Rotterdamsche Courant, Rotterdam	2.10. 0.
Berlingske Tidende, Copenhagen	5. 0. 0.
Tidens Tegn, Oslo	5. 0. 0.
Dagsposten, Trondheim	1.10. 0.
Stavanger Aftenblad, Stavanger	1.10. 0.

Dagens Nyheter, Stockholm	7.10. 0.
Helsingin Sanomat, Helsinki	3. 0. 0.
Briwa Zeme, Riga	2.10. 0.
Paevaleht, Tallinn	1. 0. 0.
Lietuvos Aidas, Kaunas	1. 0. 0.
Narodni Osvobozeni, Prague	1.10. 0.
Neue Freie Presse, Vienna	2. 0. 0.
Thurgauer Zeitung, Frauenfeld	1. 8. 0.
St. Galler Tagblatt, St. Gallen	1. 8. 0.
Pesti Hirlap, Budapest	5. 0. 0.
Pester Lloyd, Budapest	2. 0. 0.
Le Moment, Bucharest	1. 0. 0.
La Nacion, Buenos Aires	10. 0. 0.
La Bourse Egyptienne	2. 0. 0.

Total	£81.10. 0.

Emery Reves to Winston S. Churchill

7 September 1937   Paris

Dear Mr. Churchill,

Kindly find enclosed statements regarding the publication of your third and fourth articles.

I am also enclosing a cheque of £90.0.0. (Ninety Pounds).

Should you have received 60% of the gross proceeds of all publications, so I think the figures would have been as follows:

1° article:	£56. 6.0.	instead of	£57. 4.0.
2° article:	46.10.0.	– –	51.11.0.
3° article:	50. 7.0.	– –	52. 5.0.
4° article:	41.14.0.	– –	45. 0.0.

I note what you tell me regarding Paris-Soir and the French rights. I am leaving in a few days for Geneva where I shall stay during the Assembly. So I shall only be able to start conversations with newspapers on my return. It is evident that I shall leave everything as it stands and shall not undertake anything until I was able to discuss the matter with you.

I am sending you enclosed another copy of Het Laatste Nieuws, with another article published by Opera Mundi.

I am also enclosing you two telegrams from the Neue Freie Presse in Vienna, which I beg to kindly return to me. These telegrams refer to your last article on the Far Eastern crisis. The first telegram says "Churchill accepted", and later I received a second telegram saying "Cancel acceptation Churchill as article already published London Friday."

I think there is one more proof how important it would be to arrange simultaneous publications all over the world. After having received the two telegrams I have telephoned to Vienna trying to persuade the Editor to publish the article but he said that the whole Vienna press has published already quotations of it, and that he would make himself ridiculous in publishing an article, which is known by everybody. I beg, therefore, to kindly consider the following two suggestions:

1°—The simple remark "World copyright reserved" does not prevent unauthorised reproductions in other countries. The press moral in Central and Eastern Europe as well as in South America is very low, and an article published as the Evening Standard is publishing your articles, is immediately taken by the London correspondents of many foreign papers. To prevent this the only way would be to print at the end of each article the following quotation:

"Copyright by Evening Standard, outside the British Empire by Cooperation. Reproduction, even partially, strictly forbidden."

So agencies and newspaper correspondents would see who has the Copyright, and being afraid of legal consequences would not dare to reproduce without authorisation the most important passages of the articles.

I have discussed this question with Mr. Robertson, who told me that he believes Lord Beaverbrook [1] has some prejudice against copyright remarks. But I am convinced this could be settled if you would express the desire, as otherwise we shall have to suffer many losses and cannot prevent unauthorised publications.

2°—To avoid such incidents with newspapers the best solution would be of course if you would see a possibility to write the articles four–five days before their publication.

I am sending enclosed a small cutting from a newspaper, still in connection with your article on Germany. The chairman of the Foreign Nazi Organisations, Herr Bohle, announces that he will visit England in October and should like to have a talk with you in order to convince you about the innocence of Nazi organisations in other countries.

We have received the last two articles without title. I should be grateful if you would send us the articles with a title as much depends upon a good headline. When I am in Paris, I think I could arrange this, but while I am away, I am afraid that some difficulties might arise here to find a good title in English language.

Yours very sincerely,
I. Révész

1.   Lord Beaverbrook, one of Churchill's friends since the First World War, was the owner of the *Evening Standard*. In May 1940, Churchill appointed him Minister of Aircraft Production, in which capacity he remarkably increased the output of fighter planes.

Emery Reves to Winston S. Churchill

12 September 1937   Paris

Dear Mr. Churchill,

This afternoon I have had a telephone conversation with the Editor of
LE SOIR in Brussels, and he told me how disappointed he is of our arrangement. He accepted an unusually high fee in Belgium for your articles, believing that he will have exclusive rights, and two Belgian papers—HET LAATSTE
NIEUWS and XXème SIECLE—in Flemish and in French—are publishing
simultaneously your articles supplied by Opera Mundi. He said the explanation I have given him over a month ago would have been satisfactory if these
publications had been stopped. But we are in the third month of our contract, and these publications are still going on. He said that he cannot believe
that such a thing is possible without your authorization, and you have certainly made two arrangements, one with Opera Mundi, and one with us.

I have told him that this is out of question, but I really believe that a letter
from you would be very useful to clear the atmosphere. I wonder therefore
whether you could write a letter to the Editor of LE SOIR, explaining that
incident. I think the best would be if you would send this letter to me as I
shall have to go to Brussels as soon as I am back from Geneva. But in my
opinion it would be equally necessary to write letters to the two Belgian
papers publishing the Opera Mundi series asking them to finish as quickly as
possible these publications which are disturbing the publication of your fresh
articles. Such a letter could greatly facilitate future arrangements with these
two papers too.

I am expecting your next article at the beginning of this week. If you permit me a suggestion, I think it would very much interest the international
press if you would deal with the naval situation in the Mediterranean.

I beg to remain,
Yours very sincerely,
I. Révész

Winston S. Churchill to Emery Reves

14 September 1937

I send you herewith the answer I have received from Colonel McCormick[1]
of the Chicago Tribune. In these circumstances if you should be making the
journey to the United States I should be quite ready to place the marketing
of these fortnightly articles in the United States in your hands, subject however to the condition that nothing must be done to complicate my position
with Collier's Magazine for which I do important work every year, and that
any proposals you may make must be submitted to me beforehand so that I
might consider how they affect my market in the United States which is a

more valuable one for me in respect of magazine work than it could ever be as the result of these topical articles.

I have forwarded your complaints about Het Laatste Nieuws to Curtis Brown. I can do no more.

I enclose you a letter for the Editor of the Brussels Le Soir.

1. Robert McCormick, who had seen active service on the Western Front in 1918, was both Editor and Publisher of the strongly anti-British *Chicago Tribune* from 1919 until his death in 1955.

Winston S. Churchill to the Editor of Le Soir

14 September 1937   Chartwell
Private

DRAFT[1]

Dear Sir,

I hear from Dr. Revesz that you have been vexed by the fact that some articles of mine have been appearing in the Het Laatste Nieuws and XXeme Siecle. These are part of an old contract made by Opera Mundi in respect of the second serials of some articles published many months ago in England. They have nothing to do with the new original topical articles which I write every fortnight for the Evening Standard and which are so widely reproduced in Europe. Steps are being taken to bring the Opera Mundi publications to a close. It was thought that they had ended nearly six weeks ago.

I desire to assure you that Dr. Revesz will in future have entire control of my Continental business, and I trust this will be satisfactory to you.

1. For correspondence relating to this letter, as finally sent, see 7 and 11 October 1937.

Violet Pearman to Emery Reves

16 September 1937

Dear Dr. Revesz,

Herewith the article for this week's Evening Standard,[1] which I hope reaches you safely in time. It has to be sent to London by train to be posted at Victoria station, and today it should catch an early air mail. I have also telegraphed to you that it was coming.

Yours faithfully,
[Violet Pearman]
Private Secretary

1. "Friendship with Germany," published in the *Evening Standard* on 17 September 1937.

Cooperation to Winston S. Churchill

[17 September 1937]   Paris

FRIENDSHIP WITH GERMANY

(Diffusion disturbed by early publication in London.)

Published by	Gross proceeds
Paris-Soir, Paris (not published)	£10. 8. 0.
Pariser Tages Zeitung, Paris	0.16. 0.
Le Soir, Bruxelles	10. 0. 0.
Nieuwe Rotterdamsche Courant, Rotterdam	3. 0. 0.
Berlingske Tidende, Copenhagen	5. 0. 0.
Tidens Tegn, Oslo	5. 0. 0.
Dagens Nyheter, Stockholm	7.10. 0.
Paevaleht, Tallinn	1. 0. 0.
Neues Wiener Tagblatt, Vienna	2. 0. 0.
Neue Zürcher Zeitung, Zurich	4. 0. 0.
Le Moment, Bucharest	1. 0. 0.
La Nacion, Buenos-Aires	10. 0. 0.
O Estado de Sao Paulo	7. 0. 0.
Total	£66.14. 0.
60%	£39.14. 0.

Cooperation to Winston S. Churchill

18 September 1937   Paris

1. Telegram from PESTI HIRLAP, Budapest
"Pester Lloyds of the 18th September has published an extensive resumé
of Churchill article and consequently, we are not publishing it any more."
—Pesti Hirlap.

TRANSLATION FROM THE GERMAN

2. Letter from Neues Wiener Tagblatt, Vienna
TO COOPERATION Paris,   Vienna, 18.9.1937
     To our very great regret, we must draw attention to the fact that another
case has occurred in which both the copyright of COOPERATION as well
as the agreement in regard to the specified date for the publication of an
article have become quite an illusion. The latest article by Winston Churchill,
which we accepted by telegram, was reserved by you for Monday the 20th or
the 21st. Actually it appeared however as late as yesterday, the 17th inst. in the
Evening Standard. But what makes it more annoying is that the Telegraph
Company in spite of the copyright and despite the prohibition to pass on

extracts from the article, has placed at the disposal of its subscribers a detailed extract from the Evening Standard and this extract has in fact appeared today in several Vienna newspapers whereas we wanted to keep to the date. We are of course no longer bound to this time of publication. Apart from this, we must draw attention to the fact that your articles are practically valueless if newspapers, who have not acquired them from you, are in the position to accept them and publish them through a telegraph agency without the payment of any money, which has happened in this the second instance.

Emery Reves to Winston S. Churchill

20 September 1937   Hôtel de la Paix
                                                                                      Geneva

Dear Mr. Churchill,

This morning, when I entered the press-room of the League of Nations, several editors staying here received me with bad news.

Your article has been published in London Friday afternoon. The same evening various German stations have broadcasted it, and a German telegraphic agency has diffused all over Europe an extract of 400 words of the article. I am enclosing a cutting of Pester Lloyd of Saturday morning containing this comment. All this happened before the original article has reached the newspapers, though we have translated and despatched it 4 hours after its reception in Paris. Now many papers will decline the publication of this article.

I am terribly sorry that I have to trouble you once more with this problem, but I feel obliged to inform you that we shall lose the greater part of our contracts by the end of the year if we cannot alter this situation. Your articles are far too important that they could be published in London without being remarked elsewhere. And once the news-agencies diffused large extracts of them, the papers refuse to publish the original version.

I do beg, under these circumstances, to kindly consider my two proposals to avoid such incidents in the future, which may spoil the whole international market:

1. The articles ought to be published in England and on the Continent on the same days.

2. The Evening Standard, just like all other papers do, ought to publish the articles with a clear and detailed Copyright-line in order to prevent even partial reproductions. The quotation which could safeguard your rights is as follows: "Copyright by Evening Standard, outside the British Empire by Cooperation." "Reproduction, even partially, strictly forbidden."

Besides this business point of view, I think you have the greatest political interest to prevent the quotation of parts of your articles. Please, read carefully this extract of 400 words. It is a most able and diabolic work, which carries the sign of the method of Dr. Göbbels. They extracted phrases of your article in such a manner that the effect of this comment is exactly the contrary to that of the whole article! It reads as a tribute to Herr Hitler, as a kind of a "Mea Culpa" after your previous article. And in those countries where this has appeared, we cannot publish anymore the integral text of the article!

I have received copy of your letter regarding U.S.A. As soon as I shall be back in Paris, I shall study the possibilities.

I met here in Geneva the Editor of the "Hungarian Quarterly" of Budapest. This is a quarterly to promote relations between Hungary and the English speaking world, published in English language. It is published by a society, the Chairman of which is Count Bethlen.[1] They should very much like to publish an article by you of about 3000 words. You would be entirely free to choose the subject which should be a general political subject, interesting Central Europe. They only ask that the article should not be very "anti-nazi", as this would be delicate for them to publish at the moment. They were prepared to pay £50.-.- (Fifty Pounds) which is for them a quite unusually high fee.

I should be grateful if you would inform me by returning air-mail (Hôtel de la Paix, Genève), whether you are accepting this proposal. I think that I could use such an article also in some other countries, so that the article could bring more than what they alone can pay.

I beg to remain,
Yours very sincerely
I. Révész

---

1.   Count Stephen (István) Bethlen was one of the counterrevolutionary leaders in postwar Hungary. He served as Prime Minister from 1921 to 1931, when he promoted the economic reconstruction of Hungary.

Emery Reves to Winston S. Churchill

21 September 1937   Geneva

A Lithuanian Paper equally refused the article on that reason.[1] This article, which could have had a very great success, will not be published but half as well as the previous ones. And this incident has caused such excitement among our clients that I am afraid if it happens once more, existing contracts will be cancelled.

It is therefore of the greatest importance that already the next article should be released on the same day all over the world, and that the Evening Standard should publish it with a detailed Copyright-line. Even so, I am afraid that the next articles will not be published as well as until now, and I shall be satisfied if the consequences of this incident will not exceed 100 Pounds.

It is evident that the news-agencies had no right to publish such large parts of the article, and you or the Evening Standard could require an indemnity. Should this article have been published under the Copyright I have indicated already several times, I would immediately open a legal action on my part, and I am sure I would get a high indemnity.

I have hoped that your articles will be published <u>regularly</u>, and with increasing interest in all countries, during a long period, and that I shall be able to secure for you regularly about 1000.- Pounds a year.[2] It is really a great pity that we are going to destroy this already organized market on account of a secondary, technical question which could be easily settled.

I should be most obliged if you would be kind enough to let me know whether you can arrange that the publications in London shall take place in such a form that they shall not prevent international publications. I must calm some editors in giving them a formal assurance for the future.

1. Churchill's article "Friendship with Germany" had been refused by some papers because it had been distributed by the news agencies, as a news item.
2. One thousand pounds a year in 1937 was the equivalent of £25,000 in 1996.

Winston S. Churchill to Emery Reves: telegram

23 September 1937

Please send instances of copyright infringements as Standard will prosecute

Churchill

Winston S. Churchill to Emery Reves

23 September 1937

The Evening Standard cannot alter their copyright line. They say they would have to make a special exception in this case which would cast a slur on all their "world copyright" protection. On the other hand they are willing to take up with the offending papers the breach which has occurred. Will you kindly send me whatever instances are possible.

I hope to send you the next article on Monday.

Violet Pearman to Emery Reves

26 September 1937

Dear Doctor Révész,

I send you herewith a letter I have received from Mr. Robertson of the "Evening Standard", and shall be glad if you will comply with the request he makes in the second paragraph.

The translations of the documents you sent me certainly show that we have been seriously pirated. The German synopsis does not appear to have been unfair, except from the point of view of the plagiarism and the violation of copyright. I think you should write to the "Neues Wiener Tagblatt" and explain that vigorous measures are being taken to protect the copyright.

I hope to let you have the next article on Monday or Tuesday, which ought to give you a good start.

Emery Reves to Winston S. Churchill

28 September 1937   Hôtel de la Paix
                                                                  Geneva

Dear Mr. Churchill,
   I think it would be useful if the EVENING STANDARD would ask the London representative of the German News Agencies, especially Europa-Press, not to use your next articles as they did the last one. Such a warning in advance might have some effect.

                                                       Yours most respectfully,
                                                              I. Révész

Winston S. Churchill to Emery Reves

3 October 1937

Dear Doctor Révész,
   I have found an article written some years ago on "The United States of Europe", which I think would be very suitable, if adapted and brought up-to-date, for The Hungarian Review.
   What commission would you propose upon a fee of £50 which they offer? I should not consider this matter upon the same basis as our regular fortnightly articles.
   Pray let me know your views.

Emery Reves to Winston S. Churchill

7 October 1937   Paris

Dear Mr. Churchill,
   I am just back in Paris. Yesterday, I have seen in Marseille, in a local paper, a picture of you together with Herr Bohle. Your expression shows that the conversation must have been a very amusing one.
   I am happy that you have found an article which you believe to be suitable for the Hungarian Quarterly. Has this article been published in Europe? Pub-

lication in America would not disturb, but I should not like that they should discover later that the article is an old one. If you will adapt it and bring it up-to-date, this question will not arise. Regarding the conditions, I shall be pleased to arrange this publication for you without any commission.

In reply to a letter of Mr. Robertson asking for further instances of the copyright infringement, I can only refer to a previous letter of mine, containing the three agencies which have diffused on the continent extracts of your articles. They are, 1) Europa-Press in Frankfurt and their two sub-agencies, 2) Telegraphen Companie in Vienna and 3) Információ Hirlaptudósító in Budapest. Quite a great number of newspapers have published these comments, but there is nothing to do against them as they have acted in good faith.

Having left Geneva, I visited French provincial towns (Lyon, Marseille, Montpellier, Perpignan, Saint-Etienne) to discuss matters with newspaper editors. At present, the situation of the French provincial press is almost catastrophic; the social legislation of the Blum government made in the newspaper business more difficulties than in any other economic branch. To all this comes a rise of 60% of the paper price and a considerable fall in the advertisements. There will be an important meeting next week of the French Newspaper Proprietors Association to discuss the situation.

Under these circumstances, I prefer not even to mention your collaboration; I believe it is better to wait a month or two to see what will be the development.

I hope to be able to come over to London in the second part of this month for about a fortnight, and shall be glad to give you some further information on the situation and also to discuss with you some plans regarding the United States.

I beg to remain
Yours very sincerely,
I. Révész

P.S. I am leaving here for Brussels in a few days. The letter which you were kind enough to send me to the Editor of Le Soir is excellent.[1] I only beg to kindly change two words. You say in the letter that you write these articles "every fortnight for the Evening Standard . . ." I think it is not a good policy to make believe newspaper editors that you are writing these articles specially for the Evening Standard and they have only second rights to reproduce them. I wonder therefore whether you would have the kindness to say "articles which I write every fortnight for the international press and . . ." etc.

Pray return me this letter at your earliest convenience.

Thanks,
R.

1.   For the text of this letter, see 14 September 1937.

Arnold K. Maplesden[1] *to Emery Reves*

11 October 1937   7 Museum Mansion
                                                          Great Russell Street
                                                          London W.C.1.

Dear Sir,
   In reply to your letter of October 8th, I wish to state that you have been
misinformed when you say that a "very considerable part" of the article by
Mr. Churchill has been "lifted" by me.
   I merely reported the fact that the EVENING STANDARD had published the article in question and quoted a few sentences which seemed to me
to have a political significance.
   Naturally, I had no intention whatever of infringing the copyright in the
article. I considered that the publication of the article as such constituted a
news item of considerable importance.
   If, however, you object to the dissemination of such news items, I will
undertake not to mention in my news reports any further articles of Mr.
Churchill published in the EVENING STANDARD.
                                                          Yours faithfully,

   1.   Arnold K. Maplesden, head of the London office of Europa Press.

Violet Pearman to Emery Reves

13 October 1937

Dear Dr. Revesz,
   Herewith the article for this week's Evening Standard,[1] as promised on the
telephone to you today by Mr. Churchill himself.
                                                          Yours faithfully,
                                                          [Violet Pearman]
                                                          Private Secretary

   1.   "War Is Not Imminent," published in the *Evening Standard* on 15 October
1937.

Winston S. Churchill to Emery Reves: telegram

13 October 1937

   Article corrections sixth line leave out from this fear down to proving itself
true two and a half lines Stop Second page fifth line should read my belief
that major war is not imminent leaving out in the next six or eight months
Stop third page ninth line after Libya leave out to threaten and insert which
cannot fail to cause concern in Egypt
                                                          Churchill

Emery Reves to Winston S. Churchill: telegram

14 October 1937

Regret telegram arrived this morning. Article despatched during night.

Revesz

Emery Reves to Winston S. Churchill

14 October 1937   Paris

Dear Mr. Churchill,

We have really made a great effort to translate and despatch your article. It was nearly 4 o'clock this morning when I have sent 37 letters to the Air France Headquarters that they may reach the first morning planes.

Unfortunately your telegram was received only this morning at 8 o'clock so I was no more able to make the corrections. It is a pity that these corrections have not been transmitted to us by telephone last night.

Usually telegrams after 10 p.m. are not delivered in Paris unless before the address there is indicated "NUIT". But I have examined the telegram and see that it was despatched in Westerham at 8.30 p.m. and received at the Telegram Head Office in Paris at 9.45 p.m. So I shall submit this telegram to the Minister of Postes, Télégraphes & Téléphones and shall ask for an inquiry.

After the fatigues of last night my office is rather sleepy to-day but I shall certainly let you have a cheque and a statement concerning the last two articles before the end of the week.

Yours very sincerely,
I. Révész

Emery Reves to Winston S. Churchill

18 October 1937

Dear Mr. Churchill,

Kindly find enclosed a cheque of £100.- and statements regarding the publications of your last three articles.

As you see the incident has caused a considerable drawback in the publications. And should we receive your articles only 2 or 3 days before their publication in London, I see no way to get the same results as with the first articles.

May I resume briefly the situation?

There is only a small number of newspapers with which we have contracts for the publication of all of your articles. The major part of them takes separate decisions for each article. This is natural and it is only on that basis that we are reaching considerable circulation for all the articles we are publishing. We are in touch in every country with 4–5 newspapers and it is a statistical rule that important articles are accepted by the 2nd or 3rd paper if the first or second declines them. But to pursue these negotiations we must have about a week's time as at the very moment when the article is published anywhere, there is no use in offering it any longer, as such proposals irritate only the Editors. So all arrangements have to be made before the release date which has to be the same for all countries. If we must rely upon one single proposal, the business becomes a kind of a gamble. It is impossible to foresee which paper will be interested in a special article as this depends mostly upon local circumstances.

Please consider, for example, what has happened just now with your last article, "The war is not imminent" in Central Europe. We have received this article on Wednesday night, dispatched it before Thursday morning but the earliest date by which the greater part of the papers could receive this article was Friday evening. So I released it for Saturday. I have sent it to a German and a Czech paper in Prague, to a paper in Vienna and in Budapest. The German paper in Prague has accepted it, the three others declined it. I have immediately offered it to other papers in the respective cities, two of them have turned it down because in the meantime the German paper in Prague published it. I have spent more than £2.0.0.- for telephone conversations to try to change their mind. But it was useless, I was only told that they would have been glad to publish the article, should they have received it earlier.

The first few articles have had a wide circulation because I have released them about a week after the publication in the Evening Standard and so it was possible to arrange for publication in practically all the countries. But this method has led to the incidents about a month ago and is no more practicable. The articles must be released in London and on the Continent simultaneously. With the last two articles I made an experience in releasing them the day following their publication in London. The result is a fall of about 40% in the publications.

There are two reasons: 1°—To offer an article on Friday for publication on Saturday is almost hopeless as I know that most papers take already Thursday their dispositions regarding their leaders for Sunday. Anything coming later is automatically returned. 2°—It is impossible to submit articles to other papers in case of refusal.

To all this comes a new difficulty. During the winter months the Air-mail is under normal conditions (without taking into consideration fog and bad weather) half as good as during the summer. During the summer months, for instance, the big line Central-Eastern Europe leaving Paris every morning arrived on the same day in Budapest, Belgrade and even Bucarest. Since the 1st of October this line stops at Prague and continues its route only the following day. This means that until 1st of April the quickest way to get letters to Vienna, Budapest, and further on, takes two days.

I have given to that problem the most careful consideration as I see that you do not like to write your articles sooner, but unfortunately I see no solution to come over these technical difficulties. Either we can dispatch to all countries your articles Monday in the morning for publication on Friday or Saturday or we must be content with half results.

I should be most grateful, therefore, if you would consent to make a trial in writing your two or three next articles on Sunday so that we may receive the MS by Monday morning. Should any event necessitate some alterations, this we could easily communicate to the papers having accepted the article even until Thursday.

I do hope that you will understand my insisting upon that point as I feel that we have common interests. We must avoid technical difficulties and small incidents as such unnecessary discussions trouble very much our relations with the Editors, and I am afraid, even what has happened during the last weeks have diminished their enthusiasm.

Yours very sincerely,
I. Révész

P.S. Please ask Mrs. Pearman to control the figures on the statements, as nothing is more complicated for us continentals than to count in British currency.

Emery Reves to Winston S. Churchill

18 October 1937   Paris

Dear Mr. Churchill,

A few minutes after I have mailed my letter of this morning, I received a letter from the Editor of LIDOVE NOVINY in Prague of which I enclose a copy. The letter translated into a poor English is as follows:

> "In reply to your letter of 15th inst. I take the liberty to inform you that I have received the Churchill-article on the 15th inst. at 5 p.m. As its release date has been fixed for the 16th it was technically impossible for us to translate the m.s. and to dispatch it in time to Bruenn in our printing-house. Neither was it possible for us to delay its publication as you are in touch also with Prager Tagblatt which has, indeed, published the article on Saturday.
>
> I must underline once again that we cannot bind ourselves to publish all the articles which you are submitting to us. This regards naturally also the articles of Mr. Churchill though we estime particularly this author. Should this condition not be acceptable for you, it would be rather difficult for our newspaper to continue our free collaboration.
>
> signed
The Editor."

I think this letter adds nothing to what I have said in my letter of this morning. I am also enclosing a letter for you which I have received through Paris-Soir.

Yours sincerely,
I. Révész

Winston S. Churchill to Emery Reves

20 October 1937

Dear Dr. Revesz,

Many thanks for your letter and cheque.

I have heard from the Evening Standard that the Newspaper Proprietors' Association are taking action to restrain pillaging "world copyright articles" and the Evening Standard have also communicated with the offenders.

I will endeavour to send you the articles as early as possible and the next one will be despatched on Sunday.

I have not yet been able to find a suitable article for the Hungarian Review but I will try and do so in the near future.

I am sending you a copy of my new book by this mail.[1]

I do not understand what you mean by your postscript. We have no means here of checking the exchanges.

---

1.   This was *Great Contemporaries,* a collection of twenty-one biographical articles that Churchill had written between October 1929 and January 1936, for the *Pall Mall, News of the World, Strand, Daily Mail,* and *Sunday Pictorial.* The book had been published on 4 October 1937. After the Second World War, under Reves's guidance, it was translated into French, German, Italian, Swedish, Portuguese, Norwegian, Dutch, and Hebrew.

Henri Haïm[1] to Emery Reves

20 October 1937   30 rue Kasr-el-Nil
                                                                        Cairo

Messieurs,

Par votre lettre du 29 juin 1937, vous avez bien voulu nous offrir l'exclusivité des articles de Mr. Winston Churchill.

Nous avons accepté votre offre par notre lettre du 3 juillet 1937 et vous confirmions cette acceptation en date du 19 juillet 1937 comme suit:

"nous nous empressons de vous informer que nous acceptons les droits de reproduction exclusive pour nos éditions du Caire et d'Alexandrie de la série d'articles que vous donnera Mr. Winston Churchill, à raison de £2.- par article pour une période de six mois."

Quelle ne fut pas notre surprise après avoir été offert et obtenu l'exclusivité de ces articles de découvrir dans les colonnes de THE EGYPTIAN GAZETTE d'hier l'article du grand homme politique anglais intitulé "War is not imminent", que nous allions faire paraître le même jour chez nous et qui était déjà composé sur le marbre.

J'attends vos explications, par retour du courrier, sur cette grave infraction à nos accords.

En attendant, veuillez agréer, Messieurs, nos salutations distinguées.

Henri Haïm

1.   Director-Administrator of *La Bourse Egyptienne,* the largest circulation French-language newspaper in the Middle East. It was under the same ownership as the English-language *Egyptian Mail,* the rival to the *Egyptian Gazette.*

Emery Reves to Winston S. Churchill

21 October 1937 Paris

Dear Mr. Churchill,

Many thanks for your letter. I am glad that your next article will be dispatched on Sunday. I have not yet received your book, but I thank you most heartily in advance.

I am sorry that my postscript was not clear. The exchange rates have been checked here. I only ask you to control whether the 60% have been well counted from the total.

Kindly find enclosed the letters from the Evening Standard which you were kind enough to send me.

Yours very sincerely,
I. Révész

Winston S. Churchill to Emery Reves

23 October 1937

Dear Doctor Révész,

I send you the article "Yugo-Slavia and Europe" in very good time.[1] It will not be published here until Friday, 29th October. You can have it translated as soon as possible, but there may be a few corrections, which I will telephone at latest on Monday. Thus you could despatch it for certain by the night mails of Monday, for release Saturday morning.

I think my next article will probably study the problems of Czecho-Slovakia.

1.   Churchill's article on Yugoslavia was published in the *Evening Standard* on 29 October 1937 as "A Key State in Europe." In it, he urged Yugoslavia not to range itself

"among the dictatorial or totalitarian States." Far "safer and wiser," he wrote, "would it be for this new kingdom of the Southern Slavs to throw in her lot boldly upon the side of Peace, Freedom and Parliamentary democracy. In this way alone would she realize the internal strength and unity which is vital to her in these critical decades of her life."

Emery Reves to Winston S. Churchill

24 October 1937   Paris

Dear Mr. Churchill,

Please, accept my heartiest thanks for your book which I have received yesterday. You gave me a great pleasure in having sent it.

Kindly find enclosed a copy of to-day's HET LAATSTE NIEUWS publishing again an article from the old Opera Mundi series. This is about the 25th publication. I cannot imagine what they have done with the 6 articles, but they seem to have manufactured an almost inexhaustible stock of articles out of them.

I have received this morning by air-mail a most unpleasant letter from the Editor of LA BOURSE EGYPTIENNE in Cairo, of which I am enclosing a copy.[1] As you know, I have made a contract with this paper for the regular publication of your articles, since the beginning of our collaboration. Now, a competitor of theirs, the EGYPTIAN GAZETTE, has published your last article "War is not imminent", just the day when they wanted to publish it (la BOURSE EGYPTIENNE and THE EGYPTIAN MAIL are under the same proprietorship).

How did the EGYPTIAN GAZETTE get this article? Should it not be a pillage, so they could only have received it from the EVENING STANDARD. Please, do enquire by Mr. Robertson what has happened, and inform me about the situation by returning mail, as I must answer to Cairo without delay to give a satisfactory explanation.

After these two bad news, a good one: I have raised the fee of PARIS SOIR, from now on they will pay 2.000.- francs per article.

I hope it was possible for you to despatch your article to-night, and that we shall receive it to-morrow, Monday, by the first mail. I have prepared already everything for its translation and immediate expedition.

Yours sincerely,
I. Révész

1.   See the letter from Henry Haïm to Emery Reves of 20 October 1937.

Violet Pearman to Winston S. Churchill

25 October 1937

Mr. Churchill,

I have telephoned Dr. Revesz (because of his office shutting at 7 p.m.) and told him the two small amendments. He is delighted to have the article so soon, and hopes this will always be done wherever possible.

Winston S. Churchill to Emery Reves: telegram

27 October 1937

Have received offer serialisation my new book Scandinavian countries Will this affect your sales

Churchill

Emery Reves to Winston S. Churchill

27 October 1937   Paris

Dear Mr. Churchill,

The Editor of SVENSKA DAGBLADET in Stockholm, Mr. Trygger,[1] has written to me that he will be in Paris at the end of this week and intends to go to London about the end of next week. He is a very distinguished Swedish gentleman, the son of the Conservative leader and for many years Prime Minister of Sweden. His family is the principal shareholder of SVEN-SKA DAGBLADET which is the most important conservative newspaper in Sweden, called the "the TIMES of Scandinavia".

Mr. Trygger is a great admirer of you. He asks me to introduce him to you and requests for an appointment. I should be most grateful indeed if you would be kind enough to receive him between the 4th and the 10th of November, as we have rather delicate things to discuss with him. The situation in Stockholm is as follows:

I have very good relations with both the DAGENS NYHETER and SVENSKA DAGBLADET which are the two most important papers in Sweden. DAGENS NYHETER is liberal, SVENSKA DAGBLADET is conservative. DAGENS NYHETER has a little higher circulation, SVENSKA DAGBLADET is a little more serious and heavier. I happened to be in Stockholm when our collaboration started and as you know, DAGENS NYHETER signed at once a contract with me, concerning all of your articles and accepted to raise considerably the fee which has been fixed for 150 Swedish Crowns per article.

As soon as Mr. Trygger learned of this arrangement, he insisted to secure for his paper your articles. I tried to frighten him saying that DAGENS NYHETER pays 200 Crowns per article, but he, at once, said: "O.K."

There is a great competition and jealousy between these two papers, and the only thing I could do was to convince him, that there is nothing to do in this year, but we can discuss the matter later. He accepted this solution but said at once that this is a condition sine qua of our further collaboration, and if I cannot secure for him your articles, he will denounce his general contract with COOPERATION concerning all our other articles. Indeed, in the letter in which he announces his coming to Paris and London he reminds me this situation.

It is a rather delicate matter because I have the feeling that it would be really unfair to take away the articles from DAGENS NYHETER who has always published them and who is very much interested in them; on the other side, we have to give some kind of satisfaction to SVENSKA DAG-BLADET. The problem is very much like the Spanish Non-Intervention, the ideal solution would be to lay it before the Non-Intervention Committee. We must try to postpone decisions as long as possible. Or, perhaps, we could give him some special articles outside this series? I should be grateful if you would kindly let me know your opinion on this question.

Should you prefer it, I should be glad to come over to London with Mr. Trygger to have a talk together.

Yours very sincerely,
I. Révész

1.   Carl Trygger, the son of a Swedish Foreign Minister, was Chief Editor of *Svenska Dagbladet* from 1934 to 1940.

Emery Reves to Winston S. Churchill

27 October 1937   Paris
Express

Dear Mr. Churchill,

Having received your telegram I have tried to telephone to you, but, unfortunately, I could not reach you neither in London nor in Westerham.

I have written to you this morning a letter concerning our Stockholm business which is in a certain degree already a reply to your telegram of this evening (the letter was addressed to Chartwell).

Yes, I firmly believe that a serialisation of your book in Scandinavia undertaken without taking into consideration our existing contracts and our negotiations with other newspapers would very much affect our sales. So I should beg not to accept this proposal.

On the other hand, should you like to serialise the book, I should be glad to undertake it in the whole world. This might interest in Stockholm the SVENSKA DAGBLADET (please, c.f. to my letter of this morning), and many other papers. Having read the book, I think that some portraits are particularly suitable for international publication. I think: the Ex-Kaiser, Shaw, Chamberlain, Hindenburg, Asquith, Lawrence, Foch, Trotsky, Alfonso, Hitler and Clemenceau.

Should you agree in principle, we could discuss the matter next week.

Yours very sincerely,
I. Révész

Winston S. Churchill to Emery Reves

28 October 1937

Dear Dr. Revesz,

Yours of October 27, about the serials of Great Contemporaries on the Continent. Will you please communicate with my publisher H. Thornton Butterworth, 15 Bedford Street, Strand, W.C.2. upon the subject. He has received an offer of £35 from a Denmark newspaper. I have told him that you are in charge of all my Continental business at the present time. He will be glad therefore to transfer this offer to you.

I do not recommend separate arrangements for serialisation with one single paper. I prefer your plan of a general serialisation of some of the most suitable articles. Will you therefore make me your proposals and explain how such an addition could be effected with our existing arrangements. We must not compromise the fortnightly articles on any account. I could not entrust you with the whole world business as I have other arrangements in the United States and in the British Empire; but I should be glad to discuss with you a plan for serialising limited to your present sphere.

I also send you a letter I have received from Mr. Robertson about the Egyptian Gazette. I have no doubt that you and he have now settled the difficulty.

Finally I send you, in confidence, some papers I have received from the Evening Standard showing how very effectively they have taken up the complaints which you made against the papers which pillaged my German article.

Emery Reves to W. H. Robertson

28 October 1937   Paris

Dear Mr. Robertson,

Many thanks for your letter. The Egyptian incident is most unfortunate indeed, and I cannot understand how it happened.

I have made a contract with "La Bourse Egyptienne" (which is now under the same proprietorship as the "Egyptian Mail") for the regular publication of <u>all</u> the articles of Mr. Churchill. They are paying £2.0.0. per article, i.e.

£4.0.0. per month. This is a contract of which I informed Mr. Churchill in
July already and which he approved. They have regularly published all the
articles and it seems to me that the article "War is not imminent" was the
first article the "Egyptian Gazette" published since three months, as this was
the first protest I have received from Cairo.

Under these circumstances, I do beg to cease to supply the "Egyptian
Gazette" with Mr. Churchill's articles as I think the other arrangement is far
more regular and advantageous for Mr. Churchill. I shall try to explain the
matter to the Editor of "La Bourse Egyptienne". But it would be disastrous
if the "Egyptian Gazette" would publish another article from Mr. Churchill.
So I beg to kindly send at once a cable to this paper cancelling the last article
which you have sent them already. I am sure you will understand this request.

I shall probably come over to London in November and hope very much
to see you.

Yours sincerely

Cooperation to Winston S. Churchill

[29 October 1937]   Paris

YUGOSLAVIA AND EUROPE [1]

Published by	Gross proceeds
Paris-Soir (not yet published)	£13.10. 0.
Pariser Tages Zeitung, Paris	0.16. 0.
Europe, Paris	2. 0. 0.
Le Soir, Bruxelles	10. 0. 0.
Berlingske Tidende, Copenhagen	5. 0. 0.
Tidens Tegn, Oslo	5. 0. 0.
Dagens Nyheter, Stockholm	7.10. 0.
Paevaleht, Tallinn	1. 0. 0.
Zydu Balsas, Kaunas [2]	0. 8. 0.
Pestry Tyden, Prague	1.10. 0.
Neue Freie Presse, Vienna	2. 0. 0.
Tages Anzeiger, Zurich	4. 0. 0.
Le Moment, Bucharest	1. 0. 0.
La Bourse Egyptienne, Le Caire	2. 0. 0.
O Estado de Sao Paulo, Sao Paulo	7. 0. 0.
Total	£62.14. 0.
60%	£37.12. 0.

1.   See 23 October 1937, note 1.
2.   *The Voice of the Jews*, the main paper of the Jewish community in Kaunas
(Kovno). It was published in Yiddish. Reves also sold Churchill's articles to a number
of other Jewish papers, including the prestigious Warsaw Yiddish daily, *Hajnt*.

Winston S. Churchill to Emery Reves

29 October 1937

Dear Dr. Revesz,

I send you a letter I have had from the Editor of the Evening Standard.[1] You will see that it is not always possible to fix an article so far in advance. After all the Evening Standard is the parent paper and I must satisfy them first.

The apologies I sent you from the various papers and agencies which had pirated our German article seem to me thoroughly satisfactory. I wonder whether you should not try a later release date as you did in the first instance. I do not think we shall be pirated again. However you must be the judge of this. I really can do no more at this end.

I shall be very glad to see Mr. Trygger with you or without you as soon as I know when he has come.

   1.   Percy Cudlipp, the Editor from 1933 to 1938.

Emery Reves to Winston S. Churchill

29 October 1937   Paris

Dear Mr. Churchill,

I have received your letter of October 28th, and I am writing to your publisher asking him to let me know which newspaper in Danemark has made him the offer.

I am absolutely of your opinion that we must not compromise the fortnightly articles on any account. And my first impression is that the Danish proposition might have such an effect. To give the serialisation rights of the whole book for £35.0.0. without knowing what the paper intends to do is a rather doubtful business. They might make out of the book thirty or forty articles and publish them during many months. Such an inflation of publications would certainly compromise the fortnightly articles.

I would suggest that we should arrange ourselves a limited number of articles, eight or maximum ten, about 13–1400 words each, and release them simultaneously. I would also suggest to make arrangements only on such a basis that newspapers should not get these articles cheaper than your fortnightly articles. As soon as I hear from your publisher I shall write you on the subject.

I thank you very much for having sent me the enclosed papers.

Mr. Robertson has written to me saying that he believed he could go on sending your articles to Egypt. He offers me to withdraw these articles should I desire so. I am enclosing for your information a copy of my reply.

I should be most grateful if you would kindly give me a reply to my sec-

ond letter of October 22nd, as I am expecting the visit of the Editor of Svenska Dagbladet on Monday.

Yours very sincerely,
I. Révész

Emery Reves to Winston S. Churchill

2 November 1937   Paris

Dear Mr. Churchill,

Many thanks for your letter of the 21st, which I have received to-day only.
I quite understand the point of view of Mr. Cudlipp, but I think that it will
be easy to find a compromise. Should you deal with a very topical subject,
you could certainly not write it a week before, but many of your articles will
not suffer at all if they were prepared a few days earlier. Regarding the articles
we have published during the past three months, I believe that the majority
of them belong to the second category. I hope to be able to discuss with you
this matter in a few days.

Mr. Trygger is in Paris. I have lunched with him to-day, and I believe
that with the assistance of a good French "déjeuner" I have arranged already
many things with him. At least, I have prepared such an arrangement.

I told him that though you and me, we both very much appreciate his
interest, it is a rather delicate matter to take away your fortnightly articles
from DAGENS NYHETER who has published them since a rather long
time. We must find an outway without bloodshed. I proposed him that we
should secure for him from time to time a special article from you outside
this series. I thought on the articles you are writing for COLLIERS or other
magazines (he could use articles of 2,000 words or more). Should these publications be possible, so both papers will be satisfied. Should DAGENS
NYHETER protest against such publications in his paper, which is not very
probable, so we could consider—if the situation permits—to make an
arrangement with him for all the articles.

My impression was that this solution will find his approval, should it be
possible for us to secure for him Swedish rights of such special articles. I told
him that we could not give him such special articles for less than £20.0.0.—
which he accepted in principle.

I have tried to sell him the serial rights of your book, but he said this is
not possible anymore in Sweden. The book is already on sale there, his own
paper has even commented it, so now it is no more possible to publish a
series out of this book. He would have been glad to do so before the book
appeared, and will be very pleased to serialize your next book before its
publication.

Mr. Trygger will arrive in London on Saturday. I am coming either
together with him, or via Brussels on the same day. Could we see you on

Sunday, or would you prefer a week day, Saturday or Monday? Please, let me know this by returning mail.

Yours very sincerely,
I. Révész

Winston S. Churchill to Emery Reves: telegram

4 November 1937

Let me know when you arrive will arrange luncheon either country or London

Churchill

Winston S. Churchill: engagement cards

10 November 1937   11 Morpeth Mansions

Dr. Revesz at flat.

Cooperation to Winston S. Churchill

[11 November 1937]   Paris

ARMISTICE OR PEACE [1]

Published by	Gross proceeds
Paris-Soir	£13.10. 0.
Pariser Tages Zeitung, Paris	0.16. 0.
Le Soir, Bruxelles	10. 0. 0.
Luxemburger Zeitung, Luxembourg	1. 0. 0.
Rotterdamsche Courant, Rotterdam	2.10. 0.
Berlingske Tidende, Copenhagen	5. 0. 0.
Tidens Tegn, Oslo	5. 0. 0.
Stavanger Aftenblad, Stavanger	1.10. 0.
Dagsposten, Trondheim	1.10. 0.
Dagens Nyheter, Stockholm	7.10. 0.
Lietuvos Aidas, Kaunas	1. 0. 0.
Neues Wiener Tagblatt, Vienna	3. 0. 0.
Neue Zürcher Zeitung, Zurich	4. 0. 0.
Pester Lloyd, Budapest	2. 0. 0.
Politika, Belgrade	4. 0. 0.
La Bourse Egyptienne, Le Caire	2. 0. 0.
La Nacion, Buenos Aires	10. 0. 0.
Total	£74. 6. 0.

1.   "Armistice—or Peace?" was published in the *Evening Standard* on 11 November 1937.

Emery Reves to Winston S. Churchill

13 November 1937   89 Piccadilly
                                                             London W.1.

Dear Mr. Churchill,

Kindly find enclosed the two versions of the divorce article. As I have told you on the telephone, I think the American version would be more suitable for Continental publication. The small alterations I venture to suggest are the following:

1) It is advisable to present the article in two parts, in case a newspaper would prefer to publish it in two issues. I would suggest to terminate the first part on page 9. In this first part there is nothing to change, except to cut out six lines on page 8 which are obviously addressed to Americans.

2) I would suggest to cut the last paragraph on page 9, the whole page 10, and the first paragraph on page 11, as this would be too much about America.

3) Regarding Part II., I think it would be a good start the 3rd paragraph on page 4 of the English version: "There are three main divisions of the Christian world . . ." until page 5, line 2 "Wycliffe . . ." Then it goes on the American version again (p. 11.) "Wycliffe . . ."

4) The small corrections on pages 15 and 16 are made after the English version, as the American one is very much addressed to American readers.

I think after these small corrections the article will be very suitable for Svenska Dagbladet, and perhaps also for other papers.

Winston S. Churchill: engagement cards

23 November 1937   Chartwell

   10.30 a.m.   Dr. Revesz.

Emery Reves to Winston S. Churchill

24 November 1937   Paris

Dear Mr. Churchill,

I just arrived in Paris and am sending you enclosed the statements regarding the two last articles on Yugoslavia and on the Armistice. I am also enclosing a cheque of £80.- in respect of these articles.

I confirm our agreement regarding the serialization of your book on the Continent.

I shall arrange the serialization in Copenhagen without any charge for COOPERATION. The fee agreed upon is £45.-. I shall reserve 10% for the Agent of Mr. Butterworth and let you have the rest.

Should I be able to arrange in some other countries serialization so it would be on the usual 60/40 basis as this gives even more work than the regular articles.

Before leaving London I have had another talk with Mr. Butterworth and he told me to send the money from Denmark to him and not directly to you. I should be grateful if you would make quite clear the position with your publisher to avoid any misunderstanding. I think the best solution would be if you could reserve for yourself the serialization rights abroad in order to avoid any interference.

I thank you once more for your kind invitation at Chartwell and beg to remain,

Yours vy sincerely,
I. Révész

Winston S. Churchill to Emery Reves

25 November 1937

Yours of November 24. You should send the cheque for the Danish serialisation through Mr. Butterworth.

It is not my intention to authorise any serialisation or publication on the Continent, other than volume rights, except through you while our present agreement lasts.

Cooperation to Winston S. Churchill

[26 November 1937]   Paris

THE FUTURE OF SPAIN [1]

Published by	Gross proceeds
Paris-Soir, Paris (not yet published)	£13.10. 0.
Le Soir, Bruxelles	10. 0. 0.
Berlingske Tidende, Copenhagen	5. 0. 0.
Dagens Nyheter, Stockholm	7.10. 0.
Tidens Tegn, Oslo	5. 0. 0.
Dagsposten, Trondheim	1.10. 0.
Helsingin Sanomat, Helsinki	3. 0. 0.
Briwa Zeme, Riga	2.10. 0.
Lietuvos Aidas, Kaunas	1. 0. 0.

Zydu Balsas, Kaunas	0. 8. 0.
Neue Freie Presse	2. 0. 0.
St. Galler Tagblatt, St. Gallen	1. 8. 0.
Pester Lloyd, Budapest	1. 0. 0.
Le Moment, Bucharest	1. 0. 0.
La Nacion, Buenos Aires	10. 0. 0.
Bourse Egyptienne, Alexandria	1.10. 0.
Egyptian Mail, Cairo	1.10. 0.
Total	£67.16. 0.
60%	£40.12. 0.

1.   Published in the *Evening Standard* on 26 November 1937 as "Spain's Road to Peace."

Violet Pearman to Emery Reves

5 December 1937

Dear Dr. Revesz,
    Herewith Mr. Churchill's article for the Evening Standard this week,[1] which we hope reaches you in time. It has been specially posted by me today in the late fee box at Victoria station, and I have come up to London from the country to do this.

Yours faithfully,
[Violet Pearman]
Private Secretary

1.   "Europe's Plea to Roosevelt," published in the *Evening Standard* on 10 December 1937.

Emery Reves to Violet Pearman

6 December 1937   Paris

Dear Mrs. Pearman,
    Many thanks for the article which arrived here this morning by the first mail. It has been translated in three languages and it was dispatched to all countries before 3 p.m. We must maintain this system of expedition as it is the only one working without any surprise.
    May I ask you to remind Mr. Churchill the photograph he has kindly promised me. I should be grateful if you could send it to me this week.

Yours very sincerely,
I. Révész

Winston S. Churchill to Emery Reves: telegram

7 December 1937

Corrections which please make if think necessary First paragraph insert upon before words the Japanese aggression delete vast same sentence Third paragraph delete vast in 2nd sentence substitute gigantic for vast in next sentence

Churchill

Emery Reves to Winston S. Churchill: telegram

8 December 1937

Please send two hundred words, though for many papers late.

Revesz

Emery Reves to Winston S. Churchill

8 December 1937   Paris

Dear Mr. Churchill,

I hope you have received in time my telegram asking you to kindly let me have the extra 200 words. Indeed, this article was rather short. Unfortunately, it is too late to submit this new paragraph to all our newspapers, but I shall send it everywhere it might arrive before Friday.

The two small corrections have no importance for continental publication, as they are merely stylistical. As all our newspapers publish the articles in a foreign language, such linguistic nuances naturally disappear in the translation.

I beg to remain,
Yours very sincerely
I. Révész

Violet Pearman to Emery Reves

8 December 1937

Dear Dr. Revesz,

I send herewith as asked by telegram, the extra two hundred words for the article. I daresay it will go into Paris-Soir and Le Soir, and maybe some other nearby papers, but Mr. Churchill knew it could not go into the others because of the time. By some oversight the article was shorter than usual,

though of course usually Mr. Churchill gives them an extra hundred or more
words in each article more than the requisite thousand words.

Yours sincerely,
[Violet Pearman]
Private Secretary

Cooperation to Winston S. Churchill

10 December 1937   Paris

GREAT BRITAIN AND AMERICA[1]

Published by	Gross proceeds
Paris-Soir, Paris (not yet published)	£13.10. 0.
Pariser Tages Zeitung, Paris	0.10. 0.
Le Soir, Bruxelles	10. 0. 0.
Luxemberger Zeitung, Luxemburg	1. 0. 0.
Algemeen Handelsblad, Amsterdam	2.10. 0.
Berlingske Tidende, Copenhagen	5. 0. 0.
Dagens Nyheter, Stockholm	7.10. 0.
Tidens Tegn, Oslo	5. 0. 0.
Paevaleht, Tallinn	1. 0. 0.
Neues Wiener Tagblatt, Vienna	3. 0. 0.
Tages Anzeiger, Zurich	4. 0. 0.
Journal des Nations, Geneva	0.10. 0.
Ujsag, Budapest	0.16. 0.
Nowy Dziennik, Cracovie	0.14. 0.
Le Moment, Bucharest	1. 0. 0.
La Nacion, Buenos Aires	10. 0. 0.
Bourse Egyptienne, Alexandria	1.10. 0.
Egyptian Mail, Cairo	1.10. 0.
Total	£69. 0. 0.
60%	£41. 8. 0.

1.   The British title of this article was "Europe's Plea to Roosevelt."

Emery Reves to Winston S. Churchill

12 December 1937   Paris

Dear Mr. Churchill,
    As you were kind enough to ask me, I venture to make a suggestion
regarding the subject of your next article.

The changements in the high command of the army undertaken by Mr. Hore-Belisha have been widely commented abroad but General Gort and his colleagues are hardly known.[1] I think if you could write an article on the reorganization of the army it would be of great interest. I am all the more convinced of that as every information regarding British rearmament is always published by the great newspapers abroad.

Yours very sincerely,
Révész

1. Leslie Hore-Belisha, Secretary of State for War; and Lord Gort VC, Chief of the Imperial General Staff (and later Commander-in-Chief of the British Expeditionary Force).

Violet Pearman to Emery Reves

16 December 1937

Dear Dr. Revesz,

Mr. Churchill thanks you for your letter and thinks your suggestion about British rearmament and the Army very good. He will if possible follow it out and write something in that sense.

Would you be very kind and send him the cheque for November, also let him have the list for the last three articles.

The signed photograph was sent to you yesterday, and I hope it reaches you safely.

Yours sincerely,
[Violet Pearman]
Private Secretary

Winston S. Churchill to Emery Reves

19 December 1937

Dear Dr. Revesz,

Herewith the article for this week, which is a resumé of the year 1937, and not upon the changes in the army here.[1] You should get it first thing on Sunday morning this time, as I am putting it on the boat-train tonight, i.e. the late-fee box in Victoria Station.

1. "Panorama of 1937" was published in the *Evening Standard* on 23 December 1937. The article "Britain Rearms" was published in the *Evening Standard* on 7 January 1938.

Emery Reves to Winston S. Churchill

22 December 1937   Paris

Dear Mr. Churchill,

Kindly find enclosed statements regarding your last two articles, "The future of Spain" and "Great Britain and America". I am also enclosing a cheque for £104.0.0. in respect of these two articles and the extra-fee of £24.0.0. for the publication of the Divorce article in Svenska Dagbladet in Stockholm.

As you were kind enough to ask my opinion by telephone this morning regarding the interview you have given to Pester Lloyd in Budapest, the situation is as follows: Should this newspaper be among those which are publishing regularly your articles, I think it would be a good thing to show them a friendly spirit and give them an interview if they desire so. Unfortunately, our relations with this newspaper are very unsatisfactory. In the arrangement with them in July last, it was understood that they would regularly publish all your articles. But in fact they do not publish more than one out of three or four. The other day, I have written to the Editor for an explication. He replied that the reasons are political: your articles are usually against Nazism and Fascism and they want to keep friendship with Berlin and Rome. Under these circumstances, it seems to me that the asking for this interview is a small political manoeuvre in order to publish an article from you (in the form of an interview) not on the problems which you consider to be important, but on subjects which they are putting. My conviction is that in this special case, the best reply would be that you have charged Cooperation to send to Budapest your fortnightly articles and that you would be only too glad if they would publish them. Should they get this interview, so they will be even less interested in the coming articles. It is a bad Central European habit to ask interviews by leading Statesmen and refuse their articles, which is an excellent method to get their views without payments. Should it be no more possible to withdraw this interview so I think it would be a good thing if you would let the Editor of Pester Lloyd know that you wished to be agreeable to them in according this interview and that you hope that in reply for this courtesy they will publish more regularly your fortnightly articles which we are sending them.

Please let me know your opinion on this question.

Yours very sincerely,
I. Révész

Emery Reves to Winston S. Churchill: telegram

23 December 1937   Paris

Budapest refuses even Christmas article. Considered too anti-Nazi.
Cooperation

Cooperation to Winston S. Churchill

[23 December 1937]   Paris

BETTER OUTLOOK FOR 1938 [1]

Published by	Gross proceeds
Paris-Soir, Paris	£13. 2. 0.
Le Soir, Bruxelles	10. 0. 0.
Algemeen Handelsblad, Amsterdam	2.10. 0.
Berlingske Tidende, Copenhagen	5. 0. 0.
Dagens Nyheter, Stockholm	7.10. 0.
Tidens Tegn, Oslo	5. 0. 0.
Briwa Zeme, Riga	2.10. 0.
Paevaleht, Tallinn	1. 0. 0.
Zydu Balsas, Kaunas	0. 8. 0.
Prager Tagblatt, Prague	1.10. 0.
Tages Anzeiger, Zurich	4. 0. 0.
St. Galler Tagblatt, St. Gallen	1.10. 0.
Le Moment, Bucharest	1. 0. 0.
Bourse Egyptienne, Alexandria	3. 0. 0.
El Diario, Buenos Aires	10. 0. 0.
Total	£68. 0. 0.
60%	£40.16. 0.

1. Published in the *Evening Standard* as "Panorama of 1937." In this article, Churchill saw hope for 1938 in Anglo-French unity and in "the goodwill extended towards the free governments of Europe by the United States," which had become "more apparent as the months have passed." His article ended, "On Christmas Day, 1914, the German soldiers on the Western Front ceased firing. They placed small Christmas trees on their trenches and declared that on this day there would be peace and goodwill among suffering men. Both sides came out of their trenches and met in the blasted No-man's Land. They clasped each other's hands, they exchanged gifts and kind words. Together they buried the dead inaccessible and deprived of the rites which raise man above the brute. Let no man worthy of human stature banish this inspiration from his mind."

Emery Reves to Winston S. Churchill

29 December 1937   Paris

Dear Mr. Churchill,

I hope you have received my previous letter and the cheque.

I should like to inform you briefly about what has happened in Stockholm between the two rival newspapers. A few days after I have sent the "Divorce" article to SVENSKA DAGBLADET, I have received a telegram from the Editor of DAGENS NYHETER saying that their competitor, the SVENSKA

DAGBLADET, announces your regular contribution for 1938 in a most sensational way and asking for explication. Three hours later another telegram came from the SVENSKA DAGBLADET informing me that the Editor of DAGENS NYHETER asked them by telephone how did they get your article, but they have refused to give him any information. After these two telegrams, I have written two long letters to the two jealous editors on the following lines:

To SVENSKA DAGBLADET: I urged them to stop sensational publicity and not to announce that your contribution will be a regular one. Our agreement in Chartwell was that the regular fortnightly articles will be reserved further on for DAGENS NYHETER, but that they will get from time to time Swedish rights in the reproduction of your special articles which you will write for magazines and which will be of another type. I told them that any exaggeration which might prejudice our existing relations with the other newspaper might make us difficult to submit to them further articles.

To DAGENS NYHETER: I told them that the situation remains as it was without any changement and they will have exclusive rights in Sweden further on for your fortnightly articles. I explained them that your journalistic activity has two aspects. You are writing fortnightly articles, on topical political events, and besides, special articles for reviews and magazines, usually dealing with non-political subjects. I also explained that SVENSKA DAGBLADET has approached you in the past several times for articles, but the reply was always that nothing can be done in view of the existing arrangement with DAGENS NYHETER. But their insistence was always growing, and now you have given them a magazine article and have promised them to allow reproductions in Sweden for such articles from time to time. Any competition is out of question, as these articles are of a different type and they can only make publicity for the regular articles.

The reply of the SVENSKA DAGBLADET was, that he will certainly abstain to insist advertising the word "regular", and saying that this word has in Swedish not as clear meaning as in English or French.

DAGENS NYHETER has replied that they find my explications fully satisfactory.

So Christmas brought peace, both papers are satisfied, and our position in Sweden is stronger than ever.

I am enclosing the advertisement which has caused the storm in the water-glass.

I should be most grateful if you could let me have your next article before Saturday if possible, on account of the New Year's Day. Should you deal with the armament problem, I think you might be able to write it one or two days before.

I am terribly interested to know whether Sunday Referee was right in announcing your entering in the Cabinet. As I fully agree with Oscar Wilde that a question can never be indiscreet, only the reply, I venture to ask you this question.[1]

I very much hope that you will let me know if you have a few moments in Paris when going to the Riviera.

With my best wishes for the New Year,

I beg to remain
Yours very sincerely,
I. Révész

1.   Churchill was not to enter Neville Chamberlain's Cabinet until the outbreak of war in September 1939. He had been out of office since the summer of 1929, although, after the general election in 1935, many people had expected Stanley Baldwin to appoint him Minister for the Coordination of Defence.

Winston S. Churchill to Emery Reves

29 December 1937

Many thanks for the cheque received.

I gave this interview as an act of courtesy at the request of the Foreign Office to Lady Listowel,[1] and I cannot bargain about it with Pester Lloyd, though I agree with you they do not deserve any consideration.

I shall be in Paris on the 3rd and 4th at the British Embassy. Perhaps you will ring me up there and we can have a talk.

1.   Lady Listowel (Judith), the Hungarian-born daughter of Raoul de Marffy-Mantuano. In 1933 she married the fifth Earl Listowel, Junior Whip of the Labour Party from 1937 to 1941 and Whip of the Labour Party in the House of Lords from 1941 to 1944. He was Parliamentary Under Secretary of State for India in the final year of Churchill's wartime premiership and held Cabinet office (including Minister of State for Colonial Affairs) throughout Clement Attlee's postwar Labour government.

FORGING A PARTNERSHIP

1938

Cooperation to Winston S. Churchill

[1 January 1938]   Paris

CONTRACTS MADE IN THE EMPIRE PRESS

Publication	£ per article
South African Morning Newspapers	7. 7. 0.
The Sydney Morning Herald	3. 3. 0.
The Melbourne Argus	3. 3. 0.
The Advertiser, Adelaide	2. 2. 0.
West Australian, Perth	2. 2. 0.
The Press, Christchurch	2. 2. 0.
The New Zealand Herald, Auckland	2. 2. 0.
Evening Post, Wellington	2. 2. 0.
Otago Daily Times, Dunedin	2. 2. 0.
Nassau Guardian, Nassau	0.14. 0.
Toronto Star, Toronto	8. 0. 0.
African Morning Post, Accra	0.10. 6.
Times of Malta, Malta	0.10. 6.
East African Standard, Nairobi	1. 1. 0.
Total	£37. 0. 0.

Cooperation to Winston S. Churchill

[7 January 1938]   Paris

PROGRESS OF BRITISH REARMAMENT [1]

Published by	Gross proceeds	
Paris-Soir, Paris	£13. 2. 0.	(2.000 Fcs)
Pariser Tages Zeitung, Paris	1. 0. 0.	

Le Soir, Bruxelles	10. 0. 0.	
Luxemburger Zeitung, Luxembourg	1. 0. 0.	
Berlingske Tidende, Copenhagen	5. 0. 0.	
Dagens Nyheter, Stockholm	7.10. 0.	
Tidens Tegn, Oslo	5. 0. 0.	
Helsingin Sanomat, Helsinki	3. 0. 0.	
Briwa Zeme, Riga	2.10. 0.	
Paevaleht, Tallinn	1. 0. 0.	
Lietuvos Aidas, Kaunas	1. 0. 0.	
Zydu Balsas, Kaunas	0. 8. 0.	
Neues Wiener Tagblatt, Vienna	3. 0. 0.	
Neue Zürcher Zeitung, Zurich	4. 0. 0.	
Pesti Hirlap, Budapest	5. 0. 0.	
Kurjer Warszawski, Varsovie	5. 0. 0.	
Le Moment, Bucharest	1. 0. 0.	
Bourse Egyptienne, Alexandria	3. 0. 0.	
La Nacion, Buenos Aires	8. 0. 0.	

Total	£79.10. 0.
60%	£47.14. 0.

1.   This article was published in the *Evening Standard* on 7 January 1938, entitled "Britain Rearms." Churchill wrote it a few days before going on a month's holiday at Maxine Elliot's villa, the Château de l'Horizon, at Golfe Juan in the South of France.

Emery Reves to Winston S. Churchill

11 January 1938   Paris

Dear Mr. Churchill,

Miss Scialtiel,[1] whom I believe you know, submitted me yesterday the following proposition on behalf of LA NOUVELLE REVUE CRITIQUE for the publication of "Great Contemporaries" in French:

    6% royalty until 3,000 copies
    7% royalty until 6,000 copies
    8% royalty until 15,000 copies
    10% royalty after 15,000 copies.

Payment in advance: 3.500.-- francs.

Miss Scialtiel asks for herself 20% commission.

I do not think this offer is a very brilliant one, but it is a fact that there is a great crisis at the moment in the French publishing business. Should you accept this offer, I would not take any commission.

The war is raging again in Stockholm. The Swedish people are real warriors, they have maintained their mentality since the religious wars. About a fortnight ago, everything was settled, and both Editors have promised me by letter and on the telephone that they will keep quiet and stop the fight. This morning, in reading SVENSKA DAGBLADET, I saw on the first page this huge publicity which I am enclosing. It is obviously directed against the DAGENS NYHETER, and it says that if the public wants to read your articles, they should read them in SVENSKA DAGBLADET.

I really believe that they are exaggerating, and that it is not quite fair that they are involving your person in a pure competition fight. I have written to-day a rather severe letter to our friend, Mr. Trygger, urging him to stop this exaggerated publicity. I am enclosing copy of this letter for your information, asking you to kindly let me know whether you agree with my point of view. I should be grateful if you kindly return me the enclosed newspaper cutting.

I hope to receive your next article Sunday or Monday morning. Shall we get it from Cannes or from London? Regarding the subject, I think it would be rather interesting to explain the British position in the Far East. Hong Kong, Singapore, the British interests in Shanghai, are in the news to-day, but very few people know exactly what these places mean for the Empire. At the moment of writing, I do not know yet the result of the Imperial Conference in Tokyo, but if Japan declares war to China, this will be the most topical subject during the coming days.

I wish you fine sunshine and beg to remain,

Yours very sincerely,
I. Révész

1.   Marguerite Scialtiel, a Paris literary agent, was the French representative of the London literary agency Curtis Brown.

Cooperation to Winston S. Churchill

[12 January 1938]   Paris

THE ANGLO-GERMAN NAVAL AGREEMENT [1]

Published by	Gross proceeds
Le Soir, Bruxelles	£10. 0. 0.
Berlingske Tidende, Copenhagen	5. 0. 0.
Paevaleht, Tallinn	1. 0. 0.
Helsingin Sanomat, Helsinki	3. 0. 0.
Paris-Soir, Paris	15. 0. 0.
Pariser Tages Zeitung, Paris	0.14. 0.
Eleftheron Vima, Athens	1. 1. 0.
Arbeiderspers, Amsterdam	3. 0. 0.

Zydu Balsas, Kaunas	0. 8. 0.
Luxemburger Zeitung, Luxemburg	1. 0. 0.
Bergens Tidende, Bergen	2. 0. 0.
Dagens Nyheter, Stockholm	7.10. 0.
La Nacion, Buenos Aires	8. 0. 0.
O Estado de Sao Paulo, Sao Paulo	7. 0. 0.
Diarios Asociados, Rio de Janeiro	3. 0. 0.
Total	£67.13. 0.

BRITISH EMPIRE

Melbourne Argus, Melbourne	2. 2. 0.
Telegraph, Brisbane	2. 2. 0.
Advertiser, Adelaide	2. 2. 0.
Times of Ceylon, Ceylon	2. 2. 0.
East African Standard, Nairobi	1. 1. 0.
Total	£9. 9. 0.

1.   This agreement, negotiated by Neville Chamberlain at the start of his premiership, had been denounced by Churchill in the House of Commons, earning him the particular hostility of the mass of Conservative MPs, who regarded the agreement as an important act of statesmanship by their new leader. After the signing of the Munich Agreement at the end of October 1938, Chamberlain specifically linked the Munich and Anglo-German naval agreements as joint signs of Britain and Germany's intention "never to go to war with one another again."

Winston S. Churchill to Emery Reves

18 January 1938

Dear Dr. Revesz,

I do not think very much of Miss Scialtiel's offer. As far as I can make out it is practically the same as Payot's. At the present rate of exchange it is about £23. I think it is better to wait a little longer.

Emery Reves to Winston S. Churchill[1]

21 January 1938

Dear Mr. Churchill,

Many thanks for your letter. I quite agree with you and shall communicate with Miss Scialtiel that, for the moment, her offer is not interesting.

I have told you in Paris that LA NACION in Buenos-Aires has only published 12 articles from the series and they have stopped the publication at the end of December. Now I was able to make with them a new arrangement. It was the result of rather complicated negotiations on various matters, and I have signed a new contract for all of your articles for a fee of £8.0.0. each. I had to make them these concessions as they must pay all the articles even if they do not publish the one or the other. But this time the contract is for a whole year, and includes 26 articles. I hope you will find this solution satisfactory.

So between the two contracts only two articles have not been published in LA NACION, and one of them I was able to place in another Buenos-Aires newspaper, EL DIARIO, for 10£. I think that this publication helped me very much to sign a new contract with LA NACION.

Yours very sincerely,
I. Révész

1. Churchill had returned to London and Chartwell from the South of France.

Cooperation to Winston S. Churchill

21 January 1938   Paris

JAPAN AND THE WHITE RACE

Published by	Gross proceeds	
Paris-Soir, Paris	£13. 2. 0.	(2.000 Fcs)
Le Soir, Bruxelles	10. 0. 0.	
Luxemburger Zeitung, Luxembourg	1. 0. 0.	
Berlingske Tidende, Copenhagen	5. 0. 0.	
Dagens Nyheter, Stockholm	7.10. 0.	
Tidens Tegn, Oslo	5. 0. 0.	
Paevaleht, Tallinn	1. 0. 0.	
Lietuvos Aidas, Kaunas	1. 0. 0.	
Zydu Balsas, Kaunas	0. 8. 0.	
Neues Wiener Tagblatt, Vienna	3. 0. 0.	
Thurgauer Zeitung, Frauenfeld	1.10. 0.	
Pesti Hirlap, Budapest	5. 0. 0.	
Le Moment, Bucharest	1. 0. 0.	
La Nacion, Buenos Aires	8. 0. 0.	
Total	£62.10. 0.	
60%	£37.10. 0.	

Cooperation to Winston S. Churchill

4 February 1938   Paris

GREAT POWERS, SMALL POWERS AND THE LEAGUE [1]

Published by	Gross proceeds
Paris-Soir, Paris	£12.10. 0.
Le Soir, Bruxelles	10. 0. 0.
Arbeiderspers, Amsterdam	3. 0. 0.
Luxemburger Zeitung, Luxembourg	1. 0. 0.
Berlingske Tidende, Copenhagen	5. 0. 0.
Dagens Nyheter, Stockholm	7.10. 0.
Tidens Tegn, Oslo	5. 0. 0.
Paevaleht, Tallinn	1. 0. 0.
Lietuvos Aidas, Kaunas	1. 0. 0.
Zydu Balsas, Kaunas	0. 8. 0.
Neue Freie Presse, Vienna	0. 0. 0.[2]
Journal des Nations, Geneva	0. 8. 0.
Ujsag, Budapest	0.12. 0.
Nowy Dziennik, Cracovie	0.12. 0.
Le Moment, Bucharest	1. 0. 0.
La Nacion, Buenos Aires	8. 0. 0.
O Estado de Sao Paulo, Sao Paulo	7. 0. 0.
Bourse Egyptienne, Cairo	3. 0. 0.
Total	£67. 0. 0.

1.   Published in the *Evening Standard* on 4 February 1938 as "The League Is Not Yet Dead."
2.   Following the German annexation of Austria in March 1938 and the imposition of Nazi rule, no money was transferred to Cooperation for this article.

Emery Reves to Winston S. Churchill

4 February 1938   Paris

Dear Mr. Churchill,
    I think I have found the ideal man for the work you need. He is M. Paul Henri Michel, the librarian of the "Bibliothèque de documentation internationale contemporaine" at Vincennes. This is the greatest library in the world of post-war history and has the richest collection of documents. So M. Michel is just at the source of the documents where he can make the best research work.
    He is himself a writer of political and historical works. I am sending as printed matter three books of him; the one only in proofs as this book on the Adriatic question is under print and will appear next week only. He is an

excellent linguist and has translated many books from German, Italian and Spanish. He is doing since many years translations for me too. I have talked with him today about the work you need without mentioning your name. I think he would be much interested. I am sure that he will be of absolute discretion as it was he himself who told me that he could undertake this work only if nobody would know about it, being an official of a State Library.

I think he would be better than the man I had first in mind when we have talked about the matter yesterday.

Have you written already your long article on Mr. Neville Chamberlain?[1] I think it would be time to give something for publication to Svenska Dagbladet. Besides I feel sure that this article will have a very wide circulation all over Europe. I should be grateful if you would kindly send me a collection of your magazine articles which you think suitable for publication abroad.

I have unfortunately forgotten yesterday to mention the position with the Hungarian Quarterly. I have exchanged several letters with them in the past weeks and they say they could not publish an article which would appear equally in an English or American Magazine. They are very anxious to get an article from you and are prepared to pay a fee of £50.- which is for them a quite exceptional rate. But they ask for exclusive rights having half of their circulation in England and half in America. Could you accept this offer? Personally I believe that this article would be easy to publish afterwards even in England and in America, as this review has a very limited circulation.

Yours very sincerely,
I. Révész

1.   Churchill did not write any "long article" on Neville Chamberlain. His most sustained character appreciation was his obituary oration in the House of Commons on 12 November 1940.

Winston S. Churchill to Emery Reves

11 February 1938

Many thanks for the trouble you have taken. I expect that the contract for this work will be signed during March,[1] and should this be so, I will ask you to put me in touch with M. Henri Michel and perhaps he could come over to London to see me. It is not worth while troubling him until something definite is arranged, and therefore I should like to make a personal contact before deciding. Meanwhile I will endeavour to read his books.

I am afraid I cannot undertake three thousand words of original matter for the Hungarian Review. I will consider whether it is possible to make a variant of some of the articles I have already written.

1.   Churchill was about to sign a contract with Cassell and Company Limited, of London, for a four-volume book, *A History of the English-Speaking Peoples.* The book

was almost finished by the time of the outbreak of war in September 1939 but was then set aside. Churchill did not take it up again until after he had completed his war memoirs, and the first volume, which had been ready to be printed in 1940, was not published until 1956.

Emery Reves to Winston S. Churchill

12 February 1938   Paris

Dear Mr. Churchill,

As soon as I have received Mrs. Pearman's letter, I made inquiries at the Bibliothèque Nationale regarding the picture of the Duke of Marlborough showing him in the uniform of a French colonel.[1]

Unfortunately, the Bibliothèque Nationale has not published such a picture post-card. They say it might be that some private publishers did so, but there are so many of them, that it is impossible to find out without knowing the publisher's name.

To-day I went myself to the "Cabinet d'Estampes" of the Bibliothèque Nationale and have regarded all the etchings they possess about the Duke. There are over 50, some of them most beautiful. But, unfortunately, no one is representing him as French colonel. I found only one picture which shows him in French uniform. It is a charming small etching with the following inscription:

"Mr. de Marleborough"
"tel qu'il était en 1668 quand il servait en qualité d'enseigne dans le .
Régiment des Gardes Françaises."
(gravée d'après Vander-meulen)

Should you like to see this picture, I could easily get made a photographic reproduction. I have had a talk with the director of the Cabinet d'Estampes, who will make some further research next week.

The situation is the following: all the etchings are classified:

1) after the artists
2) after the subjects.

So, should there be only one copy of the etching you are looking for, this is not to be found under "Marlborough" but under the name of the graveur. Should you know who was the graveur, it would be easy to find the portrait. In any case, I shall try again next week to find the picture.

Yours very sincerely,
I. Révész

1. Churchill was looking for illustrations for the fourth and final volume of his biography of his ancestor John Churchill, first Duke of Marlborough. The volume was published on 2 September 1938.

Violet Pearman to Emery Reves

16 February 1938

Dear Dr. Revesz,

   I am asked by Mr. Churchill to thank you for going to so much trouble over the photograph of the Duke of Marlborough about which you wrote to him on the 12th instant. The one in the French uniform about which you speak in the third paragraph of that letter is the one he wants, and if you would get a good (though not expensive) photographic reproduction, Mr. Churchill would be very pleased to have it. He thinks it is the one which he is looking for, as its inscription, which you kindly give, would point to this being so. The illustrations of the fourth volume of the book are now being assembled, and therefore the sooner we can have the photograph, the better.

Yours sincerely,
[Violet Pearman]
Private Secretary

Cooperation to Winston S. Churchill

17 February 1938   Paris

IT IS NOT ALL OVER YET [1]

Published by	Gross proceeds
Paris-Soir, Paris	£12.10. 0.
Le Soir, Bruxelles	10. 0. 0.
Dagens Nyheter, Stockholm	7.10. 0.
Tidens Tegn, Oslo	5. 0. 0.
Briwa Zeme, Riga	2.10. 0.
Paevaleht, Tallinn	1. 0. 0.
Zydu Balsas, Kaunas	0. 8. 0.
Prager Tagblatt, Prague	1.10. 0.
Journal des Nations, Geneva	0. 8. 0.
Le Moment, Bucharest	1. 0. 0.
La Nacion, Buenos Aires	8. 0. 0.
O Estado de Sao Paulo, Sao Paulo	7. 0. 0.
Total	£56.16. 0.

   1.   "It Is Not All Over Yet" was published in the *Evening Standard* on 4 March 1938.

Emery Reves to Winston S. Churchill

18 February 1938   Paris

Dear Mr. Churchill,

I have received a letter from Mr. Trygger, of Stockholm, who is rather anxious to be able to publish a second article from you, as two months have passed since he has published the Divorce article.

Could you let me have the article on Neville Chamberlain you mentioned to me in Paris? I should be grateful if you would kindly let me have a copy of it at your earliest convenience. Should you not be able to release this article yet, please send me anything you find suitable for publication in Svenska Dagbladet.

I shall order a photographic reproduction of the Marlborough portrait. I hope this will be ready in 2/3 days.

Yours very sincerely,
I. Révész

Winston S. Churchill to Emery Reves: telegram

21 February 1938

Cannot release Chamberlain article yet.

Churchill

Emery Reves to Winston S. Churchill

22 February 1938   Paris

Dear Mr. Churchill,

I am sorry that I called you on the telephone this morning in a bad moment.[1]

Kindly find enclosed the reproduction of the Marlborough picture. I hope it is the right one. I have also the photographic plate which I could forward to you, should you need it.

I note that you cannot release yet the Neville Chamberlain article. But could you send me something else for SVENSKA DAGBLADET? Mr. Trygger is urging very much to get an article from you, and I think we must not disappoint him and give him at least every second month one or two magazine articles as he is paying very well. When we met in Paris, you have suggested that you will let me have a collection of your magazine articles which we might get reproduced on the Continent. I would be most grateful if you would be good enough to send me some of these articles at your earliest convenience. As Mr. Trygger is asking for an article since about three weeks, I have promised him to give a concrete reply in the course of this week.

May I ask your advice regarding a rather delicate matter? Now, that Mr.

Eden has resigned, he will certainly be approached by newspapers or agencies and will probably undertake some journalistic work. I am thinking since several years to secure his contribution for COOPERATION. Sir Austen Chamberlain wanted to introduce me to him once, but it was no use for me to approach him as long as he was in Office.

I think it would not be discreet if I would write to him directly, immediately after his resignation; on the other hand there is a risk that, if I am waiting some weeks, he will make some other commitments. As I believe that you know him very well I venture to ask you what way you think would be the best. Should you by chance have an opportunity to mention to him COOPERATION and my desire, I should be most grateful. I do hope that you will not mind in asking you this favour.

I wonder what will be the subject of your next article. I think that an article on British Foreign Policy would be even more interesting and topical than an article on Austria.

I am leaving for a trip to Central Europe: Switzerland, Austria, Czechoslovakia, Hungary and Yugoslavia. Recent events have made publications extremely difficult in these countries and I must try to save as much as possible. During my absence I shall be, as usual, in daily touch with my Office and every communication will be forwarded to me without delay.

Yours very sincerely,
I. Révész

1.   Churchill was preparing his speech for the debate later that day on Anthony Eden's resignation as Foreign Minister. He ended his speech with the words: "I predict that the day will come when at some point or other, on some issue or other, you will have to make a stand, and I pray God that when that day comes we may not find that, through an unwise policy, we are left to make that stand alone."

Violet Pearman to Emery Reves

25 February 1938

Dear Dr. Revesz,

Mr. Churchill has asked me to write to thank you for the charming photograph of the Marlborough picture which you have procured for him, which he certainly intends to use in his book. Would you therefore now kindly obtain the necessary permission to reproduce the picture, and inform the Bibliothèque Nationale that, as is usual, mention would be made under the illustration as to its source. I daresay they will require a small fee for this permission.

Mr. Churchill will consider about the article for Svenska Dagbladet and let you know later.[1]

Mr. Eden would not, Mr. Churchill thinks, wish to take up journalistic work at the present time, but if there is a good opportunity for Mr. Churchill to mention it to Mr. Eden, he will certainly do so and recommend your assistance to him.

The article this week end will most probably be upon the British foreign policy.

Yours faithfully,
[Violet Pearman]
Private Secretary

1.   Churchill had written an article, "Women in War," for the *Strand* magazine. Reves sold it to *Svenska Dagbladet* (Stockholm) for £25, to *Berlingske Tidende* (Copenhagen) for £15, and to the *Illustrated Weekly of India* (Bombay) for £8 (a total that is the equivalent in 1996 of £1,200). Reves also sold *Svenska Dagbladet* three other magazine articles by Churchill ("The Problem of the Labour Unemployed," "Parliamentary Democracy," and "Challenge in the Pacific") for £25 each.

Winston S. Churchill to Emery Reves: telegram

2 March 1938

Kindly delete words black defeatism in sentence about Flandin.

Churchill

Emery Reves to Winston S. Churchill

7 March 1938   Suvretta House
                                                         St. Moritz
                                                        Switzerland

Dear Mr. Churchill,

Svenska Dagbladet is rather impatient. I have just received a new letter from Mr. Trygger. He says that he has seen an article in STRAND MAGAZINE 'Women in War'.[1] This article would be quite suitable for him, should you not be able to give him something else, as 3 months have already passed since he has published your Divorce article, and announced with great publicity your collaboration.

Please, let us have a copy of this STRAND MAGAZINE article or anything else at your earliest convenience. I am sure you will agree with me that we should not disappoint Mr. Trygger, as he is a great admirer of yours, and pays really well.

I am leaving for Vienna, Prague, Budapest and Belgrade within the next days.

Yours very sincerely
I. Révész

P.S. I am glad that you like the Marlborough picture.

1. "Women in War" was published in the February 1938 issue of the *Strand* magazine.

Winston S. Churchill to Emery Reves: telegram

7 March 1938

No objection let Svenska Dagbladet have article suggested in your letter received today Am sending copy off tonight

Churchill

Violet Pearman to Emery Reves

7 March 1938

Dear Sir,
    I am desired by Mr. Churchill to thank you for your letter received today, and to send a copy of the article "Women in War" as requested.

Yours faithfully,
[Violet Pearman]
Private Secretary

Rachel Gayman to Winston S. Churchill

14 March 1938   Paris

Dear Mr. Churchill,
    We thank you very much for your wire, which, of course, we expected because of the Session of the House of Commons and the Declaration of Mr. Neville Chamberlain.
    If it is possible, we should be most grateful if you could wire to-morrow the subject of your next article, and if you could dispatch the M.S. to-morrow night, either by air-mail express, or post it in the special letter-box at Victoria Station before the departure of the last mail train, so that we could receive it on Wednesday morning.
    Of course, we are transmitting by wire the contents of your own telegram to Mr. Révész, who is now in Budapest.

Very sincerely yours,
R. Gayman

Winston S. Churchill to Cooperation: telegram

15 March 1938

Subject article despatched tonight from Victoria is Austrian Eye-opener.

Churchill

Cooperation to Winston S. Churchill

[18 March 1938]   Paris

THE AUSTRIAN EYE-OPENER [1]

Published by	Gross proceeds
Paris-Soir, Paris	£12.10. 0.
Le Soir, Bruxelles	10. 0. 0.
Arbeiderspers, Amsterdam	3. 0. 0.
Berlingske Tidende, Copenhagen	5. 0. 0.
Dagens Nyheter, Stockholm	7.10. 0.
Tidens Tegn, Oslo	5. 0. 0.
Paevaleht, Tallinn	1. 0. 0.
Lietuvos Aidas, Kaunas	1. 0. 0.
Kurjer Warszawski, Varsovie	5. 0. 0.
National Zeitung, Bâle	2. 6. 0.
Journal des Nations, Geneva	0. 8. 0.
Le Moment, Bucharest	1. 0. 0.
La Nacion, Buenos Aires	8. 0. 0.
Jornal do Brasil, Rio de Janeiro	2. 0. 0.
La Bourse Egyptienne, Cairo	3. 0. 0.
Total	£66.14. 0.

1. "The Austrian Eye-Opener" was published in the *Evening Standard* on 18 March 1938.

Winston S. Churchill to Lord Camrose [1]

4 April 1938

My dear Camrose,

I am very glad you have returned to these troubled scenes.

There is a matter of business which I want to discuss with you. For the last two years I have written fortnightly mainly on foreign politics for the Evening Standard. They have paid £70 per article of 1,000 to 1,100 words. In addition they have syndicated it in England for my benefit to the papers on the attached list A, yielding from £25 to £30 per article. Besides this outside the United Kingdom they have syndicated it for my benefit to the papers on list B, yielding about £15 per article.[2] This they have done through their own office without any trouble or expense to me.

Finally however a remarkable development has grown up on the Continent for translations of these articles. These I now manage myself through the agency of Co-operation, and the yield on a 60/40 basis is between £40 and £50 per article. The list of Continental papers taking these articles

includes those on list C.[3] As you will see it is a very fine platform, though as
Nazi power advances, as in Vienna, planks are pulled out of it. The accep-
tances vary slightly from fortnight to fortnight, but I should think on the
whole the articles have reached £140–£150 apiece.[4] I have not made any
satisfactory arrangement about the American rights, though occasionally an
article is sold. I am looking into this and hope to develop syndication there
during the course of the present year.

    1.   Lord Camrose was the Proprietor of the *Daily Telegraph* and one of Churchill's
closest friends. The *Evening Standard* having objected to the anti-German and anti-
appeasement tone of Churchill's articles, Camrose acquired the fortnightly series for
the *Daily Telegraph*. The last *Evening Standard* article, "Red Sunset in Spain," was
published on 5 April 1938, the first *Daily Telegraph* article nine days later.
    2.   List A included the *Glasgow Evening News,* the *Aberdeen Evening Express,* and
the *Belfast Telegraph,* all of which regularly printed Churchill's fortnightly articles. List
B included the *Adelaide Advertiser,* the *East African Standard,* the *Times of Malta,* and
the *Madras Mail.*
    3.   List C sent by Churchill to Lord Camrose consisted of the articles for which
Reves was responsible. It included newspapers in Holland (Rotterdam), Belgium (Brussels), Denmark (Copenhagen), Sweden (Stockholm), Norway (Oslo and Trondheim),
Estonia (Tallinn), Lithuania (Kaunas), Switzerland (Lausanne, Lucerne, and Zurich),
Czechoslovakia (Prague), Hungary (Budapest), Poland (Warsaw and Cracow), Romania (Bucharest), and Argentina (Buenos Aires).
    4.   The equivalent value in 1996 of £150 in 1938 was £3,750.

Cooperation to Winston S. Churchill

[5 April 1938]   Paris

RED SUNSET[1]

Published by	Gross proceeds	
Paris-Soir, Paris	£11.10. 0.	(2.000 frs)
Le Soir, Bruxelles	10. 0. 0.	
Nieuwe Rotterdamsche Courant, Rotterdam	2.10. 0.	
Berlingske Tidende, Copenhagen	5. 0. 0.	
Dagens Nyheter, Stockholm	7.10. 0.	
Tidens Tegn, Oslo	5. 0. 0.	
Paevaleht, Tallinn	1. 0. 0.	
Zydu Balsas, Kaunas	0. 8. 0.	
Gazette de Lausanne, Lausanne	1.10. 0.	
Neue Zürcher Zeitung, Zurich	4. 0. 0.	
Lidove Noviny, Prague	1.10. 0.	
Le Moment, Bucharest	1. 0. 0.	
Nowy Dziennik, Krakow	0.10. 0.	
La Nacion, Buenos-Aires	8. 0. 0.	
Total	£59. 8. 0.	

1.   Churchill's article "Red Sunset in Spain" was first published in the *Evening Standard* of 5 April 1938. It was subsequently published in the book *Step by Step* (London, 1939), pages 227–230. For this bibliographic information, I am grateful to Ronald I. Cohen, who is in the final stages of preparing *Sir Winston Churchill: A Bibliography of His Published Writings* (London: Cassell, 1998).

Violet Pearman to Winston S. Churchill

[5 April 1938]

CONTINENTAL PAPERS TO WHICH COOPERATION SENT CHURCHILL'S ARTICLES [1]

√ *Paris-Soir,* Paris
√ *Berlingske Tidende,* Copenhagen
√ *Dagens Nyheter,* Stockholm
√ *Tidens Tegn,* Oslo
√ *Le Soir,* Bruxelles
  Luxemburger Zeitung
  Helsingin Sanomat
  Briwa Zeme, Riga
√ *Paevaleht,* Tallinn
  Lietuvos Aidas, Kaunas
√ *Lidove Noviny,* Prague
√ *Neue Zuercher Zeitung,* Zurich
  Neues Wiener Tagblatt, Vienna
  Kurjer Warszawski, Warsaw
  Pesti Hirlap, Budapest
  Politika, Belgrade
  Bourse Egyptienne, Cairo
√ *La Nacion,* Buenos Aires
  O Estado de Sao Paulo
  De Telegraaf, Amsterdam
  Pariser Tages Zeitung
  Pester Lloyd, Budapest
  Europe, Paris
√ *Nieuwe Rotterdamsche Courant,* Rotterdam
  Dagsposten, Trondheim
  Prager Tagblatt, Prague
  Tages Anzeiger, Zurich
  St. Galler Tagblatt
  Journal des Nations, Geneva
  Uzsaag, Budapest
  Algemeen Handelsblad, Amsterdam
  Stavanger Aftenblad
  Narodni Osvobozeni, Prague

Neue Freie Presse, Vienna
　　Thurgauer Zeitung, Frauenfeld
√ *Le Moment,* Bucharest
√ *Zydu Balsas,* Kaunas
　　Pester Tyden, Prague
√ *Nowy Dziennik,* Krakow
　　Arbeiderspers, Amsterdam
√ *Gazette de Lausanne*
　　Tribune de Lausanne
　　Luzerner Tagblatt, Luzern

　　1.　Mrs. Pearman indicated with a tick the fourteen papers (of the forty-three in this list) which had published "Red Sunset."

Emery Reves to Winston S. Churchill

5 April 1938   Paris

Dear Mr. Churchill,
　　Kindly find enclosed statements regarding the publication of the last four articles and a cheque of £160.0.0. (One Hundred Sixty Pounds), in payment for them.
　　I should be glad if you would let me have some of your magazine articles which you find suitable for publication abroad, as we agreed upon in Paris.

Yours very sincerely,
I. Révész

Winston S. Churchill to Emery Reves

8 April 1938

Dear Dr. Revesz,
　　The Evening Standard notified me of their wish to terminate the series of articles at a month's notice on account of divergence from the policy of the paper. I replied that in these circumstances I did not wish to write any more for them.
　　I have now transferred the publication of the parent article on the same terms to the Daily Telegraph. I gather they would prefer Wednesday for publication instead of Friday, and also that they will insert any line safeguarding copyright which I may require. I will therefore insert it in the form you wish, thus there will not be the same difficulty about concerting the publications abroad.
　　Obviously the first article will be about the French Government which should command special interest in view of my visit.

I am sending under separate cover, a letter enquiring about the various newspapers which have not taken the last four articles at particular times.

It may amuse you to know that there was a rush of papers to secure the articles the moment it was rumoured in Fleet Street that the Standard had stopped them. Both the News Chronicle and the Sunday Pictorial were eager with offers, but the Daily Telegraph is a far more powerful and suitable platform for me.

Emery Reves to Winston S. Churchill

9 April 1938   Paris

Dear Mr. Churchill,

I should like to repeat the copyright line the DAILY TELEGRAPH has always used in publishing our articles:

WORLD COPYRIGHT 1938 BY THE DAILY TELEGRAPH & MORNING POST AND COOPERATION
Reproduction even partially strictly forbidden.

If Mrs. Pearman would quote this line regularly at the end of each article, they would print it without discussion.

We must take care as the DAILY TELEGRAPH is far more dangerous regarding pillage than the EVENING STANDARD was. Until now unauthorized reproductions were only due to some unscrupulous foreign correspondents in London. But the DAILY TELEGRAPH has a very wide circulation all over Europe, it arrives in practically all the capitals by air-mail in a few hours, and is read by all the newspaper redactions. So it is much more important that publications should be simultaneous in London and on the Continent in future. However, I am convinced that this will be easy to arrange as I have always collaborated with Mr. Watson[1] most cordially. When we have published Sir Austen Chamberlain's articles under the same circumstances, we always consulted each other by telephone or on the wire and sometimes they waited one or two days when it was necessary.

May I ask you how do you intend to organize the publication of the articles in the British Dominions? I should be glad if I could take over this work and I think it would have some advantages for you if all foreign publications would be centralized. I imagine this work on the following basis:

1) We would open special accounts for the Dominions.

2) We would take over all the existing arrangements with Dominion newspapers, and the fees paid by these papers would be remitted to you without any deduction.

3) Should we be able to improve the existing arrangements or to make new arrangements, so this would make part of our general contract and the proceeds would be shared on the basis 50/50.

I should be most grateful if you would kindly consider these suggestions, and let me know your opinion about it.

Yours very sincerely,
I. Révész

1.   Arthur E. Watson, Editor of the *Daily Telegraph* for a quarter of a century, from 1924 to 1950.

Emery Reves to Winston S. Churchill

12 April 1938   Paris

Dear Mr. Churchill,

I forgot to ask you tonight at the telephone to try to arrange that the DAILY TELEGRAPH shall not publish the article before Friday. The earliest day by which we could release the article on the continent is Saturday and I am afraid many papers would decline it, if it appeared in London two days before.

Yours very sincerely
I. Révész

Cooperation to Winston S. Churchill

[14 April 1938]   Paris

THE NEW FRENCH GOVERNMENT [1]

Published by	Gross proceeds
Paris-Soir, Paris	£11.10. 0.
Le Soir, Bruxelles	10. 0. 0.
Luxemburger Zeitung, Luxemburg	1. 0. 0.
Nieuwe Rotterdamsche Courant, Rotterdam	2.10. 0.
Berlingske Tidende, Copenhagen	5. 0. 0.
Dagens Nyheter, Stockholm	7.10. 0.
Tidens Tegn, Oslo	5. 0. 0.
Dagsposten, Trondheim	1.10. 0.
Paevaleht, Tallinn	1. 0. 0.
Luzerner Tagblatt, Luzern	1.10. 0.
Tribune de Lausanne, Lausanne	1. 0. 0.
Lidove Noviny, Prague	1.10. 0.
Prager Tagblatt, Prague	1.16. 0.
Pesti Hirlap, Budapest	5. 0. 0.
Pravda, Belgrade	4. 0. 0.
Le Moment, Bucharest	1. 0. 0.
La Nacion, Buenos Aires	8. 0. 0.
Total	£68.16. 0.

1.   Published as "France's New Government" in the *Daily Telegraph,* on 14 April 1938. Edouard Daladier had succeeded Léon Blum as Prime Minister four days earlier.

Violet Pearman to Emery Reves

14 April 1938

Dear Dr. Revesz,

Herewith an article which was written for a series in a Sunday newspaper, but it was thought wiser not to publish it at the time it was written in 1937. Therefore it is an entirely new article, and Mr. Churchill would like to know whether the Stockholm people would like to have it or not. It is about 4,500 words long.[1]

Regarding the article which arrived late yesterday, this was I am sure entirely due to delay at the Paris end of the journey, owing possibly to the unsettled state of workers in Paris. It was put on the aeroplane which leaves London at 6 a.m. and which is <u>entirely composed of mails,</u> being a General Post Office regular service. It was actually seen to be put in the bag put on their aeroplane, extra money was paid for Express service at your end, and therefore you should have had it early. This was the method I had to adopt once before when the 8 p.m. boat train had gone before the article was ready, and that time it got to you early and everything was alright. I tell you this in order to clarify the position, as the telephone was extremely difficult to hear or to make oneself understood on a bad line.

Yours sincerely,

1.   The article, "The Effect of Aerial Transport on Civilization," was published later that year by *Svenska Dagbladet* in Stockholm and *Berlingske Tidende* in Copenhagen (see Cooperation to Churchill, 20 October 1938).

Emery Reves to Winston S. Churchill

21 April 1938   Paris

Dear Mr. Churchill,

I am coming over to London tomorrow or after tomorrow, but I am not quite sure by which train. I am writing to ask you to kindly dispatch your next article on Friday night so that we shall receive it on Saturday morning, should the article be for publication on Wednesday next. I wonder which subject you will deal with. I imagine probably on Anglo-Italian relations. You will certainly read tomorrow in the Daily Telegraph an article by Gayda[1] which we are publishing. This is the official Italian interpretation though a rather funny one.

I venture to suggest also another subject. The British mission to the United States and Canada. The general opinion on the Continent is that the air-force production on the other side of the Ocean strengthens considerably the position of Great Britain in France.[2]

You would very much oblige me if you would kindly inform us by telegram, if possible before Friday evening, whether we could expect the article so as to prepare everything for translations and expedition.

Yours very sincerely,

I. Révész

1. Virginio Gayda, Editor of the *Giornale d'Italia* since 1926 and known outside Italy as "Mussolini's mouthpiece." He was killed during an American air raid on Rome in March 1944.

2. On 28 April 1938 Churchill published, as his second *Daily Telegraph* article, "Britain's Deficiencies in Aircraft Manufacture." In it he wrote of the British government's decision "to make important purchases of aircraft in the United States and to set up large aircraft factories in Canada": "Such a resolve on the part of the Government is wholly admirable, and must be vigorously supported by all who wish to see the gathering dangers warded off." The article was circulated by Reves as "The Air Defence of Great Britain."

Cooperation to Winston S. Churchill

[28 April 1938]   Paris

THE AIR-RESERVE OF GREAT BRITAIN

Published by	Gross proceeds
Paris-Soir, Paris	£15. 0. 0.
Pariser Tages Zeitung, Paris	0.15. 0.
Le Soir, Bruxelles	10. 0. 0.
Luxemburger Zeitung, Luxemburg	1. 0. 0.
Der Telegraaf, Amsterdam	5. 0. 0.
Berlingske Tidende, Copenhagen	5. 0. 0.
Dagens Nyheter, Stockholm	7.10. 0.
Tidens Tegn, Oslo	5. 0. 0.
Paevaleht, Tallinn	1. 0. 0.
Lietuvos Aidas, Kaunas	1. 0. 0.
Gazette de Lausanne, Lausanne	1.10. 0.
National Zeitung, Bâle	2. 0. 0.
Thurgauer Zeitung, Frauenfeld	1.10. 0.
Le Moment, Bucharest	1. 0. 0.
La Nacion, Buenos Aires	8. 0. 0.
O Estado de Sao Paulo, Sao Paulo	7. 0. 0.
O Jornal, Rio de Janeiro	3. 0. 0.
Total	£75. 5. 0.

Cooperation to Winston S. Churchill

[28 April 1938]   Paris

Article	Gross proceeds
"Red Sunset"	£59. 8. 0.
"The New French Government"	68.16. 0.
"The Air-Reserve of Great-Britain"	75. 5. 0.
Total for 3 articles	£203. 9. 0.
60% of £203.9.0	£122. 2. 0.[1]

1. In the money values of 1996, £122 is approximately £3,000.

Emery Reves to Winston S. Churchill

1 May 1938   89 Piccadilly
                                                  London S.W.1.

Dear Mr. Churchill,
    Your last two articles have been published as follows:

Red Sunset
Paris-Soir
Le Soir, Bruxelles
Nieuwe Rotterdamsche Courant
Berlingske Tidende, Copenhagen
Dagens Nyheter, Stockholm
Tidens Tegn, Oslo
Päevaleht, Tallinn
Zydu Balsas, Kaunas
Neue Zürcher Zeitung, Zurich
Gazette de Lausanne
Lidove Noviny, Prague
Le Moment, Bucharest
Nowy Dziennik, Cracovie
La Nacion, Buenos Aires

The New French Government
Paris-Soir
Le Soir, Bruxelles
Luxemburger Zeitung
Nieuwe Rotterdamsche Courant
Berlingske Tidende, Copenhagen
Dagens Nyheter, Stockholm
Tidens Tegn, Oslo

Dagsposten, Trondheim
Päevaleht, Tallinn
Luzerner Tagblatt, Luzern
Tribune de Lausanne
Lidove Noviny, Prague
Prager Tagblatt, Prague
Pesti Hirlap, Budapest
Pravda, Belgrade
Le Moment, Bucharest
La Nacion, Buenos Aires

As soon as I am back in Paris, I shall control these publications and let you have a check with the definite statements.

I have seen Mr. Robertson, and have now the detailed statements regarding the publication of the 15 last articles in the Dominions. I should very much like to show you these figures. Whereas the average gross proceeds amounted six months ago to about £15.-.-, this has fallen during the past three months to an average of £3.- to £6.- per article for the whole Empire.

I have met here in London the Editor of the CHINA PRESS of Shanghai whom I know well from Paris and Geneva. He is an unusually intelligent Chinese, close to the Government, and very well informed. As you have told me that you are gathering some facts for your next article on the Far East, I wonder whether you would like to meet him. I think he could give you some useful information. Should you have some time Tuesday or Wednesday, I could bring him to your flat any time you wish.

Yours very sincerely
I. Révész

Violet Pearman to Emery Reves

1 May 1938

Dear Dr. Revesz,

Herewith I send you, at Mr. Churchill's request, the articles which were arranged when you last visited here. You will see that I have numbered them in the order in which they will appear in the News of the World this year, and I have added the dates on which they will be published, as far as these are known for the first six. The remaining six articles will be published some time in the autumn, and I will let you have the exact dates for these as soon as they are known.[1] You will see that No. 8 and No. 10 of the set of 12 are not sent to you, as they are too British to appeal to any foreign country, (i.e. the Penal System and Social Services respectively).

Mr. Churchill wishes me to stress very strongly that these articles, if taken by any Continental newspaper, cannot be published until they have already

appeared in the News of the World, and he wishes you to be very particular
in this respect.

Yours sincerely,
[Violet Pearman]
Private Secretary

1. Churchill's *News of the World* articles and the dates on which they were published (under the general title "The Effects of Modern Amusements on Life and Character") were: "Sport Is a Stimulant in Our Workaday Society" (4 September), "Preven-
tion of Crime Is Vital as Punishment" (11 September), "System That Guarantees This
Freedom" (18 September), "The Childless Marriage Threatens Our Race" (25 September), "Workers of Britain Have Come into Their Own" (2 October), "Health Comes
First in Social Progress" (October 9), and "What Other Secrets Does the Inventor
Hold?" (October 23). At the end of the year the *News of the World* published three
articles in the series "Parliament from the Inside": "Memories of Parliament as a
Novitiate Member" (18 December), "On Making a Maiden Speech in the House"
(25 December), and "Parliament Is a Stage of Empire" (1 January 1939).

Winston S. Churchill: engagement cards

5 May 1938

Dr. Revesz at Lady's Gallery Entrance.[1]
Debate.

1. At the House of Commons. During the debate, Churchill spoke against the
decision to transfer control of Britain's three naval bases in Southern Ireland to the
Irish Free State (Churchill himself had secured the bases for Britain as part of the Irish
Treaty in 1922). Churchill told the House, during the debate which Reves attended,
"In a war against an enemy possessing a numerous and powerful fleet of submarines,
these are the essential bases from which the whole operation of hunting submarines
and protecting incoming convoys is conducted." Interrupted by hostile cries, he continued, "I am very sorry to have to strike a jarring note this afternoon, but all opinions
should be heard and put on record."

Emery Reves to Winston S. Churchill

5 May 1938   London S.W.1.

Dear Mr. Churchill,
   Confirming our conversation this afternoon in the House of Commons, I
would suggest that the gross proceeds resulting from the publications in British Dominions and Colonies should be divided between you and COOP-
ERATION on the basis of 2/3 for you and 1/3 for COOPERATION. Air
mail expenses, etc. will be on our charge. I hope you will find this proposal
satisfactory, and would be grateful if you would let me know whether you are
accepting it.
   I think this is the most practical way, as publications during the past

months have been so reduced in the Empire that we cannot base upon them a calculation. The one contract I have signed with the South African group brings more than the total average of the last month. Mr. Robertson told me on the telephone this afternoon that several newspapers in Australia (Sydney Morning Herald, Courier Mail in Brisbane) have given notice recently to terminate the publications. The principal reason is that the articles are out of date when they are arriving.

I am actually in negotiations with a Dutch broadcasting company, who has offered us to broadcast our articles to India, Australia, New Zealand and possibly to South Africa. Should this be possible, so it would mean quite a new proposal to oversea newspapers which I think they will appreciate.

I am leaving Friday afternoon. Should you have a few moments, I should be grateful if we could discuss the policy in handling these newspapers.

Enclosed I am sending a letter which has been submitted to me by Paris-Soir.

Yours very sincerely,
I. Révész

Winston S. Churchill to Emery Reves

6 May 1938

As these articles will not have to be translated, and the air mail expenses are not very serious, I think it would be fairer if we divided 75/25%, and I hope you will agree to this.

I do not see how your broadcast plan is going to help exclusive sales to particular papers.

I will send you the new article at the earliest moment.

Emery Reves to Winston S. Churchill

9 May 1938   Paris

Dear Mr. Churchill,

I have received your letter of May 6th suggesting that the remunerations obtained in the British Empire should be divided 75/25%.

I accept this proposal as long as we shall diffuse the articles by air-mail. Should it be possible to go over to the broadcasting method we shall have to reconsider the situation.

If this method will be practical it will multiply the value of the articles in oversea countries. The plan we are going to study is the Hell-System, which is the most modern system of distributing news. It is a radio-telegraphic method by Morse-signs captured only by special apparatus. The Havas-Agency has that installation and the news they are broadcasting from Paris can be printed in a few minutes later in China as well as in Argentina. The telegram can be captured only by their officers in the respective countries having the necessary installation. Now a Dutch Company has established the same system in order of quick transmission of news to the Dutch East Indies. The Director of that Company is an old friend of mine and he suggested to me the other day to transmit our articles to the oversea countries by their system. I have a meeting with him Friday in Brussels and shall see whether this scheme is practical. Should this be the case, so this would give to our articles an unusual value as it will be for Australian and South African papers a sensational achievement if they could publish the articles on the same day as the London papers without paying the full cable expenses.

In the coming weeks I shall be travelling very much and beg to kindly send us your articles with a title. An attractive title is very important, and in my absence I could not give you the guarantee that your articles will be submitted to the papers with an adequate title.

Yours very sincerely
I. Révész

Cooperation to Winston S. Churchill

[12 May 1938]   Paris

THE CONSEQUENCES OF THE
ANGLO-ITALIAN AGREEMENT [1]

Published by	Gross proceeds
Paris-Soir, Paris	£15. 0. 0.
Le Soir, Bruxelles	10. 0. 0.
Luxemburger Zeitung, Luxemburg	1. 0. 0.
Berlingske Tidende, Copenhagen	5. 0. 0.
Dagens Nyheter, Stockholm	7.10. 0.
Tidens Tegn, Oslo	5. 0. 0.
Briwa Zeme, Riga	2.10. 0.
Paevaleht, Tallinn	1. 0. 0.
Zydu Balsas, Kaunas	0. 8. 0.
Journal des Nations, Geneva	0. 8. 0.
Lidove Noviny, Prague	1.10. 0.
Ujsag, Budapest	0.16. 0.
Politika, Belgrade	4. 0. 0.
Le Moment, Bucharest	1. 0. 0.
Bourse Egyptienne, Cairo	2. 0. 0.
La Nacion, Buenos Aires	8. 0. 0.
Agencia Meridionale, Rio de Janeiro (10 journaux)	3. 0. 0.
Total	£68. 2. 0.

1.   This article was published in the *Daily Telegraph* as "Premier's Work for a Non-War System in Europe."

Emery Reves to Winston S. Churchill

18 May 1938   Paris

Dear Mr. Churchill,

Kindly find enclosed statements regarding 3 articles and a cheque of £120.0.0. (one hundred and twenty Pounds).

I must apologize for not having sent you these statements before, but I have had unusually busy days since I am back in Paris.

Regarding your last article on Anglo-Italian Relations, it is too early yet to see the result. I would prefer to give you a statement by the next occasion.

I wonder on what subject you will write your next article. After your meeting with Henlein,[1] I think an article on Czechoslovakia would be of great interest. Should you by chance be able to write the article before the week-end, I should be grateful if you could dispatch it by Saturday night.

Yours very sincerely
I. Révész

1.   Konrad Henlein, leader of the Nazi sympathizers among the German-speaking majority in the Sudetenland, had visited Churchill at Chartwell, where he sought to assure Churchill that his party had no designs on the integrity of Czechoslovakia and no desire for the annexation of the Sudetenland by Germany.

Emery Reves to Winston S. Churchill

19 May 1938   Paris

Dear Mr. Churchill,

The Editor of the BERLINGSKE TIDENDE in Copenhagen who is regularly publishing all your articles, is in London for a few days. He is anxious to make your personal acquaintance after many years of collaboration and he asked me to introduce him to you.

I think it would be a good thing if you could spare a few moments and receive him. The BERLINGSKE TIDENDE is the most important newspaper in Danemark and he is regarded as the greatest Danish political writer. His name is:

Nicolaj Blaedel

and he is staying at the moment:

Mount Royal
Marble Arch

I have asked him to telephone one day to Mrs. Pearman hoping that you will be able to give him a short interview.[1]

With many thanks,
yours very sincerely,
I. Révész

1. Mrs. Pearman noted on this letter Churchill's response: "No. Deeply regret."

Cooperation to Winston S. Churchill

[26 May 1938]   Paris

AN "INCIDENT" IN CHINA [1]

Published by	Gross proceeds
Paris-Soir, Paris	£15. 0. 0.
Pariser Tages Zeitung, Paris	0.14. 0.
Le Soir, Bruxelles	10. 0. 0.
Nieuwe Rotterdamsche Courant, Rotterdam	2.10. 0.
Berlingske Tidende, Copenhagen	5. 0. 0.
Dagens Nyheter, Stockholm	7.10. 0.
Tidens Tegn, Oslo	5. 0. 0.
Briwa Zeme, Riga	2.10. 0.
Lietuvos Aidas, Kaunas	1. 0. 0.
Zydu Balsas, Kaunas	0. 8. 0.
Kurjer Warszawski, Varsovie	5. 0. 0.
Hajnt, Varsovie	0. 8. 0.
Tages Anzeiger, Zurich	4. 0. 0.
Tribune de Lausanne, Lausanne	1. 0. 0.
Lidove Noviny, Prague	1.10. 0.
Pesti Hirlap, Budapest	5. 0. 0.
St. Galler Tagblatt, St. Gallen	1. 8. 0.
Politika, Belgrade	4. 0. 0.
Le Moment, Bucharest	1. 0. 0.
Bourse Egyptienne, Cairo	2. 0. 0.
La Nacion, Buenos Aires	8. 0. 0.
O Estado de Sao Paulo, Sao Paulo	7. 0. 0.
Agencia Meridionale, Rio de Janeiro (10 papers)	3. 0. 0.
Total	£92.18. 0.

1. Published in the *Daily Telegraph* on 26 May 1938 as "How Japan's Military Enterprise Is Shackled."

Emery Reves to Winston S. Churchill

27 May 1938   Paris

Dear Mr. Churchill,

Except the SOUTH AFRICAN MORNING NEWSPAPERS I have
made until now contracts for 6 months with the following three Empire
newspapers:

TIMES OF MALTA (10/6 per article)
EAST AFRICAN STANDARD, Nairobi (1 Guinea per article)
THE ADVERTISER, Adelaide (2 Guineas per article)

The fees are the old ones, but the advantage is that now these newspapers
have taken the obligation to publish all of your articles. I hope there will be
some more such arrangements.

I am leaving Monday for the Scandinavian and Baltic countries and shall
be away from Paris for about a month. During my absence my Office is naturally working as usual. All communications from you will be forwarded to me
immediately. Besides, I shall be in daily telephone communication with Paris,
so that you can reach me everywhere within a few hours. From Monday until
Thursday next, I shall stay at Hôtel d'Angleterre, in Copenhagen.

I should be grateful if you could despatch your articles by Saturday nights
and "Express". I have made arrangements that they shall be translated on
Sundays and despatched everywhere by Monday morning.

Yours very sincerely,
I. Révész

Emery Reves to Winston S. Churchill

31 May 1938   Paris

Dear Mr. Churchill,

I have arranged that my Office shall work during the holidays, so your
article will be dispatched Monday morning. It would be a great facility, however, if you could mail your article, like last week, Saturday night, by express.

I have written some days ago a letter to Mr. Eden, inviting him to contribute articles to COOPERATION. I should be most grateful to you if
you would be kind enough to speak with him by an occasion, and say a few
words upon COOPERATION. Last week I have seen already an article by
him in the French press and I would very much regret if our invitation would
come late.

Needless to say that these articles would not interfere at all with the publication of your fortnightly articles, and this by two reasons: first, he is not a
journalist and I would not suggest him to write regularly and very frequently;
second, I would offer his articles to other newspapers than yours.

I had to stay in Paris another day and am leaving for Copenhagen tomorrow.

Yours very sincerely
I. Révész

Cooperation to Winston S. Churchill

[9 June 1938]   Paris

CONSCRIPTION IN ENGLAND [1]

Published by	Gross proceeds
Paris-Soir, Paris	£15. 0. 0.
Le Soir, Bruxelles	10. 0. 0.
Luxemburger Zeitung, Luxemburg	1. 0. 0.
Berlingske Tidende, Copenhagen	5. 0. 0.
Dagens Nyheter, Stockholm	7.10. 0.
Tidens Tegn, Oslo	5. 0. 0.
Stavanger Aftenblad, Stavanger	1.10. 0.
Helsingin Sanomat, Helsinki	3. 0. 0.
Briwa Zeme, Riga	2.10. 0.
Paevaleht, Tallinn	1. 0. 0.
Lietuvos Aidas, Kaunas	1. 0. 0.
Zydu Balsas, Kaunas	0. 8. 0.
Kurjer Warszawski, Varsovie	5. 0. 0.
Neue Zürcher Zeitung, Zurich	4. 0. 0.
Journal des Nations, Geneva	0. 8. 0.
Gazette de Lausanne, Lausanne	1. 0. 0.
Pesti Hirlap, Budapest	5. 0. 0.
Politika, Belgrade	4. 0. 0.
Le Moment, Bucharest	1. 0. 0.
Bourse Egyptienne, Cairo	2. 0. 0.
La Nacion, Buenos Aires	8. 0. 0.
O Estado de Sao Paulo, Sao Paulo	7. 0. 0.
Agencia Meridionale, Rio de Janeiro (10 papers)	3. 0. 0.
Total	£93. 6. 0.

1. Published by the *Daily Telegraph* on 9 June 1938 as "Perfecting Britain's Strength by National Service."

Winston S. Churchill to Emery Reves

22 June 1938

I shall be coming over to Paris next week on the 27th, staying until the 30th, and I shall hope to see you during my visit.

Will you very kindly have prepared statements about the Empire and other sales since you took them over from the "Evening Standard".

I hope you liked the last article.

Cooperation to Winston S. Churchill

[23 June 1938]   Paris

ASSURANCES OF PEACE [1]

Published by	Gross proceeds
Paris-Soir, Paris	£15. 0. 0.
Pariser Tages Zeitung, Paris	0.14. 0.
Le Soir, Bruxelles	10. 0. 0.
Luxemburger Zeitung, Luxemburg	1. 0. 0.
Berlingske Tidende, Copenhagen	5. 0. 0.
Dagens Nyheter, Stockholm	7.10. 0.
Tidens Tegn, Oslo	5. 0. 0.
Bergens Tidende, Bergen	2. 0. 0.
Helsingin Sanomat, Helsinki	3. 0. 0.
Paevaleht, Tallinn	1. 0. 0.
Briwa Zeme, Riga	2.10. 0.
Lietuvos Aidas, Kaunas	1. 0. 0.
Zydu Balsas, Kaunas	0. 8. 0.
Kurjer Warszawski, Varsovie	5. 0. 0.
Neue Zürcher Zeitung, Zurich	4. 0. 0.
Lidove Noviny, Prague	1.10. 0.
Prager Tagblatt, Prague	1.10. 0.
Politika, Belgrade	4. 0. 0.
Le Moment, Bucharest	1. 0. 0.
La Nacion, Buenos Aires	8. 0. 0.
Agencia Meridionale, Rio de Janeiro	3. 0. 0.
(10 papers)	
Total	£82. 2. 0.

1.   This article appeared in the *Daily Telegraph* on 23 June 1938 as "Factors Which Sway Europe's Fate over Czechoslovakia."

Emery Reves to Winston S. Churchill

27 June 1938   Paris

Dear Mr. Churchill,

I am back in Paris from my journey which was in every respect
satisfactory.

Sir Charles Mendl told me this morning that you will probably not come
over to Paris this week on account of the postponement of the Royal visit.
Please, do let me know whether this is so, in which case I shall send you
cheque and statements in a next letter.

I would be glad, however, if you would come over to Paris these days,
as there are several matters I should like to discuss with you.

Yours very sincerely
I. Révész

Emery Reves to Winston S. Churchill

28 June 1938   Paris

Dear Mr. Churchill,

I have received a letter from Mr. Watson asking me to agree that your next
article shall be published in the DAILY TELEGRAPH exceptionally on
Wednesday July 6th instead of July 7th. I naturally agreed with that suggestion, hoping very much that it will be possible for you to help us in trying
to write this article by Friday, so that we shall receive it Saturday morning.

Have you decided already the subject of the next article? I think it would
be interesting if you could write on the political significance and importance
of the coming Royal visit to Paris. Should you like this subject, so I hope you
will find some leisure to dictate the article before Saturday.

I think you have not yet been in my office in Paris. I happen to have one
of the largest terraces on the Champs-Elysées overlooking the whole Avenue
of the Etoile until the Concorde. Should it be useful to you, or for your
friends, to watch the entry of the King, it is entirely at your disposal. It is
probable that Sir Charles Mendl will also use it for some of the guests of the
Embassy.

Supposing that you are not coming over to Paris before the Royal visit,
I shall send you the statements within one or two days.

Yours very sincerely,
I. Révész

Emery Reves to Winston S. Churchill

1 July 1938   Paris

Dear Mr. Churchill,

Kindly find enclosed a cheque of £240.8.6. in respect of your last four articles.[1] I am enclosing statements regarding the publication of these articles, as well in the international press as in the Empire press. As you will see the general trend is going upward and the last articles have been better published than the previous ones.

The situation in the Dominion press is the following:

As you will remember when I took over the handling of the Dominion rights there was not one single contract in existence and publications sank constantly, so that the average gross proceeds of the five last articles have been between 3–6 Guineas per article for the whole Empire. I have endeavoured since the first day to come to definite contracts with these newspapers which was rather difficult as they have received in the past years your articles without any obligation, they have rejected a great number of them and have paid rather small fees for those only which they have freely accepted. Until to-day I have signed five contracts which are now definite for a 6 months period. The market was particularly spoiled in Australia. For some time the SYDNEY MORNING HERALD has published the articles, but Mr. Robertson told me that they did not want them any more and so he was submitting them lately to the SYDNEY SUN for £3.3.0. per article accepted. This is a very small fee for Sydney, as those papers are always paying me £5.5.0. per article, less interesting than yours. Nevertheless, I have tried to come to an arrangement with the SYDNEY SUN and have submitted them the first two articles in May. The result was negative; they rejected to alter the situation and wanted to receive your articles free of any obligation. So I came back to the SYDNEY MORNING HERALD and am glad to say that we have come to an arrangement for a 6 months period for all your articles on the basis of £3.3.0. each. It would have been possible to get £5.5.0. for some of the articles, but it was impossible to get higher fees and a contract simultaneously.

Besides the SYDNEY MORNING HERALD I have signed another contract with the ADVERTISER in Adelaide, which paper is paying £2.2.0. (Two Guineas) per article. So we have now at least £5.5.0. per article sure coming from Australia. I shall now try to make some other arrangements with local papers in Australia, though they have stopped publication in the last period, while they were handled by the EVENING STANDARD.

As you know there is a contract with the SOUTH AFRICAN MORNING NEWSPAPERS on the basis of £7.7.0. per article. I also signed contracts with the EAST AFRICAN STANDARD in Nairobi on the basis of £1.1.0. per article, and the TIMES OF MALTA on the basis of 10/6 per article.

These five newspapers secure us an income of £14.3.6. per article for a six months period, which is already considerably more than the average of the previous six months.

Needless to say that I do not consider this result as complete and hope to make new arrangements also in other parts of the Empire. What I am aiming at are definite contracts and I have not sent out your last four articles to such newspapers with which we have no contracts. I shall do so only when I shall see that there is no more chance in a certain part of the Empire to come to fix arrangements.

Regarding the other parts of the world everything is going all right, and I hope that my last journey in the Nordic countries has strengthened our position. The Editors are very satisfied with the articles, the only remark I have heard from an Editor is that some of your articles are written obviously for British public.

In Stockholm we have to expect at the end of this year the renewal of the fight between the two rival newspapers. SVENSKA DAGBLADET is satisfied with the present situation in publishing from time to time your magazine articles, but the Editor of the DAGENS NYHETER is anxious that your articles shall not be published in another Swedish newspaper. He urges me to stop that by the end of this year. It will be a hard job to satisfy these two papers, but we have still time to think it over.

PARIS-SOIR told me yesterday that they have written to you asking for a short special article on the occasion of the Royal visit. What they want is not really an article but a short message of 30–50 lines addressed to the French people which they would like to publish on the front page the day of the King's arrival. Could you comply with that request? If yes, please let me have these few lines at an early convenience, so that we shall be able to remit them to PARIS-SOIR in time.

I wonder whether you will be able to despatch your next article one day sooner than usually, as the DAILY TELEGRAPH wishes to publish it on Wednesday already.

Yours very sincerely
I. Révész

1. The 1996 money value of £240 in 1938 was £6,000.

Cooperation to Winston S. Churchill

1 July 1938   Paris

PUBLICATIONS OF THE BRITISH EMPIRE

"The Consequences of the Anglo-Italian Agreement"
Times of Malta, Valetta-Malta   £ 0.10. 6.
South African Morning Newspapers   7. 7. 0.

East African Standard, Nairobi	1. 1. 0.
Advertiser, Adelaide	2. 2. 0.
	£11. 0. 6.
"An 'Incident' in China"	
Times of Malta, Valetta-Malta	£ 0.10. 6.
South African Morning Newspapers	7. 7. 0.
East African Standard, Nairobi	1. 1. 0.
Associated Newspapers of Ceylon	1. 1. 0.
Advertiser, Adelaide	2. 2. 0.
	£12. 1. 6.
"Conscription in England"	
Sydney Morning Herald, Sydney	£ 3. 3. 0.
Times of Malta, Valetta-Malta	0.10. 6.
South African Morning Newspapers	7. 7. 0.
East African Standard, Nairobi	1. 1. 0.
Advertiser, Adelaide	2. 2. 0.
	£14. 3. 6.
"Assurances of Peace"	
Sydney Morning Herald, Sydney	£ 3. 3. 0.
Times of Malta, Valetta-Malta	0.10. 6.
South African Morning Newspapers	7. 7. 0.
East African Standard, Nairobi	1. 1. 0.
Advertiser, Adelaide	2. 2. 0.
	£14. 3. 6.
Total	£51. 9. 0.

INTERNATIONAL PUBLICATIONS

"The Consequences of the Anglo-Italian Agreement"	£ 68. 2. 0.
"An Incident in China"	92.18. 0.
"Conscription in England"	93. 6. 0.
"Assurances of Peace"	82. 2. 0.
Total	£336. 8. 0.
60% of £336.8.0.	£201.16.10.

Winston S. Churchill to Emery Reves

3 July 1938

Many thanks for your letter about which I am writing you tomorrow.

In the meantime I would suggest that you should not send important communications in these very flimsy envelopes which resemble circulars, of which I receive scores in the week. Actually your letter was discovered in a bundle of these, which are never brought before me until they are examined in detail.

I enclose the envelope in which your letter was sent.

Emery Reves to Winston S. Churchill

4 July 1938   Paris

Dear Mr. Churchill,

I wonder whether my letter with the statements and cheque dispatched Friday last has arrived already.

I have received the "Acute Indigestion" Sunday evening[1]—it is excellent. The article has been dispatched already in all countries, but it is technically impossible that newspapers shall publish it before Thursday. I am rather afraid that some incident will occur again as this article might arouse some sensation.

The Editor of the new French weekly "Messidor" is preparing a special number on Great Britain and British Institutions on the occasion of the Royal visit in Paris, and they are anxious to get the opinion of some leading British Statesmen on the following problem

"England is the only country in the world in which the ruling classes have never waited to consent or to accept reforms until it was too late. How do you explain this singular and unique phenomenon?"

"Messidor" would be most grateful if you would kindly explain your opinion on that question briefly in 15–20 lines. "Messidor" is, as you may know, a new popular weekly of the Confédération Générale du Travail under the personal direction of Mr. Léon Jouhaux. It reaches some 5,000,000 members of the C.G.T.

They did not want to disturb you directly and asked me to submit to you this request. I very much hope that you will be able to comply with that request, as this publication reaches an important section of the French public. As "Messidor" is obliged to close this number at the end of this week, I would be grateful if you would kindly address these few lines to COOPERA-TION latest on Friday next.

Yours very sincerely,
I. Révész

1. "Acute Indigestion" was published in the *Daily Telegraph* on 6 July 1938 as "Germany's Discipline for the Old Austria."

Cooperation to Winston S. Churchill

6 July 1938   Paris

AN ACUTE INDIGESTION

Published by	Gross proceeds
Paris-Soir, Paris	£15. 0. 0.
Le Soir, Bruxelles	10. 0. 0.
Nieuwe Rotterdamsche Courant, Rotterdam	2.10. 0.
Berlingske Tidende, Copenhagen	5. 0. 0.
Dagens Nyheter, Stockholm	7.10. 0.
Tidens Tegn, Oslo	5. 0. 0.
Bergens Tidende, Bergen	2. 0. 0.
Helsingin Sanomat, Helsinki	3. 0. 0.
Briwa Zeme, Riga	2.10. 0.
Zydu Balsas, Kaunas	0. 8. 0.
Hajnt, Warsaw	0.10. 0.
Nowy Dziennik, Krakow	0. 8. 0.
Journal des Nations, Geneva	0. 8. 0.
Le Moment, Bucharest	1. 0. 0.
La Nacion, Buenos Aires	8. 0. 0.
O Estado de Sao Paulo, Sao Paulo	7. 0. 0.
Agencia Meridionale, Rio de Janeiro	3. 0. 0.
Total	£73. 4. 0.

Winston S. Churchill to Emery Reves

7 July 1938

Dear Doctor Revesz,

I hope you have already received an acknowledgement from me of the receipt of your statement and cheque.

I was very hard pressed last week; hence the fact that we were a day behind in the delivery of the article.

I fear I could not undertake to send the message you suggest to "Messidor".

Yours sincerely,

Winston S. Churchill to Emery Reves

10 July 1938

Dear Doctor Revesz,

Many thanks for your letter of July 1. The sales of the articles are growing well under your care, and I am very satisfied with all you do for me. I now address myself to the other points mentioned therein.

I think all you have done about the Dominion rights is very good. I only wish you could develop something of the same kind in the United States. It is incredible that this market has not been tapped. There must be at least half a dozen papers who would pay from five to ten guineas apiece. I am not so sure that I am going there this Autumn after all.

At present I have put the marketing of the articles in the hands of the representative of Curtis Brown.[1] He does not appear to have achieved anything so far.

I am very glad that the last few articles have had a wider circulation on the Continent.

With regard to Sweden I think you should try to keep the two going on the present basis. Anyhow, I leave it entirely to you.

I am coming over on July 18 and shall be in Paris until 21 or 22. I shall probably do one of the Daily Telegraph articles on the Royal Visit. In these circumstances it would be difficult for me to write a preliminary puff for the PARIS-SOIR.

I hope you liked the last article about Austria. I see that the Daily Telegraph was confiscated in Germany for publishing it.

I shall look forward to seeing you in Paris.

1. Allan M. Collins, of Curtis Brown, New York, whom Churchill replaced with Reves as his United States literary agent five months later.

Emery Reves to Winston S. Churchill

12 July 1938   Paris

Dear Mr. Churchill,

Many thanks for your kind letter of July 10th.

I am glad you find the results in the Dominions satisfactory. There is a new small arrangement with the AFRICAN MORNING POST in Accra, Gold Coast, for a 6 months period on the basis of 10/6 per article. Though rather modest, it is a contract.

I am absolutely of your opinion that it is incredible that the American market is not yet opened for your articles. I am still hoping to go over later in the autumn and to be able to do something.

I am sorry to hear that Curtis Brown has not yet been able to achieve anything in the States. Under these circumstances I wonder whether you allow me an advice. I think that nothing can spoil the market more than constant offerings by agents. Such a thing must be a success within a few days. If somebody is on the spot and cannot get at least one contract within eight days, so there are either great political and financial difficulties or the man is unable to negotiate and to conclude. I am very much afraid that they have sent out a great number of written offers which is a bad tactic. The only way is to negotiate personally with the newspaper proprietors or the editors. Offers by letters diminish considerably the value of the articles.

I should be happy if they could achieve a result but if nothing has been done yet, I think you ought to withdraw your option and not to let them make further offers for your articles. It will be very difficult to convince editors in the United States to take your articles if they have turned them down a few weeks or months ago.

I hope very much to talk with you on the matter in Paris. Will you stay at the Embassy this time too?

Yours very sincerely,
I. Révész

P.S. Should your next article deal with the Royal visit I do beg to write it at once and let us have the manuscript by to-morrow or the day after to-morrow. Such an article can only have a wide publication if it reaches the newspapers <u>before</u> the visit takes place, and it takes about 8 days until the articles arrive in the Dominions and in South America.

Allan M. Collins to Winston S. Churchill

15 July 1938

Curtis Brown Ltd
18 East 48th Street
New York

Dear Mr. Churchill,

I reluctantly admit defeat on the Telegraph series. I approached some twenty newspapers and although some were interested, from none could I get sufficient indication of meeting the required price.

I have no doubt that if someone had the opportunity to visit the editors of these papers individually that something could be done, although whether on a large enough scale or not I can not be sure.

For your records I did try one more syndicate, that of the Register and Tribune Syndicate of Des Moines, Iowa.

Sincerely yours

Cooperation to Winston S. Churchill

[26 July 1938]

THE ROYAL VISIT IN PARIS [1]

Published by	Gross proceeds
Paris-Soir, Paris	£15. 0. 0.
Le Soir, Bruxelles	10. 0. 0.
Luxemburger Zeitung, Luxembourg	1. 0. 0.
Berlingske Tidende, Copenhagen	5. 0. 0.
Dagens Nyheter, Stockholm	7.10. 0.
Tidens Tegn, Oslo	5. 0. 0.
Bergens Tidende, Bergen	2. 0. 0.
Stavanger Aftenblad, Stavanger	1.10. 0.
Dagsposten, Trondheim	1.10. 0.
Helsingin Sanomat, Helsinki	3. 0. 0.
Briwa Zeme, Riga	2.10. 0.
Paevaleht, Tallinn	1. 0. 0.
Lietuvos Aidas, Kaunas	1. 0. 0.
Zydu Balsas, Kaunas	0. 8. 0.
Kurjer Warszawski, Warsaw	5. 0. 0.
Hajnt, Warsaw	0.10. 0.
Nowy Dziennik, Krakow	0. 8. 0.
Gazette de Lausanne, Lausanne	1.10. 0.
Journal des Nations, Geneva	0. 8. 0.
Prager Tagblatt, Prague	1.10. 0.
Pester Lloyd, Budapest	2. 0. 0.
Pesti Hirlap, Budapest	5. 0. 0.
Politika, Belgrade	4. 0. 0.
Le Moment, Bucharest	1. 0. 0.
La Nacion, Buenos Aires	8. 0. 0.
O Estado de Sao Paulo, Sao Paulo	7. 0. 0.
Agencia Meridionale, Rio de Janeiro	3. 0. 0.
Total	£95.14. 0.

1. Published in the *Daily Telegraph* on 26 July 1938 as "What Freedom Means for France."

Violet Pearman to Emery Reves

27 July 1938

Dear Sir,
    I am desired by Mr. Churchill to send you the attached letter [not found] from Curtis Brown Ltd. of New York, for your information.
    Kindly return after perusal.

Yours truly,
[Violet Pearman]
Private Secretary

Winston S. Churchill: engagement cards

30 July 1938

Dr. Revesz. Lunch. To be confirmed.

Cooperation to Winston S. Churchill

[4 August 1938]   Paris

THE UNITED STATES AND EUROPE [1]

Published by	Gross proceeds
Paris-Soir, Paris	£15. 0. 0.
Pariser Tages Zeitung, Paris	0.14. 0.
Le Soir, Bruxelles	10. 0. 0.
Luxemburger Zeitung, Luxembourg	1. 0. 0.
Berlingske Tidende, Copenhagen	5. 0. 0.
Dagens Nyheter, Stockholm	7.10. 0.
Tidens Tegn, Oslo	5. 0. 0.
Bergens Tidende, Bergen	2. 0. 0.
Dagsposten, Trondheim	1.10. 0.
Helsingin Sanomat, Helsinki	3. 0. 0.
Briwa Zeme, Riga	2.10. 0.
Paevaleht, Tallinn	1. 0. 0.
Lietuvos Aidas, Kaunas	1. 0. 0.
Zydu Balsas, Kaunas	0. 8. 0.
Hajnt, Warsaw	0.10. 0.
Neue Zürcher Zeitung, Zurich	4. 0. 0.
Prager Tagblatt, Prague	1.10. 0.
Politika, Belgrade	4. 0. 0.
Le Moment, Bucharest	1. 0. 0.
La Nacion, Buenos Aires	8. 0. 0.

O Estado de Sao Paulo, Sao Paulo		7. 0. 0.
Diarios Asociados, Rio de Janeiro		3. 0. 0.
Total		£84.12. 0.

1.   Published in the *Daily Telegraph* on 4 August 1938 as "Influence the U.S. May Wield on Europe's Destiny."

Cooperation to Winston S. Churchill

[4 August 1938]

PUBLICATIONS IN THE BRITISH EMPIRE

"An Acute Indigestion"	
Sydney Morning Herald	£ 3. 3. 0.
Times of Malta	0.10. 6.
South African Morning Newspapers	7. 7. 0.
East African Standard, Nairobi	1. 1. 0.
Advertiser, Adelaide	2. 2. 0.
Daily News, Ceylon	1. 1. 0.
African Morning Post, Accra	0.10. 6.
	£15.15. 0.
"The Royal Visit in Paris"	
Sydney Morning Herald	£ 3. 3. 0.
Times of Malta	0.10. 6.
South African Morning Newspapers	7. 7. 0.
East African Standard, Nairobi	1. 1. 0.
Advertiser, Adelaide	2. 2. 0.
African Morning Post, Accra	0.10. 6.
	£14.14. 0.
"The United States and Europe"	
Sydney Morning Herald	£ 3. 3. 0.
Times of Malta	0.10. 6.
South African Morning Newspapers	7. 7. 0.
East African Standard, Nairobi	1. 1. 0.
Advertiser, Adelaide	2. 2. 0.
African Morning Post, Accra	0.10. 6.
	£14.14. 0.

PUBLICATIONS IN THE INTERNATIONAL PRESS

"An Acute Indigestion"	£ 73. 4. 0.
"The Royal Visit in Paris"	95.14. 0.

"The United States and Europe"	84.12.	0.
"Women in War"	48. 0.	0.
Total	£301.10.	0.
60%	£180.18.	0.

PUBLICATIONS IN THE BRITISH EMPIRE

"An Acute Indigestion"	£ 15.15.	0.
"The Royal Visit in Paris"	14.14.	0.
"The United States and Europe"	14.14.	0.
Total	£ 45. 3.	0.
75%	£ 34. 4.	0.
Total of percentages	£215. 2.	0.

Erland Echlin[1] *to Winston S. Churchill: telegram*

5 August 1938   9 Latimer Road,
Strictly Confidential   London W.6

Undertaking behalf my newspaper, agreement with Cooperation, Paris, to publish articles by you throughout Canada. As I have never before heard of Cooperation, could I have assurance from you that Cooperation is completely authorised in this matter.

Reply by return much appreciated, as it is desired to complete negotiations this morning. Many thanks.

    1.   London representative of the *Toronto Star.*

Winston S. Churchill to Erland Echlin: telegram

5 August 1938

Doctor Revesz and Cooperation have my full authority.

                                                          Churchill

Emery Reves to Winston S. Churchill

16 August 1938   Paris

Dear Mr. Churchill,

This time we have had many technical difficulties. The article arrived here to-day, Tuesday morning, only. The air-mail has not much value for a short distance like London-Paris. The only possibility to get over a letter by the night is the late fee box at Victoria Station before 8 p.m.

The telegram which you sent me Sunday evening announcing the article arrived here late Monday evening, and only by the courtesy of a gentleman whom I did not know before. The telegram was addressed: BALSAC 5700, DR. REVESZ, PARIS. Unfortunately, there is another Dr. Revesz in Paris, a physician, and the telegram was delivered to him as the telephone number is no telegram address in France as it is in England. My telegram address is: COOP-ERATION PARIS. It is not necessary to add anything to these two words. On the contrary, anything in addition might delay the delivery.

I shall certainly let you have statements regarding the last articles before the weekend.

Cooperation to Winston S. Churchill

[18 August 1938]   Paris

GERMAN MANOEUVRES [1]

Published by	Gross proceeds
Le Soir, Bruxelles	£10. 0. 0.
Berlingske Tidende, Copenhagen	5. 0. 0.
Paevaleht, Tallinn	1. 0. 0.
Helsingin Sanomat, Helsinki	3. 0. 0.
Paris-Soir, Paris	15. 0. 0.
Utrechtsch Nieuwsblad (and 10 Dutch provincial papers)	7. 0. 0.
Briwa Zeme, Riga	2.10. 0.
Zydu Balsas, Kaunas	0. 8. 0.
Luxemburger Zeitung, Luxemburg	1. 0. 0.
Tidens Tegn, Oslo	5. 0. 0.
Bergens Tidende, Bergen	2. 0. 0.
Dagsposten, Trondheim	1.10. 0.
Hajnt, Warsaw	0.10. 0.
Le Moment, Bucharest	1. 0. 0.
Dagens Nyheter, Stockholm	7.10. 0.
Die Weltwoche, Zurich	4. 0. 0.
Lidove Noviny, Prague	1.10. 0.
Oran Republicain, Oran	1. 0. 0.
La Nacion, Buenos Aires	8. 0. 0.
O Estado de Sao Paulo, Sao Paulo	7. 0. 0.
Diarios Asociados, Rio de Janeiro	3. 0. 0.
Total	£86.18. 0.

1. Published in the *Daily Telegraph* on 18 August 1938 as "Thoughts on Germany's Big-Scale Manoeuvres."

Emery Reves to Winston S. Churchill

18 August 1938   Paris

Dear Mr. Churchill,
    Kindly find enclosed a cheque of £215.-.- (Two Hundred Fifteen Pounds)
and statements regarding the publication of the three last articles.

Yours very sincerely,
I. Révész

Winston S. Churchill to Emery Reves

25 August 1938

    Many thanks for your letter and cheque.
    Do you happen to know anything about a Monsieur Ferdinand Lot.[1] He
is an archaeologist and a great authority on Roman and Anglo-Saxon Britain.
He delivered a lecture here in 1931 which was greatly esteemed. I gather he is
now very old. Could you find out for me what his circumstances are? Because
if I could get in touch with him it might help in the work upon which I am
now engaged.
    What has happened to the Japanese Naval article? Did the Swedes take it?
I was very pleased to see how well you had disposed of the article 'Women in
War'. The sales of the articles are growing well under your care, and I am
very satisfied with all you do for me.
    I do not like the look of things at all.

    1.   Ferdinand Lot, 1866–1952. A professor at the Sorbonne, historian, and philolo-
gist, he published his first book, on the later Carolingians, in 1891. His widely ac-
claimed history of the end of the ancient world and the beginning of the middle ages
was published in 1927, after which he wrote a history of the invasions of the German
tribes (1935) and a study of the barbarian invasions and the settlement of Europe (1937).
His last book, on Gaul, was published in 1947.

Emery Reves to Winston S. Churchill

25 August 1938   Paris

Dear Mr. Churchill,
    I am glad to inform you that in the past days I have signed 3 more con-
tracts in the British Empire, with the ARGUS in Melbourne, THE WEST
AUSTRALIAN in Perth and THE NASSAU GUARDIAN on the Bahamas.
    We now have already 9 contracts in the Empire and I hope to come to
some further arrangements during the coming month.
    On the other hand one contract has been cancelled by TIDENS TEGN
in Oslo. I think this newspaper became bankrupt and it has been taken over
by a new proprietor and a new Editor. The new people have denounced all

the old arrangements. I think it will be possible a little later to come to a new contract with the new principals or, in the negative, to make an arrangement with another newspaper in Oslo.

I believe that from October on I shall be able to transmit your articles to oversea countries through the Radio station, Koswijk in Holland. This is one of the most modern and powerful stations in Europe and their terms are rather reasonable. We are undertaking the first experiments in October when I shall be in America.

I am going over with a view to establish a regular exchange of views between the American Press and the Press of the European democracies. I think such an exchange might create a better understanding between the democratic countries on the two Continents. I should like to arrange for regular publication of our articles in the American Press in order to inform directly the American public about the opinion of leading European states-men on international affairs. On the other side, I should like to invite some of the most important American statesmen to explain their views which I would like to publish in the international press abroad.

This idea interests here in Paris everybody and I hope that I shall be able to get the moral support of President Roosevelt.

To the newspapers my proposition will be a pure business proposition, saying that they could get on every event of international importance the authoritative comment of the leading European statesmen transmitted by Radio-telegram, which is an entirely new and interesting complement to their news gathering system. I think such a proposal made directly to the important newspapers might interest them, and after my first contract with the Toronto Star I am rather hopeful.

I should be much obliged, should you approve this plan, if you would confirm me that you transfer to COOPERATION the exclusive handling of your articles in the United States of America. Should there be no satisfactory result within a period of six months you can, of course, withdraw this author-ization. But it is very important for me in view of my coming negotiations that from now on nobody shall have the right to offer your articles in the United States. Needless to say that this arrangement will not interfere with your direct contribution to Collier's.

Yours very sincerely
I. Révész

P.S. The situation in Paris is not good, the days of Daladier seem to be counted. His speech was a great mistake, the Trade-Unions were prepared to make every concession, but instead of negotiating he has made this public attitude which awoke the fighting spirit on both sides again. People say that Daladier acted under the influence of Patenôtre. A crisis could be rather awk-ward in view of the news coming from Germany and Spain. Herriot is appar-ently requested by everybody to form a National Government but this would spoil his further ambitions.[1]

1.   Edouard Herriot had been Prime Minister of France three times: from June 1924 to April 1925, for two days in 1926, and from June to December 1932. He was never Prime Minister again. In 1942 he was imprisoned by the Gestapo. From 1947 to 1953 he was President of the French National Assembly.

Winston S. Churchill to Emery Reves

27 August 1938

My dear Revesz,

Many thanks for your letter, and I am glad to hear of the new contract you have made for the British Dominions.

The great thing is to have settled agreements to take a series for a particular period. This picking and choosing is no use.

I am glad also you have decided to go to the United States, if the European situation does not prevent you.

I hereby give you full authority for the exclusive handling of my articles in the United States of America for six months, from October 1, and I am notifying Curtis Brown and the "Evening Standard" to this effect. This, of course, excludes the Collier articles, or any special magazine articles which I may make at a similar fee. However, apart from Collier's, I do not think there will be any.

I am sorry to hear what you say about Daladier. Any weakening of the French Government at this moment would add to our dangers.

Winston S. Churchill to Emery Reves: telegram

28 August 1938

Article dispatched express post tonight.

Churchill

Cooperation to Winston S. Churchill

[1 September 1938]   Paris

IS AIR POWER DECISIVE? [1]

Published by	Gross proceeds
Le Soir, Bruxelles	£10. 0. 0.
Berlingske Tidende, Copenhagen	5. 0. 0.
Paevaleht, Tallinn	1. 0. 0.
Helsingin Sanomat, Helsinki	3. 0. 0.
Paris-Soir, Paris	15. 0. 0.
Pariser Tages Zeitung, Paris	0.14. 0.

Utrechtsch Nieuwsblad (and 10 Dutch provincial papers)	7. 0. 0.
Lietuvos Aidas, Kaunas	1. 0. 0.
Luxemburger Zeitung, Luxemburg	1. 0. 0.
Tidens Tegn, Oslo	5. 0. 0.
Bergens Tidende, Bergen	2. 0. 0.
Stavanger Aftenblad, Stavanger	1.10. 0.
Le Moment, Bucharest	1. 0. 0.
Dagens Nyheter, Stockholm	7.10. 0.
Der Bund, Bern	2. 0. 0.
Tages Anzeiger, Zurich	3. 0. 0.
Gazette de Lausanne, Lausanne	1.10. 0.
Prager Tagblatt, Prague	1.10. 0.
Politika, Belgrade	4. 0. 0.
La Nacion, Buenos Aires	8. 0. 0.
O Estado de Sao Paulo, Sao Paulo	7. 0. 0.
Diarios Asociados, Rio de Janeiro	3. 0. 0.
Total	£90.14. 0.

1.   On 1 September 1938 the *Daily Telegraph* published Churchill's article "Is Air Power Decisive in War?" As well as in the newspapers listed here, the article was published in *Journal des Nations* (Geneva), South African Morning newspapers, *Advertiser* (Adelaide, Australia), *Sydney Morning Herald, Nassau Guardian* (Bahamas), *African Morning Post* (Accra, Gold Coast), *Toronto Star, Times of Malta,* and the *East African Standard* (Nairobi).

Emery Reves to Winston S. Churchill

1 September 1938   Paris

Dear Mr. Churchill,

Many thanks for your letters of August 25th and 27th.

Kindly find enclosed some information regarding M. Ferdinand Lot including the list of his works. He is no more lecturing. His address is: 53, rue Boucicaut, FONTENAY-AUX-ROSES (Seine). I hope this information will be of use to you.

I am glad you were pleased to see how I have disposed of the article "Women in War". I think this will be possible several times a year but I should not like to submit to newspapers too many of your magazine-articles as they might disturb the publication of the fortnightly articles.

The Japanese Naval article has been just sent to Stockholm. I have no reply yet, but I feel sure they will publish it.

I am confident that I shall be able to give you some further good news from the Dominions in the near future.

I thank you for your authorization for the United States. I shall ask you for a special letter for the case it would be necessary to show it to some American editors. But I shall certainly come over to London before I am leaving. It is possible that I shall come over for one or two days around the 10th of September.

Yours very sincerely,
I. Révész

Winston S. Churchill: engagement cards

11 September 1938

Dr. Revesz for tea.

Winston S. Churchill to Emery Reves

12 September 1938

Dear Doctor Revesz,
I confirm our arrangement whereby Cooperation has the exclusive right to handle my articles in the United States of America. This is in addition to other contracts which I have made with you.

Cooperation to Winston S. Churchill

[15 September 1938]   Paris

CRISIS [1]

Published by	Gross proceeds
Le Soir, Bruxelles	£10. 0. 0.
Paevaleht, Tallinn	1. 0. 0.
Helsingin Sanomat, Helsinki	3. 0. 0.
Paris-Soir, Paris	15. 0. 0.
Pariser Tages Zeitung, Paris	0.14. 0.
Utrechtsch Nieuwsblad (and 10 Dutch provincial papers)	7. 0. 0.
Briwa Zeme, Riga	2.10. 0.
Lietuvos Aidas, Kaunas	1. 0. 0.
Zydu Balsas, Kaunas	0. 8. 0.
Bergens Tidende, Bergen	2. 0. 0.
Stavanger Aftenblad, Stavanger	1.10. 0.
Hajnt, Warsaw	0.10. 0.
Le Moment, Bucharest	1. 0. 0.
Dagens Nyheter, Stockholm	7.10. 0.

Tages Anzeiger, Zurich	4. 0. 0.
Lidove Noviny, Prague	1.10. 0.
Prager Tagblatt, Prague	1.10. 0.
La Nacion, Buenos Aires	8. 0. 0.
O Estado de Sao Paulo, Sao Paulo	7. 0. 0.
Diarios Asociados, Rio de Janeiro	3. 0. 0.
Total	£78. 2. 0.

PUBLICATIONS IN THE BRITISH EMPIRE

"German Manoeuvres"

South African Morning Newspapers	£ 7. 7. 0.
Advertiser, Adelaide	2. 2. 0.
Sydney Morning Herald, Sydney	3. 3. 0.
West Australian, Perth	2. 2. 0.
African Morning Post, Accra	0.10. 6.
Toronto Star, Toronto	7.10. 0.
Ceylon Daily News, Colombo	1. 1. 0.
Times of Malta, Malta	0.10. 6.
The Hindu, Madras	1.10. 0.
East African Standard, Nairobi	1. 1. 0.
	£26.17. 0.

"Air Force"

South African Morning Newspapers	£ 7. 7. 0.
Advertiser, Adelaide	2. 2. 0.
Sydney Morning Herald, Sydney	3. 3. 0.
West Australian, Perth	2. 2. 0.
Nassau Guardian, Nassau	0.14. 0.
African Morning Post, Accra	0.10. 6.
Toronto Star, Toronto	7.10. 0.
Times of Malta, Malta	0.10. 6.
East African Standard, Nairobi	1. 1. 0.
Evening Post, Wellington	2. 2. 0.
The Press, Christchurch	2. 2. 0.
	£29. 4. 0.

"Crisis"

South African Morning Newspapers	£ 7. 7. 0.
Advertiser, Adelaide	2. 2. 0.

Sydney Morning Herald, Sydney	3. 3. 0.
West Australian, Perth	2. 2. 0.
New Zealand Herald, Auckland	2. 2. 0.
Evening Post, Wellington	2. 2. 0.
The Press, Christchurch	2. 2. 0.
Daily Times, Dunedin	2. 2. 0.
Ceylon Daily News, Colombo	1. 1. 0.
Straits Times, Singapore	1. 1. 0.
African Morning Post, Accra	0.10. 6.
East African Standard, Nairobi	1. 1. 0.
Nassau Guardian, Nassau	0.14. 0.
Daily Gleaner, Kingston	0.14. 0.
Trinidad Guardian, Port of Spain	0.14. 0.
Times of Malta, Malta	0.10. 6.

£29. 8. 0.

PUBLICATIONS IN THE INTERNATIONAL PRESS

"German Manoeuvres"	£ 86.18. 0.
"Air Force"	90.14. 0.
"Crisis"	78. 2. 0.
"Challenge in the Pacific"	40. 0. 0.
Total	£295.14. 0.
60%	£177. 9. 0.

PUBLICATIONS IN THE BRITISH EMPIRE

Total	£ 85. 9. 0.
75%	£ 64. 1. 0.
Total of percentages	£241.10. 0.

1.   On 15 September 1938 the *Daily Telegraph* published Churchill's article "Can Europe Stave Off War?"

Winston S. Churchill to Emery Reves: telegram

15 September 1938

FOR DISTRIBUTION TO THE EUROPEAN PAPERS

The personal intervention of Mr. Chamberlain and his flight to see Herr Hitler, does not at all alter the gravity of the issues at stake. We must hope that it does not foreshadow another complete failure of the Western Democracies to withstand the threats and violence of Nazi Germany.

Emery Reves to Winston S. Churchill

16 September 1938   Paris

Dear Mr. Churchill,

Thank you very much for your letter concerning America.

I am sorry for the misunderstanding as to the release of your last article. When I saw Mr. Watson Monday last, I told him that you have not yet written your article. I said that I hope to receive the MS by Tuesday, but should we be able to despatch it only Wednesday so I might be obliged to ask him to release it on Friday only. I said that in this case I shall telephone from Paris.

I am glad to say that I was able to make today two further contracts in the Empire. The one is with the STRAITS TIMES in Singapore, paying £1.1.0. (One Guinea) per article and the other is with the TRINIDAD GUARDIAN in Port of Spain, paying 14/- (Fourteen Shillings) per article. Both contracts are running for 6 months. Please add these two newspapers to the list I have submitted to you in London.

The situation in the Empire is now the following:

We have now 16 contracts compared with none when I have taken over the handling of the Dominions rights. The income per article is now about £39.- compared with the average of £6.- prior to our arrangement.

I hope that after this result you will agree with me that the income from the Dominion publications should be divided between us on the same basis as the proceeds from the other countries. Sixty per cent from the new income is about four times as much as what you have received in the last months before our arrangement.

But I would not ask you for this change if the handling of the Dominions rights would not be much more expensive than the handling of the Continental rights. The fees each paper is paying are relatively small and we have a great number of papers to deal with. This means a rather large volume of work. Besides, the air-mail postage to over-seas countries is rather high from France and the dispatching of some thirty air-mail letters costs about £3.- (Three Pounds) per article.

I should also like to mention that to come to the present result I have spent for cables over £40.-.

I should be grateful if you would kindly let me know your opinion on that suggestion.

The atmosphere in Paris is rather bad though the morale of the population is excellent. I think Flandin is wrong and should there be a mobilization he will probably hardly dare to speak in the Chamber. The act of Mr. Chamberlain was of course a great surprise but opinions are rather divided as to the practical results. One Cabinet Minister whom I saw this morning said to me: "England must feel very strong that she can allow such a step." Most people

believe that the psychological moment to stand firm has come and that a
capitulation before Hitler would mean the definite loss of all the Central and
Eastern European countries today prepared to fight on our side.

Yours very sincerely,
I. Révész

Emery Reves to Winston S. Churchill

17 September 1938   Paris

Dear Mr. Churchill,

It would be excellent if the negotiations with the Sudeten German Party
would go on as well as our negotiations with the Dominion Press.

To-day, I have to report another contract, in Hong Kong. It is with The
Newspaper Enterprise Ltd. (I do not know exactly the name of the newspaper) paying £1.10.0 per article, and running for 6 months. This is the seven-
teenth contract in the Empire, bringing the income for the Dominion rights
to £40.0.0. per article.

Yours very sincerely
I. Révész

Violet Pearman: Churchill diary note

22 September 1938   Paris

Saw Dr. Revesz personally.

Emery Reves: recollection [1]

[22 September 1938]

Churchill came to Paris during the Munich crisis to try to get a few sup-
porters in Paris. Everybody was against him. At the Ritz, in front of a dozen
people, the Minister of Marine[2] said, "He is a war monger. He wants to go
to war." I accompanied him by taxi to Le Bourget. During the journey he
said to me, "The articles I write are much more important than my speeches
in Parliament. The press print one or two short paragraphs from the
speeches, and that is all."

1. In a telephone conversation with Martin Gilbert on 11 November 1975.
2. César Campinchi, French Minister of Marine from March 1938 to June 1940
and, from September 1939 to May 1940, Churchill's ministerial opposite number at the
Admiralty.

Emery Reves to Winston S. Churchill

22 September 1938   Paris

Dear Mr. Churchill,

I hardly came back from Le Bourget when I have received a cable from the
DAILY TELEGRAPH of Brisbane accepting a 6 months contract for £2.2.0
per article. This is another new contract, which I beg to add to the list of the
existing arrangements.

With this arrangement we have now 5 contracts in Australia, in Sydney,
Melbourne, Adelaide, Perth and Brisbane. This is a 100% success, as there
are no more centers in Australia where newspapers are published.

Your declaration[1] has made a deep impression here. All the newspapers
have published it.

Yours very sincerely
I. Révész

1.   Churchill's press statement of the previous day, in which he declared, "The
partition of Czechoslovakia under Anglo-French pressure amounts to a complete surrender by the Western democracies to the Nazi threat of force."

Emery Reves to Winston S. Churchill

25 September 1938   Paris

Dear Mr. Churchill,

The news coming to Paris from Germany through private channels, of
which I have communicated to you some this evening on the telephone,
prove that the Russian note to Poland has made the greatest impression in
Berlin, and that the German General Staff is very much troubled about the
possibility of any move of the Russian army.

In view of this fact I think there is something which might stop Hitler and
change the situation at once. And this is an immediate meeting between
Daladier, Hore-Belisha and Marshal Vorochiloff, the three war Ministers.[1]
Vorochiloff has never left Russia, and if he would be invited to fly to Paris
or to London, this would be an even greater sensation than the flight of Mr.
Chamberlain to Hitler. It is quite the same what would be the result of such
a meeting, it would make a tremendous impression in Germany, and frighten
them more than any Anglo-French declaration. It is obvious that the usual
diplomatic methods have no effect in Germany, and I believe that such a
demonstration would be "a lightning in the night", to use Hitler's own
words.

I wonder whether you believe that such a step could be suggested to the
English and French Governments.

I very much hope that you will be able to despatch your article to-morrow

Monday night. In any case, I beg to kindly let me know by a telegram early in the afternoon of Monday whether we can expect your article Tuesday morning or not.[2]

Yours very sincerely,
I. Révész

1.   Edouard Daladier was the French War Minister, Leslie Hore-Belisha was the British Secretary of State for War, and Marshal Kliment Vorochiloff (normally written Voroshilov) was the Soviet Union's Commissar for Defense.
2.   The article was "France, Britain, and the Future Fate of Europe," published in the *Daily Telegraph* on 4 October 1938.

Winston S. Churchill to Emery Reves: telegram

27 September 1938

Article will be despatched Friday or Saturday. Will telegraph later.

Winston Churchill

Winston S. Churchill to Emery Reves: telegram

2 October 1938

Reference article France & Crisis please delete word "ride" and substitute "rise like Antaeus".

Winston Churchill

Ditto till 'delete word "point" in last sentence and substitute "spirit".'

Cooperation to Winston S. Churchill

[4 October 1938]   Paris

FRANCE AND THE CRISIS

Published by	Gross proceeds
Le Soir, Bruxelles	£10. 0. 0.
Berlingske Tidende, Copenhagen	5. 0. 0.
Paevaleht, Tallinn	1. 0. 0.
Helsingin Sanomat, Helsinki	3. 0. 0.
Paris-Soir, Paris	15. 0. 0.
Utrechtsch Nieuwsblad (and 10 Dutch provincial papers)	7. 0. 0.
Zydu Balsas, Kaunas	0. 8. 0.
Luxemburger Zeitung, Luxemburg	1. 0. 0.
Tidens Tegn, Oslo	5. 0. 0.

Bergens Tidende, Bergen	2. 0. 0.
Stavanger Aftenblad, Stavanger	1.10. 0.
Kurjer Warszawski, Warsaw	5. 0. 0.
Le Moment, Bucharest	1. 0. 0.
Dagens Nyheter, Stockholm	7.10. 0.
St. Galler Tagblatt, St. Gall	1.10. 0.
La Esfera, Caracas	1.10. 0.
La Nacion, Buenos Aires	8. 0. 0.
O Estado de Sao Paulo, Sao Paulo	7. 0. 0.
Diarios Asociados, Rio de Janeiro	3. 0. 0.
Total	£85. 8. 0.

BRITISH EMPIRE PUBLICATIONS

South African Morning Newspapers	7. 7. 0.
Advertiser, Adelaide	2. 2. 0.
Telegraph, Brisbane	2. 2. 0.
West Australian, Perth	2. 2. 0.
Ceylon Daily News, Colombo	1. 1. 0.
Straits Times, Singapore	1. 1. 0.
The Hindu, Madras	1.10. 0.
Hong Kong Herald, Hong Kong	1. 1. 0.
East African Standard, Nairobi	1. 1. 0.
The Press, Christchurch	2. 2. 0.
Total	£21. 9. 0.

Emery Reves to Winston S. Churchill

6 October 1938   Paris

Dear Mr. Churchill,

Your speech in the House was grand.[1] It made a very big impression over here on all those who still can be impressed. The debate in the Chamber was rather dull. Everybody voted for the Government to avoid to be called a "bellicist", but this vote does not show at all the real sentiment of the Deputies. There will come a great reaction one day in France, but, of course, too late.

I am writing to you to-day to ask you two questions:

1) When are you writing your next article? Sunday next or only the following Sunday?

2) I should be grateful if you would let me have your reply to my suggestions regarding the Dominion rights, as I should like to prepare now the statements for your last articles.

Yours very sincerely,
I. Révész

1.   Churchill's speech on 5 October 1938, during the third day of the Munich debate, in the course of which he said, "Silent, mournful, abandoned, broken, Czechoslovakia recedes into the darkness. She has suffered in every respect by her association with the Western democracies and with the League of Nations, of which she has always been an obedient servant."

Winston S. Churchill to Emery Reves

7 October 1938

Dear Dr. Revesz,
    The next article will be written on Sunday and published on Thursday.[1]
    With regard to the Dominion rights, I agree to the 60-40 basis, in view of all the new business you have brought, but I think it should begin only from this date.

1.   Churchill's next published article was "Palestine at the Crossroads," which appeared in the *Daily Telegraph* on 20 October 1938.

Winston S. Churchill: engagement cards

13 October 1938

    Dr. Revesz to lunch.

Cooperation to Winston S. Churchill

20 October 1938   Paris

PALESTINE AT THE CROSSROADS

Published by	Gross proceeds
Le Soir, Bruxelles	£10. 0. 0.
Berlingske Tidende, Copenhagen	5. 0. 0.
Paevaleht, Tallinn	1. 0. 0.
Paris-Soir, Paris	15. 0. 0.
Utrechtsch Nieuwsblad (and 10 Dutch provincial papers)	7. 0. 0.
Lietuvos Aidas, Kaunas	1. 0. 0.
Zydu Balsas, Kaunas	0. 8. 0.
Luxemburger Zeitung, Luxemburg	1. 0. 0.
Tidens Tegn, Oslo	5. 0. 0.
Bergens Tidende, Bergen	2. 0. 0.
Kurjer Warszawski, Warsaw	5. 0. 0.
Le Moment, Bucharest	1. 0. 0.
Dagens Nyheter, Stockholm	7.10. 0.
Tages Anzeiger, Zurich	3. 0. 0.

Politika, Belgrade	3. 0. 0.
La Nacion, Buenos Aires	8. 0. 0.
Diarios Asociados, Rio de Janeiro	3. 0. 0.
Bourse Egyptienne, Cairo	2. 0. 0.
Total	£79.18. 0.

BRITISH EMPIRE PUBLICATIONS

South African Morning Newspapers	7. 7. 0.
Advertiser, Adelaide	2. 2. 0.
Telegraph, Brisbane	2. 2. 0.
Toronto Star, Toronto	8. 0. 0.
Ceylon Daily News, Colombo	1. 1. 0.
Times of Malta, Malta	0.10. 6.
Daily Gleaner, Kingston	0.14. 0.
East African Standard, Nairobi	1. 1. 0.
The Press, Christchurch	2. 2. 0.
Total	£24.19. 6.

Cooperation to Winston S. Churchill

20 October 1938   Paris

THE EFFECT OF AERIAL TRANSPORT ON CIVILIZATION [1]

Published by	Gross proceeds
Svenska Dagbladet, Stockholm	£25. 0. 0.
Berlingske Tidende, Copenhagen	15. 0. 0.
Total	£40. 0. 0.

1.   Churchill had written this article in 1937; see his secretary's letter to Reves of 14 April 1938.

Kathleen Hill[1] to Emery Reves

20 October 1938

Dear Doctor Revesz,

   Mr. Churchill notices that the last cheque he received from you was on August 20, two months ago, and he hopes you will be good enough to send him the accounts very shortly.

Yours truly,
[Kathleen Hill]
Private Secretary

1.   Kathleen Hill, Churchill's Resident Secretary at Chartwell from 1936, was his Principal Personal Secretary throughout the Second World War.

Emery Reves to Winston S. Churchill

23 October 1938   Paris

Dear Mr. Churchill,
    Kindly find enclosed a cheque of £241.10.0 (Two hundred forty one pounds and ten shillings) in respect of your articles published in August and September. I also enclose statements regarding these publications.
    I would be grateful if you would agree that I shall send you statements always in the second month after the publication of the articles. Now that we are working in more and more overseas countries, it is almost impossible for me to have a complete picture of the publication of an article in the following month. Regarding the publications in South America, in Australia and in New Zealand, I only get replies or copies of the newspapers 6–8 weeks after having mailed the article. Even if I have contracts, I cannot be quite sure of the result before, as it will sometimes happen that an article will become out of date when it reaches some newspapers and will not be published. In such a case I cannot ask for payments, even if we have a contract. I hope you will understand this situation and agree with my suggestion.
                                                            Yours very faithfully,
                                                                    I. Révész

Winston S. Churchill to Emery Reves

29 October 1938

    Many thanks for your letter of the 23rd instant and cheque.
    I think it would be a better arrangement if you send me the statement about the Continental publications you have always handled, as you have hitherto done—viz. every month. The overseas countries could come in a month later, as you suggest.

Emery Reves to Winston S. Churchill

1 November 1938   Paris

Dear Mr. Churchill,
    Your article has been safely received here and despatched to all countries during the night. We naturally gained time in transmitting the article on the telephone, but I would very much prefer if during my absence in America we could come back to the old method and if you could mail the articles always on Sunday night. Though I am sure that during my absence my office will work exactly as well as if I would be here, it would be more sure if we could receive the articles in typescript.

I would be most grateful if you could give me a letter of introduction to Mr. Baruch,[1] as you have kindly promised me, asking him to put me in touch with some people in America and to help me in my task.

I have an idea regarding America and should be very much interested to learn your opinion about it. I think that one of the most dangerous consequences of the Munich agreement is the renewed campaign for isolation in the United States. Some great and impressive manifestations are to be organized in America to support the cause of Democracy and Freedom. I am thinking on the following:

During the coming New York World Fair a "Week of Liberty" ought to be organized in New York. During 6 or 7 evenings huge mass meetings ought to take place in which the most outstanding representatives of the free nations should deliver speeches on the problems of Liberty. Two sections could be made: those who still have their liberty to defend, England, United States and France; and those who have lost already their liberties, Germany, Italy, China, Spain, Austria, etc . . . Great Britain ought to be represented by you, France by Herriot or Blum,[2] U.S.A. by one or two political leaders to be decided upon, Italian democracy by Count Sforza,[3] German democracy by Thomas Mann,[4] Spanish democracy by Madariaga[5] (or someone else), and so on.

I should like to proceed in the following way: To form a Committee of 5–6 outstanding American public men who would have the charge to raise the funds of organization. This committee shall have to ask the patronage of President Roosevelt, who probably will accept to deliver the inaugural speech. Naturally all the speeches shall be broadcasted in several languages all over the world.

I firmly believe that such a scheme would very much interest the Americans, as this might be one of the greatest attractions of the World Fair. On the other hand, for the Statesmen of the various countries this might be a unique occasion to address to millions on a spot where world interest will be focused next year. It would be something positive, to show the whole world the strength and the solidarity of the great democratic nations. Since years we have been passive and it seems really that the time has come to start an offensive. And I have the feeling that in view of the unfortunate situation in England and France such a renaissance could only be initiated in America.

Please, let me know what do you think of this idea.

Yours very sincerely,
I. Révész

1.   Bernard Baruch, an American financier and public servant (head of the United States Raw Materials Board in the First World War). When Churchill was Minister of Munitions, the two men worked closely without ever meeting, and Churchill subsequently befriended him.

2.   Léon Blum, leader of the French Popular Front left-wing coalition and Prime Minister from June 1936 to June 1937 and March to April 1938. He was interned by

the Germans from 1941 to 1945. He became Prime Minister for a third time, for two months, at the end of 1946.

3.   Count Sforza, an Italian diplomat who had resigned as Ambassador to France in 1922 in protest against Mussolini's Fascist regime. The Count lived in exile in Belgium until 1939, then in the United States, returning to Italy in 1943, after the fall of Mussolini. Minister of Foreign Affairs, 1947–1951. His influence was a determining factor in Italy's participation in the Organization for European Economic Cooperation and the North Atlantic Treaty Organization (NATO).

4.   Thomas Mann, German novelist and essayist. In 1929 he was awarded the Nobel Prize for Literature. He lived in exile in the United States from 1933, was deprived of his German citizenship in 1936, and became a United States citizen in 1944.

5.   Don Salvador de Madariaga, former Spanish Ambassador in Paris and Permanent Spanish Representative at the League of Nations (1931–1936). An exile from Franco's Spain, he lived in Oxford from 1939 to 1976, when he returned to Spain. He died in 1978.

Cooperation to Winston S. Churchill

3 November 1938   Paris

ALL IS NOT LOST IN CHINA [1]

Published by	Gross proceeds
Le Soir, Bruxelles	£10. 0. 0.
Berlingske Tidende, Copenhagen	5. 0. 0.
Paevaleht, Tallinn	1. 0. 0.
Helsingin Sanomat, Helsinki	3. 0. 0.
Paris-Soir, Paris	15. 0. 0.
Zydu Balsas, Kaunas	0. 8. 0.
Luxemburger Zeitung, Luxemburg	1. 0. 0.
Bergens Tidende, Bergen	2. 0. 0.
Tidens Tegn, Oslo	5. 0. 0.
Kurjer Warszawski, Warsaw	5. 0. 0.
Le Moment, Bucharest	1. 0. 0.
Dagens Nyheter, Stockholm	7.10. 0.
Gazette de Lausanne, Lausanne	1.10. 0.
Der Bund, Bern	2. 0. 0.
Eleftheron Vima, Athens	1. 1. 0.
Bourse Egyptienne, Cairo	2. 0. 0.
Palestine Post, Jerusalem	1. 0. 0.
La Nacion, Buenos Aires	8. 0. 0.
O Estado de Sao Paulo, Sao Paulo	7. 0. 0.
Diarios Asociados, Rio de Janeiro	3. 0. 0.
Total	£81. 9. 0.

BRITISH EMPIRE PUBLICATIONS

South African Morning Newspapers, Johannesburg	7. 7. 0.
Advertiser, Adelaide	2. 2. 0.
Telegraph, Brisbane	2. 2. 0.
Toronto Star, Toronto	8. 0. 0.
Times of Ceylon, Ceylon	2. 2. 0.
Times of Malta, Malta	0.10. 6.
Straits Times, Singapore	1. 1. 0.
Newspaper Enterprise, Hong Kong	1. 1. 0.
East African Standard, Nairobi	1. 1. 0.
The Press, Christchurch	2. 2. 0.
Total	£27. 8. 6.

1. Published in the *Daily Telegraph* on 3 November 1938 as "Japan's Precarious Gains from Recent Successes."

Emery Reves to Winston S. Churchill

4 November 1938   Paris

Dear Mr. Churchill,
    The Editor of BERLINGSKE TIDENDE in Copenhagen, Mr. Nic. Blaedel, is in Paris at the moment. As you know, he is publishing since many years all your articles, his newspaper is the most important conservative paper in Denmark and he is regarded as the greatest political journalist of his country.
    Mr. Blaedel is a great champion of democracy and is fighting for British influence in Scandinavia and against Nazism.
    Quite confidentially I can tell you that he is on a holiday and it is doubtful whether he will return to his newspaper. His case is a great scandal in the Scandinavian countries. A few days after the Munich agreements the German Minister has paid a visit to the Danish Foreign Minister and spoke to him about it in the following terms: As you will understand, the situation is completely changed now. Germany has got Czechoslovakia, her influence in Hungary, Rumania, Yugoslavia is growing every day, so that Germany can get all food and raw materials she wants from those "friendly countries". Germany has no need anymore to buy anything in Denmark and she will probably stop importations from that country. However, should the Danish government wish to continue selling their goods in Germany, and then came the conditions, mostly of political nature, among them that Mr. Blaedel should leave his newspaper.
    In Sweden a few days after the Munich agreement the socialist Prime

Minister has written personal letters to all the newspaper editors asking them to be extremely careful not to criticize Germany and not to publish anything which might hurt the German government.

I have received similar information last week from Norway, from the President of the Storting, Mr. Hambro, who is also leader of the Conservative party.

As you see, the terror is spreading all over Europe. This complete change of the situation in the Scandinavian countries is a direct consequence of the Munich agreements. Until that modern peace treaty the Scandinavian countries were courageous fighting against Nazism, now they are helpless and have to capitulate. Direct German intervention is an accomplished fact.

I think if the majority of the English people does not care a bit what is going on in Central Europe, they ought to be interested of what is happening in Scandinavia as these countries have been since more than a century in the British sphere of influence.

Mr. Blaedel could give you many interesting information and facts regarding the events in the Northern countries which I think might be useful for one of your speeches in Parliament. Could you receive him for a conversation? He will arrive in London Monday next and stay about a fortnight at:

MOUNT ROYAL, MARBLE ARCH.

If you could let him know when you are in London, he would be happy to go and see you whenever you have a moment to spare for him.

Yours very sincerely
I. Révész

Winston S. Churchill to Emery Reves

5 November 1938

Yours of the 1st instant. It will not always be possible to send the articles on Sunday, though I will try to do so.

I am afraid I am too much occupied here to take part in the scheme which you mention in the last paragraph of your letter.

Emery Reves to Winston S. Churchill

16 November 1938   Paris

Dear Mr. Churchill,

I am leaving Saturday morning on the "Normandie". During my absence Mademoiselle R. Gayman will be in charge of our office. You can trust that everything will go on exactly as usual.

I have arranged that while I am away an amount of £100.-.- should be remitted to you at the end of each month, as I should like to see that statements are exact on my return.

My address in New York will be: THE PLAZA (cable: REVESZ PLAZA NEW-YORK). I shall certainly keep you in touch with the developments of my negotiations.

Yours very sincerely,
I. Révész

Cooperation to Winston S. Churchill

[17 November 1938]   Paris

ENGLAND AFTER MUNICH [1]

Published by	Gross proceeds
Le Soir, Bruxelles	£10. 0. 0.
Paevaleht, Tallinn	1. 0. 0.
Paris-Soir, Paris	15. 0. 0.
Pariser Tages Zeitung, Paris	0.14. 0.
Eleftheron Vima, Athens	1. 1. 0.
Zydu Balsas, Kaunas	0. 8. 0.
Luxemburger Zeitung, Luxemburg	1. 0. 0.
Bergens Tidende, Bergen	2. 0. 0.
Kurjer Warszawski, Warsaw	5. 0. 0.
Dagens Nyheter, Stockholm	7.10. 0.
Palestine Post, Jerusalem	1. 0. 0.
La Nacion, Buenos-Aires	8. 0. 0.
O Estado de Sao Paulo, Sao Paulo	7. 0. 0.
Diarios Asociados, Rio de Janeiro	3. 0. 0.
Total	£62.13. 0.

BRITISH EMPIRE PUBLICATIONS

South African Morning Newspapers, Johannesburg	7. 7. 0.
Times of Ceylon, Ceylon	2. 2. 0.
Newspaper Enterprise, Hong Kong	1. 1. 0.
East African Standard, Nairobi	1. 1. 0.
Advertiser, Adelaide	2. 2. 0.
Telegraph, Brisbane	2. 2. 0.
Daily Gleaner, Kingston	0.14. 0.
Straits Times, Singapore	1. 1. 0.
Times of Malta, Malta	0.10. 6.
Total	£18. 0. 6.

1. Published in the *Daily Telegraph* on 17 November 1938 as "Nation's Hopes and Misgivings since Munich."

Emery Reves to Winston S. Churchill

18 November 1938   Paris

Dear Mr. Churchill,

Before leaving I should like to ask a question.

Are your NEWS OF THE WORLD articles free for publication in America? I shall certainly not offer them to Collier's or to any other publication which might compete with that magazine. But I think they might interest many dailies, particularly for their Sunday editions.

Please let me know your opinion about that directly at THE PLAZA in New York.

Yours very sincerely,
I. Révész

Winston S. Churchill to Emery Reves

21 November 1938

The "News of the World" articles are certainly free for publication in the United States once they have been published here. On the other hand, my relations with Collier's, through Mr. Chenery, the Editor, are of the first importance to me, and I am now negotiating with him for the renewal of another contract next year and would do nothing contrary to his wishes.

Generally speaking, it would be a great mistake to sell second serials in the United States. This would only detract from the very high price I obtain for the Collier's articles. Do not, therefore, take any steps in the matter. All I want you to do for me is to sell the fortnightly articles as well as you can, consulting me before making any final contract.

Winston S. Churchill to Violet Pearman

24 November 1938

Mrs. Pearman.

For Dr. Revesz: all except British Penal System and British Social Services.

But he can only publish them in foreign languages, & <u>after</u> they have appeared in N of W.[1]

Please collect them for him & let me see before despatch.

WSC

1. Between April 1938 and the outbreak of war in September 1939, Churchill wrote a total of twenty-one articles for the *News of the World*.

Cooperation to Winston S. Churchill

[25 November 1938]   Paris

EMIGRATION [1]

Published by	Gross proceeds
Berlingske Tidende, Copenhagen	£15. 0. 0.
Eleftheron Vima, Athens	2. 2. 0.
Kurjer Warszawski, Warsaw	10. 0. 0.
Svenska Dagbladet, Stockholm	25. 0. 0.
Total	£52. 2. 0.

1. One of Churchill's *News of the World* articles, published on 22 May 1938 as "Peopling the Wide Spaces of Empire."

Emery Reves to Winston S. Churchill: telegram

25 November 1938   New York

Your letter confirming I have exclusive American rights unfortunately lost. Please send copy quickest. Meanwhile cable confirmation. Thanks.

Revesz

Winston S. Churchill to Emery Reves: telegram

26 November 1938

You have exclusive right to handle fortnightly series articles subject to my confirmation (stop). But see Chenery, nothing must conflict with Collier's interests. (stop). Deprecate second serials of other material as unduly cheapening.

Churchill

Emery Reves to Winston S. Churchill: telegram

26 November 1938   New York

Your cable understood but please send cable containing only confirmation American exclusivity like original letter which might show editors

Revesz

Winston S. Churchill to Emery Reves: telegram

27 November 1938

I confirm our arrangement whereby Cooperation has exclusive right to handle my articles in America. (stop) This is in addition to other contracts made with you.

Winston Churchill

Cooperation to Winston S. Churchill

[1 December 1938]   Paris

FRANCE AND ENGLAND [1]

Published by	Gross proceeds
Le Soir, Bruxelles	£10. 0. 0.
Berlingske Tidende, Copenhagen	5. 0. 0.
Paevaleht, Tallinn	1. 0. 0.
Helsingin Sanomat, Helsinki	3. 0. 0.
Paris-Soir, Paris	15. 0. 0.
Eleftheron Vima, Athens	1. 1. 0.
Zydu Balsas, Kaunas	0. 8. 0.
Luxemburger Zeitung, Luxemburg	1. 0. 0.
Tidens Tegn, Oslo	5. 0. 0.
Bergens Tidende, Bergen	2. 0. 0.
Le Moment, Bucharest	1. 0. 0.
Dagens Nyheter, Stockholm	7.10. 0.
Palestine Post, Jerusalem	1. 0. 0.
La Nacion, Buenos Aires	8. 0. 0.
O Estado de Sao Paulo, Sao Paulo	7. 0. 0.
Diarios Asociados, Rio de Janeiro	3. 0. 0.
Total	£70.19. 0.

BRITISH EMPIRE PUBLICATIONS

Advertiser, Adelaide	2. 2. 0.
Times of Ceylon, Ceylon	2. 2. 0.
Newspaper Enterprise, Hong Kong	1. 1. 0.
Daily Gleaner, Kingston	0.14. 0.
East African Standard, Nairobi	1. 1. 0.
Times of Malta, Malta	0.10. 6.
The Press, Christchurch	2. 2. 0.
Straits Times, Singapore	1. 1. 0.
Total	£10.13. 6.

1. Published in the *Daily Telegraph* on 1 December 1938 as "How Stand Britain and France since Munich?"

Emery Reves to Winston S. Churchill

2 December 1938   The Plaza
                                            Fifth Avenue at 59th Street
                                                        New York

Dear Mr. Churchill,

Many thanks for your letter of November 21st and for the two cables.

I have had a talk with Mr. Chenery, and explained him the situation. I told him that I am trying to get published your fortnightly articles in the American press, but that this work does not interfere at all with his direct relations with you. He said that he would not like to see his direct competitors (Saturday Evening Post, Liberty, American, Time) publishing articles from you, but he has no objection at all that other type of periodicals or newspapers should publish your articles. Publications in the daily press, or in the Sunday sections of the daily newspapers, do not interfere at all with his interests. The conversation was very cordial and he was thankful for my visit.

I shall certainly not offer your "News of the World" articles so that they might deprecate the fortnightly articles. I am interested to make a market for these features. I only think that should I be able to come to an arrangement with one or several papers, they might be interested to have some articles from you for their Sunday sections too. And for that purpose we could use some of your "News of the World" articles. But this is a minor question.

The problem of getting published our articles over here, is a problem of transmission. Topical political articles arriving here 10–12 days after their publication in London, have absolutely no interest for the American press. I think that the wireless service I have in mind might help.

I am going now for a few days to Washington, as I should like to gather as much information as possible regarding the complicated press conditions here, before I enter negotiations with some Editors.

Wherever I am in America, the best way to reach me is The Plaza, as long as I am over here.

                                            Yours very sincerely,
                                                   I. Révész

Cooperation to *Winston S. Churchill*

[15 December 1938]   Paris

DANGERS IN THE EAST OF EUROPE [1]

Published by	Gross proceeds
Le Soir, Bruxelles	£10. 0. 0.
Berlingske Tidende, Copenhagen	5. 0. 0.
Paevaleht, Tallinn	1. 0. 0.
Paris-Soir, Paris	15. 0. 0.
Oran Republicain, Oran	1. 0. 0.
Zydu Balsas, Kaunas	0. 8. 0.
Luxemburger Zeitung, Luxemburg	1. 0. 0.
Tidens Tegn, Oslo	5. 0. 0.
Bergens Tidende, Bergen	2. 0. 0.
Le Moment, Bucharest	1. 0. 0.
Dagens Nyheter, Stockholm	7.10. 0.
Gazette de Lausanne, Lausanne	1.10. 0.
National Zeitung, Basle	2. 0. 0.
Palestine Post, Jerusalem	1. 0. 0.
La Nacion, Buenos Aires	8. 0. 0.
O Estado de Sao Paulo, Sao Paulo	7. 0. 0.
Diarios Asociados, Rio de Janeiro	3. 0. 0.
Total	£71. 8. 0.

BRITISH EMPIRE PUBLICATIONS

Telegraph, Brisbane	2. 2. 0.
Advertiser, Adelaide	2. 2. 0.
Times of Ceylon, Ceylon	2. 2. 0.
Newspaper Enterprise, Hong Kong	1. 1. 0.
East African Standard, Nairobi	1. 1. 0.
Times of Malta, Malta	0.10. 6.
Straits Times, Singapore	1. 1. 0.
Total	£9.19. 6.

1. Published in the *Daily Telegraph* as "Eastern Europe on the Morrow of Munich."

Rachel Gayman to Winston S. Churchill

21 December 1938   Paris

Dear Mr. Churchill,

As you are surely well aware, the day following Xmas day is always consid-ered as a holyday in France, and it is the case for next Monday when we expect your next article.

Of course, our staff, at least in part, is disposed to come and work in order to despatch your article without delay; so are our translators. But, our English stenograph is just going over to London in her family for a couple of weeks. We are afraid to not be able to find a good substitute to her, able to take your article without mistake on the telephone. So we beg to kindly come back to the old method, and to send us your article by regular mail, so that we get it on Monday morning and arrange its despatch during the day.

We should be most grateful to kindly wire on Saturday whether we can expect your article on Monday, and which subject you intend to deal.

With our most grateful thanks in advance, and with our most sincere compliments for Xmas and the New Year,

we beg to remain,
Yours most sincerely,
R. Gayman

Cooperation to Winston S. Churchill

[30 December 1938]   Paris

THE SPANISH ULCER [1]

Published by	Gross proceeds
Le Soir, Bruxelles	£10. 0. 0.
Berlingske Tidende, Copenhagen	5. 0. 0.
Paevaleht, Tallinn	1. 0. 0.
Paris-Soir, Paris	15. 0. 0.
Pariser Tages Zeitung, Paris	0.14. 0.
Zydu Balsas, Kaunas	0. 8. 0.
Luxemburger Zeitung, Luxemburg	1. 0. 0.
Tidens Tegn, Oslo	5. 0. 0.
Bergens Tidende, Bergen	2. 0. 0.
Dagens Nyheter, Stockholm	7.10. 0.
Tages Anzeiger, Zurich	3. 0. 0.
St. Galler Tagblatt, St. Gall	1.10. 0.
Palestine Post, Jerusalem	1. 0. 0.
La Nacion, Buenos Aires	8. 0. 0.
Diarios Asociados, Rio de Janeiro	3. 0. 0.
Total	£64. 2. 0.

BRITISH EMPIRE PUBLICATIONS

Telegraph, Brisbane	2. 2. 0.
Advertiser, Adelaide	2. 2. 0.
Times of Ceylon, Ceylon	2. 2. 0.
Newspaper Enterprise, Hong Kong	1. 1. 0.
East African Standard, Nairobi	1. 1. 0.
Times of Malta, Malta	0.10. 6.
Total	£8.18. 6.

1.   Published in the *Daily Telegraph* on 30 December 1938 as "Let the Spaniards Make Peace Lest Spain Loses All."

MOVING TOWARDS WAR

1939

Emery Reves to Winston S. Churchill: telegram

21 January 1939   New York

Sarnoff chairman Radio Corporation accepted principle my suggestion organising daily short broadcast through all national broadcasting stations by leading European democratic statesmen on international affairs Stop Scheme great political importance please cable whether principle accepting deliver fortnightly American broadcast on contract basis naturally remunerated and ask Eden Duff Cooper whether willing undertake same task should scheme realise thanks.

Revesz Plaza

Emery Reves to Winston S. Churchill: telegram

24 January 1939   New York

Please cable whether broad-casting suggestion interesting. Thanks.

Revesz

Winston S. Churchill to Emery Reves: telegram

26 January 1939

Impossible form opinion broadcast plan without details how often each speaker how long each speech duration of contract. How much paid for each delivery.

Churchill

Emery Reves to Winston S. Churchill: telegram

28 January 1939   New York

Planning you, Eden, Duff Cooper and three Frenchmen fortnightly, others monthly, and occasionally each speech 5 to 10 minutes. Unable fix payment this stage negotiation. Asking only approval in principle. Forward acceptance depending on final offer later.

Would help if you cable scheme interesting, but acceptance depends on payment and duration of contract.

Revesz

Winston S. Churchill to Emery Reves: telegram

28 January 1939

Scheme interesting but acceptance depends on payment and duration contract.

Churchill

Winston S. Churchill to Emery Reves: telegram

29 January 1939

Had hoped you would make arrangements for sale of fortnightly articles. Cannot help you in framing this new plan.

Churchill

Emery Reves to Winston S. Churchill: telegram

29 January 1939   New York

Thanks for cable. Would be grateful if you could consult by occasion Eden, Duff Cooper, and cable whether feel same.

Revesz

Cooperation to Winston S. Churchill

[30 January 1939]   Paris

WHAT DOES MUSSOLINI MEAN? [1]

Published by	Gross proceeds
Le Soir, Brussels	£10. 0. 0.
Berlingske Tidende, Copenhagen	5. 0. 0.
Paevaleht, Tallinn	1. 0. 0.
Helsingin Sanomat, Helsinki	3. 0. 0.

Paris-Soir, Paris	15. 0. 0.
Luxemburger Zeitung, Luxemburg	1. 0. 0.
Bergens Tidende, Bergen	2. 0. 0.
Le Moment, Bucharest	1. 0. 0.
Dagens Nyheter, Stockholm	7.10. 0.
Gazette de Lausanne, Lausanne	1.10. 0.
La Nacion, Buenos Aires	8. 0. 0.
O Estado de Sao Paulo, Sao Paulo	7. 0. 0.
Diarios Asociados, Rio de Janeiro	3. 0. 0.
Total	£65. 0. 0.

BRITISH EMPIRE PUBLICATIONS

South African Morning Newspapers	7. 7. 0.
Sydney Morning Herald	3. 3. 0.
Melbourne Argus	2. 2. 0.
Advertiser	2. 2. 0.
Times of Ceylon	2. 2. 0.
Hong Kong Herald	1. 1. 0.
East African Standard	1. 1. 0.
Times of Malta	0.10. 6.
Evening Post, Wellington	2. 2. 0.
The Press, Christchurch	2. 2. 0.
Total	£23.12. 6.

1. Published in the *Daily Telegraph* on 30 January 1939 as "Counting the Cost of Italy's Policies Abroad."

Emery Reves to Winston S. Churchill: telegram

8 February 1939 New York

Contract Herald Tribune signed today they will also syndicate whole country publications start March owing great promotion campaign regard arrangement big success writing

Revesz

Cooperation to Winston S. Churchill

[9 February 1939] Paris

THE LULL IN EUROPE [1]

Published by	Gross proceeds
Le Soir, Bruxelles	£10. 0. 0.
Berlingske Tidende, Copenhagen	5. 0. 0.

Paevaleht, Tallinn	1. 0. 0.
Paris-Soir, Paris	15. 0. 0.
Eleftheron Vima, Athens	1. 1. 0.
Lietuvos Aidas, Kaunas	1. 0. 0.
Zydu Balsas, Kaunas	0. 8. 0.
Luxemburger Zeitung, Luxembourg	1. 0. 0.
Bergens Tidende, Bergen	2. 0. 0.
Stavanger Aftenblad, Stavanger	1.10. 0.
Hajnt, Varsovie	No payment
Le Moment, Bucharest	No payment
La Bourse Egyptienne, Le Caire	2. 0. 0.
Dagens Nyheter, Stockholm	7.10. 0.
Gazette de Lausanne, Lausanne	1.10. 0.
La Nacion, Buenos Aires	8. 0. 0.
O Jornal, Rio de Janeiro	3. 0. 0.
Palestine Post, Jerusalem	1. 0. 0.
Argus, Melbourne	2. 2. 0.
Advertiser, Adelaide	2. 2. 0.
Telegraph, Brisbane	2. 2. 0.
South African Morning Newspapers	7. 7. 0.
Times of Ceylon, Ceylon	2. 2. 0.
Hong Kong Herald, Hong Kong	1. 1. 0.
Daily Gleaner, Kingston	0.10. 6.
East African Standard, Nairobi	1. 1. 0.
Times of Malta, Malta	0.10. 6.
Total	£79.17. 0.

1.   Published in the *Daily Telegraph* on 9 February 1939 as "Light and Shade in Europe since Herr Hitler Spoke."

Winston S. Churchill to Emery Reves: telegram

9 February 1939

Let me know terms

Emery Reves to Winston S. Churchill: telegram

9 February 1939   New York

Contract very complicated but excellent exactly what wanted guarantee local New York rights only twenty pounds each article whole country considerably more please have confidence my judgment believe my greatest success detailed letter coming Queen Mary

Revesz

Emery Reves to Winston S. Churchill

10 February 1939   The Plaza
                                                                   New York

Dear Mr. Churchill,

It was a very hard battle. Three months continuous fighting, but the result is a hundred per cent success. I know that it was a long time, but with less patience and tenacity I could only return, like everybody returned before, saying that there is "nothing to do" in the United States. The contract I have signed is the exact realisation of the scheme I have worked out during the past year and I think that within a year it might double our publications and our proceeds.

The situation in this country is briefly the following:

1) The daily papers are written by staff writers and foreign correspondents. Signed articles by important public men have not yet been published in the American press with regularity. Such articles are reserved for the Sunday supplements and for magazines.

2) The magazine field was closed to me on account of your contract with Collier's and on account of the fact that magazines need the manuscript of the articles 5–6 weeks before their publication abroad. Your fortnightly articles are too topical and can therefore never be regularly placed in American magazines. They are newspaper-articles.

3) All the American syndicates are declining, they have no authority before publishers, and none of these organizations is able and prepared to contract any such series. On the other hand, you can only get high fees in this country through syndication, as all the daily papers are local and pay only very low fees for local rights. No daily paper is prepared to pay anything like the magazines as they are not interested in exclusive American rights.

These were the main reasons why nobody whom you gave options during the past years was able to make an arrangement for the regular publication of your fortnightly articles.

I knew this particular situation and believed that the only chance of success lies in an entirely new wireless service of international opinions to supplement the American newsgathering system. I have told you about this plan before I left Europe, and enclose a short exposé about my proposition to the American press.

I had to proceed very carefully and have had first informal conversations with a very great number of officials, statesmen, businessmen, newspapermen, etc. to have an exact impression of the situation. Everybody said that the scheme is very interesting, but that it will be hard to start with, as it really means a kind of a revolution in the American press. I want them to do something which they did not do until now and this will be very difficult.

There were two important points: a) A new idea must be presented in this country by new people, an arrangement with Hearst or any similar organization would have killed the whole scheme. b) It was essential to make a contract with one of the big New York papers, as nothing can be a success in the country regarding foreign services which is not accepted first by a New York paper. And the difficulty is that there are only two such papers, the Times and the Herald.

For many weeks I was negotiating with a group of influential and wealthy people who wanted to create a new Company for the handling of our articles, and there were already $120,000 at our disposal to start with work, when my negotiations with the Herald Tribune took a concrete form and led finally to a success.

From the two New York papers, the Herald Tribune is for us far better than the Times. The Times is owned by Jews, and today this would have meant that many Americans would have become suspicious that we are making "European propaganda". The Herald Tribune has the same position here as the Daily Telegraph in London. It is the most important conservative paper, very influential, and nobody can suspect them that they are undertaking something which is "un-American". It is THE best newspaper for us to reach the influential public, and to get many other American papers to take the series and to subscribe to our service.

Besides, the Herald Tribune Syndicate has made the two greatest successes in this country: Walter Lippmann and Dorothy Thompson.[1] Dorothy Thompson told me that when they have started, the Herald Tribune has only offered her $10,000 a year for three articles per week and 50% of the syndication revenue. After the first year her income was over $70,000.

That was the reason that I have accepted from the New York Herald Tribune a relatively small amount, under the condition that they will make a promotion campaign worthy to the value of these articles. We have had many long conferences with the whole General Staff of the Herald Tribune, Ogden Reid, Mrs. Reid and their son Whitelaw Reid (the proprietors), their Editors, the Business Manager, their Syndicate Manager, etc. They are very keen on the scheme and will start immediately a promotion campaign which promises a great success. They will spend considerable capital for this campaign. There will be advertisements in the other newspapers. They are preparing a beautiful album which will be sent to all the Universities, Libraries, Schools, etc. The Manager of their Syndicate is starting in three days for a trip all over the country to negotiate with all the important publishers personally.

One of the main features of the scheme, is the short-wave transmission from Holland. We have made yesterday the first experiments, the reception was perfect. This is the first service in this country of that type. It would mean that all the subscribing newspapers will be able to pick up the articles directly from Europe, and that they will receive everything you and the other European statesmen write within a few hours and directly. I have offered this wireless transmission free of charge. It will cost me about £1,500 a year but I believe it is a good investment.

I am afraid I could not explain to you all details without making out of this letter a volume. I shall give you all further information personally in the beginning of March. As to the financial possibilities, we have a guarantee of £20 per article from the Herald Tribune for the local New York rights.[2] But I would be surprised if we would not have within 3–4 months £40–50 and in about a year considerably more. In any way the articles will be regularly published in the New York Herald Tribune, and this in itself is a great success.

I think you were rather satisfied with the results of the last two years. I have the feeling that what I have achieved in the U.S.A. is more than all the other arrangements together. Of course, I may have a wrong impression, but I must take this risk. My belief is that within a few months we shall not only have a considerable income from this country, but also a unique and nationwide tribune which you will find useful in reaching the American public.

The regular transmissions will start on March 10th. I would be grateful if you would take into consideration the American public when writing your articles in March and April. Much will depend upon the interest of these articles. My contract is for a year, but the Herald Tribune has the right to stop it after 90 days, should the service not be satisfactory. This is natural. But I am confident this is merely a precaution, as they are spending in advance much money for the promotion, and are also buying special machines for recording the short-wave transmissions.

I shall be back in Paris either on March 1st (Ile de France) or latest March 8th (Normandie). Within a few days I shall come over to London and shall tell you all my American adventures.

I shall also explain you the broadcasting scheme which I hope will interest you.

I am going to-morrow to Canada for a few days to make some arrangements.

Yours very sincerely,
I. Révész

1.   Walter Lippman was Special Writer to the *New York Herald Tribune* syndicate from 1931 to 1962. Dorothy Thompson, the former head of the Berlin bureau of the *New York Evening Post*, was, in 1934, the first American correspondent to be expelled from Nazi Germany, on Hitler's personal orders. From 1936 to 1958 she published an "On the Record" column in the *New York Herald Tribune,* which was syndicated to as many as 170 newspapers.
2.   This guarantee of £20 per article was the equivalent of £500 in 1996.

Winston S. Churchill to Emery Reves: telegram

17 February 1939

Your letter February 10 could not sanction publication America any article of mine for less than 125 dollars net to me.

Churchill

Emery Reves to Winston S. Churchill: telegram

18 February 1939 Chicago, Illinois

Accept guarantee minimum 125 dollars net to you[1]

Revesz

1. In 1939 $125 was the equivalent of $780 (£520) in 1996.

Winston S. Churchill to Emery Reves: telegram

20 February 1939

Much obliged.

Churchill

Cooperation to Winston S. Churchill

[23 February 1939] Paris

HOPE IN SPAIN [1]

Published by	Gross proceeds
Le Soir, Bruxelles	£10. 0. 0.
Paevaleht, Tallinn	1. 0. 0.
Paris-Soir, Paris	15. 0. 0.
Eleftheron Vima, Athens	1. 1. 0.
Zydu Balsas, Kaunas	0. 8. 0.
Luxemburger Zeitung, Luxembourg	1. 0. 0.
Bergens Tidende, Bergen	2. 0. 0.
Hajnt, Varsovie	No payment
Le Moment, Bucharest	No payment
Dagens Nyheter, Stockholm	7.10. 0.
Tages Anzeiger, Zurich	3. 0. 0.
La Nacion, Buenos Aires	8. 0. 0.
O Jornal, Rio de Janeiro	3. 0. 0.
La Bourse Egyptienne, Le Caire	2. 0. 0.
Argus, Melbourne	2. 2. 0.
South African Morning Newspapers	7. 7. 0.
Advertiser, Adelaide	2. 2. 0.
Telegraph, Brisbane	2. 2. 0.
Times of Ceylon, Ceylon	2. 2. 0.
Trinidad Guardian, Port of Spain	0. 7. 6.
Hong Kong Herald	1. 1. 0.
Times of Malta, Malta	0.10. 6.
Total	£71.13. 0.

1. Published in the *Daily Telegraph* on 23 February 1939 as "Can Franco Restore Unity and Strength to Spain?"

Emery Reves to Winston S. Churchill: telegram

2 March 1939   New York

Further contracts already signed Washington Philadelphia Boston Buffalo Cleveland SanFrancisco LosAngeles Toronto Much will now depend upon interest first articles please make your next article hot close to news will be first wired here sailing

Revesz

Emery Reves to Winston S. Churchill

8 March 1939   Paris

Dear Mr. Churchill,

I was very sorry that I have disturbed you this evening during dinner time. But I have just arrived in Paris and wanted to know whether I shall wire your last article "Is it peace?" as the first one to America.

I am very glad (even proud) that my American trip was a full success and that I was able to open the American press for the first time for European opinions. I shall come over to London early next week, and shall give you full information about all my negotiations and about the results.

In the meantime, I am sending you enclosed the proof of the first full page advertisement which appeared in New York last Sunday. As you see the NEW YORK HERALD TRIBUNE believes that this scheme means "a new era in American newspaper publishing".[1]

I am also enclosing copies of two letters which I have received on the "Normandie" before leaving New York from Mrs. Ogden Reid, the proprietor of the paper, and from Mr. Wilbur Forrest who is the acting Editor. I am sending these copies as they will show you more clearly than anything I could say what importance they attach to this new venture both from political and publishing point of view, and what type of articles we must try to send them so that this great American tribune should be at our disposal for a long time.[2]

I am also despatching under separate cover a promotion album the NEW YORK HERALD TRIBUNE has issued for the other American newspapers and for many public institutions, schools, universities, libraries, etc . . .

I should be grateful if you would kindly look through these documents until I shall be able to give you more information personally.

I beg to remain,

Yours very sincerely,
I. Révész

1.   The advertisement announced, "Europe's Leading Statesmen, Europe's Leading Writers will wireless their comments on Europe's news to the weekday *New York
Herald Tribune*." Listing the "new *Herald Tribune* writers," it said of Churchill, who
headed the list, "Probably the most powerful commentator in British public life."

2.   In her letter welcoming the new series, Mrs. Ogden Reid told Reves, "I cannot
impress on you too strongly, however, that the publication of the material, either in
this paper or the others throughout the country to whom our syndicate has sold the
series, will continue only if the articles are interesting. For my own part I have high
hopes that all will go well, but please keep in mind that there are many doubting
editors."

Cooperation to Winston S. Churchill

[9 March 1939]   Paris

IS IT PEACE? [1]

Published by	Gross proceeds
Le Soir, Bruxelles	£10. 0. 0.
Berlingske Tidende, Copenhagen	5. 0. 0.
Paris-Soir, Paris	15. 0. 0.
Pariser Tages Zeitung, Paris	1. 0. 0.
Eleftheron Vima, Athens	1. 1. 0.
Lietuvos Aidas, Kaunas	1. 0. 0.
Zydu Balsas, Kaunas	0. 8. 0.
Luxemburger Zeitung, Luxembourg	1. 0. 0.
Bergens Tidende, Bergen	2. 0. 0.
Hajnt, Varsovie	No payment
Le Moment, Bucharest	No payment
Dagens Nyheter, Stockholm	7.10. 0.
La Bourse Egyptienne, Le Caire	2. 0. 0.
La Nacion, Buenos Aires	8. 0. 0.
Estampa, Bogota	1. 1. 0.
South African Morning Newspapers	7. 7. 0.
Argus, Melbourne	2. 2. 0.
Telegraph, Brisbane	2. 2. 0.
Advertiser, Adelaide	2. 2. 0.
Times of Ceylon, Ceylon	2. 2. 0.
Hong Kong Herald, Hong Kong	1. 1. 0.
East African Standard, Nairobi	1. 1. 0.
Times of Malta, Malta	0.10. 6.
Straits Times, Singapore	1. 1. 0.
New York Herald Tribune and the other American newspapers	50. 0. 0.[2]
Total	£124. 8. 6.

1. Published in the *Daily Telegraph* on 9 March 1939 as "Are the Prospects of Peace in Europe Brighter?"
2. This was the first payment under the scheme Reves had devised for Churchill's articles in the United States.

Emery Reves to Winston S. Churchill

11 March 1939   Paris

Dear Mr. Churchill,

I was very glad that you have agreed to telephone the few more lines on Hore-Belisha's declaration which made the article up to date.[1]

Thursday morning, I have cabled to the NEW YORK HERALD TRIBUNE that your first article will deal on the armament position of the European Powers. Half an hour after we have received the additional lines the following cable came from New York: CHURCHILL ON ARMAMENT POSITION EUROPEAN POWERS GOOD STOP URGE CURRENTEST ANGLE IN LEAD EXAMPLE BRITISH DECISION SEND NINETEEN DIVISIONS CONTINENT EVENT WAR.

You see how right I was in asking you for these few lines.

I have taken the night train to Amsterdam and assisted to this first transmission. It is a very exciting procedure. We have been in contact with New York for about 50 minutes; first they have started to send 25 words a minute. Then, after ten minutes came the message from New York that the reception was good and they speeded it up until 75 words per minute. About an hour later I received already the following message: ARTICLE FINE RECEPTION PERFECT THANKS.

So this was a good start and I came back to Paris this morning. I have to settle here some of the most urgent matters which have accumulated during my 4 months absence, and then I shall come over to London. I hope to arrive on Thursday.

Yours very sincerely,
I. Révész

1. Leslie Hore-Belisha was Secretary of State for War from May 1937 to January 1940.

Kathleen Hill: Chartwell Literary Account

19 March 1939

Meeting Dr. Revesz (literary agent) also Dr. Ripka[1] & Miss Grant Duff[2] at Oxted, 3 luncheons, and car back to Oxted Stn.

1. Hubert Ripka, Editor of the Prague daily newspaper *Lidove Noviny* from 1934 to 1939. In March 1939 he escaped to Paris, where he organized pro-Czech propaganda. Escaping to London in June 1940, he served as Deputy Secretary of State for Foreign

Affairs to the Czech government-in-exile. Czechoslovak Minister of Foreign Trade (Prague, 1945 to 1948), he escaped from Czechoslovakia after the Communist takeover and lived in exile in England until his death in 1958.

2.   Shiela Grant Duff, a cousin of Clementine Churchill. Her father had been killed in action on the Western Front in September 1914, when she was only a year old. From 1936 to 1938 she lived in Prague as a journalist for various British newspapers. In 1938 she published a Penguin Special, *Europe and the Czechs*. She later recalled "that French was mostly spoken for Ripka's sake for he knew no English at that time" (letter to Gilbert, 12 July 1994).

Cooperation to Winston S. Churchill

[24 March 1939]   Paris

THE EUROPEAN CRUNCH [1]

Published by	Gross proceeds
Le Soir, Bruxelles	£10. 0. 0.
Paris-Soir, Paris	15. 0. 0.
Zydu Balsas, Kaunas	0. 8. 0.
Hajnt, Varsovie	No payment
Dagens Nyheter, Stockholm	7.10. 0.
La Bourse Egyptienne, Le Caire	2. 0. 0.
Palestine Post, Jerusalem	1. 0. 0.
La Nacion, Buenos Aires	8. 0. 0.
O Estado de Sao Paulo, Sao Paulo	7. 0. 0.
O Jornal, Rio de Janeiro	3. 0. 0.
Argus, Melbourne	2. 2. 0.
Telegraph, Brisbane	2. 2. 0.
Advertiser, Adelaide	2. 0. 0.
South African Morning Newspapers	7. 7. 0.
Times of Ceylon, Ceylon	2. 2. 0.
Hong Kong Herald	1. 1. 0.
East African Standard, Nairobi	1. 1. 0.
Daily Gleaner, Kingston	0.10. 6.
Times of Malta, Malta	0.10. 6.
New York Herald Tribune and the other American newspapers	50. 0. 0.
Total	£122.14. 0.

1.   Published in the *Daily Telegraph* on 24 March 1939 as "Herr Hitler Faced with a New Spirit of Resistance."

Emery Reves to Winston S. Churchill

27 March 1939   Paris

Dear Mr. Churchill,

1—Before I left London I have had a talk with the Editor of the NEWS CHRONICLE[1] who might be interested to undertake in England the same service of opinions three times weekly as the NEW YORK HERALD TRIBUNE and the other American newspapers. When he saw the list of the Contributors he immediately said that he would be most interested to get also your fortnightly articles. I told him that this is not impossible; however, should you agree some time in the future to give them the publication of your fortnightly articles, these ought to be paid separately and at a rate of £100.- per article.

Please let me know whether your contract with DAILY MIRROR is already definitive or whether you might still consider the NEWS CHRONICLE.[2] Perhaps their public would be more interesting particularly if they are undertaking a great promotion campaign for these articles all over the country. I shall not do anything until I hear from you but if you believe this suggestion to be interesting I could indirectly encourage them to make to you a proposition on that basis. Needless to say that for these payments from an English newspaper COOPERATION would renounce to its share of 40 per cent.

2—I have not yet received your magazine articles. Please let me have them all as soon as you can as we have no more in stock and there is a certain market for them in the Continental Press.

3—Have you dispatched already the letter to Mr. Blaedel, Editor of BERLINGSKE TIDENDE, in Copenhagen, a draft of which I have dictated to your Secretary? I would be grateful if you would send me a copy of this letter as on its basis I hope to arrive to a complete reconciliation with him.

Yours very sincerely,

I. Révész

1. From 1936 to 1948 the *News Chronicle* was edited by G. Barry.
2. Churchill committed himself to write for the *Daily Mirror,* his first article being "Hitler Sells the Pass!" about the German-Italian border (27 July 1939).

Kathleen Hill to Emery Reves

27 March 1939   Chartwell

Dear Doctor Revesz,

I am sending you six articles which Mr. Churchill has written for the 'News of the World.' You will see that the three articles on 'The House of Commons' have already been published. I will let you know as soon as the remaining three are published.[1]

I am sorry that Mr. Churchill did not agree to sending the suggested letter to Mr. Nicolas Blaedel. You may perhaps think it advisable to write to him yourself explaining that it was not possible to fit in an appointment, but that Mr. Churchill hopes to see him on his next visit to England.

Yours truly,
[Kathleen Hill]
Private Secretary

1.   There were in fact four more *News of the World* articles: "The Man Who Has to Say No" (the Treasury), published on April 30; "Sombre Memories of the Home Office," May 7; "Our Rule Britannia Office of State" (Admiralty), May 14; and "The Cinderella of Our Fighting Services" (War Office), May 21.

Winston S. Churchill to Nicolas Blaedel

6 April 1939   Chartwell

Dear Mr. Blaedel,

I much regret to hear from our common friend, Doctor Revesz, that your plans for meeting me when you were last in London fell through. I do not now remember the circumstances, but I can assure you it would have been a pleasure for me to have seen you and had a talk.

I trust when you are next in England, you will not fail to advise me beforehand.

Yours very truly,

Winston S. Churchill to Emery Reves: telegram

11 April 1939

Can you wireless four thousand words for Collier's[1] this week, and how much would it cost.

Churchill

1.   This was "War, Now or Never," published in *Collier's* on 3 June 1939.

Emery Reves to Winston S. Churchill

12 April 1939   Paris

Dear Mr. Churchill,

I have received your telegram asking whether we could transmit by wireless an article for Collier's. I have asked for you on the telephone but was unable to reach you. So I am writing you as it would be too complicated to explain the situation in a telegram.

In principle, I could easily transmit the article by the Amsterdam station but everything depends whether Collier's could arrange the reception. I could not possibly ask the New York Herald Tribune to undertake such a work for another newspaper as they are very busy in receiving day and night their news from all the parts of the world and the reception of 4,000 words takes a considerable time.

The best solution would be the following: Collier's should make an understanding with the Radio Corporation of America who are in contact with the Holland Radio and charge them to receive this transmission. The Radio Corporation could easily arrange with the Holland Radio all details (wave-length, speed, time of transmission etc). They should cable Holland Radio that this article will be remitted by Cooperation in Paris and the transmission paid by us.

If you cable this to Collier's and if the Radio Corporation in America will get in touch with Holland Radio in Amsterdam, they could fix all technical details within a few hours.

The costs of the transmission depend entirely on the speed. The 4,000 words would cost at a speed of 30 words per minute about £15–20, at a speed of 70 words per minute about £8–10. The speed would depend upon the ability of the receivers and on atmospheric conditions. These figures only include the transmission of the wireless message, the costs of the reception ought to be paid by Collier's. But these are usually not very high.

In general, such wireless transmissions are only advantageous in case of a regular service. For an isolated transmission the ordinary presscable or Press Wireless might be preferable though considerably more expensive. Nevertheless, if you wish we can make a trial.

Please let me know about your decision.

Yours very sincerely,
I. Révész

Cooperation to Winston S. Churchill

[13 April 1939]   Paris

MUSSOLINI'S CHOICE [1]

Published by	Gross proceeds
Le Soir, Bruxelles	£10. 0. 0.
Berlingske Tidende, Copenhagen	5. 0. 0.
Paevaleht, Tallinn	1. 0. 0.
Paris-Soir, Paris	15. 0. 0.
Pariser Tages Zeitung, Paris	1. 0. 0.
Der Telegraaf, Amsterdam	5. 0. 0.
Zydu Balsas, Kaunas	0. 8. 0.
Luxemburger Zeitung, Luxembourg	1. 0. 0.

Bergens Tidende, Bergen	2. 0. 0.
Stavanger Aftenblad, Stavanger	1.10. 0.
Tidens Tegn, Oslo	5. 0. 0.
Dagens Nyheter, Stockholm	7.10. 0.
Sydney Morning Herald, Sydney	3. 3. 0.
Argus, Melbourne	2. 2. 0.
Telegraph, Brisbane	2. 2. 0.
Advertiser, Adelaide	2. 2. 0.
Times of Ceylon, Ceylon	2. 2. 0.
Hong Kong Herald, Hong Kong	1. 1. 0.
East African Standard, Nairobi	1. 1. 0.
Times of Malta, Malta	0.10. 6.
The Press, Christchurch	2. 2. 0.
Otago Daily Times, Dunedin	2. 2. 0.
Bourse Egyptienne, Le Caire	2. 0. 0.
Palestine Post, Jerusalem	1. 0. 0.
La Nacion, Buenos Aires	8. 0. 0.
O Jornal, Rio de Janeiro	3. 0. 0.
South African Morning Newspapers	7. 7. 0.
Group *New York Herald Tribune*	50. 0. 0.

Total   £144. 2. 6.

1.   Published in the *Daily Telegraph* on 13 April 1939 as "Would War or Peace Better Serve Mussolini's Interests?"

Winston S. Churchill to Sir Alexander Cadogan [1]

17 April 1939

I think this may be of interest to you.[2] It is of no consequence to me as the sums paid by these papers are insignificant. Nevertheless the growing German control of the Press of all these neutral countries seems to me to be a serious matter.

1.   Permanent Under Secretary of State for Foreign Affairs from 1938 to 1946, including the whole of Churchill's wartime premiership.
2.   A letter from Reves, in which he indicated the countries that were no longer willing to take Churchill's articles, on political grounds. For a full account, see the letter that Reves sent Reginald Leeper (at the Foreign Office) on 31 May 1939.

Winston S. Churchill to Emery Reves

18 April 1939

Thank you so much for your letter, which I have read with great interest. I have sent a copy of it to the Foreign Office.

Cooperation to Winston S. Churchill

[20 April 1939]   Paris

PRESIDENT ROOSEVELT AND FRANCO'S CHOICE [1]

Published by	Gross proceeds
Le Soir, Bruxelles	£10. 0. 0.
Paevaleht, Tallinn	1. 0. 0.
Paris-Soir, Paris	15. 0. 0.
Oran Republicain, Oran	1. 0. 0.
Lietuvos Aidas, Kaunas	1. 0. 0.
Zydu Balsas, Kaunas	0. 8. 0.
Bergens Tidende, Bergen	2. 0. 0.
Stavanger Aftenblad, Stavanger	1.10. 0.
Le Moment, Bucharest	No payment
Dagens Nyheter, Stockholm	7.10. 0.
Advertiser, Adelaide	2. 2. 0.
Telegraph, Brisbane	2. 2. 0.
Hong Kong Herald, Hong Kong	1. 1. 0.
East African Standard, Nairobi	1. 1. 0.
Times of Malta, Malta	0.10. 6.
La Nacion, Buenos Aires	8. 0. 0.
O Estado de Sao Paulo, Sao Paulo	5. 0. 0.
O Jornal, Rio de Janeiro	3. 0. 0.
South African Morning Newspapers	7. 7. 0.
Sydney Morning Herald	3. 3. 0.
Group *New York Herald Tribune*	50. 0. 0.
Total	£122.14. 6.

1.   Published in the *Daily Telegraph* on 20 April 1939 as "Shadow of the Axis over Franco's Next Moves."

Kathleen Hill to Emery Reves

2 May 1939

Dear Dr. Revesz,

This is to let you know that the "NEWS OF THE WORLD" published Mr. Churchill's article—"The Exchequer" on Sunday last, April 30, and the article—"The Home Office"—will be published on Sunday next May 7.

Mr. Churchill intends to bring the 'Admiralty' article up to date, and it will not be published until he has done so, but I will let you know.

Yours truly,
[Kathleen Hill]
Private Secretary

A. de Premio Real[1] to Winston S. Churchill

2 May 1939   13 Quai Voltaire,
                                                                    Paris VII

Sir,

We had the great pleasure of publishing, in our issue of April 26—a copy of which is sent to you by the same mail—your most interesting article entitled "Hitler commettra-t-il les mêmes erreurs que Napoléon".

It has met with a total appreciation from our readers and we do hope that in a close future we shall prove able to give them other writings of yours.

They seem the best way to reenforce the mutual understanding and friendliness between your people and our people.

Therefore, we would feel deeply grateful if you kindly accept to receive just for a few minutes one of our best reporters, whom we intend to send to London within a fortnight.

In the case you agree on the principle, we shall be glad to know it, so as to ask you to fix an appointment a few days before our reporter leaves.

We beg you, Sir, to believe us,

                                                                    Yours truly,
                                                                    A. de Premio Real

1.   Chief Editor of *Vu, L'Illustré Français*.

Emery Reves to Winston S. Churchill

6 May 1939   Paris

Dear Mr. Churchill,

Last week I have received the visit of an English gentleman who came to see me on behalf of the Foreign Office. He wanted some information regarding the matter about which I have written to you already and which you have communicated with the Foreign Office.

During the past weeks the situation became worse in many countries and I should like to give you some new information regarding Poland, Rumania and Greece, our new allies:

1°) Poland. Your last article 'Poland's Peril' was not published in Warsaw and in spite of the change in policy no British article was published in the Polish press during the past weeks.

2°) Rumania. The German control over the press has become complete during the past weeks. Even the most francophile newspaper UNIVERSUL is now pro-nazi. The method of pressure is the following: there is an Under-secretary for Press and Propaganda, the Head of which is Mr. Titeanu. Mr. Titeanu is a great friend of a German lady, Frau Erika von Kohler, who is in

Bucharest since several months and who happens to be the sister of Himmler, the Head of the Gestapo. This governmental organisation has monopolized the publicity in Rumania and newspapers can only get publicity through this department. The consequence is that the publicity revenue of a francophile paper has sunk from 400,000 Lei per month to practically zero. On the other side, the publicity revenue of the newspaper CURENTUL, controlled entirely by the Germans, has risen from 100,000 Lei to over 300,000 Lei per month. I think it is not necessary to comment this situation. I only should like to add that there are 22 German language newspapers in Rumania controlled directly by the Propaganda Ministry in Berlin.

3°) Greece. During the past months I have made a very interesting arrangement with leading Greek newspapers ELEFTHERON VIMA, PROIA and ETHNOS, and though half of our articles have been censored by the Government I was always able to publish 6–8 articles in a month which was something. I have now received the April-report from my agent in Athens which is disastrous. Since Italy occupied Albania and Great Britain guaranteed the independence of Greece, no article criticizing fascism or nazism has been allowed to be published by the Greek press. The only three articles the publication of which the Government permitted were the following: an article by Virginio Gayda, an article by Señor de Madariaga (rather favourable to Franco) and an English article which has shown some understanding of Germany. Since the 1st of April all the articles written by Winston Churchill, Anthony Eden[1], Duff Cooper, Wickham Steed,[2] Major Attlee,[3] Admiral Usborne[4] and all the French statesmen have been prohibited by the Greek censorship.

I have definite proofs that all these articles have been accepted by the newspapers for publication and that their publication has been prohibited afterwards by the Greek Government.

I am giving you this information because I feel sure you will agree with me that this situation is intolerable. I have also given some of this information to M. Daladier. I hope to see him next week.

Something from Scandinavia: last week I received in Paris the visit of Mr. Trygger, the Editor of the great conservative newspaper SVENSKA DAGBLADET in Stockholm. You certainly remember him, we have lunched together in Chartwell last year. He was tremendously anxious to get your articles. Now he says that he cannot publish them anymore unless on non-political subjects. He also denounced my contract for Mr. Eden's articles which he was anxious to sign last summer. He says that he cannot ruin his newspaper and if he would go on to publish articles by statesmen who 'do not understand Germany', he would get no more publicity at all and would be unable to pay any dividend to his stockholders. This is the situation.

Yours very sincerely,

I. Révész

P.S. I have read that you have delivered a broadcast to America last week. May I ask you for which network and whether you have received a fee for this broadcast or not? I want to take up my negotiations for the regular broadcasting service for America and it would be helpful for me if I would know under what conditions you have delivered that speech. I am sending you enclosed two letters which have been addressed to you by readers of PARIS-SOIR.

    1.   Anthony Eden had been Secretary of State for Foreign Affairs from December 1935 to February 1938 (when he was succeeded by Lord Halifax). He had first entered the Cabinet as Minister without Portfolio for League of Nations Affairs in June 1935.

    2.   Henry Wickham Steed, a former Editor of the *The Times* (London), and from 1937 a regular broadcaster on world affairs for the Overseas Service of the BBC.

    3.   Clement Attlee, Leader of the Labour Party since 1935. From 1942 to 1945 he was Deputy Prime Minister in Churchill's wartime coalition, and from 1945 to 1951 was Prime Minister of the third Labour government.

    4.   Rear-Admiral Cecil Vivian Usborne, a former Director of Naval Intelligence (1930–1932). He had retired from the Royal Navy in 1933 but returned to public service in 1939 as Director of the Censorship Division of the Press and Censorship Bureau.

Winston S. Churchill to Emery Reves

8 May 1939   Chartwell

Dear Doctor Revesz,

    Butterworth is publishing in volume form the articles of the last three years, and I enclose you a copy of the Preface which I have written.[1]

    You will see that I have made a number of statements about the circulation of these articles in Europe, which I shall be very much obliged if you will check or amplify in a manner to produce the effect desired, namely of a world-wide circulation for the articles.

    I shall certainly work in a reference to Cooperation in the course of the final text.

    Could you let me have this back in a week with any notes you wish to make about the circulation? Please pay particular attention to the reference to the American plan, which I may not have stated quite correctly.

    In a footnote the names of all the papers who have accepted us sh'd be given. Can you kindly supply this.

    1.   This was *Step by Step*, published in Britain by Thornton Butterworth on 27 June 1939 and in the United States by Putnam two months later, on 25 August 1939. The volume was translated into French, German, Italian, Swedish, Danish, Norwegian, and Spanish. The German-language edition was published in Amsterdam by Allert de Lange in 1940.

Kathleen Hill to A. de Premio Real

8 May 1939

Dear Sir,

I am desired by Mr. Winston Churchill to thank you for your letter of May 2nd and to say how glad he is that you were pleased with the article in question.

Mr. Churchill asks me to let you know that with regard to future articles in the press, he would like you to get in touch with his literary agent, Dr. Revesz, Cooperation, Paris.

In answer to the penultimate paragraph of your letter Mr. Churchill is so pressed with public work that he fears at the present time it would be very difficult for him to see your reporter, much as he would like to do so.

Yours faithfully,
[Kathleen Hill]
Private Secretary

Winston S. Churchill to Emery Reves

8 May 1939   Chartwell

Dear Doctor Revesz,

I am indeed sorry to hear that the net is closing round our activities, through fear of Germany. Luckily, you have already called in the New World to redress the balance of the Old.

I gave a broadcast to the United States, gratis and on public grounds, and it was a condition that the two great Agencies linked up together, which they did.

I have not yet received the accounts of the last four articles, and if their circulation has prospered. Will you please let me have them at your convenience.

When answering my previous letter about the Preface to the new book, perhaps you will give me a list of all the papers in all the countries which have at any time taken the articles in the series.

Emery Reves to Winston S. Churchill

9 May 1939   Paris

Dear Mr. Churchill,

Many thanks for your letter of May 8th to which I reply immediately. I am very glad indeed to hear that you are going to publish in volume form the articles of the last three years. I have had this idea since a long time and I am happy that you are going to realize it now.

Regarding the preface I should like to make the following remarks:

1) You say that the articles published by the EVENING STANDARD and the DAILY TELEGRAPH may be called "parent articles". I know that you are accustomed to call this series after the newspaper publishing it in London. This is natural but if you would publish this, the other newspapers would not like it at all. Most of the newspapers publishing your articles are exactly as important in their respective countries as the London papers and they would never have signed contracts if the proposition would have been that they had merely to reproduce articles which are written for an English newspaper. I think the right formula is to say that you have written these articles for the world press and the British rights have been reserved for the EVENING STANDARD and the DAILY TELEGRAPH.

2) You say that in Europe the articles have been published in more than 20 newspapers, in a dozen countries, and in 6−7 languages. This is far too modest. In fact, the articles have been published in Europe in more than 40 newspapers, in 20 countries, and in 19 languages (English, French, Flemish, Dutch, Danish, Norwegian, Swedish, Finnish, Estonian, Latvian, Lithuanian, Polish, German, Czech, Rumanian, Hungarian, Serbian, Greek and Yiddish).

3) In mentioning the three Scandinavian countries you ought to add Finland and to the Balkan States Greece.

4) I do not understand what you mean by "the famous Noyer-Preyer Press of Vienna and Hungary". This must be an error as I have never heard of them. [It was Churchill's mispronunciation of "Neue-Freie."]

5) As to the British Empire press, please add to the Dominions Canada and to the Colonies Ceylon, Hong Kong, Singapore, Trinidad, Gold Coast, Bahamas, where your articles are also more or less regularly published.

6) I think you could also mention South America saying that many South American papers are publishing regularly your articles, particularly LA NACION in Buenos Aires, O JORNAL in Rio de Janeiro and O ESTADO in Sao Paulo. The articles reach them partly by radio short waves, partly by air-mail.

7) Regarding the United States it might be interesting to give some more details, that all the articles are transmitted by short wave wireless from Paris to New York and so they appear all over the American continent the next day after you have written them in London. There are fourteen important newspapers who have signed contracts for the regular publication of these articles, from coast to coast, from New York to Los Angeles (If you like I can give you the list of the newspapers.).

I am glad that you will work in a reference to Cooperation in the course of the final text. Perhaps you can say either at the beginning or at the end of these statements that outside Great Britain all these arrangements have been

made by Cooperation who also have established the wireless service to the
United States. I am leaving this entirely to your judgment. I only want to say
that all compliments will be gladly accepted.

I should be happy if you would send me a copy of the revised new version
of the preface so that I may see whether there is anything further to add.

I shall let you have statements and the cheque during this week.

> Yours very sincerely
> I. Révész

P.S. I shall let you have a complete list of all the newspapers in one or
two days.

Winston S. Churchill to Emery Reves: telegram

12 May 1939

Many thanks for letter, but let me have Preface back with your suggested
amendments.

> Churchill

Emery Reves to Winston S. Churchill

14 May 1939   Paris

Dear Mr. Churchill,

Kindly find enclosed statements for the articles published in February and
March, and a cheque of £269.3.6, in respect of these articles.

I am also returning the Preface indicating with numbers the passages to
which the remarks in my letter of May 9th refer.

I have submitted to an Australian magazine your article "Will Hitler make
Napoleon's mistakes?".[1] To my greatest surprise I have received now a reply
from the Editor of that magazine saying that he is unable to publish this article because it has appeared already in the SYDNEY MORNING HERALD.
The SYDNEY MORNING HERALD has not received this article from us,
and I wonder where they have taken it from. Do you know anything about
this case, and have you received any payment in respect of this article?

Please, let me know by returning mail what you know about this publication so that I may take up the case at once with the SYDNEY MORNING
HERALD.

> Yours very sincerely,
> I. Révész

---

1. "Will Hitler Repeat Napoleon's Mistakes?" was first published in *Illustrated* on
4 March 1939.

Winston S. Churchill to Emery Reves

17 May 1939

Many thanks for your letter, cheque and accounts, which last I am studying.

It was decided by the publishers not to refer to the previous publication as they thought it would do harm.

I am inquiring about the "Sydney Morning Herald".

Cooperation to Winston S. Churchill

[18 May 1939]   Paris

TURKEY AND THE PEACE BLOC [1]

Published by	Gross proceeds
Le Soir, Bruxelles	£10. 0. 0.
Berlingske Tidende, Copenhagen	5. 0. 0.
Paevaleht, Tallinn	1. 0. 0.
Paris-Soir, Paris	15. 0. 0.
Algemeen Handelsblad, Amsterdam	2. 0. 0.
Zydu Balsas, Kaunas	0. 8. 0.
Luxemburger Zeitung, Luxembourg	1. 0. 0.
Bergens Tidende, Bergen	2. 0. 0.
Stavanger Aftenblad, Stavanger	1.10. 0.
Le Moment, Bucharest	No payment
Dagens Nyheter, Stockholm	7.10. 0.
Argus, Melbourne	2. 2. 0.
Telegraph, Brisbane	2. 2. 0.
Advertiser, Adelaide	2. 2. 0.
West Australian, Perth	2. 2. 0.
Times of Ceylon, Ceylon	2. 2. 0.
Hong Kong Herald, Hong Kong	1. 1. 0.
East African Standard, Nairobi	1. 1. 0.
Times of Malta, Malta	0.10. 6.
Bourse Egyptienne, Le Caire	2. 0. 0.
Group *New York Herald Tribune,* New York	50. 0. 0.
O Jornal, Rio de Janeiro	3. 0. 0.
La Nacion, Buenos Aires	8. 0. 0.
South African Morning Newspapers	7. 7. 0.
Sydney Morning Herald	3. 3. 0.
Total	£132. 0. 6.

1. On 18 May 1939 the *Daily Telegraph* published this article as "Turkey's Significance as a Partner in the Peace Bloc."

Winston S. Churchill: engagement cards

27 May 1939

Dr. Revesz to tea.

Winston S. Churchill to Emery Reves [1]

27 May 1939   Chartwell

Dear Dr. Revesz,
    I confirm our agreement whereby you have full authority to negotiate with
the American Broadcasting Company my broadcast to the United States.
    I am quite prepared to undertake monthly, or if necessary fortnightly,
broadcasts on topical events under the conditions agreed upon.
    You have already exclusive rights for handling of such and to sign con-
tracts for a trial period of six months.
    This arrangement does not include public speeches which might be gener-
ally released also for broadcast.

1. This letter was dictated by Reves while he was at Chartwell for Churchill to
sign.

Emery Reves to Winston S. Churchill

31 May 1939   Paris

Dear Mr. Churchill,
    I am sending you enclosed for your information copy of the memoran-
dum I have sent to Mr. Rex Leeper [1] at his request.

Yours very sincerely,
I. Révész

1. Reginald Leeper, Head of the News Department of the Foreign Office and
later, during Churchill's wartime premiership, Ambassador to Greece.

Emery Reves to Reginald Leeper

31 May 1939   Paris
Confidential

Dear Sir,
    Referring to our conversation the other day, I give you herewith some
information regarding the press conditions in several European countries and
the difficulties in publishing British articles.

There are two categories of countries:

A) Countries in which the German influence is direct, and in which the Governments, through their press control and active censorship, prohibit the publication of any articles which might criticize Germany, Nazism or any form of dictatorship.

To this category belong the Baltic countries, Poland, Rumania, Hungary, Jugoslavia, Bulgaria and Greece.

B) Countries in which Germany, through constant pressure and frequently repeated protests, has created an atmosphere of uncertainty in which newspapers feel that it is dangerous to publish anything that might displease the Germans.

In this category belong Sweden, Denmark, Holland, Switzerland and several South American countries.

I should like to give all the facts I have gathered during the past months concerning the situation in each of the above mentioned countries:

1) <u>Baltic countries</u>. In Latvia it is practically impossible to publish any articles by British statesmen. I had arrangements with two government newspapers BRIWA ZEME and RITS in Riga which were cancelled about six months ago at the direct order of the Latvian Foreign Office, and since that time not one article by a British statesman has been published in the Latvian press. To illustrate the situation in this country I should like to mention— apart from our own experiences—a most characteristic event. For several years the leading Latvian newspaper JAUNAKAS ZINAS has had as correspondent in Paris, M. Arved Arenstam, probably the best known Latvian journalist. In his correspondence, he has invariably given prominence to the policy of the western democracies. A few weeks ago, the German minister in Riga protested personally to the Latvian Foreign Minister against the journalistic activity of this correspondent and asked for his immediate dismissal if the Latvian government wished to entertain good relations with Germany. A few days ago, the publishers of JAUNAKAS ZINAS informed Mr. Arenstam that they are unable to maintain him as their Paris correspondent. They have already sent another man who is informing his paper entirely in the sense required by the Nazis. Latvia is at present completely closed to us, and no articles by British or other democratic statesmen can be published in a press which is entirely under the control of the government.

In Estonia and in Lithuania the situation is much better. Though some of our articles cannot be published in these two countries, the greater part of our articles regularly appear in the leading newspapers in Tallinn and Kaunas.

2) <u>Poland</u>. The Polish governmental press was for many years closed to British and French articles. My agreement with the GAZETA POLSKA was denounced after the German-Polish Press Agreement signed in 1934. This agreement provides that the two governments shall prohibit the publication of any news, comment or articles which might be prejudicial to good rela-

tions between the two countries. The consequence of this agreement was that the Polish press became indirectly under the complete control of Germany. The only newspaper that published during the past years an article by British statesmen from time to time was the opposition newspaper KURJER WAR-SZAWSKI. The publisher of this newspaper, Konrad Olchowicz, was nominated Senator a few months ago and—curious coincidence—since that time our co-operation has ceased and not a single British or French article has been published.

The situation in Poland today is that the entire Polish press (with the exception of the Jewish newspapers) is hermetically closed to our articles. The Anglo-Polish Agreement has had no consequence at all, and all the articles we have offered by British statesmen—many of them most favourable to Poland—have been refused by the newspapers. The newspapers still follow the instructions given them by the government press department in accordance with the Polish-German Press Agreement. Only a change of the official Polish press policy could enable the newspapers to publish the views of the leading British statesmen.

3) In <u>Hungary</u> and in <u>Bulgaria</u>, the press is forced entirely into the service of Germany. It seems to me that there is little hope of changing the situation in these two countries for the time being.

4) <u>Rumania</u>. The press in this country has during the past few months come entirely under government control, and the press department follows a purely pro-German policy. Even Universul, the most pro-French newspaper since the war, has now changed its management and is pro-Nazi. The method of pressure upon the newspapers is most peculiar. There is a newly inaugurated Undersecretariat for Press and Propaganda of which the head is Mr. Titeanu. He is a great friend of a German lady, Frau Erika von Kohler, who has been in Bucharest for several months and who—as far as I am informed—is the sister of Herr Himmler, the head of the Gestapo. His organization has monopolized commercial publicity in Rumania, and newspapers can only secure advertisements through this department. Consequently, the advertising revenue of the newspaper CURENTUL, which is entirely controlled by the Germans, has risen from 100.000 lei to over 300.000 lei per month. On the other hand, the only pro-French newspapers that remained in Rumania, the French language paper LE MOMENT in Bucharest, has lost almost all its advertising revenue, which has sunk from an average of 400.000 lei per month to practically zero. This last newspaper which still publishes our articles but only in French and consequently with but little effect in Rumania—has the greatest difficulties, and it is to be foreseen that it will soon disappear. Its publication is very often prohibited for several days, and its publisher, Mr. A. Hefter is in a kind of a "preventive exile" in London at the moment. On the other hand, there are over twenty German newspapers in Rumania, which all enjoy the greatest facilities on the part of the Gov-

ernment. All these German newspapers are directly controlled from Berlin. The Anglo-Rumanian Agreement has made no change in the situation, and no Rumanian newspaper is for the time being publishing British articles.

5) <u>Greece</u>. For several years there has been strict government censorship in this country, but in spite of this censorship we were able to publish about half of our articles and the leading Greek newspapers—ELEFTHERON VIMA, PROIA and ETHNOS—have published an average of 7–8 articles per month. Since Italy occupied Albania, and Great Britain guaranteed the independence of Greece, no British or French articles have passed the Greek censorship. I have definite proofs that almost all the articles we have submitted since the Anglo-Greek Agreement written by Winston Churchill, Anthony Eden, Lord Lloyd,[1] Duff Cooper, Wickham Steed, Major Attlee, Admiral Usborne and all the French statesmen have been accepted by the newspapers for publication, but that their publication was prohibited afterwards by the Greek government censorship.

6) <u>Yugoslavia</u>. Since the Stoyadinowitch regime, the press has suffered under a terrible censorship and has to adopt a pro-German policy. Only one newspaper in Belgrade—POLITIKA—has had the courage and the power to fight against this policy and to follow a democratic, pro-English and pro-French line. I have had a contract with this newspaper which for many years published all our articles. Then followed a period when on account of our article the newspaper was several times confiscated and about 6 months ago the publisher of POLITIKA, M. Vladimir Ribnikar, who is a convinced democrat and who put up a heroic fight during the past years, informed me that he is unable to carry out our contract. Since that time no article by British or French statesmen has been published in Yugoslavia.

I am coming now to the second category of countries.

7) In the Scandinavian and the other neutral countries the situation is about the same. Constant pressure on behalf of Germany and the German diplomatic representatives forces the governments and the newspapers to be very careful in publishing any view which might lead to a German protest. You certainly know the case of Mr. Nikolas Blaedel, foreign Editor of Berlingske Tidende in Kopenhagen, the leading Danish journalist, who has been forced to spend several months abroad in consequence of German protests against his pro-English and pro-democratic policy. I was told that the Swedish Prime Minister himself had written private letters to the leading editors urging them to be very careful and not to publish anything which might call forth a German protest. My case with the Dutch government is another sign of this fear-produced dependence on Germany. We started on the tenth of March last a regular four times weekly wireless service for the American newspapers through the Amsterdam Station. I was urged by the Dutch to transmit our articles through their wireless station and signed a purely commercial contract with them on that purpose. Three weeks later I have received an official telegram from The Hague informing me that in view of

the international situation they had given orders to the Amsterdam Post Office to stop immediately the transmission of our articles. On inquiries I have learnt that the Dutch Foreign Minister and the Minister of Interior have decided to forbid immediately the transmission of these articles which are regarded to be "one-sided propaganda" and "dangerous for the neutrality of Holland".

During the past weeks I received several cancellations from Scandinavia and neutral countries saying that our contributors "do not understand Germany".

This situation in the majority of the European countries is the consequence of the active press policy pursued since several years by the German government imposing their will on the press of all these small countries by various means.

In the first category of countries, it is the consequence of direct press agreements. In most of those countries, there is no freedom of press and the governments are in sympathy with an anti-democratic policy. So they are an easy instrument for the German propaganda. Most of the newspaper editors I know in these countries are opposing this policy, but they are helpless and under administrative terror. The guarantees Great Britain has given to Poland, Rumania and Greece did not change the situation at all. Only special diplomatic representations on this behalf might re-establish normal conditions. The Germans have obtained their position by force. Hardly any political or commercial negotiation has taken place during the past years with these countries without imposing this "press truce". As there was never any pressure by England or France, the Germans have obtained what they wanted and control the press. The situation is most paradoxical, and the policy of these countries can be expressed in the following phrase: "We must be agreeable to the Germans until the very last moment, when we shall ask England and France to make war for us". I think that by strong diplomatic representations, the situation could be changed, as it is certainly not too much to convince those governments that now that they are virtually the allies of Great Britain and France in the event of war, some kind of co-ordination of policy is indispensable and their public ought to be informed about British views on international affairs.

As to the second category of countries, there is no question of any hostility towards Great Britain. It only happens that, whenever something appears in the newspapers, there is an official German protest which if necessary is repeated daily. They apply the principle: "A force d'embêter les gens ils cèdent". This diplomatic pressure in the neutral countries is supported by a very able policy in the distribution of German commercial publicity in the neutral countries. Newspapers in the neutral countries have considerable revenues from the publicity of the German tourist organizations and some powerful chemical trusts like "Bayer"; motorcar and Radio-Manufacturers like "Opel" and "Telefunken". Newspapers which are not agreeable to

Germany do not get these advertisements. The Editor of a leading Swedish newspaper who recently denounced our contract for Mr. Anthony Eden's articles and said that he could only publish articles by Mr. Winston Churchill on "non-political subjects" told me quite openly that he must do so as his shareholders are expecting dividends.

Diplomatic representations as well as the proper distribution of British commercial advertisements might quickly change the situation and make possible again the regular publication of British articles in these small democratic countries.

I am giving all these information in best faith, having collected them from authentic sources. Nevertheless, I cannot be responsible for their absolute correctness. I am leaving entirely to your judgment how you will use these information, but believe it would be more advisable not to communicate names, neither my name nor the other names mentioned in this letter to the governments. All the editors, journalists and civil servants who gave me this information when I had personal talks with them, asked me to consider it as absolutely confidential. They believe that if published or directly put to the governments, the latter would deny the facts, and the incident would only aggravate the situation. I beg you therefore kindly to consider this information as strictly confidential and to use them only in such a way as to cause no prejudice to any person or newspaper involved.

Yours sincerely,

1.   Lord Lloyd, a leading Conservative politician and former High Commissioner for Egypt and the Sudan, was to become Secretary of State for the Colonies during Churchill's wartime premiership.

Emery Reves to Winston S. Churchill

1 June 1939   Paris

Dear Mr. Churchill,

I received today good news from New York regarding the broadcasting scheme, and some further complication regarding the articles.

These two information made me decide to take the "Normandy" Wednesday morning and go over to New York. I hope that a fortnight will be sufficient to settle both matters.

Under such circumstances I should be most grateful if you would kindly send me the letter we agreed upon as your letter is the only one I have not yet received.

As I have told you, Sir Robert Vansittart [1] was very much in favour that you and Mr. Eden should accept this invitation. I am sending you enclosed copy of a letter which I have received already from Mr. Eden and which is similar to the draft I have dictated in Chartwell.[2] I very much hope that it will be possible for you to send me such a letter latest Sunday.

As I have told you, it is natural that this letter is only an option, and should I not be able to make satisfactory arrangements within six months, which would guarantee for you £50.- for each broadcast to be delivered at your house or in London conforming to your desire, it will lose its validity.

This letter shall only help me to make arrangements in the United States just as the letter you gave me regarding the fortnightly articles has very much helped me to come to a contract with the New York Herald Tribune.

I very much hope that you will dispatch your next article by Sunday night. Should you still believe that it would be delicate to write on Russia, I think some subject in connection with the progress of British rearmament would be very interesting. My opinion is that the best subject would be the progress of Air Force production. Another subject might be the new British Army if you could give some information, what has been done already, how the army will be organized, etc.

But these are merely suggestions. You will know best what subjects would interest the public next week.

1. Chief Diplomatic Adviser to the government.
2. See 27 May 1939.

Emery Reves to Winston S. Churchill

1 June 1939

Dear Mr. Churchill,

I thank you for your letter.[1]

It is natural that this letter is only an option, and should I not be able to make satisfactory arrangements within six months, which would guarantee for you £50 for each broadcast to be delivered at your house or in London conforming to your desire, it will lose its validity.

This letter shall only help me to make arrangements in the United States just as the letter you gave me regarding the fortnightly articles has very much helped me to come to a contract with the New York Herald Tribune.

1. This was the letter of 27 May 1939, which Reves had dictated.

Emery Reves to Winston S. Churchill

2 June 1939   Paris

Dear Mr. Churchill,

I am definitely leaving Wednesday on the "Normandie" for New York.

I shall have to fight a big battle there with the NEW YORK HERALD TRIBUNE and the group of newspapers taking our articles. As you know, these articles have had a very great success in the United States. Not only the public appreciates them very much, but all the Editors and particularly the Editor of the NEW YORK HERALD TRIBUNE has congratulated me several times upon the quality, the importance and the news value of the articles. The contract I have signed with them three months ago for a year provided a trial period of 3 months which ends on June 13th. I accepted such a trial period as a matter of course because the newspapers did not know what kind of articles we shall send them, and it was natural that they could not take a long engagement without knowing the quality of the service. This doubt has disappeared as the success of the articles is general and complete. I have just heard from New York that Mr. Ogden Reid, the proprietor of the NEW YORK HERALD TRIBUNE said to somebody that the service was "wonderful", and that the success was much greater than he expected.

I was really surprised to-day in receiving from the business manager of the NEW YORK HERALD TRIBUNE a cable denouncing our contract for the end of the trial period and proposing another contract which would practically reduce our income by about 35 to 40%. This is a manoeuvre of the various business managers and a kind of a blackmail. I think that they believe that the service being now introduced in the American press, you and the other Statesmen are anxious to continue anyhow and so they can get your contributions cheaper.

I am going to New York to fight against this attitude and to decline any reduction of the fees which have been certainly not too high on the basis of my old contract. I think that on the contrary they must be anxious to continue with these publications, and they would make themselves ridiculous to stop it after such a success and such a big publicity. As I have told you, it is a typical Munich problem, and we have to risk war if we want to save peace with honour.

My position would be much stronger if I could prove that you feel the same. It would be a great help for me if you could send me a letter in about the following terms:

"You were rather astonished to hear that the NEW YORK HERALD TRIBUNE has cabled and denounced the contract suggesting another contract with considerably reduced fees. It happens for the first time to you that an important newspaper to which you are contributing suggests a reduction of fees which you could not accept. I have told you at the beginning that the fees of the articles will be higher with the time, as indeed what the NEW YORK HERALD TRIBUNE and the other American newspapers have paid until now were rather low in comparison with the fees you are receiving from the big newspapers in other countries. You are anxious to keep the standing you have in the international press and you would rather prefer not to contribute to the NEW YORK HERALD TRIBUNE than to accept such a treatment though you would particularly regret if this great American newspaper would be the first which would show so little appreciation for your contributions. You ask me to explain your attitude to the NEW YORK HERALD TRIBUNE and to let you know by cable the result of my negotiation. In any case you cannot authorize me to accept less remuneration than during the first three months of our collaboration with the NEW YORK HERALD TRIBUNE."[1]

The more disappointment this letter will express, the better its effects will be.

Please, have the kindness to despatch to me this letter to Paris on Monday. Should you be unable to write it before Monday evening, so please, send it on board of "Normandie" at Southampton. The ship will stop at Southampton early in the afternoon on Wednesday.

I do feel that I can settle this matter in a satisfactory way, but please, help me with this letter. Naturally, I am asking similar letters from all the principal contributors of COOPERATION.

With many thanks,
Yours very sincerely,
I. Révész

1.   For Churchill's letter as sent to Reves, see 5 June 1939.

Kathleen Hill to Emery Reves

3 June 1939   Chartwell

Dear Doctor Revesz,

I send you herewith the typescript of an article on Mr. Anthony Eden which Mr. Churchill has written for the STRAND MAGAZINE. The article will probably appear in their <u>September</u> number, so it must not be re-sold yet.[1] I will let you know later the exact date when it will be published.

Regarding your recent statement of account, Mr. Churchill notices that there is no amount from the Empire Press for: "What does Mussolini mean?" published on 26 January 1939, although the Empire Press took all the other articles. Would you please let him know about this.

Yours faithfully,
[Kathleen Hill]
Private Secretary

1.   "The Rt. Hon. Anthony Eden P.C." was published in the August number of *Strand*. Eden, who had resigned from the government as Foreign Secretary in February 1938, rejoined the Cabinet on the outbreak of war in September 1939 as Secretary of State for the Dominions. During Churchill's wartime coalition he served as Secretary of State for War (May to December 1940) and Foreign Secretary (December 1940– May 1945).

Cooperation to Winston S. Churchill

[4 June 1939]   Paris

POLAND'S PERIL [1]

Published by	Gross proceeds
Le Soir, Bruxelles	£10. 0. 0.
Berlingske Tidende, Copenhagen	5. 0. 0.
Paevaleht, Tallinn	1. 0. 0.
Helsingin Sanomat, Helsinki	3. 0. 0.
Paris-Soir, Paris	15. 0. 0.
Pariser Tages Zeitung, Paris	1. 0. 0.
Zydu Balsas, Kaunas	0. 8. 0.
Tidens Tegn, Oslo	5. 0. 0.
Bergens Tidende, Bergen	2. 0. 0.
Dagens Nyheter, Stockholm	7.10. 0.
Argus, Melbourne	2. 2. 0.
Telegraph, Brisbane	2. 2. 0.
Advertiser, Adelaide	2. 2. 0.
Times of Ceylon, Ceylon	2. 2. 0.
Straits Times, Singapore	1. 1. 0.
Bourse Egyptienne, Le Caire	2. 0. 0.
Palestine Post, Jerusalem	1. 0. 0.
Group *New York Herald Tribune*, New York	50. 0. 0.
La Nacion, Buenos Aires	8. 0. 0.
O Jornal, Rio de Janeiro	3. 0. 0.
South African Morning Newspapers	7. 7. 0.
Sydney Morning Herald	3. 3. 0.
Total	£133.17. 0.

1. This article was published on 4 June 1939 in the *News of the World* as "Will There Be War in Europe—and When?"

Emery Reves to Winston S. Churchill

5 June 1939   Paris

Dear Mr. Churchill,

Thank you for having drawn my attention to the fact that the fees from the Empire Press have not been counted in my statements for your article "What does Mussolini mean?" published in January last. When the statement for this article was established, there was no news yet from the Empire, and when I have established the next statement, it was forgotten to come back to this article. It has been published in the following Empire newspapers:

South African Morning Newspapers
Sydney Herald
Melbourne Argus
Advertiser
Times of Ceylon
Hong Kong Herald
East African Standard
Times of Malta
Evening Post, Wellington
The Press, Christchurch.

I shall add the amount for these publications in the next statement.

Yours very sincerely,
I. Révész

Winston S. Churchill to Emery Reves

5 June 1939

I send you enclosed the two letters for which you ask.[1] As soon as I hear from the Post Office their explanation of the delay, I will send the envelope, so that you can have similar complaint made by your office to the French department.

Will you kindly make arrangements for the prompt payment while you are away of the fees which are due to me. To-day's article makes five for which no account has yet been rendered. Perhaps you will look into this.

I am posting to you direct at the Savoy Plaza a series of articles which have appeared in the News of the World. These you could sell to monthly magazines without affecting Collier's. There are three articles about life in the House of Commons and four upon my experience in different public Departments of State, all of which are well adapted for American consumption, and written in a popular way. In consideration of the fact that these have all appeared already in the News of the World, I should be prepared to sell the American copyright for 750 dollars each.[2]

Pray do not make any contract without advising me beforehand, and also make sure that Mr. Chenery of Collier's knows what you are doing, and is satisfied therewith.

All good wishes for success on your journey. I am sure you are right to go.

1. The two letters, dated 5 June 1939, that follow.
2. The value of those $750 in 1996 is $5,700 (£3,800).

Winston S. Churchill to Emery Reves

5 June 1939

Dear Dr. Revesz,

I was surprised to hear that the New York Herald Tribune has cabled denouncing the contract, and suggesting another contract with considerably reduced fees. I understood that the Tribune was very much pleased with the series of articles, which will probably acquire greater importance as the European situation moves towards its climax. I should certainly not be prepared to allow my work to be syndicated on any terms less favourable than those upon which we have been working.

For two years I did not allow these articles to be syndicated in the United States, and it is only the arrangement you made with the New York Herald Tribune, which has made this possible. I cannot, therefore, authorise you to accept less remuneration than what has ruled during the first three months of this new arrangement.

Winston S. Churchill to Emery Reves [1]

5 June 1939

Dear Dr. Revesz,

I am much interested in your proposal to negotiate with the American broadcasting companies for my special broadcasts to the United States.

These would not exceed ten minutes, and would be either monthly or fortnightly. I shall be very glad to consider any concrete proposals you may lay before me after your discussions on the spot, and for this purpose I accord you exclusive rights of handling the matter. This, of course does not apply to any public broadcasts I may give in the meanwhile.

1.   This letter was drafted in its entirety by Reves.

Kathleen Hill to Emery Reves

5 June 1939

Dear Doctor Revesz,

Below I give you the publishing dates of the "News of the World" articles:—

April 30.	1939	. . .	"The Exchequer"
May 7.	"	. . .	"The Home Office"
" 14.	"	. . .	"The Admiralty"
" 21.	"	. . .	"The War Office".

Yours faithfully,
[Kathleen Hill]
Private Secretary

Kathleen Hill to Emery Reves

5 June 1939

Dear Doctor Revesz,

I enclose herewith a copy of Mr. Churchill's article "Will there be War".

This was published in Collier's on June 3, and also appeared in the News of the World on June 4. It is, of course, for European sale only.

Yours faithfully,
[Kathleen Hill]
Private Secretary

Emery Reves to Winston S. Churchill: telegram

5 June 1939   Paris

Shall spend few hours London Wednesday afternoon. Please prepare articles. Wire where can telephone you.

Revesz

Winston S. Churchill to Emery Reves: telegram

5 June 1939

Articles available telephone Westerham 81.

Churchill

Cooperation to Winston S. Churchill

[8 June 1939]   Paris

TRIPLE BULWARK OF PEACE [1]

Published by	Gross proceeds
Le Soir, Bruxelles	£10. 0. 0.
Berlingske Tidende, Copenhagen	5. 0. 0.
Paris-Soir, Paris	15. 0. 0.
Pariser Tages Zeitung, Paris	1. 0. 0.
Lietuvos Aidas, Kaunas	1. 0. 0.
Zydu Balsas, Kaunas	0. 8. 0.
Luxemburger Zeitung, Luxembourg	1. 0. 0.
Bergens Tidende, Bergen	2. 0. 0.
Hajnt, Varsovie	No payment
Dagens Nyheter, Stockholm	7.10. 0.
Melbourne Argus, Melbourne	2. 2. 0.
Telegraph, Brisbane	2. 2. 0.
Advertiser, Adelaide	2. 2. 0.

West Australian, Perth	2. 2. 0.
Times of Ceylon, Ceylon	2. 2. 0.
Newspaper Enterprise, Hong Kong	1. 1. 0.
East African Standard, Nairobi	1. 1. 0.
Times of Malta, Malta	0.10. 6.
South African Morning Newspapers, Johannesburg	7. 7. 0.
Sydney Morning Herald, Sydney	3. 3. 0.
Bourse Egyptienne, Le Caire	2. 0. 0.
Palestine Post, Jerusalem	1. 0. 0.
La Nacion, Buenos Aires	8. 0. 0.
O Jornal, Rio de Janeiro	3. 0. 0.
Group *New York Herald Tribune*	50. 0. 0.
Total	£130.10. 6.

1.   This article was published in the *Daily Telegraph* on 8 June 1939 as "Towards a Pact with Russia." Churchill, formerly an implacable opponent of Bolshevism, had since 1936 advocated bringing Soviet Russia into a European defense system. Despite the start of negotiations between Britain and Russia during the summer, in August a pact was signed in Moscow between Germany and the Soviet Union (the Molotov-Ribbentrop Pact), which effectively gave Hitler a free hand against Poland that September and led to the partition of Poland between the Soviet Union and Germany a month later.

Kathleen Hill to Emery Reves

9 June 1939   Chartwell

Dear Doctor Revesz,

   With reference to your letter of May 14, Mr. Churchill has not given permission to any newspapers to reproduce the article "Will Hitler make Napoleon's Mistakes?" which originally appeared in "Illustrated." Therefore as it would appear that the SYDNEY MORNING HERALD reproduced the article without permission, I would suggest that you should send them an account.

Yours very truly,
[Kathleen Hill]
Private Secretary

Emery Reves to Winston S. Churchill: telegram

20 June 1939   New York

   NBC agreement made starting September fortnightly broadcasts fifty pounds each your part trial period five months believe great success returning Normandie twentyeight

Revesz

Cooperation to Winston S. Churchill

[22 June 1939]   Paris

ENCIRCLEMENT AND PROPAGANDA [1]

Published by	Gross proceeds
Le Soir, Bruxelles	£10. 0. 0.
Paris-Soir, Paris	15. 0. 0.
Zakenwereid, Amsterdam	3. 0. 0.
Lietuvos Aidas, Kaunas	1. 0. 0.
Zydu Balsas, Kaunas	0. 8. 0.
Bergens Tidende, Bergen	2. 0. 0.
Dagens Nyheter, Stockholm	7.10. 0.
Melbourne Argus, Melbourne	2. 2. 0.
Telegraph, Brisbane	2. 2. 0.
Times of Ceylon	2. 2. 0.
Newspaper Enterprise, Hong Kong	1. 1. 0.
East African Standard, Nairobi	1. 1. 0.
Times of Malta, Malta	0.10. 6.
South African Morning Newspapers, Johannesburg	7. 7. 0.
Sydney Morning Herald, Sydney	3. 3. 0.
Bourse Egyptienne, Le Caire	2. 0. 0.
Palestine Post, Jerusalem	1. 0. 0.
La Nacion, Buenos Aires	8. 0. 0.
O Jornal, Rio de Janeiro	3. 0. 0.
O Estado de Sao Paulo, Sao Paulo	5. 0. 0.
Group *New York Herald Tribune*	50. 0. 0.
Total	£127. 6. 6.

1. Published in the *Daily Telegraph* on 22 June 1939 as "Germany's Use of Tactics of Encirclement." This was Churchill's thirty-first, and last, article in the *Daily Telegraph* since they had taken over the publication of Churchill's fortnightly articles from the *Evening Standard* in April 1938.

Chartwell Literary Accounts [1]

10 July 1939   Chartwell

Lunch to Dr. Revesz (Literary Agent) and Mrs. Ogden Reid (New York Herald Tribune).

1. This document is from the Literary Accounts, which Churchill had to keep for income tax purposes, regarding entertaining and meals at Chartwell. These accounts were kept by Kathleen Hill.

Winston S. Churchill: engagement cards

11 July 1939   Chartwell

   6.30   Dr. Revesz.

Winston S. Churchill and Emery Reves: agreement

11 July 1939   Chartwell

Agreement made this 11th day of July, 1939, between Mr. Winston Churchill, of Chartwell, Westerham, Kent, and Me. E. Revesz, of No. 33 Champs-Elysées, Paris, France.[1]

   1. Mr. Churchill transfers to Mr. Revesz the exclusive rights for handling his broadcasts outside Great Britain. It is understood that this agreement only includes special broadcasts delivered directly to broadcasting companies and that Mr. Churchill is entirely free to release for broadcasting purposes speeches or addresses made before a public audience.

   2. Mr. Churchill agrees to deliver monthly broadcasts to the National Broadcasting Company in New York on dates to be agreed in each month. Each such address shall be a discussion of international topics or events of worldwide interest and shall not be less than seven nor more than fifteen minutes in length of delivery. Mr. Churchill will furnish a copy of each address as soon as possible before the broadcast is delivered, to be transmitted to New York in advance if requested. The time and place of delivery of the broadcasts are to be agreed upon, but it is anticipated that the broadcasts to the United States will be delivered between eleven and twelve p.m. G.M.T., and at the studios of the B.B.C. in London, or other broadcasting companies, should Mr. Churchill be away from London, on the day of delivery of such broadcast. Should Mr. Churchill so desire, the National Broadcasting Company will install its microphones and radio broadcasting pickup equipment in the house or office of Mr. Churchill.

   3. These broadcasts to America shall be delivered regularly every month. Should the international situation so require, additional broadcasts might be delivered, on mutual agreement between Mr. Churchill and the broadcasting company.

   4. Mr. Revesz will remit to Mr. Churchill a fee of One Hundred Pounds (£100.0.0)[2] for each broadcast delivered monthly to the United States. Should these broadcasts also be released for broadcasting companies in other countries, additional payments will be made, which are to be agreed upon. Payments will be made monthly.

   5. This agreement enters into force on the tenth of September 1939 and shall be valid for a trial period of five months. This agreement may be extended by mutual agreement for six additional months from the tenth of February 1940, and from the tenth of August 1940 from year to year. Should

the international situation so require, the starting date of this agreement may be advanced upon mutual consent.

6. It is understood that the broadcasting of the addresses herein referred to shall not be commercially sponsored, either in the United States or in any other country, without the special written consent of Mr. Churchill.

7. It is understood that should Mr. Churchill be prevented, by becoming a Cabinet Minister or for any other major reason, from delivering such broadcast addresses regularly, this agreement will be suspended for such period. It is also understood that this agreement shall be suspended should the United States Government in Washington have any objection to the delivery of such broadcasts.

1.   Emery Reves was still using his original name, Imre Révész, when signing letters but had begun using E. Revesz (without accents) in contracts and agreements.
2.   In 1939 £100 was the equivalent of £2,500 in 1996.

Winston S. Churchill to Emery Reves

12 July 1939

I return you copy of the agreement duly signed by me.
I am keeping the original as signed by you.
Many thanks for all the care you are bestowing upon my affairs.

Cooperation to Winston S. Churchill

[13 July 1939]   Paris

THE HUSH IN EUROPE [1]

Published by	Gross proceeds
Le Soir, Bruxelles	£10. 0. 0.
Berlingske Tidende, Copenhagen	5. 0. 0.
Paris-Soir, Paris	15. 0. 0.
Nieuwe Rotterdamsche Courant, Rotterdam	2. 0. 0.
Zydu Balsas, Kaunas	0. 8. 0.
Luxemburger Zeitung, Luxembourg	1. 0. 0.
Bergens Tidende, Bergen	2. 0. 0.
Tidens Tegn, Oslo	5. 0. 0.
Hajnt, Varsovie	No payment
Dagens Nyheter, Stockholm	7.10. 0.
Weltwoche, Zurich	3.10. 0.
South African Morning Newspapers	7. 7. 0.
Argus, Melbourne	2. 2. 0.

Advertiser, Adelaide	2. 2. 0.
Telegraph, Brisbane	2. 2. 0.
West Australian, Perth	2. 2. 0.
Times of Ceylon, Ceylon	2. 2. 0.
Hong Kong Herald, Hong Kong	1. 1. 0.
East African Standard, Nairobi	1. 1. 0.
Times of Malta, Malta	0.10. 6.
Bourse Egyptienne, Le Caire	2. 0. 0.
Palestine Post, Jerusalem	1. 0. 0.
O Jornal, Rio de Janeiro	3. 0. 0.
O Estado de Sao Paulo, Sao Paulo	5. 0. 0.
Group *New York Herald Tribune*	50. 0. 0.
La Nacion, Buenos Aires	8. 0. 0.
Total	£140.17. 6.

1. This article was published in the *Daily Mirror* on 13 July 1939, the first of four articles that Churchill was to write for the *Daily Mirror* between then and 24 August 1939.

Emery Reves to Winston S. Churchill

17 July 1939   Paris

Dear Mr. Churchill,

I wonder how did you like the Military Parade in Paris.[1] I think the most amazing was the spirit of the public. I have never seen such a crowd on the Champs Elysées, not even on the occasion of the Royal visit. Six months ago there was complete confusion. Now the determination to resist is unanimous. I think that in another six months there will be a spirit of offensive.

I have great troubles this time with your last article which has been published in the DAILY MIRROR without "Copyright" and which has been quoted and partially reprinted all over Europe without authorization. I have received many protests from our clients and several papers have refused its publication after its content has been published by various telegraphic agencies.

I have a kind of a gentlemen's agreement with the Havas Agency and they do not touch any article which appears under the copyright of COOPERATION. But this article has been widely circulated by them. I have protested but they have just shown me the following telegram from their London Office:

"Article Churchill porte aucune mention Copyright".

You remember how much trouble we have had two years ago when the Evening Standard did not quote the copyright line. Almost every second article was stolen abroad and we could not safeguard the rights of our clients.

Since the Evening Standard and later the Daily Telegraph have published the articles with the usual copyright line—since about a year and half—not one single incident has occurred. Obviously, this is the right method if we want international circulation.

I very much hope that you will agree with me that we must avoid that these conflicts with our newspapers should start again. Please, therefore, tell the DAILY MIRROR that at the end of each article the following copyright line must be quoted:

"WORLD COPYRIGHT BY THE DAILY MIRROR AND COOPERATION"
"Reproduction even partially strictly forbidden."

I should be most grateful if you will kindly let me know whether this formality is settled and whether I can assure our newspapers that the incident of last week will not occur again.

Yours very sincerely,
I. Révész

1.   On July 14 Churchill flew to Paris, as a guest of the French government, to watch the annual military review. After the ceremony was over, Consuelo Balsan, who was with him, commented on the size of the tanks in the parade. They were so large that they had shaken the Champs Elysées in their progress. In her memoirs she recorded Churchill's response: the French government had to show its people "that their economics had been transferred from the idleness of the stocking to the safety of the tank."

Kathleen Hill to Emery Reves

20 July 1939   Chartwell

Dear Doctor Révész,

I am requested by Mr. Churchill to thank you for your letter of July 17.

Mr. Churchill is sorry to hear of the trouble you have had over the last article, but he has now arranged with THE DAILY MIRROR to have the copyright line quoted at the end of each article in future.

Yours truly,
[Kathleen Hill]
Private Secretary

Emery Reves to Winston S. Churchill

24 July 1939   Paris

Dear Mr. Churchill,

I am now preparing to publish your series on British Institutions (House of Commons, Admiralty, etc. . . .).

All the articles are already translated with the exception of the one on The

War Office. I only had one copy of this article which I have left in America. Please let me have another copy of this article by returning mail.[1]

I also beg to tell me whether it is right that the series consist of 7 articles: 3 on the House of Commons, 1 on the Admiralty, 1 on the Home Office, 1 on the Exchequer, 1 on the War Office.[2]

I think much would depend upon a good general title under which all the articles ought to be published. As you are explaining in this series your personal souvenirs, I wonder whether "Political Souvenirs" would not be a suitable common title for all the articles.[3]

I should be grateful if you would kindly let me know what you think about this suggestion and whether you have a better and more attractive headline. I think it ought to be personal.

Yours very sincerely,
I. Révész

1.   Churchill noted in the margin of this paragraph, "Send."
2.   Churchill noted in the margin of this paragraph, "Yes."
3.   Churchill noted in the margin of this paragraph, "Yes."

Kathleen Hill to Emery Reves

25 July 1939   Chartwell

Dear Doctor Revesz,

This is just to let you know that Mr. Churchill's article on Mr. Anthony Eden has now been published in the August number of the STRAND MAGAZINE.

Yours truly,
[Kathleen Hill]
Private Secretary

Kathleen Hill to Emery Reves

26 July 1939   Chartwell

Dear Doctor Révész,

I write on behalf of Mr. Churchill to thank you for your letter of July 24.

I enclose herewith a copy of the War Office article, and confirm that the series consists of seven articles:—The House of Commons (Nos. I, II and III), The Admiralty, The Home Office, The Exchequer, and The War Office.

Mr. Churchill is willing for you to publish the articles under a general title, and thinks "Political Souvenirs" would be suitable.

Yours very truly,
[Kathleen Hill]
Private Secretary

Cooperation to Winston S. Churchill

[27 July 1939]   Paris

WHAT OF THE TYROL? [1]

Published by	Gross proceeds
Paris-Soir, Paris	£15. 0. 0.
Le Soir, Bruxelles	10. 0. 0.
Berlingske Tidende, Copenhagen	5. 0. 0.
Zydu Balsas, Kaunas	0. 8. 0.
Bergens Tidende, Bergen	2. 0. 0.
Stavanger Aftenblad, Stavanger	1.10. 0.
Tidens Tegn, Oslo	5. 0. 0.
Hajnt, Varsovie	No payment
Dagens Nyheter, Stockholm	7.10. 0.
Argus, Melbourne	2. 2. 0.
Telegraph, Brisbane	2. 2. 0.
Advertiser, Adelaide	2. 2. 0.
Nassau Guardian, Nassau	0. 7. 6.
Times of Ceylon, Ceylon	2. 2. 0.
Hong Kong Herald, Hong Kong	1. 1. 0.
East African Standard, Nairobi	1. 1. 0.
Times of Malta, Malta	0.10. 6.
The Press, Christchurch	2. 2. 0.
Otago Daily Times, Dunedin	2. 2. 0.
La Nacion, Buenos Aires	8. 0. 0.
O Estado de Sao Paulo, Sao Paulo	5. 0. 0.
O Jornal, Rio de Janeiro	3. 0. 0.
Group *New York Herald Tribune*	50. 0. 0.
Total	£128. 0. 0.

1.   Published in the *Daily Mirror* on 27 July 1939 as "Hitler Sells the Pass!"

Emery Reves to Winston S. Churchill

27 July 1939   Paris

Dear Mr. Churchill,

I have just received a cable from the Vice-President of the National Broadcasting Company in New York, informing me that they have announced yesterday for the first time our radio-talks, and that he has learnt that Mr. Kaltenborn [1] of the Columbia Broadcasting System is already flying over to Europe to get interviews with you and with our other speakers for the radio.

He says in his cable that he hopes you will not grant such a radio interview before we start our series of broadcasts, as this would take the edge off our first talks.

I am forwarding to you this information just received from New York though I feel sure that in view of our arrangement with the National Broadcasting Company you would not accept any suggestion from a competing American broadcasting company, as they obviously only want to make our start less interesting in disturbing the promotion campaign of the N.B.C. introducing your regular broadcasts.

I should be most grateful if you would kindly let me know how you feel about this and also if you would be good enough to inform me should you be approached later on by the Columbia Broadcasting Company.

Yours very sincerely,
I. Révész

1.   H. V. Kaltenborn, a pioneer news reporter, worked with CBS from 1930 to 1939 and with NBC from 1940 until 1958, where he was known as the Dean of Radio Commentary. During the war he gave regular broadcast accounts of the war on all fronts.

Kathleen Hill to Emery Reves

3 August 1939   Chartwell

Dear Doctor Révész,
    I send you herewith a copy of Mr. Churchill's article entitled 'How the War Began', which has been published in PICTURE POST this week.

Yours very truly,
[Kathleen Hill]
Private Secretary

Kathleen Hill to Winston S. Churchill

3 August 1939   Chartwell

Mr. Churchill,
    I am not sure whether Dr. Revesz took a copy of this Air Raids article the other day. Shall I send it to him?[1]
    Collier's paid for the article, but they have not advised the publishing date.

K.H.

1.   Churchill noted at this point, "Yes."

Kathleen Hill to Emery Reves

6 August 1939   Chartwell

Dear Doctor Révész,

As I am not sure whether you took a copy of Mr. Churchill's article "Air Raids and the Population" the other day, I am sending you one herewith.

The article has been published in THE NEWS OF THE WORLD and COLLIER'S MAGAZINE.[1]

Yours very truly,
[Kathleen Hill]
Private Secretary

1. The article had been published by *Collier's* on 17 June 1939 as "Bombs Don't Scare Us Now" and on the following day by the *News of the World* as "Air Bombing Is No Road to World Domination."

Emery Reves to Winston S. Churchill

6 August 1939   Paris

Dear Mr. Churchill,

I hope that the London Office of the National Broadcasting Company has got already in touch with you, and that everything will be all right Tuesday evening. Please, do not tell anybody that the microphone has been brought to your house, as it is a principle of all the broadcasting companies (particularly the B.B.C.) not to do this any more. All our speakers shall deliver their broadcasts in the B.B.C. studios in London. The N.B.C. agreed on my request to make an exception in your case, but they hope that this will remain between us.

I shall probably not be able to listen to your broadcast, so please, let me have a copy of it at your earliest convenience, if possible by the night-mail of Monday.

I am grateful to you that you have kindly promised me not to entertain for the time being offers coming from other American broadcasting companies without consulting me.

I shall let you have statements and the cheque in the course of this week.

Yours very sincerely,
I. Révész

Emery Reves to Winston S. Churchill

11 August 1939   Paris

Dear Mr. Churchill,

Kindly find enclosed statement for two articles and a special publication in a Paris Weekly.[1]

I also enclose cheque of £170.- (One Hundred and Seventy Pounds) in respect of these articles.

Your next article "The Hush in Europe" was published in the middle of July so I am unable to give you full information on further articles to-day.

Yours very sincerely
I. Révész

P.S. I think your broadcast was brilliant![2]

1.   "Towards a Pact with Russia" (8 June 1939), "Encirclement and Propaganda" (22 June 1939), and "Will There Be War?" published in *La Tribune de France* on 13 July 1939 (for which Churchill received £25, the equivalent in 1996 of £625).

2.   On 8 August 1939 Churchill made an eight-minute broadcast to the United States, the first in a regular series negotiated by Reves. "No wonder there is a hush among all the neighbours of Germany," Churchill said, "while they are wondering which one is going to be 'liberated' next." The coming of war on 3 September 1939, and Churchill's entry into the War Cabinet, as First Lord of the Admiralty, meant that this first broadcast was also the last.

Cooperation to Winston S. Churchill

[11 August 1939]   Paris

A WORD TO JAPAN [1]

Published by	Gross proceeds
Le Soir, Bruxelles	£10. 0. 0.
Berlingske Tidende, Copenhagen	5. 0. 0.
Paevaleht, Tallinn	1. 0. 0.
Helsingin Sanomat, Helsinki	2. 0. 0.
Paris-Soir, Paris	15. 0. 0.
Pariser Tages Zeitung, Paris	1. 0. 0.
Eleftheron Vima, Athens	1. 0. 0.
Der Telegraaf, Amsterdam	5. 0. 0.
Zydu Balsas, Kaunas	0. 8. 0.
Luxemburger Zeitung, Luxembourg	1. 0. 0.
Bergens Tidende, Bergen	2. 0. 0.
Hajnt, Varsovie	No payment
Dagens Nyheter, Stockholm	7.10. 0.
Weltwoche, Zurich	3.10. 0.
Argus, Melbourne	2. 2. 0.
Telegraph, Brisbane	2. 2. 0.
West Australian, Perth	2. 2. 0.
Nassau Guardian, Nassau	0. 7. 6.
Times of Ceylon, Ceylon	2. 2. 0.
Straits Times, Singapore	1. 1. 0.
Hong Kong Herald, Hong Kong	1. 1. 0.

Times of Malta, Malta	0.10. 6.
Palestine Post, Jerusalem	1. 0. 0.
O Estado de Sao Paulo, Sao Paulo	5. 0. 0.
O Jornal, Rio de Janeiro	3. 0. 0.
Group *New York Herald Tribune*	50. 0. 0.
La Nacion, Buenos Aires	8. 0. 0.
Total	£132.16. 6.

1. "A Word to Japan!" was published in the *Daily Mirror* on 27 July 1939.

Emery Reves to Winston S. Churchill [1]

21 August 1939   Paris

Dear Mr. Churchill,

I have just received your article which is excellent.[2] I wish the declaration of Chamberlain and Daladier would be in the same terms. This might still save the situation. I have just had a long talk with Dr. Rauschning, the former national-socialist Head of the Danzig Government, who has very good relations to the Reichswehr. He said that the German army cannot make war against England and France and Hitler knows that. So, should England be absolutely firm, probably nothing would happen in Danzig. But if there is the slightest interpretation possible as to the willingness of England to make war, they will undoubtedly attack Poland.

I have received to-day a telephone call from St-Jean-Cap-Ferrat from one of the Editors of the READERS DIGEST who has just arrived from America. As you know, this is one of the most successful American publications with a circulation of over three million. They want to change their policy and not to publish merely cuttings from other magazines, but also some original features. They pay very well, and I think I shall be able to get from them $1,500 to $2,000 for an article. The Editor is anxious to explain to you what type of articles they desire, and whether it would be possible for them to get such articles from you. This magazine being a monthly, there is no interference with COLLIER'S. He will be in Paris Thursday next. Do you think it would be possible for you to receive him for a short talk when you pass through Paris? I should be glad if you would let me know when you arrive in Paris and whether I could see you here.

I hope you have received the statements and the cheque I have sent you to Chartwell before you left for France.

Yours very sincerely,
I. Révész

P.S.—The chauffeur who has brought your article presented a note of Frs 280 and 7 frs for stamps. We have paid him this amount. I am telling you this to avoid that you should pay him again on his return.[3]

1.   Churchill was then staying at the Château de Saint-Georges-Motel, west of Paris, as the guest of Consuelo Balsan (formerly Duchess of Marlborough, the divorced wife of Churchill's cousin Sunny, ninth Duke of Marlborough). Another guest was the painter Paul Maze, with whom Churchill painted.

2.   "At the Eleventh Hour!" was published in the *Daily Mirror* on 24 August 1939.

3.   At that time 280 French francs was the equivalent of £38 in 1996. Churchill received 2,000 francs (worth £375 in 1996) for each of his fortnightly articles in *Paris-Soir*.

Cooperation to Winston S. Churchill

[24 August 1939]   Paris

AT THE ELEVENTH HOUR

Published by	Gross proceeds
Le Soir, Bruxelles	£10. 0. 0.
Berlingske Tidende, Copenhagen	5. 0. 0.
Paris-Soir, Paris	15. 0. 0.
Zydu Balsas, Kaunas	0. 8. 0.
Bergens Tidende, Bergen	2. 0. 0.
Tidens Tegn, Oslo	5. 0. 0.
Stavanger Aftenblad, Stavanger	1.10. 0.
Illustrowany Kuryer Codzienny, Cracovie	No payment
Hajnt, Varsovie	No payment
Dagens Nyheter, Stockholm	7.10. 0.
Tages Anzeiger, Zurich	3. 0. 0.
Gazette de Lausanne, Lausanne	1.10. 0.
Freie Ratier, Chur	0.10. 0.
Advertiser, Adelaide	2. 2. 0.
Argus, Melbourne	2. 2. 0.
Nassau Guardian, Nassau	0. 7. 6.
Times of Ceylon, Ceylon	2. 2. 0.
Hong Kong Herald, Hong Kong	1. 1. 0.
Daily Gleaner, Kingston	0.14. 0.
Times of Malta, Malta	0.10. 6.
Palestine Post, Jerusalem	1. 1. 0.
La Nacion, Buenos Aires	8. 0. 0.
O Estado de Sao Paulo, Sao Paulo	5. 0. 0.
O Jornal, Rio de Janeiro	3. 0. 0.
Group *New York Herald Tribune*	50. 0. 0.
Total	£127. 8. 0.

Emery Reves to Winston S. Churchill

26 August 1939   Paris

Dear Mr. Churchill,

I am very much perturbed about your telling me on the telephone that
Lady Diana Cooper[1] has asked you how much you receive for the broadcasts
to America and your intention to tell it to her.

I do hope that you have not yet told to her our agreement, and that you
will not tell the figure. I would be in a most painful situation, as what I have
agreed to pay to you is more than three times as much as what I can pay to
the other British Statesmen, and more than four times as much as I can grant
to French and continental Statesmen.

You will no doubt remember that when I have accepted your suggestion of
£100.0.0 per broadcast, I have told you that I could make such an agreement
only under the condition that <u>nobody</u> will know its terms except yourself and
me. You have given me a formal promise that the terms of this agreement will
be kept secret, and that nobody will have any information about it.

I am relying on your promise and do beg you not to place me in a most
awkward situation. Should this letter arrive too late, and should you have
already told the figure, please, do let me know, so that I may avoid even more
unpleasant complications.

Yours very sincerely,
I. Révész

Kindly find enclosed a cheque of £100.0.0 for your first broadcast.

1. The wife of Alfred Duff Cooper, who had resigned from the Cabinet at the
time of Munich and whom Churchill brought into his wartime government as Minister of Information.

Emery Reves to Winston S. Churchill

1 September 1939   Paris

Dear Mr. Churchill,

I hope this letter will reach you.[1]

I have arranged already that you shall broadcast to the United States next
Tuesday (Sept 5th). Not being able to telephone or to send a telegram to
London, I beg to kindly get in touch with Mr. Bate of the NATIONAL
BROADCASTING COMPANY to arrange all technical details.

I do hope that you will be able to arrange with Lord Lloyd that permission
should be given for me to come over to London. I am most anxious to settle
various important questions with the British authorities regarding the diffusion into overseas countries of our views. No activity is possible any more

without official consent and I am very much afraid that my whole organization all over the world will collapse, if I am unable to maintain the service. I am expecting with great impatience your news.

I beg to remain,
Yours very sincerely,
I. Révész

1.   Hitler had invaded Poland that morning. Two days later Britain and France declared war on Germany. Despite a brief disruption of mail services, Reves's letter reached its destination.

Winston S. Churchill to Emery Reves: telegram [1]

4 September 1939

Continuance of articles most uncertain anyhow none this fortnight.

Churchill

1.   On 3 September 1939 Churchill had entered Neville Chamberlain's War Cabinet as First Lord of the Admiralty.

Winston S. Churchill to Emery Reves: telegram

5 September 1939

Regret must cancel future broadcasts.

Churchill

Emery Reves to Winston S. Churchill: telegram [1]

6 September 1939   Paris

Merci vos telegrammes sans vous service americain echouerait espere vous donnerez votre appui grande campagne Amerique tous pays neutres essentiels pour nos interets essaierai venir London samedi soumettrai projets priere telegraphier si pouvez me recevoir

Revesh [2]

1.   This telegram was addressed, "Churchill, First Lord of Admiralty, London." It was passed by "No. 41 Censor, London."
2.   With the coming of war, all telegrams sent from France overseas had to be in French. English translation: "Thank you for your telegrams. Without you the American service would fail. Hope you will give your support to the large campaign in America. All neutral countries essential for our interests. I shall attempt to come to London Saturday and shall submit proposals. Please telegraph if you are able to receive me."

Winston S. Churchill to Emery Reves: telegram

6 September 1939

Will receive you with pleasure Saturday.[1]

Churchill

1.   Churchill saw Reves at the Admiralty on Saturday, 9 September 1939. Reves was staying at the Savoy Hotel.

Winston S. Churchill to Lord Macmillan [1]

7 September 1939   Admiralty

For the last two years and more I have been writing fortnightly articles on world politics which have been printed in the Evening Standard, Daily Telegraph and Daily Mirror, and at the same time, simultaneously, in a great many newspapers all over Europe, the British Empire, and latterly the United States. A list is attached of the papers which have printed these articles. The articles have been translated into about sixteen languages.

This process now of course stops so far as I am concerned, but my purpose in writing is to put you in contact with a very remarkable man, Mr. E. Revesz, who has built up so swiftly the whole of this organisation. He is a Hungarian by birth, and at present I believe of no nationality, though he is applying for British naturalisation. He is, of course, in the refugee class, and a strong anti-Nazi. I am sure you could not possibly find anyone who would be such help in the Neutral Press, and I beg you to see him. A large part of his peacetime work comes shortly to an end.

I may add that through his business of arranging articles, he has personal access to almost all the principal English and French politicians, and until lately he had arranged a series of broadcasts to the United States in which Mr. Eden and I were taking part, together with leading ex-Ministers.

I shall be very glad to talk to you about this at any time, if I may.

Yours sincerely,
Winston S. Churchill

1.   Lord Macmillan, a distinguished lawyer and a Lord of Appeal since 1930, had been appointed Minister of Information on the outbreak of war.

Lord Macmillan to Winston S. Churchill

8 September 1939   Ministry of Information
Private

My dear First Lord,

I am much obliged by your letter received this morning in which you recommend to my notice Mr. E. Révész.

I shall be very pleased to meet him and see what can be arranged, but before I do so I should like to take advantage of your suggestion that we might have a personal talk on the matter. No doubt we can arrange a time mutually convenient.

Yours sincerely,
Macmillan

Kathleen Hill to Winston S. Churchill

20 September 1939

Mr. Churchill,

Dr. Révész thinks he might perhaps sell the 7 articles on the House of Commons, Home Office, Admiralty, etc. to America and neutral countries. (So far they have only appeared in the NEWS OF THE WORLD.) Would this be in order now that you are in the Cabinet? [1]

Dr. Révész is asking if I could give him a copy of the letter you wrote on his behalf to Lord Macmillan. May I do this, please? [2]

I have inquired about the accounts, and Dr. Révész says he cannot make these up until he returns to Paris. He is however sending an advance.

K.H.

1.   Churchill noted at this point, "Yes, reprints may be sold."
2.   Churchill noted at this point, "Yes, but let me see it first."

Kathleen Hill to Emery Reves

21 September 1939

Dear Doctor Révész,

Mr. Churchill is much obliged to you for sending your cheque for £100.0.0. on account of the last articles.

In reply to your inquiry, reprints of the seven articles which appeared in the NEWS OF THE WORLD, namely House of Commons, Admiralty, Home Office, etc., may be sold in America and neutral countries.

Yours very truly,
[Kathleen Hill]
Personal Private Secretary

Kathleen Hill to Winston S. Churchill

22 September 1939

Mr. Churchill,

Dr. Revesz presumes it will be in order to sell the 7 articles on the House of Commons etc. to American papers which are competitors of Collier's, now that presumably your contract with Collier's has temporarily come to an end. Is this all right, please.[1]

K.H.

1. Churchill noted at this point, "Yes."

Lord Macmillan to Winston S. Churchill

25 September 1939   Ministry of Information

My dear Churchill,

I think you will be interested to read the attached copy of a letter which I have sent to Mr. Revesz who recently came to see me with a recommendation from yourself.

I am very grateful to you for putting me into touch with Mr. Revesz and I have no doubt that provided that mutually satisfactory terms can be arranged his organisation will prove of real value to the Ministry.

Yours sincerely,
Macmillan

Lord Macmillan to Emery Reves

25 September 1939   Ministry of Information

Dear Mr. Revesz,

With reference to our recent conversation I find on enquiry that you have already seen several of my official advisers, who have discussed with you the possibility that the Ministry might with advantage make use of your services and those of the very extensive and efficient organisation which you have built up for the syndicalizing of articles in the British and foreign press.

I was myself very favourably impressed, and so I understand were my advisers, by what you told me of your organisation and I trust that it may be found possible to make arrangements for the Ministry to make use of it, for the distribution of articles in the foreign press particularly, on terms which will be satisfactory to both sides. I understand that Mr. Surrey Dane, the Director of the General Production Division in this Ministry has arranged to see you again to discuss how best we can secure your collaboration.

Yours sincerely,
Macmillan

Emery Reves to Winston S. Churchill

9 October 1939   Savoy Hotel,
                                                      London

Dear Mr. Churchill,
    Confirming our telephone conversation of yesterday, I believe that the
series "My Life Story" reprinted in Sunday Dispatch could be widely repub-
lished also in many other countries in Europe, America and the British
Empire.
    I would be grateful if you would kindly authorize COOPERATION to
handle these reprints. As in the past, I would secure for you 60% of the gross
proceeds from all publications.[1]
    Should you agree with this suggestion, so please let me have a complete set
of the series, or ask Sunday Dispatch to hand over to me a copy of the whole
story. It would be useful for me to know when and in which paper this series
was originally published in U.S.A.
                                            Yours very sincerely,
                                                      I. Révész

    1.   Churchill wrote in the margin of this paragraph, "Yes."

Kathleen Hill to Emery Reves

10 October 1939

Dear Doctor Révész,
    I write on behalf of Mr. Churchill to thank you for your letter of the 9th,
and to say that he is quite agreeable for you to republish the series now running in the SUNDAY DISPATCH as you suggest. I have telephoned to Mr.
Eade, the Editor, and have asked him to let you have copies.
    The series was originally published in the NEWS OF THE WORLD in
1935, but not elsewhere as far as Mr. Churchill is aware.
                                            Yours very truly,
                                                  [Kathleen Hill]
                                            Personal Private Secretary

Kathleen Hill to Winston S. Churchill

12 October 1939

Mr. Churchill,
    Are you giving Dr. Revesz the world rights in the 3 scientific articles, or
only the American?[1]
                                                      K.H.

    1.   Kathleen Hill noted on this letter, after talking to Churchill, "American at
present."

Winston S. Churchill to Paul Reynaud

13 October 1939
Private and Personal

My dear Reynaud,

I have been wanting much to have a talk with you as there are so many things which cannot be put on paper. Alas, I am anchored here, though I hope the chance to come over for a naval conference with your colleague, the Minister of Marine, may offer before long.

The purpose of this letter is limited to a single personal point. I believe you know Doctor Revesz of Cooperation Press Service. I have come to work with him during the last two years when he has shown himself extraordinarily clever in spreading my articles and broadcasts through Europe and America. It seemed to me that his whole outlook and all his interests and sentiments were anti-Nazi. Recently I have recommended him to the Ministry of Information as a disseminator through the neutral press of pro-Ally propaganda. Naturally in these cases one wants to be quite certain of the bona-fides of an alien. I wonder whether you would make inquiries from your own French Sûreté as to whether anything is known against him, and if so, what? I should be much obliged if at your convenience you could let me know how the matter stands.

With my kindest regards,
Believe me,
Yours very sincerely,
Winston S. Churchill

Kathleen Hill to Emery Reves

13 October 1939

Dear Doctor Revesz,

As promised over the telephone this evening, I am sending you the inquiries from THE TIMES OF CEYLON and MELBOURNE HERALD herewith.

I have informed Mr. Churchill that in future you are willing to allow him 75% of the gross proceeds from all British language syndications. This applies to the British Empire and to the United States.

Mr. Churchill agrees that you should handle the American rights in the three scientific articles which he wrote for the NEWS OF THE WORLD, and which have not yet been published. I will let you have copies as soon as possible.

Yours very truly,
[Kathleen Hill]
Personal Private Secretary

The Deuxième Bureau to M.I.5: telegram[1]

21 October 1939

Reference your verbal request of 14.10

The Deuxième Bureau emphasise that they still regard Revesz as a very suspect pro-Nazi propagandist and both his activities and his opinions confirm this.

The above information comes from a very trustworthy source whose word the Deuxième Bureau cannot doubt.

1. The French Deuxième Bureau and the British M.I.5 (a branch of Military Intelligence) were the agencies responsible for monitoring the activities of enemy agents.

Sir Vernon Kell[1] *to Winston S. Churchill*

21 October 1939

Dear Mr. Churchill,

I have just received the above message from France. Which confirms what they said before about Revesz:—

If you get any reply to your own letter to France I would be glad to have a copy.

Yours sincerely,
V. Kell

1. Sir Vernon Kell, who had served in the Boxer campaign in China in 1900, had been in the Directorate of Military Intelligence from 1914 to 1924 and was the head of M.I.5 from 1924 to 1940.

Winston S. Churchill to Sir Vernon Kell

22 October 1939

Dear Sir Vernon,

I am much astonished to receive your note. I enclose the report which Monsieur Reynaud has obtained for me from the Second Bureau, which is as you see precise. The pith of this report is that his secretary and partner is the sister of the Editor of the Communist paper L'HUMANITE. Hitherto the Communists have been vehemently hostile to the Nazis, whatever may be thought about their other opinions. I am quite sure the statement 'that his activities and opinions are pro-Nazi' is not true, and that the reverse is true. He is an anti-Nazi propagandist. However I am going to Paris tomorrow, Monday, and I will make enquiries myself into what appears to me to be a very strange affair.

Emery Reves to Winston S. Churchill

24 October 1939   Savoy Hotel
                                                                 London

Dear Mr. Churchill,

I should like to thank you very much for receiving me this afternoon.[1]

I have an idea of what might be the only possible cause of this strange misunderstanding. Last summer, when I was in New York, the Editor of the "New York Herald Tribune" urged me to include into our service from time to time also a German view, so that the American papers should not believe that this service is merely Anglo-French propaganda. He said that the only way in America to publish 20 articles by Churchill, Eden, Herriot, Blum etc. is to publish from time to time also a Fascist, a Nazi and a Communist article. He showed me very strong letters from American newspapers, saying that they would cancel the contracts if we would restrict our articles to the Western countries.

I told them that I am not the best man to secure for them this type of article, as COOPERATION has been since its inception strictly anti-Nazi and in Berlin they know quite well that during the past years this organisation was a centre of the most prominent democratic and anti-Nazi statesmen of the free countries. Nevertheless, I was obliged to promise the "New York Herald Tribune" that I would try to get for them one or two German articles.

As I have never had any contact with Germany since the Nazis came into power, I went to see M. George Bonnet, who was then Foreign Minister, and M. de Ferera, who was then acting Head of the Press Department of the French Foreign Office. I told them about these requests from America and some neutral countries and asked them what I should do. We all smiled and Bonnet said: "Go ahead", naturally "avec prudence". After that I wrote a letter to the Press Attaché of the German Embassy in Paris and had a talk with him. He received me with the remark that I was the greatest enemy of Germany and that nobody was doing more harm to their reputation in the international press than I. I said that I was very sorry, but that I could not change that, but there was a unique opportunity for them, as some American and neutral papers were asking for German articles, and I would be prepared to transmit them. Needless to say that <u>nothing</u> came out of these conversations and I have one or two letters and have had two or three telephone conversations on this subject.

This was my only, and unsuccessful, contact with the Nazis since the Storm Troopers occupied my office in Berlin on the 1st April 1933 and I had to flee from Germany in the clothes I stood in, just saving my life. Since then the only Germans with whom I have had personal contacts have been the anti-Nazi leaders, Thomas Mann, Prof. George Bernhard, Dr. Rauschning and the others. It is really amusing sometimes to see misunderstandings arise of a kind which one expects to find only in cheap Hollywood films. I shall see whether this is the cause of the mystery.

When I started COOPERATION in 1930, Dr. Beneš made enquiries as to whether I was a Hungarian revisionist and the Hungarians were convinced that I was paid by the Czechs. Many democratic Germans at that time thought that I was an agent of the Quai d'Orsay and in Paris they thought that I was a Fascist propagandist. Senator Borah said in the lobby of the Senate in Washington in 1934 that I was an agent of the League of Nations and that my aim was to bring the United States into the League. All this was quite natural at the beginning, as I had published many controversial views and had been travelling constantly from one country to another. But for the last five years I have never heard any stories of this kind.

As to my 'communistic tendencies', I think they are exactly as ridiculous as all the others. I am a capitalist, or at least I would like to be one! In any case, I am a 100% individualist and hate with my whole heart any form of collective regime, under which I could not exist. I think my whole life and career is indisputable proof of that.

To connect me with the brother of one of my secretaries is completely absurd. I engage and keep my employees for the qualities of their personal work and have no idea of the political convictions of members of their families. In any case I have never met this man in my life. I only know that the girl, before she came to me, had been the secretary general of the "Petit Journal" for many years, as long as that paper belonged to Louis Loucheur, and that besides COOPERATION she has an important position to-day in the official Havas agency. She is an unusually intelligent and trustworthy person and all my French statesmen-contributors and newspaper editors in Paris are on friendly terms with her.

By a strange coincidence I have been able to get some information about this man—whom, as I have told you, I have never met—this evening already. One of the Directors of the Havas agency, M. Léon Rollin, is staying at the Savoy and I asked him whether he knew anything about the brother of our common collaboratress. He replied that the man was indeed a Municipal Councillor in Paris, but was among the first members of the Communist Party who publicly resigned immediately after the conclusion of the Russo-German pact, publishing a violent article against this volte-face of Stalin. He has joined the army on the first day of the mobilization and is at the moment a lieutenant of the French army somewhere in the Maginot Line. Well, I think this man cannot be such a criminal, but I shall enquire further as soon as I get back to Paris. I hope to be back in London in a few days.

Yours very sincerely,
E. Révész[2]

1. Churchill saw Reves at the Admiralty.
2. This is the first time that Reves signed a letter to Churchill using the initial
"E" for Emery (as opposed to Imre). For a short while the two initials were inter-
changeable. In 1940 he used the surname "Reves" for the first time (see the memorandum of 31 January 1940).

Winston S. Churchill: engagement cards

24 October 1939

4.30   Dr. Revesz.

Kathleen Hill to Winston S. Churchill

28 October 1939

Mr. Churchill,

MI5 telephoned to me this morning to say that he gave instructions to all
the ports to let Dr. Revesz through, but unfortunately he forgot to tell the
officials at Heston Airport with the result that Dr. Revesz papers were taken
away from him there. However he was allowed to proceed, and the papers are
being forwarded to me, as Dr. Revesz asked for this to be done. Apparently
the papers are unimportant—probably literary matter. MI5 apologises to you
for the omission.

K. Hill

Emery Reves to Winston S. Churchill[1]

3 November 1939   Paris
Strictly Confidential

Dear Mr. Churchill,

The mystery has been completely cleared. All the French politicians
whom I have seen (Maurice Sarraut, Léon Blum, Yvon Delbos, Flandin, Paul
Reynaud, Georges Bonnet, and various high officials at the Quai d'Orsay and
the Information Ministry) were simply shocked and amazed. Expressions like
"stupéfiant", "comique" were their reactions.

M. Berthoin, the Secretary General of the Ministry of the Interior (the
head of all the French police and information services) has personally led the
"enquête" in contact with the Deuxième Bureau. This morning M. Léon
Blum who has spoken several times to M. Berthoin during the week, telephoned to me that the enquiry has already been closed and that—as I have
thought immediately—there is nothing except my visit and telephone calls
to the German Embassy which I have undertaken on behalf of the American
and Scandinavian newspapers. A subaltern agent who is listening to the tele-

phone calls and who has no idea about Cooperation and about what I am
doing has made a remark in my "dossier". And this was sufficient. All the
French statesmen felt rather humiliated by this "gaffe" of that famous
"Bureau". The whole story is a kind of a miniature affaire Dreyfus with all
those well-known expressions: "soupçon" "Deuxième Bureau", "Ambassade
d'Allemagne", etc . . .

I cannot tell you how grateful I am that you have drawn my attention to
this funny affair so that I was able to clear the situation at once. Otherwise,
that "soupçon" would have remained in my "dossier" until the end of my
life. (Some months ago Herriot suggested the "Légion d'Honneur" for me.
It was supported by the Foreign Ministry and by most of the political leaders.
All of a sudden the procedure stopped and nobody understood why. Now
we know.)

There was some discussion here about how you should be informed of the
clearing up of this mistake. They came to the conclusion that the best way is
if the Deuxième Bureau who has committed the error transmits the rectifica-
tion officially in the same address in which they have sent the first and erroneous information.

M. Berthoin has remitted a final report yesterday which is more than a
complete rehabilitation, it is a real eulogy. . . . I have heard something about
this note which ends with this phrase: "Si Révesz n'existait pas il devrait être
inventé."

As far as I am informed the official communication will be sent to London
today or to-morrow. I shall try to arrange that you shall receive a copy of it
while you are in Paris.

Could you possibly arrange to see me for a few moments? I have worked
out a detailed memorandum about what we ought to do immediately in all
the neutral countries. I also had already first contacts with our friends in
some of the neutral countries who would all most heartily welcome such an
action.

I am really anxious to have a short talk with you on that subject as it is
obvious that nothing will be done by bureaucrats and Ministries and that
everything must be done by a few men.

Please do let me know whether you can spare a moment for me.

with all my thanks,
Yours very sincerely,
I. Révész

1.   Churchill stayed that night at the Ritz Hotel, Paris.

Kathleen Hill to Winston S. Churchill

13 November 1939

Mr. Churchill,
    Dr. Revesz is inquiring whether you would agree to his handling the
WORLD CRISIS articles now appearing in the SUNDAY CHRONICLE in
the United States British Empire and foreign countries.
    If so, may I write him a letter to this effect?[1]

K.H.

    1.   Churchill told Kathleen Hill, "I will see him."

Kathleen Hill to Winston S. Churchill

24 November 1939

Mr. Churchill,
    Dr. Revesz is coming to England next week.
    Meanwhile, (1) do you give him permission to handle the WORLD CRI-
SIS articles now appearing in the SUNDAY CHRONICLE? If so, may I tell
them to put the copyright line at the end of each future article?[1]
    (2) May I inquire from the Home Office what has happened about his
naturalization, as he has heard nothing?[2]

K.H.

    1.   Kathleen Hill noted above "SUNDAY CHRONICLE," "Done." Churchill
noted against this paragraph, "Yes."
    2.   Churchill noted against this paragraph, "Yes."

Winston S. Churchill: engagement cards

11 December 1939

    11 a.m.   Revesz.

Winston S. Churchill: engagement cards

14 December 1939

    4.15 p.m.   Revesz.

Wilbur Forrest[1] *to Winston S. Churchill*

20 December 1939   New York

Dear Mr. Winston Churchill:

As assistant editor of the Herald Tribune I have kept in close touch with Dr. Revesz and Cooperation, Inc. for a considerable time. Doubtless you have been advised that we decided to discontinue the service of Cooperation, Inc. on December 12, three months short of actual contract expiration.

I am writing to acquaint you with the circumstances attending this decision because Dr. Revesz offered at the last moment some articles by you which he described as having been written before the war. These articles were not received in New York at the time they were offered due to atmospheric difficulties and did not appear here prior to December 12. However, as early as September 25 I wrote to Dr. Revesz acquainting him with our desire to invoke a clause in our contract which anticipating war would obviously render it impossible for you and for Mr. Eden to continue your collaboration. This collaboration was considered by us the backbone of the service. With such articles we were able to build up syndicate participation with other important newspapers. Unfortunately the war wrecked the syndicate sale and rendered the service of no great value to us. Another contributor valuable from a sales viewpoint was Signor Gayda of Italy. The war also cancelled his articles. Dr. Revesz continued to send articles by lesser known personalities, some of them entirely unknown and devoid of public interest. Naturally our syndicate clients dropped out one by one.

We regretted very much to be obliged to cancel the service, a situation created by the war—a veritable misfortune of war—and due to no fault of Dr. Revesz. This has been adequately explained to Dr. Revesz in correspondence and we are sorry that he feels some injustice has been done. Under the circumstances, however, we desire to acquaint you with the facts and to say that at some later time we would again be interested in articles from you.

May I emphasize that the success of the Cooperation Service largely depended upon your articles which were current and very close to the news. We were very glad to have them and, as you know, they were given first page prominence. The service began in trying times and was then of great value. You will no doubt join with me in regretting that it became a casualty of the war.

Sincerely yours,
Wilbur Forrest

1.   Assistant Editor of the *New York Herald Tribune*.

PART TWO

~

MEETING THE DEMANDS OF WAR
1940–1944

NEGOTIATING THE WAR MEMOIRS
1945–1946

PREPARING THE WAR MEMOIRS
1947–1955

BUSINESS AND FRIENDSHIP
1956–1964

MEETING THE DEMANDS
OF WAR

~

1940 – 1944

Winston S. Churchill: engagement cards

18 January 1940

    10 a.m.   Dr. Revesz.

Emery Reves to Winston S. Churchill

23 January 1940

Lansdowne House,
Berkeley Square,
London W.1

Dear Mr. Churchill,

I think your last broadcast has an historic importance.[1] It is the first time that a leading Allied statesman has had the courage to tell the truth publicly to the so-called neutral nations. I am persuaded that this broadcast is the beginning of very important developments since it is a signal to start a movement in all the neutral countries to change their utterly immoral and unreasonable attitude.

But the first reactions in most of these countries show what a great work has yet to be done before they will open their eyes and gain the courage to do their duty.

I was all the more happy to listen to your words as you will certainly remember that when I came over in the first week of the war I told you that from the point of view of propaganda our enemies are not the Germans but the neutrals. You corrected me: "Let us not say 'our enemies' but 'our objectives'."

Since the very first day of the war, I have been convinced that one of the most important battlefields of this war lies in the neutral countries and that on that battlefield only energetic offensives can lead to success. But victory on that battlefield means a saving of millions of men and a shortening of the war.

I have for several months had complete plans of what we ought to do in this respect <u>inside</u> these countries, which is the only effective method. I cannot and will not discuss these ideas with anyone except you and I am anxiously waiting for that opportunity.

Nobody appreciates more than I how valuable your time is but now I feel it is my duty to disturb you and to ask you to give me 15–20 minutes to explain these plans to you. I have no other argument to support this request than the belief that during the years in which I have had the honour of collaborating with you, you probably have gained the impression that no idea has any value for me unless it can be transformed into practical reality.

Please let me know whether you can spare me these few moments, for which I have been waiting for several months and for which I am only insisting because I am persuaded that they will lead to concrete results similar to those of all our past conversations.

With all my thanks,
Yours very sincerely,
I. Révész

1.   In his broadcast on 20 January 1940, Churchill said of the neutral states, "Each one hopes that if he feeds the crocodile enough, the crocodile will eat him last. All of them hope that the storm will pass before their turn comes to be devoured. But I fear, I fear greatly, the storm will not pass. It will rage and it will roar, even more loudly, even more widely. It will spread to the South; it will spread to the North."

Winston S. Churchill to Kathleen Hill

[25 January 1940]

Ask him to write the outline.

Emery Reves to Winston S. Churchill

31 January 1940   Lansdowne House,
                                                   Berkeley Square,
                                                   London W.1.

I am submitting enclosed a short memorandum. This memorandum outlines merely the start of an organisation which could be created immediately and which ought to be the nucleus of further activities.

I believe the proper diagnosis of the disease is the following: Since the last war and after the establishment of the League, the small countries believed that Europe was now organised for a long period and that the victorious powers would rule and lead Europe under the Covenant. For more than a decade they have been lulled into this feeling of security.

The series of events since 1931, Manchuria, Abyssinia, Rhineland, Spain, Austria, Czechoslovakia, Lithuania, Poland and now the Baltic countries and

Finland has thrown these countries first into a state of disillusionment and then into one of terror. They feel that to become an ally of Great Britain or of France is a kind of suicide. First they felt that we do not want to help them and now they even believe that we cannot help them.

Their present state of mind is that of pathological fear and they will go on "feeding the crocodile" as long as we do not cure them of that fear and until we are able to inoculate them with the conviction that we are a stronger animal or that under certain circumstances they themselves might be stronger than the crocodile.

This pathological state of fear, which is the only explanation of the "neutrality" of at least twelve European countries, is fostered by the microbe of German propaganda, which has reached every organ of these states.

Having consulted many representatives of these countries I am convinced that the only method of cure is to produce and to inoculate urgently the counter-poison.

We have to persuade these nations that the reason why we have allowed this series of crimes by the totalitarian powers during the past eight years was that we wanted and hoped to avoid war. But now we <u>are</u> at war for purely moral reasons, and that changes the situation entirely.

We have failed to organise collective security in the past because we have been reluctant to accept the risk of a war. If we do not succeed in organising it now, <u>during</u> this war, which is being fought to punish aggression, collective security will be most difficult, if not impossible, to organise afterwards.

We have to create organisations and local movements <u>inside</u> each of these countries under the direction of prominent leaders of each nation. They would have to carry out a constant activity, for certain ideas and against certain dangers, in the press, in the cinema, on the radio, in pamphlets, in public meetings and on the most important field of all, private relations. They must throw light on every German propaganda activity in the country and produce immediately the necessary riposte. We have to see that every German bluff should be understood as such and that information about the strength of the Allies should reach every neutral citizen, since the first step towards getting them on our side is to convince them that there can be no doubt about the outcome of this war.

I am afraid that if I were to outline here all details, all possibilities and all the action necessary, this letter would contain hundreds of pages. So, although I am convinced that no plan and no principle, particularly on this highly delicate psychological field of influencing foreign masses, has any value and that only the day to day work and practical results count, I should like to re-state my ideas in a few principles:

1. If we want to shorten the war, to make the blockade completely effective and to lay the foundations of a future Europe, we shall have to win the neutral countries of Europe over to our side.
2. To achieve that aim, a very widespread activity is necessary, adapted

to the local conditions in each country and covering the press, radio, public meetings, the armies, the political parties, the churches, social life and private relations.

3. In order to be effective, these movements, though directed by a few men charged by the Allied powers, must grow up inside each of the neutral countries and must be everywhere a national movement against foreign domination, military oppression, economic exploitation and cultural dependence and must be for national independence, political freedom, security and European organisation.

4. These movements have not only to meet in every country the German propaganda and to make it ineffective, but they have also to initiate and to carry out with the utmost energy and determination on all fields, offensives for certain positive ideas and concrete aims. It is obviously not enough to fight against the monstrous Nazi lies and bestiality, but it is also essential to proclaim a new European Credo to carry with us all those many millions who would follow us if they could believe that we are truly leading them.

5. To challenge the Nazi influence and to destroy it in all the neutral countries is an all the more urgent task as we have to prevent the possibility that Germany, during the military lull, may organise, though by terroristic methods, an economic unit stretching from the Arctic to the Black Sea and from the Rhineland to the Urals.

Yours very sincerely,
I. Révész

Emery Reves to Winston S. Churchill

31 January 1940

MEMORANDUM

The situation in the neutral countries is becoming more and more dangerous and there are increasing difficulties in publishing British or Allied articles in the neutral press. I have just received personal messages from three leading newspaper editors in Sweden, Denmark and Yugoslavia informing me that they are under such pressure that for the time being they are unable to publish articles signed by British or French writers.

Whenever a British article appears in a neutral newspaper an immediate démarche is made by the German diplomatic representation, followed by menaces of severe counter-measures in the economic or political sphere. This constant German pressure makes the Governments of the small neutral countries jittery and they urge their newspapers not to publish any British views, in order to avoid further German steps. This pressure on behalf of Germany is not counterbalanced by any Allied pressure, so that the newspapers cannot but yield, against their feelings, to this German interpretation of "neutrality".

In order to overcome this situation, more subtle methods must be applied. In all the neutral countries there are a great many leading statesmen, publicists and newspaper publishers who are the devoted friends of the Allied Powers. The activity of these people must be directed and organized in the neutral press and radio.

Four organizations ought to be created in order to foster this activity:

1) in Scandinavia
2) in the Central European and Balkan countries
3) in North America
4) in South America.

The aim of these organizations ought to be to gather the leading statesmen and publicists as well as the most important newspapers in the respective areas in order to facilitate and arrange the widest possible diffusion of articles, views and comments by pro-Allied neutral writers. It is almost impossible for a Danish paper, for instance, to publish an article by a British statesman, but they could all publish articles by Finnish or Swedish statesmen. The Russo-Finnish war, for instance, the submarine warfare etc. etc. all give ample opportunity to launch a wide campaign in the northern countries against Nazism and the possibilities are great, provided that the action is made by the neutrals themselves. Such Scandinavian views and signed articles could be much more easily published also in the other neutral areas such as the Balkans and the two Americas.

The great fear of Nazism and Bolshevism existing in the south-eastern countries of Europe could easily be exploited, for they have all been brought together in their emergency, trying to form a neutral block. It is impossible at the moment for a Hungarian or Yugoslavian newspaper to publish a British article, but they would be glad to publish a mutual interchange of views and the Yugoslavian press is prepared to publish Turkish, Greek or Rumanian views. But in order for this to be effective there must be an efficient organization in the area, under local leaders, to promote these diffusions.

There is only one certain way to influence the Central and South American public and this is through Spanish and South American writers. COOPERATION has already arranged the diffusion of pro-Allied Spanish views in the South American press with considerable success. This method ought to be extended and an efficient organization created for the diffusion of the views of leading pro-Allied Spanish and South American statesmen and publicists in the South American press.

As to the United States, any direct propaganda must have a reaction contrary to the interests of the Allied cause. But between such an obviously erroneous propaganda and complete inactivity there is a large field and great opportunities of extending influence. But again, it is essential that this should be done by Americans and other neutrals and should not be regarded as official British propaganda. There are many people in the United States who could arrange that instead of Col. Lindbergh such Americans should more frequently broadcast whose views are favourable to the democracies and to the Allied cause. There is also much to be done in the American film and press in order to avoid that most dangerous of all American attitudes: boredom and apathy towards the European struggle. It is needless to say that within these channels British views and the statements of British statesmen should be diffused according to the possibilities at any given moment.

COOPERATION, through its existing relations and friendships in all these countries, could undertake in a very short time the organization of this drive to influence the neutral public all over the world in a favourable sense for the Allied cause. There are about 20–30 leading public men in these countries and about 50–60 great newspapers closely attached to COOPERATION who could form a nucleus for a rapidly developing movement. It is obvious that full success in this field can only be obtained by very discreet approaches, but at the same time with incessant activity, which must be adapted to the local conditions in each country.

The object of any Franco-British propaganda is to attempt to abridge the war and to secure an ultimate victory while economising to the utmost human life and by facilitating the task of the armies by obtaining the support for the Allies of the public opinion of the greatest possible number of countries.

In any kind of propaganda, there are two objectives:

a) to try to dislocate Germany by preparing the fall of the Hitlerian system from the inside,

b) to gain for the Allied cause the support of all neutral countries and thus to make effective the blockade and the isolation of Germany.

The situation of most of the neutral countries—the majority of whose population is whole-heartedly in favour of an Allied victory, but, owing to its fear of Germany, supplies the latter with raw materials and foodstuffs—is so absurd and contradictory that the chances for the success of really clever propaganda are very great. In any case, it would seem worth while to devote a thousandth part of the military expenditure as an insurance for the remaining 999 parts and for the lives of millions of men.

In this war, there is a new factor, which cannot possibly compare with the situation that prevailed from 1914 to 1918, and it would seem that this "fourth arm", if well organized (avoiding direct propaganda, which is doomed in advance to failure) would produce a considerable effect. However things may be, after five months of war, it is evident that our inactivity in neutral countries is an immense error, for it leaves the field free for German pressure and creates in the mass of the neutral populations a feeling of lassitude and indifference—the most dangerous of all situations.

The reaction to Mr. Churchill's broadcast appeal to the neutrals on January 20th proves what an immense and urgent work is necessary in the neutral countries before they will have the courage to proclaim openly what their real feelings are and to take an attitude corresponding to their interests. It is our duty to arouse the conscience of every citizen of the neutral countries to this axiom of any social order: "Those who have the moral capacity to recognize the wrong, and tolerate it, are more guilty than the criminal who commits it."

It is a most dangerous belief, that German propaganda has failed because the sentiments of the civilized world are against Nazism. The fact that this band of gangsters was able to provoke a world war, the fact that they have obliged the British and French Empires to mobilize all their resources, the fact that they have forced about fifteen European countries to be neutral and to supply them with foodstuffs and raw materials, are incredible successes for the German propaganda machine.

To challenge this work in all the neutral countries, to beat these German offensives and to reconquer for Europe all these powers, seems to be an immediate and most important task, at least as long as military operations on a large scale do not develop. It is commonsense, that on the military battlefields the defensive is the right strategy for the time being, but on the battlefield of ideas the defensive is already identical with defeat and only constant and vigorous offensives can lead to success.

E. Reves[1]

1. This is the first letter I have found in which Reves used under his signature the typed version "E. Reves" instead of "I. Révész."

Winston S. Churchill to Sir John Reith[1]

8 February 1940

My dear Reith,

I venture to send you a copy of a letter which I sent to Lord Macmillan about Mr. E. Révész. I will not repeat the arguments used in the letter, as they speak for themselves.

Révész is now in London, and I strongly hope some use may be made of him. I can speak from personal experience of his altogether exceptional abilities and connections.

Yours sincerely,
Winston S. Churchill

1. Sir John Reith, former Director-General of the BBC, had succeeded Lord Macmillan as Minister of Information on 5 January 1940. Churchill gave him no place in his wartime administration, formed on 10 May 1940.

Kathleen Hill to Miss Wall [1]

12 February 1940   Admiralty

Dear Miss Wall,

Many thanks for your letter of the 10th telling me of Mr. Emery Reves' naturalization.

The First Lord wishes me to thank you personally for all the trouble you have taken in this matter.

Yours sincerely,
[Kathleen Hill]
Personal Private Secretary

1.   Miss Wall, Nationality Division, Home Office, Cleland House, Page Street, Westminster.

Sir John Reith to Winston S. Churchill

21 February 1940   Ministry of Information,
Senate House,
London University Building,
Malet Street
London W.C.1.

Dear First Lord,

A line to say that I had half-an-hour yesterday with Mr. Revesz. I think myself that he should be able to help us and I am having the possibilities looked into at once.

Yours ever,
J. C. W. Reith

Emery Reves to Kathleen Hill

23 February 1940   Lansdowne House,
Berkeley Square,
London W.1 [1]

Dear Mrs. Hill,

I am expecting now any hour my Certificate of Naturalization which is under signature. As soon as I receive the certificate I must apply for a passport.

As you know one of the reasons why Mr. Churchill has supported my naturalization was that I shall be able to travel in all the neutral countries and work like before the war. I was unable to travel since the war and it is high time for me to see what can be done in all those countries where under German pressure the press cannot publish any British views at present.

For this purpose I need a passport valid for all European countries (except Germany and Russia of course) and for U.S.A. In view of the fact that there are some difficulties in getting a passport valid for several countries and for some longer period, I would be most grateful if you would ask Mr. Churchill whether he would be so kind and advise the Passport Office to give me such a passport.[2] This is absolutely indispensable for the carrying out of my activities.

Yours very sincerely,
E. Reves

1.   Reves's notepaper was headed: "Cooperation Press Service, 77 Chancery Lane, Fleet Street, London WC2."
2.   Churchill's comment on this request, as noted by Kathleen Hill, was "no."

Emery Reves to Winston S. Churchill[1]

10 May 1940
Personal
Strictly Confidential

CONVERSATION WITH FRITZ THYSSEN[2] IN MONTE CARLO ON MAY 10TH 1940

The attack upon Holland, Belgium and Luxemburg has made a considerable impression on Thyssen. He refused to believe that this was true.

Up to the present, he states, the German High Command had definitely opposed such an operation. Even Nazi generals, like Reichenau, had formally advised Hitler to abstain from invading the Netherlands and Belgium.

Thyssen cannot understand why the High Command has yielded this time. According to him, there must be very serious internal reasons, in particular economic. The lack of iron ore, in his opinion, has compelled the German smelting works to reduce their production to one-third of their capacity.

Thyssen is quite definite in regard to the Russians. At present, it is impossible to speak of an effective assistance on their part; and this will probably continue to be the case owing to their bad will and their lack of means.

Why were the generals opposed to this operation?

Here again, THYSSEN is quite definite. The number of equipped German divisions, he says, does not exceed 100 to 150. This is less than is generally believed.

I adduced the figure of five or six million men under arms. Thyssen told me that this was materially impossible; impossible in five years to manufacture the rifles, uniforms, boots and other material for a larger number. The equipment, he considers, cannot now be speeded up; for this, the resources are lacking.

From the point of view of effectives, Germany has not enough active officers and, in particular, not a sufficient number of non-commissioned officers;
these, owing to the character of the German soldier, continue to constitute
the backbone of the German army.

As for war material, Thyssen regards the present output and stocks as
inadequate. The manufacture of cannon, he says—and he is in a position to
know—only really began at Krupp's a year and a half ago. It is true that there
are now special types of steel in which tubes can be turned out more rapidly,
but the rate of production is nonetheless limited. Virtually all that remained
over from 1918 has been scrapped.

I raised the question of Skoda. Thyssen has no information on this
subject.

In the artillery, he says, as in all special arms, there is the question of
trained officers and non-commissioned officers.

The sole branch in which Thyssen regards the German efforts as adequate
is the air force. Chain production began with the year 1936. He makes certain reservations with regard to personnel. Owing to the need for economising gasoline, it has been impossible to give the latter the proper training.
In the air, he says, the difficulty of replacing the crews is the same as for the
U. boats.

Thyssen has, he says, information to the effect that, up to a quite recent
date, the German General Staff wished to do all in its power to avoid war on
the Western front including the overthrow of the regime. On this point he
was extremely reserved. But I finally succeeded in drawing from him the
statement that a certain person "whose name, if known, would come as a
surprise", had been accredited by the General Staff to enter into contact with
British circles. He does not know to what extent it has been possible to carry
out this scheme, but he was quite taken aback by the offensive on the Western front, by which all these plans are reduced to naught.

The generals, he says, would accept a war circumscribed as in Poland or
in Norway. This, from the technical standpoint, was the maximum responsibility they could assume. Thyssen told me quite definitely that he "had never
spoken to any general of sound principles who had told me that Germany
could get away with this war. Hence the absolute desire to conclude a peace
before the beginning of the war". Thyssen added "I do not believe that Germany can be victorious. Every effort should have been made to come to
terms before the real outbreak of the war. For now, the generals, not Chamberlain, would have the final word to say, and they would be less easy to deal
with than Chamberlain. Germany had everything to gain by Chamberlain's
presence in office, for he had a horror of war and would have made sacrifices
to avoid it".

Who is the mysterious intermediary to whom Thyssen refers? Dr. Schacht?

Not impossible. An interesting detail in connection with the anonymous go-between is that he carries with him on his person a poison which causes instant death and never leaves him.

Of this conversation, there are two essential points to be retained: the first is that, according to Thyssen, Hitler has perhaps the means of sustaining one "battle of material" like that of the Somme during the last war, but no more. The other is that, up to a quite recent date, attempts have been made by the German generals to negotiate a peace.

E. Reves

1. This memorandum was written on the day that Germany invaded Holland, Belgium, and France; the day on which Churchill became Prime Minister. On reading the memorandum, Churchill sent it to his principal intelligence adviser, Major Desmond Morton, who initialed it "DM." Churchill circled the figure 100 to 150 (equipped German divisions).

2. Fritz Thyssen, a German industrialist, had been one of Hitler's first financial backers, giving Hitler and the Nazi Party enormous sums of money from as early as 1923. In 1938 he resigned from the Prussian Council of State in protest against Hitler's anti-Jewish policies. He left Germany for Switzerland in December 1939, writing a letter to Hitler protesting against both the coming of war and the persecution of the Jews. Five weeks later he was stripped of his German nationality. Arrested by the Germans in France in June 1940, he was interned in various concentration camps until the end of the war.

Emery Reves to Winston S. Churchill

14 May 1940   Paris

Dear Mr. Churchill,

I cannot tell you how happy I was when I heard on the radio that the obvious has at last happened and that you have formed the Government. Everybody, on both sides of the barricade, knows that this means the beginning of our victory.

I was in Monte-Carlo on that day working with Fritz Thyssen on a manuscript which, I think, will be of great political importance. Besides many revelations, Thyssen, the greatest German industrialist and nationalist, the man who has organized passive resistance in the Ruhr in 1923 and was condemned by the French Court Martial, the man who has financed the Nazi movement and who has put Hitler into power, will publicly proclaim that there is only one way to get peace in Europe: the partition of Germany! Thyssen comes to this conclusion through purely German reasoning which is extremely interesting. I think that this document by Thyssen, well exploited, will make a great effect in Germany and in the neutral countries.

I am sending you enclosed a memorandum of my conversations with Thyssen about the German attack on Holland and Belgium. This conversation has taken place immediately after the aggression started. This was a private conversation which he did not authorise me to publish, but I am communicating to you his observations believing that Thyssen belongs to those few people who know exactly the position of German armaments and industrial production.

I should be most grateful if I could give you some more information about this work, but I am even more anxious to have an opportunity to submit to you some plans concerning our propaganda war. Since September last I was urging to create in each neutral country special organizations to counter-act German propaganda and to conquer public opinion in each country by appropriate means. Nobody has taken me seriously except yourself. The people who have been responsible for the Allied propaganda have still believed that propaganda means publishing pamphlets and delivering broadcasts. I think the events in Denmark, Norway, Holland and Belgium have shown the diabolic nature and the tremendous efficiency of this new weapon. We have to save these countries now with the blood of our soldiers without even having made the attempt to conquer them by less expensive weapons. There are still countries where we ought to challenge this German activity which is obviously the preparation for a military offensive; but this is not a literary work, this is war.

I hope you will understand my feelings. Since the first day of the war I have clearly seen where this German "white war" will lead, but as a private individual I was unable to do anything. With Rauschning and Thyssen I have furnished two documents which have been for several months the basis of the propaganda activity of the Ministries of Information in London and Paris. But all this is nothing. This warfare, the only field on which the Germans are superior to us (and this is the reason why they are making it), has raised some questions the decision of which belongs to the competency of the War Cabinet.

I do hope that the events will permit you to spare me one day twenty minutes and to allow me to explain to you some very concrete plans in which I believe.

I shall be in London next week, but I would naturally come over with the next plane should you let me know by a telegram that you can arrange this appointment.

I beg to remain,
Yours very sincerely,
E. Reves

P.S.—I am rushing now the publication in France of your Life Story in book form.[1] I hope it will be on the market at the beginning of June.

---

1.   Churchill's account of his childhood, school, and army days, *My Early Life*, first published in Britain in 1930, had been published in France in 1937. No 1940 edition is known.

Kathleen Hill to Winston S. Churchill

18 May 1940   10 Downing Street

Mr. Churchill,

This is a long letter from Mr. Reves, but I think you will be interested
to read at least the <u>enclosure</u>.

K.H.

Desmond Morton to Winston S. Churchill

23 May 1940   10 Downing Street

Prime Minister,

I have sent a copy of Mr. Rever's[1] conversation with Fritz Thyssen,
attached to his letter, to the Ministry of Economic Warfare as a Secret document, asking them to communicate it in secret to the Directors of Naval,
Military and Air Intelligence.

In his letter to you, Mr. Rever states he has some concrete plans for coun-
tering German propaganda, that he will be in London this week and hopes to
see you. Doubtless you will instruct your Private Secretary how you wish to
reply to this.

Returning to the Fritz Thyssen conversation, my reactions are that there
is a good deal in what Thyssen says about the war economic situation in Germany, but it would be a mistake to put too much weight on the obviously
optimistic features of his account.

D.M.

1.   From Reves's written signature it was easy to misread "Reves" as "Rever."

Kathleen Hill to Winston S. Churchill

25 May 1940   10 Downing Street

Mr. Churchill,

I propose acknowledging Mr. Reves' letter, saying you have read it with
interest.

But what may I say in regard to his visit to London, and his wish to see
you, please?

K.H.

Winston S. Churchill to Kathleen Hill

25 May 1940

disengage[1]

1. Churchill and the War Cabinet were confronted that week by the rapid advance of German forces through northern France, and the need to evacuate the British Expeditionary Force from the Channel ports. The Dunkirk evacuation began on 29 May 1940. On May 31, Churchill had to go to Paris for a meeting of the Supreme War Council.

Kathleen Hill to Emery Reves

6 June 1940   10 Downing Street

Dear Doctor Reves,

I am sorry that I have not had time until now to acknowledge your letter of May 14. I passed on the letter you enclosed to the Prime Minister, and he read it with interest.

At the request of your London office I send herewith the following photographs for the forthcoming French edition of Mr. Churchill's autobiography:—

1. Mr. Churchill made a prisoner by the Boers. November 1899.
2. In the South African Light Horse, 1899.

I have had these prints done for you, so you need not trouble to return them.

I also enclose, in case you might like to have it, a photograph of Mr. Churchill taken outside the garden gate of No. 10 Downing Street. This was reproduced on the cover of 'Picture Post' of May 25 last, and you would have to arrange with Planet News Ltd. about the copyright.

Yours very truly,
[Kathleen Hill]
Personal Private Secretary

Kathleen Hill to Winston S. Churchill

7 June 1940   10 Downing Street

Mr. Churchill,

Shall I ask Mr. Reves to render an account? He has not sent a cheque since the beginning of the war.

K.H.

Winston S. Churchill to Kathleen Hill

7 June 1940   10 Downing Street

Yes

Kathleen Hill to Winston S. Churchill

[end June 1940]   10 Downing Street

Is now evacuated from France
has lost all his money.

K.H.

Winston S. Churchill to Alfred Duff Cooper [1]

30 June 1940

Minister of Information,
I have long thought very highly of Mr. Reves' abilities in all that concerns
propaganda and the handling of the neutral press. The views he sets forth
here are of great interest, but much is easier said than done.[2] Pray let me
know if he is of any use to you.

W.S.C.

1.   Churchill had appointed Duff Cooper as Minister of Information, in succession to Sir John Reith.
2.   On 24 June 1940, Reves, who was back at Lansdowne House off Berkeley
Square, resubmitted his memorandum of 31 January 1940.

Emery Reves to Winston S. Churchill

10 July 1940   Lansdowne House,
                                                          Berkeley Square,
                                                          London W.1.

Dear Mr. Churchill,
Mr. Duff Cooper told me yesterday that he would like me to go over to
New York and help to build up our propaganda organization in North and
South America.
I would be more than happy to undertake this job and I believe that an
efficient machinery could be built up in a short time. But the problem is not
merely a technical one.
The success of such an offensive depends upon the right combination of
activities which are now carried out not only under the authority of the Ministry of Information but also of the Foreign Office, the Ministry of Economic
Warfare and the Intelligence Service.
It also involves questions of general policy. In my opinion we have two
aims in America:
1) To persuade them that Hitler is directly menacing the American
nations, and he will conquer them one by one, just as he conquered Europe.

This can be achieved through men like Rauschning and Thyssen, who can state authoritatively Hitler's aims in America, and by a very effective Intelligence and News Service, covering the whole American continent, through which we would have to discover and to give very wide publicity in all the American countries of Nazi activities in each American state, menacing their independence.

2) To persuade the Americans that principles like "neutrality," "isolation," "non-intervention," "defence of the national territory but no war abroad," etc, etc . . . —principles which also Great Britain has followed until she was plunged into war and which have also been the principles of some twenty European nations until they were conquered one by one—are principles of a lost world, which lead every nation to the abyss. For this campaign we must use all the political leaders of the former neutral countries, Belgians, Dutch, Norwegians etc., including King Haakon and Queen Wilhelmina.

I feel sure you will understand how grateful I would be if I could have a short conversation with you about these principles of general policy before we start our activities. I do hope therefore that you will be able to help me by giving me an interview before I sail.

I beg to remain,
Yours very sincerely,
E. Reves

Kathleen Hill: note

[after 10 July 1940]   10 Downing Street

I told Dr. Reves over the telephone that Mr. Churchill was too busy to see him, but that he was very glad to hear he had obtained the post.

Winston S. Churchill to Alfred Duff Cooper

19 August 1940

Minister of Information,

I trust you will let me know at an early date the position with regard to the Reves proposal for propaganda in the Americas.

His scheme for one central organisation powerful enough to fight the German machine had strong points, and I hope that you will not allow it to be weakened by official caution.

Please let me know how the matter stands.

W.S.C.

Winston S. Churchill to Alfred Duff Cooper

25 August 1940

Minister of Information,

    1. I had, of course, not read Mr. Reves's scheme, and I am in no way wedded to it. Is it true, however, that Mr. Harcourt Johnstone, Dr. Dalton, &c., were, in principle, in favour of something on these lines? Is it true that the Lord Privy Seal viewed it with favour?[1]

    2. Please, however, see also the note attached by Major Morton. It would seem better to buy up a going concern and to stop it from getting into enemy hands, than to try to build up a new organization of our own. I doubt whether the plan of working up a service through Reuter and L.E.F. will be sufficient. Perhaps you will put the points to Mr. Pick. No one can be content with the present system.

W.S.C.

    1.   Harcourt Johnstone, a leading Liberal and Secretary at the Department of Overseas Trade during Churchill's wartime premiership; Hugh Dalton (Labour), the recently appointed Minister of Economic Warfare; and Clement Attlee, the Labour Party Leader, then Lord Privy Seal.

Emery Reves to Winston S. Churchill

18 September 1940
Lansdowne House
Berkeley Square
London W

Dear Mr. Churchill,

    Last Tuesday night at 2.30 a.m. a 250 pound bomb exploded on the terrace of my flat less than 3 yards from where I was sitting. I cannot describe that moment of death; in a fraction of a second the entire room was in white flames and everything crashed into pieces. I was blown to the floor, have lost my voice and felt tons of weight on me while my dressing gown was already in flames. No-one of the officials who came later in the flat could understand how I was alive.

    I have lost all my fortune in France, but this escape of death was so miraculous that I beg you to accept the enclosed cheque of £250.-.- as my contribution towards our war effort. I wish it could be forged into a bomb and dropped in Germany.[1]

    I had to undergo an operation yesterday to take out a splinter from my hand, but now I am more cheerful than ever, and more anxious than I ever was to do some useful work. I still hope that one day you will find a few moments to receive me and to allow me to explain some ideas which I could not discuss with anybody except you. You must excuse me if I believe that such a short interview might bring more success and satisfaction than all the years during which you have honoured me with your collaboration.

I beg to remain,
Yours very sincerely,
E. Reves

1.   Churchill sent this cheque to the Chancellor of the Exchequer on 19 September 1940.

Emery Reves to Winston S. Churchill

13 November 1940   Lansdowne House,
Berkeley Square,
London W.1

Dear Mr. Churchill,

I have just learnt that a COUNCIL FOR DEMOCRACY has been created in New York under the Chairmanship of William Gram Swing[1] with some 90 leaders on the board and with a program rather close to the views I have expressed in my last letter to you.

I am rather anxious to get in touch with these people as quickly as possible hoping that this might be the nucleus of a useful movement.

It is almost impossible to get a passage on the Clipper without official support. I have had a talk with the American Embassy on the situation. One word from you or from Lord Lothian could arrange everything. If Lord Lothian wanted, he could easily take me over in his party, or arrange an early passage. (Mr. Kennedy[2] has also taken with him some American journalists.)

I wonder whether you feel in a position to help me in this matter. I think I need not say how grateful I would be.

I beg to remain,
Yours very sincerely,
E. Reves[3]

1.   Raymond Gram Swing, a journalist and radio commentator. During the Second World War millions in Britain listened to his four weekly broadcasts from the United States. He was known as the "radio Uncle Sam" of American government policy.

2.   Joseph P. Kennedy, the American Ambassador to Britain from 1937 to 1941 and father of Joseph (killed in action, 1944), Jack (the future President, assassinated in 1963), Robert (a Senator, assassinated in 1968), and Edward, a Senator.

3.   Kathleen Hill marked Reves's letter, "PM to see at leisure," and although Churchill did not reply to it, he did tick it as read.

Kathleen Hill to Winston S. Churchill

14 November 1940   10 Downing Street

Prime Minister,

In this letter Mr. Reves asks if you could help him get a passage on the Clipper for America.

I take it the answer is 'No.'[1]

K.H.

1. Churchill put a tick under Kathleen Hill's second paragraph.

At the end of 1940 Emery Reves left London for New York, where he set up the Cooperation Publishing Company. A year and a half passed before he wrote to Churchill again.

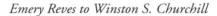

Emery Reves to Winston S. Churchill

17 June 1942   Cooperation Publishing Co., Inc.
                                                    30 Rockefeller Plaza
                                                    New York, N.Y.

Dear Mr. Churchill:

During the past months I have been trying to put on paper some ideas about democratic principles on which I have been pondering for years. It is my conviction that the cause of the second World War lies in the outdated and false interpretation of principles on which our democratic order was and still is based, and not in the weakness or short-sightedness of governments or individuals.

I believe that the peoples must understand clearly <u>why</u> we have been plunged into this second war. We must make plain what these words we use in our political language mean in 20th century terms, in order to avoid the mistakes of 1919. Such an interpretation of principles is attempted in this book.

I have shown this manuscript here to some influential people who persuaded me to print it. It will be published by Random House in a few weeks, under the title of "A Democratic Manifesto." Various Democratic Committees here are gathering signatures for a statement to recommend its wide reading, and the Office of Facts and Figures in Washington wants to secure wide distribution for it.

I very much desire to dedicate this little book to you. Would you do me
the great favor of permitting me to do so, and to print on the front page the
enclosed dedication? It is needless to say how grateful I would be if you could
accept this suggestion.

I am enclosing an airmail copy of the manuscript, and shall take the liberty to dispatch to you by airmail an advance copy of the book as soon as
I get it.

I beg to remain,
Most respectfully yours,
E. Reves

P.S.—In view of the fact that the manuscript goes to press immediately, I
should greatly appreciate it if you would be kind enough to cable me your
decision.

Emery Reves: proposed dedication

[17 June 1942]   New York

To
The Right Honorable
WINSTON S. CHURCHILL
in recollection and gratitude
for our collaboration during those
years when events forced the world
step by step into this war.

Emery Reves to Winston S. Churchill

16 November 1943   New York
Private

Dear Mr. Prime Minister,

A few days ago the New York Times published a letter by me in which I
attempted to define the notion of sovereignty in a democratic world. Among
other reactions this letter had, it was inserted in the Congressional Record by
Senator Ball.

Believing it may interest you, I take the liberty of sending you the page
from the Congressional Record containing my letter.[1]

Yours most respectfully,
E. Reves

1. On 31 October 1943 the *New York Times* published a letter by Reves (later
reprinted in the *Congressional Record*), in which he argued that sovereignty, as existing
in nation states, had "far too narrow a basis; it no longer has the power it should and

was meant to have." Not even the most powerful nation was economically self-sufficient. To preserve peace in the future, elements of national sovereignty "must be vested in and exercised by a single world body."

Emery Reves to Kathleen Hill

16 November 1943   Cooperation Publishing Co., Inc.
                                                         30 Rockefeller Plaza
                                                           New York, N.Y.

Dear Mrs. Hill:
   I should be grateful if by occasion you would be kind enough to submit the enclosed letter to the Prime Minister.
   Hoping that you are well, I am

                                                      With kind regards,
                                                        Yours sincerely,
                                                           E. Reves

Kathleen Hill to Emery Reves

2 January 1944   10 Downing Street

Dear Mr. Reves,
   Your letter of November 16 has been forwarded to me here,[1] and I will certainly hand the enclosures to the Prime Minister at the first suitable opportunity.
   Please accept my best wishes for a happy and prosperous 1944.

                                                        Yours sincerely,
                                                         Kathleen Hill

   1.   Churchill was convalescing at Marrakech, having been taken ill while visiting the troops in North Africa after the Teheran Conference.

NEGOTIATING THE
WAR MEMOIRS

~

1945 – 1946

Emery Reves to Winston S. Churchill: telegram

26 July 1945   30 Rockefeller Plaza
                                                              New York

If you intend resume journalistic activity for world press—hope you
renew prewar collaboration with Cooperation Press Service believe can assure
you better longterm arrangements than any other organization stop From
American magazines could get for special articles much higher rates than you
received before stop Regarding memoirs could make best possible offers both
British American and worldwide book and serial publication stop Trust that
in view our past successful collaboration you will give me chance discuss all
these matters before making other commitments stop Could come London
for negotiations anytime

                                                              Emery Reves

Emery Reves to Kathleen Hill: telegram

26 July 1945   New York

Please convey Mr Churchill my hope he resume collaboration with Cooperation Press Service have also cabled him directly regarding newspaper and
magazine articles book and serial rights memoirs cable possibilities would
come London anytime negotiate regards

Emery Reves to Winston S. Churchill: telegram[1]

31 July 1945   30 Rockefeller Plaza
                                                              New York

If absent please forward urgently stop After several conferences received
offer from Readers Digest for exclusive American magazine rights first series

articles unparalleled publishing history stop Publisher insists figures remain secret stop Wanted telephone you but waiting here several days can you call me Columbus five four eight naught eight or help me quick air passage London stop Urge make no arrangements until this contract considered stop Also have offers from Life et other magazines but no comparison money or influence Digest having fifty million readers stop Also received offers many newspapers dominions Europe South America all old friends hope resume collaboration please cable thanks

Emery Reves

1.   Reves's previous two telegrams had been sent to 10 Downing Street. This one was sent to Chartwell (which Churchill had not used while Prime Minister).

Emery Reves to Winston S. Churchill: telegram [1]

31 July 1945   30 Rockefeller Plaza
New York

Cabled Chartwell unique offer greatest American magazine please consider it before making other decision

1.   This telegram was sent to Claridge's Hotel.

Kathleen Hill to Emery Reves: telegram

2 August 1945   Chartwell
Strictly Private

Mr Churchill thanks you very much for cables but he is not making any plans for writing books or articles at present.

Hill
Secretary

Emery Reves to Winston S. Churchill

8 August 1945   30 Rockefeller Plaza
Private   New York

Dear Mr. Churchill:
   Many thanks for your cable message sent through Mrs. Hill telling me that at present you are not making any plans for writing books or articles. This is natural. But the reason why I sent my cables and why I am writing this letter is to ask you, in case and whenever you decide to write again, not to make any final arrangements regarding books, serial rights or magazine and newspaper articles before you give me a chance to submit to you the proposals I have.

For a long time now, and particularly since your resignation, I have been receiving a great many offers from the U.S.A., the British Empire, Europe and South America. I suppose that many of these offers were also made to you directly.

My attitude toward publishers and editors who make offers to me for your writings in the knowledge of our business relationship before the war, is that although before the war I have handled your articles in the world press, our contracts, just as the contracts I have with all the other statesmen, contained a clause according to which, at the moment you accepted a Government office, the agreements were suspended. I do hope that in case you resume your writing for the public you will continue our collaboration which, I think, you have always regarded as satisfactory. But naturally this is entirely up to you to decide.

Among the many offers received, there is one I followed up with negotiations and to which I should particularly like to draw your attention. This is The Reader's Digest.

You are no doubt aware of the unique power and influence of this magazine which is sold in more than ten million copies and which, with its readership of over fifty million, has a hold over the public incomparable with any other magazine, greater than that of the radio networks or any other opinion molder in America. I know that if the American Government wants to popularize an idea, they first try to get an article published in The Reader's Digest. Also, the huge public buying this magazine is doing so for serious reading matter only, whereas the purchasers of Life, Collier's, The Saturday Evening Post and other magazines buy them mostly to look at pictures and to read fiction, not for serious reading material.

I discussed the matter with the publisher of The Reader's Digest because I feel that if they would print your articles this would give you by far the most powerful tribune at present available in America. The publisher is most anxious to print your articles, and I was able to make him agree to pay you fees which are altogether unprecedented in American publishing history and which I do not think any other publisher could approach. The tentative draft contract I have would secure for you a large yearly amount for priority rights alone in the American magazine field and besides that, a fee per article many times what you have received before the war from American magazines. The publisher insists that the figures he is willing to agree to pay remain an absolute secret and that no American magazine or author ever learn it. Therefore I promised him not to write about it in this letter, but to come over to London to discuss the matter with you personally. I am making preparations for this trip and hope to be in London before the end of this month.[1]

Besides this offer, I have several interesting offers for your memoirs, which everybody hopes you will write, and for short, fortnightly articles on current events such as you wrote before the war, for which I could now assure you a much larger syndicate market than before the war. These include the British press.

I hope that you will be able to discuss with me all these proposals when I am in London in about three weeks. Needless to say, you alone will decide which one you would want to accept or when you would think that the time would be appropriate to start writing.

With kindest regards, I am,
Very sincerely yours,
Emery Reves

1. Kathleen Hill noted on this letter, "To see at leisure."

Emery Reves to Winston S. Churchill

9 August 1945   30 Rockefeller Plaza

Dear Mr. Churchill,

In addition to my letter of August 8th, I should like to communicate to you that regarding the possibility of publishing your war memoirs in America, I have an offer of $100,000 advance payment on a 20% royalty for the book rights alone. The serial rights could, of course, bring many times that amount.

Yours very sincerely,
Emery Reves

Emery Reves to Winston S. Churchill

17 August 1945   30 Rockefeller Plaza

Dear Mr. Churchill:

I should imagine that by now the files containing the offers you have received for your war memoirs or other writings are more voluminous than the files containing all the war documents.

In addition to my previous letters forwarding to you suggestions regarding book and magazine publications, I would merely mention that one of the leading American newspaper syndicates offered me $400,000.- for the American newspaper serial rights of your memoirs. But I think we could do better.[1]

I hope that you have received my new book, THE ANATOMY OF PEACE, a copy of which I dispatched to you several days ago.[2] Since the explosion of the atomic bomb several Senators and other public men— including physicists who actually worked on the atomic fission project— communicated to me that the conclusions reached in THE ANATOMY OF PEACE, which they thought a few weeks ago to be the concern of the future,

became an urgent and immediate necessity if we want to prevent an atomic
world war.

Yours very sincerely,
Emery Reves

1.   It was Churchill who underlined the end of this paragraph, starting at "offered
me $400,000."
2.   Reves's book *The Anatomy of Peace* was a call for world government. Of the
recently created United Nations, he wrote, "We have only gathered together many
sovereignties, and there will be no peace until there is but one sovereignty—that of a
World Order." In his concluding chapter Reves wrote, "Two per cent of the money
and effort spent for research and production of the atomic bomb would be sufficient
to carry out an educational movement that would make clear to the people what the
virus of war is and how peace can be attained in human society."

Emery Reves to Winston S. Churchill

26 October 1945   30 Rockefeller Plaza
                                                          New York

Dear Mr. Churchill,
    A few weeks ago I sent you a copy of my new book THE ANATOMY OF
PEACE which must have reached London when you were in Italy. So I wonder whether you have received it. The reason why I am asking this is that
quite extraordinary things are happening around that book.
    I am enclosing copy of an Open Letter to the American People which has
been signed by 20 of the most prominent Americans—Senators, religious
leaders, labor leaders, industrialists, writers, scientists and war veterans. It was
released last week to the American press by Supreme Court Justice Owen J.
Roberts and was printed in The New York Times, The Washington Post
and about 50 other leading American newspapers. As you see, this open letter
exhorts the American people to read and discuss THE ANATOMY OF
PEACE. This is an altogether unprecedented public action in favor of a
book, which may have very wide repercussions. The letter was also cabled
all over the world by Reuters.[1]
    You have probably read in The Daily Telegraph an article by Professor
Einstein on the political consequences of the atomic bomb. This article
is going to be published here in The Atlantic Monthly and The Reader's
Digest. In this article, Einstein arrives at the conclusion that the political
answer to the atomic bomb can be found in THE ANATOMY OF PEACE.
    I have recently been meeting regularly with the leading nuclear physicists
(Urey, Smythe, Szilard, Shapley, etc.) who are extremely worried about the
discrepancy that exists between scientific and political facts and who, one
after the other, are accepting the thesis of this book.
    The most extraordinary effect this book has had, however, is the conver-
sion of The Reader's Digest. They are going to print three installments in

three consecutive issues from THE ANATOMY OF PEACE, promoting it in a way they have never before promoted a book, calling it "the most significant articles The Digest has published in recent years." In the U.S. edition, these articles will run in the December, January and February issues. It will also be published in the English, Swedish, Finnish, Spanish, Portuguese and Arabic editions, in a total of over 12 million copies, carrying the argument of this book to 50–60 million people.

I am mentioning all this to tell you the reason I had to postpone my trip to London. I do hope, however, that I shall be able to depart soon as I have many important things to tell you.

This week I have had several conversations with the head of a four-hundred million dollar American corporation who recalls a great baccarat fight he had with you in 1935 or 1936 at Cannes. He and some others are extremely worried about the increasing deterioration in Anglo-American relations and the growing lack of understanding of Britain's position and policies. There is one man, and one man alone, who could change this trend and to whom every American would listen. This man is you. They have therefore asked me to submit to you the following proposition:

They would hire the greatest possible radio network in the best possible time once a week for fifteen minutes if you wanted to speak weekly to the American people. You would have entire freedom to say whatever you want, you would not have to submit your script in advance to anybody, and before each broadcast this fact of your complete and total independence would be announced. They would suggest a one-year contract—longer if you want—and would pay you $10,000 weekly, i.e., $520,000.00 for a year. This is an absolutely unprecedented figure for radio speaking and it is offered by friends of England so that you may have the opportunity to turn the trend and ameliorate Anglo-American relations, which they consider vital.

Besides these weekly radio talks, I have offers now for the complete exploitation of your war memoirs and other possible newspaper and magazine articles on all fields which far exceed one million dollars. So if you would consider these proposals, you would not only considerably strengthen the Sterling block, but would also do an invaluable work for the clarification of American public opinion toward Britain.

I have consulted my expert corporation lawyer here, and I believe that with regard to our several prewar contracts, it would be perfectly legal and proper to carry out all these transactions so that my corporation would purchase various rights for shares and debentures and produce capital gain instead of income. This, of course, we would have to discuss in London with your lawyers.

I should beg you only to be kind enough to let me know in a cable or a return airmail letter whether you would want me to bring to London as concrete and detailed propositions as possible without, of course, any commitment on your part in advance. I have the feeling that these projects could be carried out within the next 2–3 years in such a form that they could yield some two million dollars, the greater part of it to remain intact.

With my kindest regards,
Yours very sincerely,
Emery Reves

1. On 10 October 1945 the *New York Times,* the *Washington Post,* and fifty other American newspapers published an "Open Letter to the American People" signed by many distinguished public figures, writers, and thinkers, including Albert Einstein, warning that the Charter of the United Nations was a "dangerous illusion" unless, as they wrote, "we are ready to take the further necessary steps to organise peace." One of the nine paragraphs of the letter read: "It happens that at this anxious moment of our history a small book has been published, a very important book, which expresses clearly and simply what so many of us have been thinking. That book is THE ANATOMY OF PEACE by Emery Reves. We urge American men and women to read this book, to think about its conclusions, to discuss it with neighbours and friends, privately and publicly. A few weeks ago these ideas seemed important but perhaps reachable in the future. In the new reality of atomic warfare they are of immediate, urgent necessity, unless civilization is determined on suicide."

Winston S. Churchill to Emery Reves: telegram

3 November 1945   Chartwell

Thank you for your letters and copy of the Anatomy of Peace. If you are coming over anyway I should be glad to see you but do not make a special journey.

Churchill

Emery Reves to Winston S. Churchill

9 November 1945   30 Rockefeller Plaza
New York

Dear Mr. Churchill,
Many thanks for your cable. Naturally, I have other reasons also for coming to London.
Walter Winchell,[1] in his gossip column today, writes: "Mr. Churchill's series for a magazine is due soon." I imagine this is just another of his usual bits of gossip, as I feel certain that no American magazine could offer half as much both regarding distribution and payment as I want to submit to you.
The solutions I shall put before you comprising magazine, newspaper, radio and film rights, if acceptable to you, will, of course have to be cleared with the Treasury Departments both in London and in Washington. But I trust that a perfectly ethical and legal form can be found to carry out these operations which would leave the greater part of the profits intact for you and

your family. In any case, I do hope you will permit me to lay these propositions before you for your consideration before you make any final decisions.

I beg to remain,
Yours very sincerely,
Emery Reves

1.   Walter Winchell, a pioneer of American newspaper gossip writing, wrote a daily "On Broadway" column for the *New York Daily Mirror* from 1929 to 1963. In 1932 he introduced a weekly radio program addressed to "Mr. and Mrs. America— and all ships at sea."

Emery Reves to Winston S. Churchill

19 December 1945   30 Rockefeller Plaza
New York

Dear Mr. Churchill,

Events happening around my book almost daily have forced me to postpone my trip from week to week. It is sweeping this country in an extraordinary way. It became a textbook in several colleges, sermons are made on it in many churches, students in Harvard, Yale and Columbia began to form groups to spread it and new editions of 10,000 copies disappear in two days . . . The Reader's Digest is now organizing for January and February discussions on THE ANATOMY OF PEACE in 15,000 American clubs and discussion groups, with three speakers in each place presenting the three parts of the book. This is unprecedented in American publishing history and may have unpredictable effects. Now I must write quickly a short new book to develop certain arguments.

I am sending you this letter in great haste, having read in the papers the announcement that you are coming over to the States shortly after the New Year. I should not like to pass you in the middle of the ocean, so I shall stay here, hoping that you will be able to arrange a meeting after your arrival.

May I summarize the suggestions I should like to discuss with you.

1.   The Memoirs. Full exploitation of this work (serialization, book publication, radio and movie rights) could, in my opinion, bring about two million dollars, to be extended over a period of 4–6 years.
2.   Broadcasting. Fifteen-minute weekly broadcasts on current affairs over one of the large networks could be arranged for a period of one year or more, giving you entire liberty to say whatever you wish without any control on behalf of either the network or the sponsors. These broadcasts would reach about 25–30 million people each week. Sponsored by a large corporation whose product does not compete with any British products, such broadcasts would bring

about $500,000.- a year. If for any reason you would not want radio time to be purchased by a corporation, it could also be obtained directly from one of the networks, but in this case, of course, your income would be considerably less. However, in the eyes of the American public, commercially sponsored programs are regarded as much more "independent," much less "propaganda," than sustained programs.

3. Magazine articles. In this field, The Reader's Digest stands alone as the first choice for you. It has more than twice the circulation and four times the readership of any other American magazine. They also pay much more. A series of 10–12 magazine articles a year (3–4,000 words each) would bring about $100,000.-.

4. Fortnightly newspaper articles on current affairs (12–1500 words each) could be syndicated in a great number of American dailies and newspapers all over the world, in the same way I syndicated your articles before the war. Such articles would reach 30–40 million people and would, I presume, yield a quarter of a million dollars or more a year.

Besides these possibilities, lectures are much less effective, much less profitable and much more tiresome. You would reach a much smaller number of people, your speeches would only be local news and the other papers would print very short excerpts from them on unimportant space. City editors would distort what you say by inevitable condensations. Also, you would surely encounter at almost every meeting a Zionist, a Hindu, an Irishman, a Communist or an American Mother who would heckle you, and such incidents would be played up by many newspapers, being more "newsy" than what you would say on the platform. I feel that you should not expose yourself to this. Yet if you want to come to grips at short range with dissenters, a lecture tour could naturally be arranged easily.

This is a maximum program, the full exploitation of the possibilities. It could all be arranged at the same time. Naturally, if you think it is too much work, it can be reduced to whatever you think would be the most interesting for you. But I feel obliged to stress one point. Whatever you desire to undertake should be thought over and decided upon in advance, and all arrangements should be made before you undertake anything. Knowing the attitude of the American press, radio and publishing business, I must tell you that if you would first undertake to write a few magazine articles, to deliver a few broadcasts, and afterwards come back to some other proposals, then you would obtain much less favorable arrangements. It is, in my opinion, therefore essential to your interests that everything you may want to undertake during the coming years in these fields be contracted for before you start any writing or speaking.

I would also submit to you certain suggestions as to the forms in which these transactions could be carried out over a period of years so that a large part of the yield would remain in your possession.

Please do let me know when you intend to arrive and where we could meet. You may be certain that I shall treat any information in this connection with strict confidence. Naturally, I should be happy to come to see you wherever you will stay.

With my very best wishes for the holidays,

Yours very sincerely
Emery Reves

P.S. I am enclosing a reprint from the December Reader's Digest to show you the way they are presenting THE ANATOMY OF PEACE at the beginning and the end of the first article. E.R.

Churchill sailed for the United States on 9 January 1946. Disembarking at New York, he went by train direct to Miami, where he was the guest of Colonel Frank W. Clarke, who in 1943, after the Quebec Conference, had been his host in his Canadian lakeside house.

Emery Reves to Martin Gilbert: recollection [1]

[20 January 1946]   [Chicago]

I got a telephone call from my office in New York, "Will you please telephone the Air Attaché [2] at the British Embassy?" I thought, "What have I got to do with the Air Attaché?" I telephoned him. He said, "Mr. Churchill has arrived in Miami and asked us to take you down, to have lunch with him tomorrow. We have an embassy plane going down to Jamaica tomorrow morning. We land in Miami."

In Chicago there was a terrible snowstorm. I went to the airport which was closed and blocked by a snow blizzard. Somehow, about seven o'clock, it quieted down. A plane left about half past seven. I got to New York in time to get the midnight sleeping car train to Washington, arriving at six in the morning. The Air Attaché had sent a car to the station. I went into the plane, a small plane, only two or three seats: the pilot, the co-pilot, one young officer, and me. He was a young dashing officer. He said, "My name is Ian Fleming." [3]

The plane landed in Miami about 12 o'clock. I took a taxi and arrived five minutes before the invitation time. I expected a family gathering. There was not a soul in the house. We were alone, he and me. He asked me all sorts of questions. He asked me what happened to my mother. He burst into tears and clasped my hand.[4]

As soon as we started eating he asked the butler, will you bring in the boxes. He brought in five or six steel boxes. "Well, there it is," Churchill said. "I am going to write my memoirs."

1.   Reves dictated this recollection to me in Montreux on 3 October 1980.
2.   Group Captain (acting Air Commodore) Douglas Leslie Blackford, British Air Attaché in Washington and Panama.
3.   Ian Fleming, then a member of the British secret service, later the creator of the James Bond stories.
4.   Reves's mother, as well as one of his aunts and all his aunt's children, had been among seven hundred Jews murdered by Hungarian Fascists at Novi Sad (then in Yugoslavia, formerly part of Austria-Hungary) in January 1942. His other cousins, who were living in Hungary when the Germans occupied Hungary in March 1944, were deported to Auschwitz; only one cousin who was in Hungary during the war survived. In 1940 Reves had obtained a United States visa for his mother and sent her the necessary money and tickets so that she could travel from Novi Sad to Lisbon, but the Italian government refused to give her a transit visa.

Winston S. Churchill: engagement cards

21 January 1946   [Miami]

   1.30   Mr. Reves.

Emery Reves to Randolph S. Churchill: recollection[1]

21 January 1946   [Miami]

During the luncheon I was terribly touched by the fact that in spite of what he had done during the war he remembered everything of our relationship in the pre-war years, and quite sentimentally with tears in his eyes he said to me: "Everyone wants me to write my memoirs which I may do if I have time. And if I do, I have not forgotten what you have done for me before the war and I shall want you to handle it." I was naturally terribly touched because I knew that every American publisher wanted this and every literary agent and he could have just have had anyone. He said that for private reasons and financial reasons he was going to carry out the transaction through Lord Camrose because he had to make a capital deal and contractually I should have to deal with Lord Camrose. But that he will arrange all this and he will let me know when and how to contact him or Camrose so for the time being I should keep quiet. If I am correct Lady Churchill was there but she went out for lunch.

   1.   Reves dictated this recollection to Randolph Churchill at La Capponcina, Lord Beaverbrook's villa on the Cap d'Ail, on 4 August 1966. Five years earlier, Randolph

had begun a multivolume biography of his father, of which he published the first two volumes (covering the years 1874–1914) and two sets of supporting document volumes before his death in 1968, at the age of fifty-seven.

Winston S. Churchill: engagement cards

30 January 1946   New York

   5.30   Mr. Reves.

Emery Reves to Randolph S. Churchill: recollection

[30 January 1946]   [New York]

In New York we talked about several literary matters, mainly about an article which the Reader's Digest wanted him to write. I actually introduced him to Wallace.[1] Then we discussed a lot because I had several propositions for him from radio companies and I submitted various propositions for $25,000 for a pair of five minute speeches so he could have made a few million dollars easily if he wanted to. He was rather reluctant to speak under any commercial sponsorship and finally he decided not to do anything of that kind.

1.   DeWitt Wallace, Editor and Chairman of *Reader's Digest* from 1921 to 1973. The first issue had a circulation of 1,500. By 1929 the circulation had risen to 200,000. In the mid 1980s it was thirty million worldwide, and the magazine was published in seventeen languages.

Winston S. Churchill: engagement cards

16 March 1946   New York

   3 p.m.   Dr. Reves.

Winston S. Churchill: engagement cards

18 March 1946   New York

   5.30 p.m.   Dr. Reves.

Winston S. Churchill: engagement cards

19 March 1946   New York

   3.30 p.m.   Dr. Reves.

Winston S. Churchill: engagement cards

20 March 1946   New York

5 p.m.   Mr. Reves.
          Mr. and Mrs. de Witt Wallace.

Emery Reves to Winston S. Churchill

5 April 1946   30 Rockefeller Plaza
                                                                  New York

Dear Mr. Churchill,

The texts of the letter are exactly as we agreed upon. I have no doubt that
when the time comes to close the deal I shall be able to secure even better
conditions than these. Also I have no doubt that a similar arrangement could
be made with some other concern, should you prefer.

Yesterday I had another informal talk with Wallace of The Reader's
Digest. He is struggling between his desire to make an offer for sponsoring
your broadcasts and his financial commitments for the next 2–3 years.
Together with the radio time and promotion, these broadcasts mean, of
course, a million-dollar proposition yearly. No matter how successful The
Reader's Digest is, its financial resources cannot be compared with those of
the industrial concern in question, and now that the war is over, The Digest
is engaged in a large program of expansion, issuing the magazine in different
languages all over the world, which ties up most of their available liquid capital. I shall continue these informal conversations with Wallace and shall know
exactly what the situation is by the time I arrive in London.

· Wallace also showed me the proofs of your Pentagon Speech.[1] It is two
printed pages in The Digest, and for the reproduction of published articles
or speeches, their highest rate is $200.- per page. He asked me whether I
thought it would be all right if he remitted $2,500.- to you for this two-page
reproduction of your speech. I thought this would be all right. As it was you
personally who handed that speech over to him, he will send the check over
to you directly. This is, of course, a gesture. He is extremely anxious to get a
series of articles from you at $25,000.- apiece.[2] This also, I believe, could be
raised to the level of the Collier's offer or even beyond it if and when we can
make arrangements.

Regarding other matters, we have time to discuss them when you have
reached a decision of principle. Please do let me know when this time comes
so that I may arrange my trip to London. For the next two weeks I shall be
busy here with the preparation of the dollar edition of my book, which will
be issued early in May in a first print of 200,000 copies.

                                                      I beg to remain,
                                                    Yours very sincerely,
                                                        Emery Reves

1.   At General Eisenhower's suggestion, Churchill had spoken to a group of senior officers at the Pentagon on 9 March 1946 (four days after his Fulton "Iron Curtain" speech). He made his remarks in the room of the Secretary of War, Robert P. Patterson, telling those assembled, "The prevailing feature of our work together was the intimacy of association. Language is a great bridge. There are many, many ideas we have in common and also in practice: but there was a spirit of loyalty, of good will, of comradeship which never has been seen in all the history of war between Allied Armies, Navies and Air Forces fighting together side by side."

2.   This price for a single article, $25,000, was the equivalent of £5,000 in 1946 (£100,000 in 1996).

Claridge's: telephone message

2 August 1946   London
4.50 p.m.

Mr. Churchill telephoned to say he would be very pleased if Mr. Reves could go to his country home on Monday next between 4 p.m. and 5 p.m. The address is Chartwell, Westerham, Kent. Would Mr. Reves kindly telephone Westerham 81 to say if this is convenient.

Winston S. Churchill: engagement cards

14 September 1946   Choisi[1]

To luncheon   Count Coudenhove-Kalergi.[2]
               Mr. Reves.

1.   While preparing his Zurich speech, in which he called for a United States of Europe, Churchill stayed at the Villa Choisi on Lake Geneva.

2.   Count Richard Coudenhove-Kalergi, whose first appeal for a united Europe had been published in Vienna in 1923. The founder of the Pan-European Movement, he had visited Churchill in 1938, at the time of the publication of his book *The Totalitarian State against Man.* In 1940 he published *Europe Must Unite.* In 1953 Churchill wrote the preface to his book *An Idea Conquers the World.*

Emery Reves to Randolph S. Churchill: recollection

[14 September 1946]

He called me by telephone and asked me if I could come down for lunch to Choisi, which I did. There he said to me: "Now things are progressing but I still can't tell you anything yet but maybe in a few months the matter will be ripe for negotiations."[1]

1.   Reves later told me (at Montreux in 1980) that during the lunch at Choisi, when talk among the guests turned to Britain's black hours in 1940, Churchill pointed to Reves and said, "That man didn't believe that we were finished. He applied for British citizenship when we were finished."

Emery Reves to Randolph S. Churchill: recollection[1]

[15 October 1946]   [Paris]

I was in Paris at the Ritz and all of a sudden around three o'clock in the afternoon I get a telephone call from him from Chartwell saying, "Look here, Lord Camrose is going tomorrow on the *Queen Elizabeth* to New York to negotiate the American rights of the memoirs, and I want you to go with him. Would you come over to London and have dinner with me tonight— I want to talk to you." I was quite shocked and said, "Look here, Mr. Churchill, it is three o'clock in the afternoon—how do you expect me to get on the *Queen Elizabeth*—it is its maiden voyage if I am correct, and according to my information every cabin is sold out every trip for months." He interrupted me and said, "I shall look into that—they used to be very nice to me—so I shall call you back." I said, "Fine." He said, "Just see that you can come over." So I called up my office and my secretary and said cancel everything for appointments I have here, as I have to go to London in half an hour or an hour and tomorrow to New York.

About fifteen or twenty minutes later the telephone rings again. He said: "I have talked to the chairman of Cunard, and you have a stateroom with a bath so can you be here for dinner?" So I said, "Well, Mr. Churchill, in the meantime I have enquired and there is not a single seat on any of the flights to London. The weather is awfully bad—it is fog and rain. I don't think I can come over, but I shall see." So he said, "Well if you can't—call up the Air Attaché at the Embassy and I'll call him up to help you. If they can't manage it, I'll send over a private plane for you to come over." I was quite excited by all these arrangements, so I called up the Air Attaché, and he said, "We have already had a call from Mr. Churchill, and unfortunately the planes are all booked. The British plane has gone already, but there is one more French flight," and he would let me know. A few minutes later he called again and said there was nothing but that I should go to the airport and if anybody doesn't turn up I would have first priority over anyone else on the waiting list.

I packed a little bag and got there very fast and paid my bill at the Ritz and dashed out for a taxi to the airport—Le Bourget. It was very very bad weather—October fog—almost 6 o'clock by this time. On the way to the airport I heard that the plane was not leaving for the time being. If it cleared up later the plane may leave. So I called him up at Chartwell and said, "Look here, I am at the airport, but there is very little hope that I can come over. I don't even think that your private plane can come over because the weather is very bad." He said, "Can't you get a private plane there?" I said, "I will try."

I went around the airport and tried to find a private plane. There was a pilot there who said he had a plane—a one-motor plane. He said he would consider it and he would take me over. I eventually found someone, but he said he would charge £250 as the weather was so very poor.[2] I called Mr.

Churchill up and said, "I may be in luck—I have found a private plane and I may be in Croydon in two hours." "Fine, let me know as soon as you get here," he said. Someone took my luggage, and in the dark and the fog I was taken to a very remote hangar where there was a tiny little plane. I had the shivers when I saw it, I must tell you. So they put my luggage in and I got myself into the plane. I sat there and the pilot had to go to get some flight clearance. There was I waiting, waiting, waiting for a very long time—nearly twenty minutes. He came back, and he said he was terribly sorry but we could not leave because his motor gives sparks and he could not get clearance to fly. Again I called up Chartwell and said I was terribly sorry but I was sitting in a private plane but it could not go, so there was not the slightest hope now. I would have to leave France in the morning. Is it any sense for me to come over? He said, "Yes, come because the boat leaves at 1 o'clock. My car will wait for you at Croydon and take you down to Southampton."

Unfortunately I could not see Mr. Churchill before I left for New York. I went back to the Ritz, spent a short night, and by 4.30 in the morning I went out to the airport. This time I had already got their assurance that the first plane would take me over. There was a plane supposed to leave at 8 o'clock, which was due at Croydon shortly before 10—at that time the planes were very slow. So I thought if I get to the airport I would get to Croydon before 10 o'clock; there was a chance for me to get to Southampton by 1 but not to Chartwell. So I was at the airport waiting and waiting. The time of the departure of the plane arrived. We were seated in the plane (Air France) again waiting and waiting until 9 o'clock, and by this time I was absolutely certain that I would miss the boat. Finally a little after 9 o'clock the plane was given permission to start. We left and arrived at Croydon about ten minutes to 11 and found we could not land. We circled one, two, three times. Finally after a certain number of attempts we did land. I got off the plane very slowly with the absolute conviction that I had missed the boat.

I walked towards the airport building, and all of a sudden I looked at the clock on the airport tower and saw it was 10 minutes past 10. Like round the world in eighty days. If it had happened in a book or a play or a movie, people would say it was artificial. I looked at my watch and saw it was 10 past 11. So I stopped an official and I said, "I beg your pardon, sir, what is the time?" He shows me the clock that says 10 past 10. I said, "It is ten past eleven." So he said, "We put the clock back an hour last night." Anyway, a chauffeur-driven car was waiting for me, and the driver had instructions to take me as fast as possible to Southampton. No time to telephone to Mr. Churchill, because by this time he knew it was too late. I asked the driver, "Do you think you can manage it?" and he said, "I doubt it, sir, because there are fog patches in all the valleys, but I'll do my best. It takes me two hours from Croydon to Southampton, but I may be able to do it in a little less." Three hours could have been half past one, and the departure of the boat was 1 o'clock. We were driving, driving, and we got to the outskirts of

Southampton about 1.20, or 1.25 pm. I looked out of the window and I said to the driver, "Do you see the *Queen Elizabeth*?" and finally we discovered the two big funnels of the *Queen Elizabeth*. We dashed to the docks and were driving at the highest possible speed to the gateway. Two stewards took my luggage, and a policeman said, "You don't need to show your passport—get out." In the middle of it, all the whistles were blowing, and at the top of the gangplank was the purser, who greets me, "You are the last passenger on the first voyage of the *Queen Elizabeth*." [3]

I sent a note to Lord Camrose that I was on the boat and that I would like to see him—perhaps we could have a drink in the bar. I knew Lord Camrose very well from prewar years when I did quite a lot of business with the *Daily Telegraph,* and we met also during the first few months of the war in the Ministry of Information. We met in the bar, and he was very surprised to see me on the boat. I naturally assumed that everything was arranged between your father and him. Lord Camrose is staggered and says he has no idea why I am on the boat. I said, "Didn't Mr. Churchill tell you something?" and he said, "Absolutely nothing." I said, "He called me up yesterday in Paris asking me to come on the boat to accompany you and to help you negotiate in America." He seemed quite shocked. So we telegraphed to Mr. Churchill to clarify the situation. A few hours later we received a radiogram. I had said to him, "Camrose uninformed about my journey, could you explain it." He replied, "I am sure you will do an excellent job, but you must be very confidential and you must realize that you do not actually represent me." The signature was a capital C. Now this was even more strange. I called up Lord Camrose and I showed him.

A few minutes later a page boy knocks at my bedroom and hands me over a letter, which was signed by Camrose, saying that in view of the unusual circumstances on the boat he would like to make it clear that I was going to New York entirely on my own and that whatever I do or say I would do or say entirely on my own responsibility. I took a sheet of paper and I said, "Dear Lord Camrose—I have just received the following letter and I am in full and complete agreement with everything you say." It was probably the most embarrassing situation I have ever been in in my life. A few hours later I met Lord Camrose on the deck by chance. He was very nice and kind and smiled and we sat down and began to talk. He asked me what I had been doing in America during the war and about my organization. I had published Mr. Churchill's articles before the war in some 300–400 newspapers in some 70 countries. I told him of my relationship with newspaper publishers, and he became very interested. Suddenly I felt that he wanted to know more what I could do in America. He was more experienced in buying copyright than selling it. He asked me how much I believed one could get for this—the American rights—serial and book rights. I mentioned a figure which made him a little bit angry. "If you put such figures into the old man's head," he said, "it will be impossible to make any deal; it is absolutely childish." I told him if we could sell it to many newspapers on a royalty basis, I thought we could get between four and five million dollars. He said that that was impossible.

We became very close, and we decided that we should meet every day before lunch and dinner for an hour in the bar to discuss this matter. Lord Camrose did not drink much—he liked champagne and he liked Bordeaux wine. I was invited once for dinner with him and his wife and one of his daughters. There were about six or seven people there. We met regularly at the bar every day about 12 o'clock, and we talked until about 1 or 1.15 p.m., and every evening about 7 o'clock until about 8.30 p.m. This was during the remaining four days of our trip. The day before we arrived in New York we were very close business partners. But there was no agreement as such. He would negotiate the matter with the newspapers because he had a particularly good relationship with them, and I was supposed to negotiate the magazines and the book publishers, and we agreed.

He thought perhaps the magazines would offer more than the newspapers. We had with us a great number of offers, and I had copies of all the letters and telegrams he had received of his resignation, and it was a definite arrangement between Lord Camrose and me that we should not offer it to anyone who had not made an offer for it. So when I was in New York[4] I was staying at the Plaza Hotel and Lord Camrose at the Savoy Plaza on the other side of the square, and we agreed that every evening about 6 o'clock I should go to see him and exchange views on what we had done during the day.

Something very strange happened because I was in personal relationship with Harpers, with whom I published several books during the war, and I was hoping of course that Harpers would pay more than anyone, and that I would be partner in the American publishing. The day of our arrival in New York we read in the newspapers that Winston Churchill was suing Harpers for libel. They were foolish enough to publish a book by a Yugoslav émigré writer called Adamovitch who, in a footnote, made a remark that Winston Churchill, while he was Chancellor of the Exchequer, made some private income through Hambros Brothers while he was in office. It was a very silly thing to say. Camrose and I both felt that it was just impossible to take this to Harpers at that moment. Later on I told it to my very old friend Cass Canfield[5] and we were absolutely miserable that because of such a silly accident he was out of the deal. I think he would not have bid more than Houghton Mifflin, but I think he would have bid as much.

I talked with *Reader's Digest, Saturday Evening Post,* and with *Collier's* and a few other magazines. Camrose talked with the *New York Times, New York Herald Tribune,* with Hearst, Marshall Field, and with AP and UP about these matters. About three weeks after our embarkation he said to me, "Well I have now explored the whole situation, and the best offer I have is from Mrs. Reid,[6] and I intend to accept." This offer was for $1,100,000 for the American and world serial rights and the American book rights. I said to

Lord Camrose, "I do not think this is enough." I had explored the magazine field and found that the *Reader's Digest*—and rightly so—had said that to serialize a work of that sort was not on the lines of the *Reader's Digest.*

In view of the very strange radiogram I received from your father on the boat, I prepared an extraordinary letter, which I sent to every editor and publisher I approached. The letter was along these lines: "I would like to make it clear that I am not representing Mr. Winston Churchill and I have no rights whatever to negotiate the sale of his War Memoirs in the United States. Under these circumstances, if you are willing to talk with me I shall be very happy." I had this letter signed by Mr. Wallace of the *Reader's Digest,* then I submitted it to Mr. Ben Hibbs, who was Editor of the *Saturday Evening Post* in Philadelphia. He refused to sign it. He said, "I can't sign such a paper—it makes no sense." I wanted him to sign to say that he realized that I had no right whatsoever to offer him this. I said, "Look here, I have been negotiating Mr. Churchill's writings before the war for many years, and you probably know about my personal relationship with him. I think you can get it if you talk to me, but I have no authority to negotiate." I said, "If you want to talk with me in such a completely informal manner, I shall be happy to talk." Everyone signed except him. I think they are unique documents in the history of publishing. The best offer I got at this stage was from Mr. Chenery of *Collier's,* who was willing to pay a million dollars for the American serial rights alone. Your father wrote only one article for *Collier's.* I was quite desperate because your father made a great mistake. Chenery, who published his articles before the war, wrote him a letter and asked him for an article, which your father did without mentioning it to either Lord Camrose or me, and this was two or three days after Chenery made me a final offer of one million dollars for the American serial rights alone, which I thought was good.

So I took Lord Camrose to Chenery to negotiate on the million-dollar bid. We didn't know that the day after, Chenery received from your father his consent to write a special article for $25,000. Therefore Chenery immediately cut the discussion by saying to Lord Camrose, "Well, yes, I did say a million dollars, but I have been thinking it over, I've talked about it with my associates, and I think we cannot give more than five hundred." The moment Chenery saw that he could get the first article of your father's after the war, he saw no reason why he should pay a million dollars for the Memoirs if he could get them for half a million. I then looked at the face of Lord Camrose, who I thought was the prototype of the gentleman businessman. Lord Camrose smiled, and when Chenery mentioned half a million dollars, Lord Camrose said, "Beautiful weather in New York, isn't it—is it always so? In October, it is lovely weather." So we had a five-minute chat about the New York Indian summer and shook hands and left. That was the end of *Collier's* and Mr. Chenery.

Helen Reid's offer was $1,100,000 for the American serial rights, world serial rights, and American book rights. The *New York Times* offered very little, if I am correct something around $750,000 for the American serial rights—in a way better than Helen Reid's offer. I told Lord Camrose that this was not enough, and he said, "Well, I can't get any more. The *New York Times* doesn't want to pay, and this is the best offer." I said, "Lord Camrose, if I were you, I should not conclude anything without hearing from Luce." He said, "I have heard nothing so far, and I am not going to run after Luce." Lord Camrose had had no letter from Luce. I said, "I have just read in the papers this morning that Luce has arrived in New York from China, so he is now in New York." So he said, "Can you do something?" and I said, "I think I can." I said, "I don't know Luce very well, but I do know Claire Luce." This was on a Friday, and I said, "Can you wait until Monday to give Mrs. Reid a definite answer?" From Lord Camrose's I called up the Waldorf Towers and asked to speak to Mrs. Claire Luce. She came to the telephone, and I said, "Mrs. Luce, I want to talk to you on a very important and urgent matter." She said, "With pleasure—come and see me on Tuesday." I said, "No, I can't wait until then. It has to be today." She says, "I am going out—I am already dressed and am leaving in half an hour." I said, "Dear Mrs. Luce, believe me, I would not bother you, but this is something of vital importance for your husband, and I must see you before you leave." She said, "Good Lord, if it is that important, come right away." So I took a taxi and went to the Waldorf Towers. She opened the door of the apartment dressed in a suit and a hat and said, "What is it?" I said, "It is very secret. In the next forty-eight hours it will be decided who in America will have the rights of Winston Churchill's War Memoirs." I said, "Where is Henry?" She said, "Harry's sleeping—he spent two nights on the plane coming from China and is deadly tired." I said, "Could you wake him?" She left me, and about five or six minutes later the door opened and Henry Luce comes in in a dressing gown. He had been awakened from a deep sleep and was a little bit angry. He said, "You are the fifth or sixth or seventh agent who comes to me saying that he represents Churchill—now who is his representative?" I said, "Look here, I don't know—I can't tell you—all I can tell you is that in forty-eight hours it will be decided. You can talk to me today or tomorrow, but after tomorrow you won't get it." He said, "Can I sleep until Monday morning?" I said, "Yes." He said, "Then come to my office on Monday morning, and we will talk about it." Camrose had said to me, "Don't mention me." So Monday morning we had the first meeting—there were four or five others and I was there about an hour. At the end of it I told him that the offers were very high and if they wanted to get it they must make a bid in excess of a million dollars for the American serial rights. How much in excess? We had to talk about that later, but it must be in excess of a million dollars. I told Camrose about this meeting and that I was to see them again. It was the same afternoon. It was after the second meeting that they told me that they had agreed to pay more than a million dollars for the American serial rights. I always tried to get the maximum for your father—more than anyone else ever paid.

Both Lord Camrose and I negotiated for your father for no commission at all. We paid our own expenses for our trips. He did it to get the British rights for the *Daily Telegraph* and I did it to get the foreign rights for me, but we both acted on principle.

When Lord Camrose was ready to conclude the business I alarmed your father and told him that I was sure we could do better than that. My intervention with the Luces led to success. When they told me they were willing to pay more than a million dollars, I told them that Lord Camrose was the person with whom they would have to conclude the business and that he was here in New York. I reported to Camrose, and Camrose went and saw them the next day. I did not go to the meeting. Mrs. Reid was kept in abeyance. He had no obligations to give an answer quickly, he was just collecting offers and said we will let you know in due course. When I next saw Lord Camrose he said, "That is a very good deal," and he looked at me and said, "You are a very good salesman—thank you very much," and I said, "I wish you could do something for the *Daily Telegraph* also." It was not the least obstacle because two days after this, Lord Camrose comes and says, "They made a very good offer and are willing to offer $1,400,000 for the American serial and book rights." I said, "Lord Camrose—No! The American serial rights—yes—but not the book rights." I said, "You must stop it." I said I would like to be in on the American publishing deal (book). I have been in partnership for many years with Harpers of New York, but now Harpers are out I think I can do a deal with Houghton Mifflin. So he said, "All right, if you can bring me the same offer from Houghton Mifflin, I will do a deal with them." So I went to Boston and in 48 hours I came back with a definite offer of $250,000 for the five volumes from Houghton Mifflin. It was a few hours before the return voyage on the *Queen Elizabeth,* and most of the final arrangements were made by radiogram on the *Queen Elizabeth.*

When Lord Camrose communicated with all the prospective buyers—the *New York Times* and Mrs. Reid etc.—that they had lost the bid, I understand that General Adler on behalf of the *New York Times* went to Luce and said, "The *New York Times* just cannot afford not to publish Winston Churchill's memoirs on the Second World War." So Luce said, "What do you want me to do?" And then came the offer of the *New York Times* to publish simultaneously and that they would pay one third of the total price.

They arranged it in such a manner that they all published it differently. Then followed twelve months of unbelievable negotiations with lawyers. They chartered an entire aircraft to bring all the lawyers to London.

I think it was for the first time in history that the American copyright, which is about the craziest in the world, was taken seriously. There are certain stipulations in American copyright law according to which you cannot copyright any part of a work, only the totality of a work, so that if you start publishing an extract from the work you lose the copyright. So they had to publish the complete volume first—they printed it in a few hundred copies and sold it to their friends for money who gave the copies back to them. But they actually had to sell a few hundred copies to show that it was actually sold. Then I had a lot of trouble.

1.   Reves dictated this recollection to Randolph Churchill at Lord Beaverbrook's villa in the South of France, La Capponcina, in 1966, when Randolph was collecting material for his father's biography.

2.   That £250 would be worth £5,000 ($7,500) today.

3.   The *Queen Elizabeth* sailed from Southampton at five minutes past two on the afternoon of 16 October 1946.

4.   The *Queen Elizabeth* reached New York at eight on the morning of 21 October 1946.

5.   Cass Canfield, President, Harper and Brothers, 1931–1945; Chairman of the Board, 1945–1955; subsequently Senior Editor, Harper and Row.

6.   Helen Rogers Reid (Mrs. Ogden Reid), President of the *New York Herald Tribune* from 1947 to 1953.

PREPARING THE
WAR MEMOIRS

1947 – 1955

N. S. Sturdee[1] to Winston S. Churchill

6 January 1947

Mr. Churchill,

I gave Mr. Reves your message. He says he is seeing Lord Camrose this evening.

Mr. Reves says that there are one or two outstanding points Lord Camrose would prefer him (Mr. Reves) to consult you about direct. Mr. Reves says these points should be cleared up at least 24 hours before any announcement is made.

As I do not believe you knew that Lord Camrose wishes you to see Mr. Reves, I said I would report to you again.

N.S.

1.   N. S. Sturdee, known as Jo, one of Churchill's secretaries, who had joined him during the war and who remained with him for a decade. Later Countess of Onslow.

Winston S. Churchill: engagement cards

7 January 1947   Chartwell

noon   Reves—stay to luncheon.

Emery Reves to Winston S. Churchill: telegram

16 March 1947   Paris

Arriving Claridges Sunday would be grateful if could see you Monday
Emery Reves

Winston S. Churchill: engagement cards

19 March 1947   Chartwell

   11 a.m.   Reves.

Winston S. Churchill: engagement cards

27 March 1947   Chartwell

   10 a.m.   Mr. Reves.

Winston S. Churchill: engagement cards

23 April 1947   Chartwell

   11 a.m.   Mr. Reves.

Winston S. Churchill: engagement cards

2 May 1947   Chartwell

   11.30   Mr. Reves.

Emery Reves to Randolph S. Churchill: recollection

[May 1947]

   I came in on the foreign rights—Lord Camrose kept the British and British Empire rights and then we made a deal for the foreign rights and I made him an offer which was the highest offer anyone offered for the foreign rights. If I am correct it was about £80,000.

Lord Camrose to N. S. Sturdee

7 May 1947   The Daily Telegraph and
                                                       Morning Post

Dear Miss Sturdee,

   I have received the enclosed offer from Mr. Emery Reves.

   The territories which he mentions would be very difficult and costly to handle from here, and in my opinion the Trustees would be right in accepting it.

   Perhaps you will put Mr. Reves' letter before them and let me hear in due course.

Yours sincerely,
Camrose

Winston S. Churchill to N. S. Sturdee

[8 May 1947]   Chartwell

Say I agree.
fms[1]

1.   "Fms" ("for my signature") was a standard request for Churchill's secretary to
draft a letter for his signature.

Winston S. Churchill: engagement cards

29 July 1947   Chartwell

5 p.m.   Mr. Reves.

Emery Reves to Winston S. Churchill

22 October 1947   30 Rockefeller Plaza
                                                        New York 20, N.Y.

Dear Mr. Churchill,
    I just arrived back in New York, and for the first time in my life feel really
exhausted. Since May, I have flown about sixty thousand miles, and have
been in twenty-eight countries. The last part of my trip was a rather unpleasant experience. Atmospheric conditions over the Cordilleras[1] are such, that
there is not much difference between commercial flying and dive-bombing.
    I have not yet finished all the negotiations, but on the whole I am satisfied
with my trip. I shall let you have a list of the Latin American newspapers and
publishers very soon. There are, however, one or two important matters I
should like to take up with you immediately.
    1) The Foreign Office has approached me several times regarding the pub-
lication of your work in Germany and Japan. I wonder whether you are
aware of the publishing situation in these countries? Authors and proprietors
of literary works are not allowed to negotiate directly, or make any deal with
German and Japanese publishers. They have to negotiate with the allied military authorities. These authorities give a license to a German or Japanese
publisher for a period of two to three years, and pay the author fifty pounds
(in the United States $250) for each book.
    It is an altogether absurd situation; it is as if we had won the war so that
British and American authors should pay reparations to the Germans and
Japanese. Most authors and publishers in England and America refuse to let
their books be published under such conditions, and refuse to make such
a present to former enemy publishers, in spite of the argument by the military authorities that they should make such a sacrifice for the democratic

re-education of the German and Japanese peoples. Recently the authorities agreed that in exceptional cases British and American authors could collect blocked marks or yen, but this is meaningless since these currencies in their present form are not worth the paper they are printed on.

To the request of the Foreign Office that I give them the German rights to your book for fifty pounds (they said that as an exception they may pay two hundred to two hundred and fifty pounds) I replied that I feel it would be unfair to give away your work in Germany for nothing, when newspapers and publishers in all the other countries are paying unprecedented fees for it. I told them that I am at least as anxious as they are to see your book published in Germany and Japan, but that I feel that if the British and American governments believe that this is an important political weapon, then they should pay its market value, just as they paid the market value of the weapons produced by Vickers and General Motors while the shooting war lasted. I do not see why political weapons should be delivered to governments without remuneration, when military weapons are paid for.

I fully realise that a large-scale distribution of British and American books in Germany and Japan are a good thing to help convince the people of the superiority of our way of life. But I think it would be even more convincing to send, free of charge, a Rolls Royce or a Cadillac car to every German or Japanese family. Why not ask motor car manufacturers to deliver their products for propaganda purposes, why only authors?

I told the Foreign Office that I am certain that I could make a satisfactory arrangement in a very short time if they could give me permission to negotiate with the German and Japanese newspapers and publishers direct. I am fully aware that I could not get any dollars or sterling for the time being, but I believe I could get some real estate or shares or art objects or any tangible property which some time in the future might be transferable. To this, the answer was that authorisation for a direct dealing could not be given.

Without involving you in any way in these negotiations, I should very much appreciate it, if you would tell me, most confidentially, how you feel about this matter. If you feel that for political reasons your work should be spread in Germany and Japan, under no condition would I like to be the man who prevents it because of my property rights. I do feel, however, that the whole structure of contracts would be jeopardised, if we were to give the Japanese for nothing what the Americans paid over a million dollars for.

My feeling is that, if the military governments do not allow us to make a decent deal, we would do better to wait with the publication of your work until conditions in these enemy countries are more normal.[2]

2) A most important problem is the illustration of your book. More and more publishers desire to publish your book heavily illustrated, demanding at least one hundred illustrations per volume. Naturally, they want original material, which they urge me to obtain for them either directly from you

or from British government departments, who certainly have thousands of interesting and unpublished war pictures, which could never be used better than by illustrating your book.

I hear from Lord Camrose that Mr. Longwell[3] has been over in London and obtained from you and from government departments a great volume of illustrations. I hope to be able to meet Longwell in a few days, but I am not certain what his attitude will be regarding the use in other countries of the pictures he already has. So I should like to ask you kindly to let me know how much more illustrative material you have (photographs, cartoons, facsimiles of documents, etc.), whether you would allow me to look through this material, and whether you would facilitate my getting permission to look through the picture material of some of the more important British government departments and to use some of it to illustrate your book.

3) I am more and more pressed by the newspapers for promotional material. They are anxious to build up interest in the series by publishing, between now and the release date of the series, short articles and stories about you and your forthcoming work. As I told you during our last meeting, what is needed is about a dozen intimate snapshots, showing you working on the memoirs (dictating, reading, walking, sitting in the garden, lying in bed, etc.) and about a dozen little anecdotes and stories. I am sure Mr. Deakin[4] or somebody else among your collaborators could easily put on paper a few interesting anecdotes of amusing episodes that have taken place while you have been engaged in this work.[5]

These three points are rather urgent, and I would be most grateful if you would be kind enough to give them your attention. I shall give you a ring early next week.

Yours very sincerely
Emery Reves

1.   The Andes.
2.   Churchill wrote in the margin of this paragraph, "Yes."
3.   Daniel Longwell, Editor of *Life*. On 10 August 1947 Churchill had written to Lord Camrose, "I gave Longwell a set of proofs of Books I and II, and also showed him a great mass of official photographs, of which I have about twenty albums."
4.   Bill Deakin, Churchill's principal literary assistant from 1936 to 1939 and again from 1945 until 1950, when he became Warden of St. Antony's College, Oxford. He was knighted in 1975.
5.   Churchill wrote in the margin at this point, "Yes," and then over the top, "No."

Winston S. Churchill to Emery Reves: telegram

30 October 1947   Chartwell

Yours of 22nd received when are you coming back here.

Churchill

Emery Reves to Winston S. Churchill

2 December 1947   30 Rockefeller Plaza
                                                  New York 20, N.Y.

Dear Mr. Churchill,

Many thanks for your cable.

The meeting we had (General Adler, James, Heiskell, Laughlin [1] and myself) after the news came that you would not be able to deliver the first volume by January 1st, was most satisfactory in every respect. I strongly urged the others not to press you and to leave it entirely to you when you will deliver the first volume. I do not see any danger in publishing the book two or three months later, and it is in the interest of all of us that no part of your work be published until you are completely satisfied with it. After all, this is not supposed to be merely a news story, but a work of art.

So no matter how some newspapers or publishers may press you, please be assured that I shall always fight on your side for the quickest possible publication—but not until you feel that each volume is as perfect as it can be.

We have decided to postpone newspaper serialisation until April 1st and book publication until June—anyway, we shall make no definite plans until the final text is delivered by you.

In the meantime, I have suggested to Lord Camrose and The New York Times that they make a provisional selection of the series, based on the "provisional final" proofs which are available, in order to gain time, as I do not suppose that the final text will be substantially different from what we already have.

In view of the fact that nobody has as much actual work to do as I have, in combining the Telegraph and the American selections, getting all the articles stencilled and printed, despatching them to the remotest corners of the earth and having them translated for simultaneous publication, I shall be most grateful if you will kindly let me have copies of any texts you may deliver to Life at the same time, so that I may do as much preparatory work as possible.

I am very glad to hear that you are going to Marrakesh for a holiday. I hope there will be no by-elections there and that, under the inspiration of the local muezzin, you will cheerfully complete the first volume.

Kindly find enclosed a "provisional final" list of the newspapers and publishers who have already signed contracts. I hope to be able to improve on it. At the moment I am negotiating with Iceland, Guatemala, Liberia and similar powers.

I have an unsolvable problem in Germany and Japan. The Foreign Office offers £100 for the German serial rights and £300 for 25,000 copies of the book. This I have naturally turned down.

My original plan was to finish all work in connection with the first volume by the end of January and then come over to Europe. But with the post-

ponement, which will require my presence in New York in February, I may
come over for a few weeks before, particularly as I very much need a little rest
after my blitz-trip. Please let me know your addresses and your movements
so that I may be able to keep contact with you.

With my best wishes for a nice holiday,
Yours very sincerely,
Emery Reves

P.S. I recall that, when in London you gave me a draft of the chapter on the
Battle of the Plate River to read, there was a note from Roosevelt to you,
thanking you for the "tremendously interesting account" of the battle you
sent him. Are you going to use this Roosevelt letter in that chapter, or anywhere else? If not, I should very much like to have a copy of it, with your
permission to use it, as everybody agrees this would be a most valuable quote
in the promotion.   E.R.

1.   General Julius Ochs Adler, General Manager of the *New York Times;* Andrew
Heiskell, Publisher of *Life;* and Henry Laughlin, of the book publisher Houghton
Mifflin. I have been unable to identify James. The book in question is the first volume
of the war memoirs.

Emery Reves to Winston S. Churchill

2 December 1947

EUROPEAN NEWSPAPERS PUBLISHING
WINSTON CHURCHILL'S MEMOIRS OF THE SECOND WORLD WAR

France, *Le Figaro*
Italy, *Nuovo Corriere Della Sera*
Spain, *La Vanguardia*
Portugal, *O Seculo*
Belgium, *Le Soir* and *Het Laatste Nieuws*
Holland, *Volkskrant* and *Elsevier's Weekly*
Denmark, *Politiken*
Sweden, *Dagens Nyheter*
Norway, *Verdens Gang*
Finland, *Helsingin Sanomat*
Czechoslovakia, *Narodne Slovo*
Switzerland, *Neue Zürcher Zeitung*
Greece, *Kathimerini*
Turkey, *Vatan*
Egypt, *La Bourse Egyptienne* and *Egyptian Mail*
Palestine, *Ha-aretz* and *Palestine Post*

SOUTH AMERICAN AND OTHER NEWSPAPERS PUBLISHING
WINSTON CHURCHILL'S MEMOIRS OF THE SECOND WORLD WAR

Argentina, *La Prensa*
Uruguay, *El Dia* and *El Pais*
Brazil, *O Globo,* Rio de Janeiro, and *O Estado de Sao Paulo*
Chile, *El Mercurio*
Peru, *El Comercio*
Cuba, *El Pais*
Mexico, *Novedades*
Bolivia, *La Razon*
Philippine Islands, *Manila Chronicle*

PUBLISHERS OF WINSTON CHURCHILL'S WAR MEMOIRS
IN VOLUME FORM

French, Librairie Plon (France) and La Palatine (Switzerland)
German, Alfred Scherz (Switzerland)
Dutch, Elsevier (Holland)
Danish, Steen Hasselbalchs Forlag (Denmark)
Swedish, Albert Bonnier Förlags A.B. (Sweden)
Norwegian, J. W. Cappelen (Norway)
Czechoslovakian, Melantrich A.S. (Czechoslovakia)
Italian, Arnoldo Mondadori Editore (Italy)
Greek, Icaros Publishing Company (Greece)
Spanish, José Janes (Spain) and Casa Jacobo Peuser Ltda. (Argentina)
Portuguese, Companhia Editora Nacional (Brazil)

Emery Reves to Winston S. Churchill: telegram [1]

22 December 1947   New York

Airmailing twenty-one factual corrections first book stop Some newspapers suggest consolation for delay short New Year statement by you released exclusively through newspapers contracted serial rights Could you do this Would be nice gesture Merry Christmas

Reves

1.   Churchill was then in Marrakech, working on his war memoirs.

Emery Reves to Winston S. Churchill

22 December 1947   30 Rockefeller Plaza
                                             New York 20, N.Y.

Dear Mr. Churchill,
    As I cabled, I am sending you enclosed a few remarks on the Provisional Final text of Book I. I believe most of the corrections I suggest are valid and,

as you want the proofs to be read from a factual point of view, I presume they are not unwelcome.

May I tell you that I find Book I overwhelming. I do not think there is anything like it in the literature of history writing. There is only one remark I should like to make, although I am sure you came to the same conclusion yourself.

There are too many documents, letters and quotes from speeches in the text. Not as if every one of them would not be of importance and interest. But the narrative is so dramatic, so exciting, that one resents the many interruptions, and the average reader will certainly skip most of the documents for the simple reason that he will be anxious to continue reading the narrative. I very much hope that it will be possible for you to absorb the greatest part of the documents into the narrative, and either to eliminate the original documents or relegate them to the Appendix. I feel that, in many instances, this would not be difficult to do.

For instance, in Chapter XI, you mention a meeting with Grandi, but then, instead of telling about this meeting in your own dramatic language, you merely print a letter you sent to Vansittart about it. The same, when you mention Maisky's visit to Chartwell, and then print your letter to Halifax. It would be far more interesting if you described Maisky's visit and your talk with him as you remember it, and then merely mention that you wrote about it a letter to Halifax.[1]

In my judgement, this is the only editorial work to be done before the volume is published. If you think I could be of any use in this editorial work, I am entirely at your disposal. As a result of the delay, I shall have to be in New York in February only. I could come over for a few weeks in January (either to Marrakesh or to London), as I have nothing specific to do.

With my kindest regards, and very best wishes for the New Year,

Yours sincerely,
Emery Reves

1.   Although Churchill ticked both suggestions in this paragraph, he decided to keep to his original plan, to allow his contemporary report to Sir Robert Vansittart and his report to Lord Halifax (then Foreign Secretary) to serve as the account of his meeting with the Soviet Ambassador, Ivan Maisky.

Winston S. Churchill to Emery Reves: telegram

24 December 1947   Hotel Mamounia
                                                                            Marrakech

Look forward to receiving factual corrections. No question of any statement Christmas wishes

Winston Churchill

Emery Reves to Winston S. Churchill

[undated]   New York [1]

FACTUAL ERRORS IN THE PROVISIONAL FINAL TEXT OF VOLUME I, BOOK I
AND SUGGESTIONS MADE BY EMERY REVES [2]

    1.   Henceforth, unless otherwise stated, all Reves's letters from New York are from 30 Rockefeller Plaza.
    2.   Churchill sent these corrections and suggestions (which do not appear to have survived) to Bill Deakin, to amend the narrative as Deakin felt necessary.

Winston S. Churchill to Emery Reves: telegram

4 January 1948   Marrakech

    Many thanks for your factual corrections which I am carefully considering. The quote Almost Final unquote text of Book I should reach you soon. Pray give me your suggestions for cutting documents and speeches. Much has already been done in new text. My method is to tell the tale from current authentic documents where possible. Please reread the whole from the beginning. Shall be back in London January 22 and would gladly run through text with you thereafter. Have every hope now of delivering Books I and II for page proofs by end January. Have made immense progress out here as you will see. Every good wish.

Emery Reves to Winston S. Churchill: telegram

5 January 1948   New York

    Thanks for cable happy you're better and progressing work stop I'm more and more convinced all speeches documents should be integrated into narrative writing best wishes

Reves

Emery Reves to Winston S. Churchill

5 January 1948   New York

Dear Mr. Churchill,

    I was very happy indeed to receive your cable this morning and to see that you agree with my suggestions.
    Together with Houghton Mifflin we have been discussing the publication of the first volume with the Book-of-the-Month Club, as their cooperation would be of immense help in the distribution. They always make their decisions many months ahead of publication, and they are unable to decide with-

out their independent judges having read the books. In view of the serialisation scheme, it will be impossible to postpone book publication, therefore, as time is very short, we have decided with Houghton Mifflin to let the judges look into the Provisional Final text of Book I.

I refused to part with the copy I have, so the judges came to my office, one by one, and read the text here. These five people, considered to be the highest literary authorities in the United States (Henry Seidel Canby, Dorothy Canfield Fisher, Christopher Morley, John P. Marquand and Clifton Fadiman) are naturally bound to secrecy.

They were all tremendously impressed and the examination of this unfinished text will be sufficient basis for further negotiations.

I watched them reading while they were sitting in my room. They were completely absorbed, but they all skipped the documents and speeches, and said exactly what I indicated to you in my last letter. Encouraged by this unanimous view of the most influential American literary experts, I should now like to make the following suggestions:

1) <u>All</u> speeches, documents should be integrated into the narrative. You can very well refer to documents and speeches and make lengthy quotations from them wherever necessary, but this should be an organic part of the text, to be continued—in quotes—in the same paragraph, even in the same phrase.

2) Quotations should be reduced to a minimum. If you would refer to your past speeches, statements, etc. in a way like: "In 1937 I said in a speech in the House of Commons that . . .", nobody would doubt what you say, and reading would be greatly facilitated.

3) There should be no differentiation of type in the text. Narrative and quotes should be in the same type to avoid interruptions in the reading of one organic text.

4) All documents you wish to use should be printed in full in an appendix, which could be set in smaller type. Documents in the appendix should be classified according to the chapters to which they refer, so as to avoid interruption of the text even by footnotes.

5) I feel that almost all the documents you use are interesting and should be integrated into the text, with very few exceptions. I have only found one section that I would suggest be eliminated, viz. your lengthy exchange of letters with the Admiralty about 14″ or 16″ guns on battleships. This is a technical problem which would interest few readers and would seem to be a sidetrack off the main road. When battleship guns are treated in detail, one wonders why not also bombers, flamethrowers, torpedoes and other weapons. If you wanted to explain the technical problems of weapons, the work might be tremendously inflated and might change its character. I feel that you should concentrate on telling the human drama of the past years and not deviate into technicalities. There may be a few other short passages which

might be omitted, but nothing struck me as much as the memoranda on the gun calibre on battleships. This passage should be reduced to less than a page.

I note that an "almost final" text of Book I. is on the way. As soon as I receive it, I shall carefully re-read the whole text again.

I also hope very much that I shall be able to come over to London for a short stay after your return, if you think my suggestions and assistance might be of some use. It is hardly possible to handle the details by correspondence.

With my best wishes, and kind regards,

Yours sincerely,

Emery Reves

P.S. Do you plan to come over to America in the near future? I would naturally keep all information confidential, but would like to coordinate my plans with yours. E.R.

Sarah Churchill to Winston S. Churchill

[undated]

Darling Papa,

Forgive me butting in. I understand that perhaps you are a little depressed by the criticism of Reves? This may or may not be true. In any case—Don't listen to too many critics—Each critic criticises from a personal angle. The work is yours—from deep within you—and its success depends on it flowing from you in an uninterrupted stream.

I have made the mistake up to now (you have not I know!) of listening to too many people in my work. The only peace I find faintly credible was when I stopped up my ears and listened to myself.

Now of course—one must have critics—particularly those who can criticise the whole sincerely—not from a small window—A journalist will criticise it as being, say a little ponderous—seeing newspaper headlines and excerpts for weeklies etc. A technical man—for the technicalities—a soldier from the army view etc.—It is your story, as you moved through, what will one day be history.

You are the best historian—the best journalist—the best poet—shut yourself up and only listen to a very few, and even then, write this book from the heart of yourself—from the knowledge you have—and let it stand or fall by that—it will stand—everyone will listen to your story.

I hate to see you pale & no longer happily preoccupied—Wow Wow Wow darling—

Your darling Mule

Sarah

Winston S. Churchill to Emery Reves: telegram

[5 January 1948]   Marrakech

There is no question of altering the whole character of work in manner you suggest

Churchill

Emery Reves to Winston S. Churchill: telegram

6 January 1948   New York

Regret misunderstanding there is no question altering character work which is superb and unparalleled stop As explained my letter January fifth integration documents purely technical editorial matter which would be accomplished few days with minimum alteration in text and documents stop Of course eye[1] may be altogether wrong

Reves

---

1. The use of "eye" for "I" was common telegraphic practice.

Winston S. Churchill to Emery Reves: telegram

7 January 1948   Marrakech

Thank you for telegram You have not yet seen (quote) Almost Final (unquote) copy (stop) As these chapters reach you by all means make your suggestions in writing on the copy (stop) We will discuss them in London.

Churchill

Emery Reves to Winston S. Churchill: telegram

7 January 1948   New York

Houghton Mifflin and other publishers would like know final title first volume for catalog they feel quote Downward Path unquote sounds somewhat discouraging would prefer more challenging title indicating crescendo events How do you like quote Gathering Clouds unquote quote The Gathering Storm unquote or quote The Brooding Storm unquote But you probably have better Regards

Reves

Winston S. Churchill to Emery Reves: telegram

12 January 1948   Marrakech

Your letter of January 5 I do not agree with your suggestions but only that you may make them (stop) There is no question of changing the book in manner you suggest

Churchill

Emery Reves to Winston S. Churchill: telegram

14 January 1948   New York

Winston Churchill.

Five Almost Final chapters absolutely perfect. You have reshaped everything as I would have suggested. If other chapters edited likewise our sole criticism fully met. Strongly feel excellent chapters II and III should stay unabridged domestic picture serial for understanding coming events. Relegating documents to Appendix whenever possible making narrative more dramatic just like first five chapters is sole desire Houghton Mifflin and Book of Month Club who approved all my suggestions before I submitted them. Would gladly take QUEEN MARY Saturday but understand Graebner[1] bringing Final Text. Please advise when you expect releasing complete First Volume and whether you think I could be any use London before that date. Must come over near future anyway but am endeavouring solve problem of being simultaneously London and New York during February.

Regards
Reves

1. Walter Graebner, the London representative of Time-Life. In 1965 he published a book of recollections, *My Dear Mister Churchill*.

Chips Gemmell[1] to Winston S. Churchill

1 February 1948   Chartwell

Mr. Churchill,

Mr. Reves rang up this evening to say that he has finished reading Book I, and thinks that as it stands it is absolutely perfect. He has however three points to make, and dictated the following on them:—

1. Ch. VI, page 9, last paragraph. Should not the phrase "I lived in fact from mouth to hand" be the other way round?
2. Ch. XVII, page 2, paragraph 3. In his conversations with M. Blum in Paris Mr. Churchill in answer to a question replies, "No, but ask your Ecole Polytechnique". In my recollection the Ecole Polytech-

nique is a high school to create engineers, whereas the Headquarters of the French Artillery is the Ecole Militaire. But perhaps this point should be checked as I am not one hundred percent certain of it.[2]

3. Ch. XXII, page 7, paragraph 2. Here I think the new Soviet-Nazi documents should be worked in. I believe that Mr. Deakin is already doing this?

C.G.

1.   Chips Gemmell, one of Churchill's secretaries, worked at Chartwell and Hyde Park Gate from 1947 to 1951, and subsequently as Clementine Churchill's secretary at 10 Downing Street. Her first task, at Chartwell, had been to prepare a catalogue of Churchill's wartime documents for use in the war memoirs.

2.   Churchill asked the military adviser on his memoirs, Colonel Pownall, to examine this paragraph. He also sent a copy of Reves's letter to Pownall and Deakin. Pownall gave the answer as "General Headquarters."

Emery Reves to Winston S. Churchill

23 February 1948

This passage on the Baltic Countries still worries me. It now reads:—

"With the exception of Latvia they have not however associated themselves with Hitlerite Germany. They wished to preserve what is now called a Social Democratic Front in sympathy with the Liberal nations of the West."

I am afraid experts of Eastern European policy will challenge that passage. The Social Democratic Parties played a dominant role in the three Baltic Countries in the 1920s. But in the 1930s they decline and by 1935/36 they were completely out of power, without any influence, either banned or leading a miserable ineffective existence. In all the three Countries parliamentary democracy was suppressed and the three Presidents—Paets in Estonia, Ulmanis in Latvia and Smetona in Lithuania—ruled by decrees as absolute dictators. From the local point of view they were dictators to the same degree as Pilsudski or Mussolini. Liberals and Social Democrats in all the three Countries were oppressed. I remember in the middle 1930s I passed through Tallinn when Estonia held a fake election. President Paets two days before the election date arrested all the candidates of the Social Democratic party and held them locked up until the elections were over.

From the point of view of foreign policy it was not possible to unite the three Countries. Estonia and Latvia, having a common frontier with the Soviet Union, hated the Russians more than the Germans. Lithuania (because of Memel) hated the Germans and (because of Vilno) the Poles more than the Russians. So naturally in Geneva the three Countries mainly supported the Western Powers because they were frightened both by Germany and Russia.

Perhaps it would be advisable to omit the reference to the Social Democratic Front, and to the Liberal nations.[1]

E.R.

1. Churchill put a line along the side of this final paragraph and added on the letter, "Done."

Winston S. Churchill: engagement cards

26 February 1948   Chartwell

    11.30 a.m.   Mr. Reves.

Emery Reves to Winston S. Churchill

28 February 1948

NOTES ON PRELIMINARY MATTER BY MR. REVES[1]

1.   <u>Title Page:</u> Perfect
2.   <u>Preface:</u> OK but there is one question. In view of the fact that publishers will receive the final version only in March, and also in view of the fact that in the USA the volume will be published at the earliest at the end of June, in Britain and elsewhere in September, would it not be advisable to advance the date line at the end of the preface from 'January 30' to sometime in March?[2]
3.   <u>Moral of the Work:</u> Perfect.
4.(a) As the Moral of the Work will be repeated in each volume, the term "Work" obviously embraces all the volumes. On the other hand the "Theme of the Work" will be different in each volume. Would it not be advisable to differentiate and to call this page following the "Moral of the Work"—"Theme of the Volume"?
  (b) The layout of this page is different for the two volumes. I think the layout for Vol II is perfect. As the page for Vol I is now printed, the two lines "Volume I" and "1919–1939" should be deleted. The first line is not necessary and the second is not correct because the volume comprises also Bk II which runs until May 1940.
5.   The following <u>half-title page,</u> giving the titles of the two books:
  (a) Again the layout for the two volumes is different and I much prefer the one for Vol II. On that page, for Vol I the line "Volume I" should be deleted, and only the title printed, as in the corresponding layout for Vol II.
  (b) On this page for Vol I, under each book the years are indicated with which each book deals. In the corresponding layout for Vol II, these date lines are missing. It is a matter of taste whether you use date lines

or not under the title of each book, but the policy should be uniform for the whole work. Personally I like better the page for Vol II as it stands.

6.   <u>Contents Table</u> for <u>Maps and Diagrams</u> for the whole volume can be one page, followed by the Contents Table for Book I and Book II.

E.R.

1.   These notes were typed out by one of Churchill's secretaries. Churchill noted on the top, "For Sunday 29th Feb" (one of the regular meetings of his advisers). On the second paragraph he wrote, "Done." Against 5(b) Churchill wrote, "In vol 1 it is in years and in vol 2 only months."
2.   Churchill did as Reves suggested.

Winston S. Churchill: engagement cards

11 March 1948   28 Hyde Park Gate [1]

    11 a.m.   Mr. Reves.

1.   Churchill's London home from 1946 until his death in 1965 was at 28 Hyde Park Gate.

Winston S. Churchill: engagement cards

23 March 1948   28 Hyde Park Gate

    4.30   Mr. Reves.

Winston S. Churchill: engagement cards

22 April 1948   28 Hyde Park Gate

    10.30 a.m.   Mr. Reves.

Winston S. Churchill: engagement cards

6 May 1948 [1]   28 Hyde Park Gate

    10 a.m.   Mr. Reves.

1.   That afternoon Churchill flew from Northolt airport to The Hague, where on the following afternoon he spoke at the opening of the Hague Conference. Addressing the question of European unity, he said, "This involves some sacrifice or merger of national sovereignty. But it is also possible and not less agreeable to regard it as the gradual assumption by all the nations concerned of that larger sovereignty which can also protect their diverse and distinctive customs and characteristics and their national traditions, all of which under totalitarian systems, whether Nazi, Fascist, or Communist, would certainly be blotted out for ever."

Winston S. Churchill: engagement cards

20 July 1948   28 Hyde Park Gate

   6 p.m.   Mr. Emery Reves.

Winston S. Churchill: engagement cards

19 September 1948   Aix-en-Provence

   Mr. Reves arrives.[1]

   1.   Churchill was working on his war memoirs in Provence. As Reves arrived, Churchill's friend Lord Cherwell was leaving, but his principal literary assistant, Bill Deakin, stayed until eight that evening. On the following day, after Clementine Churchill had left for London, Churchill himself moved to Lord Beaverbrook's villa, La Capponcina, on the Cap d'Ail.

Winston S. Churchill: engagement cards

12 October 1948   Chartwell

   1 p.m.   Mr. Reves to lunch.[1]

   1.   Churchill was back at Chartwell, working on his war memoirs. Among those who were at Chartwell that week were two of his literary assistants, Bill Deakin and Denis Kelly.

Winston S. Churchill: engagement cards

17 November 1948   28 Hyde Park Gate

   10.30 a.m.   Mr. Reves.[1]

   1.   The previous caller at 28 Hyde Park Gate that morning was the osteopath Dr. Stephen Ward.

Emery Reves to Winston S. Churchill

21 January 1949   New York
Urgent

Dear Mr. Churchill,

   I received a long letter from the French publishers, asking me to draw your attention to a number of small corrections they suggest in Volume II and three more important ones. They feel that if these few errors in detail and omissions would not be corrected, the book would certainly arouse opposition in wide circles in France, and this would be a great pity in view of the unprecedented popularity you enjoy in France. I am forwarding to you enclosed the corrections and modifications they suggest, and would merely communicate to you some of the more important points in their letter.

1) In the Battle of Dunkirk you are naturally interested in the British troops, although the French feel that French troops played an important part in that battle. The "Association des Anciens Combattants de Dunkerque" has about 20,000 members, who would most certainly resent it if you, whom they consider the greatest friend of France, would leave them entirely unmentioned. In the enclosed list the publishers indicate a few additions which, in their opinion, would appease French sensitivities.

The second point concerns the role of General Prioux who, in their opinion, is judged too severely by you. They say that General Prioux has maintained in the French Army an excellent moral standing, far superior to that of General de la Laurencie. After having carefully examined this point and sounded out the feelings in French army circles, the publishers feel that all the former officers, and even soldiers, who have served under Prioux would protest against your accusation. Their suggestions are on the enclosed list.[1]

In the last chapter of Volume II you speak about the contacts with Vichy. You quote particularly one of the notes sent by you to Marshal Pétain, but you mention nowhere the secret agreements of December 1940 between Lord Halifax and Jacques Chevalier. These secret agreements are well known in France, and they are particularly mentioned in the book "OUR VICHY GAMBLE" by the American professor William L. Langer. Although nobody expects you to write a complete history of the war, the French would certainly be surprised if, in talking about Anglo-Vichy relations these agreements would remain altogether unmentioned. The publishers' suggestions are also on the enclosed list.

In view of the fact that the volume is by now translated everywhere and the plates are about to be prepared, I beg you kindly to consider this matter urgently.

If you feel that some of the corrections suggested by the French publishers should be taken care of in all the editions, please send your corrections as usual to my London office, in which case all publishers will automatically receive them.

Should you agree to make certain corrections only in the French edition, then please send one copy of these corrections directly to

M. Maurice Bourdel, Directeur-General
Librairie Plon
8 rue Garancière
Paris VI.

and another copy to me in New York.

In any case I would be most grateful if you would kindly let me know what you intend to do in this matter.

Yours very sincerely,
Emery Reves

1. The list has not been found.

Bill Deakin to Emery Reves

29 January 1949   28 Hyde Park Gate
London S.W.7

Dear Mr. Reves,

Mr. Churchill has passed to me your letter of January 21, for which he thanks you, enclosing the comments of the French publishers.

1.) Certain modifications have been made in the sense suggested and these are embodied in a new overtake correction.
2.) This has already been the subject of an overtake correction which will by now have reached your office.
3.) As the Rougier negotiations have already been referred to in the book, and as there were several other contacts apart from those relating to Chevalier, I do not imagine that Mr. Churchill wishes to be involved in these points any further.

I have embodied all the modifications made as the result of your letter and the list of points from the French publisher in a new overtake correction, which is being sent automatically to your office.

With best wishes.

Yours sincerely,
F. W. Deakin

Winston S. Churchill to Emery Reves: telegram

3 February 1949   Chartwell

Thank you your cable your point already noticed and correction on way
Churchill

Winston S. Churchill to Emery Reves: telegram

7 February 1949   Chartwell

I have today sent Cassells the final version of volume two stop There are numerous improvements in working and a few corrections of fact These are being sent to you by airmail One case will involve changes in pagination stop

Presume you will not set up till these reach you I am not troubling you with corrections in punctuation which are very numerous You should exercise a final discretion yourselves in all matters of punctuation and typography Kind regards

Winston Churchill

Winston S. Churchill to Emery Reves: telegram

14 February 1949   London

Formal date of delivery is May 1st but many improvements will require to be made after that No date for publication can be fixed at present Regards

Winston Churchill

Winston S. Churchill to Emery Reves: telegram

16 February 1949   Westerham

Final version volume two sent airmail Houghton Mifflin February eleventh stop Have asked them to share this copy with you

Winston Churchill

Winston S. Churchill to Emery Reves: telegram

22 February 1949   Chartwell
                                                               Kent

Volume two book one chapter four page fourteen last paragraph but one stop Certainly tell French publisher and all your other book publishers to delete first sentence of this paragraph about Generals Prioux and de la Laurencie stop[1] Second sentence would then read quote More than half the First French Army found their way unquote etc

Winston Churchill

1.   Churchill had written of his surprise that General Prioux (and his liaison officers) refused to bring back "at least some of his army" to join the British forces being evacuated from Dunkirk. "Not all of them could be so tired," Churchill wrote, "or so far away that it was impossible."

Emery Reves to Winston S. Churchill

23 February 1949   New York

Many thanks for your cable agreeing that the French publisher should leave out the phrase concerning General Prioux. What a pity that you did not make this decision after receiving my letter of January 21st transmitting this suggestion of the French publisher. After publication in Figaro and the violent reaction of General Prioux (I understand many other French Generals have sent protests to Figaro which they intend to publish at the same time) this correction in the book now naturally appears as an admission of a mistake.

In view of your tremendous prestige in France, the French publisher was most anxious that no controversy should arise in which you might be accused of having unjustly condemned a popular general. I wonder whether you would not think it advisable to send a short letter either to General Prioux or to Figaro, admitting this small mistake.[1]

The protests of Gamelin, Weygand and the son of General Billotte appear to me, on the other hand, quite irrelevant. Gamelin's is even stupid. He actually said in his letter that there _were_ strategic reserves, but they were so far away that they could not be used where they were needed. This puts him in a worse position than your statement does.

It seems that your Memoirs have aroused the aggressive spirit of the French generals which was so sadly lacking in 1939. Perhaps it was a mistake not to publish this second volume at the beginning of the war.

I shall have to return to Europe in a few weeks, and would like to arrange my plans so that I could see you as soon as possible in New York or in London. If the American press is correct, you are due to arrive here on the 23rd March. Could you tell me when you expect to leave New York for home? I shall naturally keep any date confidential.[2]

Yours sincerely,
Emery Reves

1.   Churchill decided not to send any such letter but to do a special preface instead (see 14 April 1949).

2.   Churchill left England on 18 March 1949 on board the _Queen Elizabeth_ for the United States, where he spoke in New York (March 25) and at the Massachusetts Institute of Technology, Boston (March 31). This latter speech had been the invitation that took him to the United States, and he returned to England immediately after it, by sea from New York.

Winston S. Churchill to Lord Camrose

23 March 1949   4 East 66th Street
                                                  New York City

The third volume which is now finished, subject to further improvement, carries the narrative through 1941 up to my return by Air from Bermuda in January 1942. The fourth volume, on which considerable progress has been made, runs from February 1942 to the final defeat and surrender of the Germans and Italians in Tunis in May 1943. As at present arranged the fifth volume will have to complete the story up to the unconditional surrender of Germany and Japan in May and August 1945. If all this has to be pressed into the fifth volume it is evident that the scale of the narrative will have to be greatly altered and only the salient features presented. In this period we have the invasion of Sicily and Italy, the Cairo and Teheran Conferences, the operations at Anzio, the great cross-channel invasion of France and the tremendous battles there, the capture of Rome by Alexander, the winter fighting in Germany and the passage of the Rhine, von Rundstedt's counter-attack, the Yalta Conference and the serious differences with Russia, the fate of Poland, the final advance into Germany with further tension between the Western Allies and the Soviets, and finally the general victory over Germany with allusion to the General Election, and the surrender of Japan under the Atomic Bomb. To compress all this into a single volume seems a pity. I therefore suggest that you and your friends should consider a sixth volume which the above features would easily fill with matters of the highest interest and importance. It is necessary for me to know whether this would be agreeable to the purchasers, and what terms they will offer, so that I can plan my work accordingly.

Please let me know. I think all the principals are available in New York. I believe Reves is anxious for a sixth volume and probably Luce and the New York Times will have the same view. All the three volumes are much longer than the stipulated number of words, but of course I cannot tell how much time will be at my disposal in the future. It seems to me this is an opportunity for testing the opinion of all concerned.

I will talk to you about this when we meet, but thought it would be convenient for you to have this <u>aide memoire</u> to show the others.

Emery Reves to Winston S. Churchill

1 April 1949   Boston [1]
Confidential!

Dear Mr. Churchill,

I understand Life and Times object to your suggestions regarding a sixth volume. When I arrived in Boston last night, Henry Laughlin told me that Longwell called him up and persuaded him to stick to the 5 volume scheme. I have talked with Laughlin for several hours and believe convinced him to change his mind. I trust that during his meeting with you he accepted to pay another full instalment on a sixth volume.

It is my strongest conviction that you should write your War Memoirs exactly as you think they should be written. Interference in your own judgement seems to me inadmissible.

As I have already told you I am prepared to pay another Ten Thousand

Pounds for a sixth volume.[2] I am convinced Lord Camrose, Houghton Mifflin, Cassell and the Dominion papers will want to do the same. This means that you are assured to receive for Volume VI over Fifty Thousand Pounds. This should be sufficient guarantee for you to construct your work the way you think best.

My feeling is that if everybody is paying a sixth instalment and you leave it to Luce and Sulzberger[3] to decide whether they want to be the only ones to publish Volume VI without payment, they might feel ashamed to maintain their present attitude. Perhaps it was premature to raise this question at this time. I strongly feel that this change of plan should not be made public until the fourth volume is published.

I am writing this letter because I am anxious to avoid that the views of a popular picture magazine should influence you in writing this monumental work.

I do hope I can see you before you leave Boston. If not—Bon Voyage! I expect to be on the other side in a few weeks.[4]

Yours ever,
Emery Reves

1.   Churchill was also in Boston that day, following his speech at the Massachusetts Institute of Technology. His publisher, Houghton Mifflin, was based in Boston, hence Reves's visit there.
2.   For the foreign-language rights: £10,000 in 1949 was the equivalent of £178,000 in 1996.
3.   Arthur Hays Sulzberger, Publisher, *New York Times,* from 1935 to 1961.
4.   There is no record that Churchill and Reves met in Boston before Churchill's return by train to New York.

Winston S. Churchill to Emery Reves: telegram

14 April 1949   London

When will the French volume edition of volume two be published I might perhaps if there is time write a short special preface of three to four hundred words for them appreciative of the French Army and soothing offence given both to French and Belgian military circles Let me know Regards

Churchill

Winston S. Churchill to Emery Reves: telegram

21 April 1949   Westerham

Would gladly have included additional note in book but see no point in merely making a communique to the French press

Churchill

Emery Reves to Winston S. Churchill

22 April 1949   New York

Dear Mr. Churchill,

As soon as I received your cable suggesting a special preface to the French edition, appreciative of the French Army and soothing the offence given to the French and Belgian military circles, I got in touch by cable with the French publisher. The idea was excellent, and the publisher welcomed it as enthusiastically as I did.

Unfortunately, the first edition was not only printed but already distributed to the book stores, so it was technically impossible to include it in the first printing. The publisher suggested that on the official publication date they would send your preface to all the French and Belgian newspapers, and then naturally include it as a preface in the second printing, which I believe will be necessary soon.

I was sorry to receive your cable this morning, declining this solution, which is the only possible one, and I beg you to reconsider your decision and carry out your original idea. It would be easy for the publisher to tell the press that this special preface, addressed to the French people, arrived too late to be included in the first edition and therefore it is released through the press. It would not be a communiqué made by you to the French press, but it would be your preface, communicated to the press by the French publisher for technical reasons.

Both the publisher and I feel very strongly that, not only for the book, but for your personal position in France, it would be advisable to make such a gesture and appease the spirits.

Yesterday I had a talk with Paul Reynaud, who is in New York. Of course he does not agree with the French generals at all, but he said that the many protests published by them have certainly created a strong impression in France, as the French people are chauvinistic and worship their Army.

Should you decide to write this preface, please let me know in a short cable and also inform Monsieur Maurice Bourdel, Directeur General, Librairie Plon, 8 rue Garanciere, Paris VI. Your preface should then be wired to Paris ELT, naturally at our expense.

I expect to leave New York on May 5th on the Queen Mary and go first to Paris, but I hope to be in London around the middle of the month.

With kindest regards,
Yours very sincerely,
Emery Reves

Winston S. Churchill: engagement cards

18 May 1949   28 Hyde Park Gate

   10 a.m.   Mr. Reves.

Emery Reves to Winston S. Churchill

4 June 1949   Geneva

Dear Mr. Churchill,

I am writing these lines from Geneva just before leaving for Germany where I want to see what are the possibilities of getting your Memoirs published in the near future. I expect to be back in Paris by the 15th of June.

Kindly find enclosed the French translation of the draft Preface you gave me in London. The French publisher suggests to leave out about ten words referring to the guilt of the Chamber and the French politicians. He says that as the purpose of this preface is to appease, it would be unwise to antagonize others.

Please do let me know whether you would approve the insertion of this text in the next French edition or whether you would want to change it.

I would be grateful if you would let me have your view on this matter at your earliest convenience.[1]

Yours very sincerely,
Emery Reves

   1.   Churchill's secretary noted on this letter his reply: "I'll agree to that."

Winston S. Churchill to Emery Reves: telegram

27 June 1949

Hope you can come to see me at Chartwell Saturday July 2 about 5 pm
Winston Churchill

Winston S. Churchill: engagement cards

2 July 1949   Chartwell

   5 p.m.   Mr. Reves.

Emery Reves to Winston S. Churchill

22 August 1949

RE. VOLUME III.

I am most grateful for having been given the opportunity to read Volume IV, as this greatly facilitates my comments on Volume III. Volume I was excellent. Volume II was better. Volume IV is superb. There is no reason why Volume III should not be a step in this crescendo. It would be dangerous for the future volumes to leave it weaker than the first two. Please forgive my mentioning the "bloody public", but I am the Sales Department in this enterprise and it is my duty to draw the attention of the Production Chief to the problems of marketing. It has always been difficult to keep up public interest in a work of many volumes issued at intervals. The only way to overcome this psychological difficulty is to make each volume more interesting than the previous one. If Volume III is not more exciting than the first two volumes were, it will be extremely difficult, if not impossible, to revive interest again for the subsequent volumes.

I do not agree with Life that Vol. III is considerably weaker than the first two volumes and that it needs radical rewriting. I believe that Chapters I, II, III, IX, X, XVII, XXI of Book One and Chapters I, III, V, VII, XII, XIII, XIV, XV, XVI, XVII, XVIII, XIX, XX, of Book Two are highlights which cannot be surpassed by any other section of the entire work.

The need for changes and condensation in Vol. III is, in my opinion, dictated by a basic principle. This work has to deal with the great political, strategic and military problems of the war, and not with the details of minor operations or secondary events, unless they are characteristic and dramatic, like the sinking of the Bismarck.

I feel that Vol. III contains too much detail on the African campaign prior to Alamein, on the Middle East and on Naval operations. I am fully aware that at that period of the war, these were all important matters. But in this work they should be handled in a proper perspective, in proportion to the more important matters to come. The entire Vol. III and Book I of Vol IV are dominated by detailed minutes and telegrams on these day to day routine operations. It seems to me too much. The importance of these events would be emphasized if telegrams on the movements of a few battalions, one or two squadrons and fifteen or twenty guns could be eliminated. In my opinion the Chapters which could be reduced by perhaps 50,000 words are mainly Chapters IV, V, VII, VIII, XI, XIII, XV, XVI, XIX of Book One and Chapters II, III, IV, X of Book Two.

On the other hand certain other chapters which I shall indicate below, should be extended and important documents, like the plans you prepared on your voyage to Washington, and which are printed in Chapt. XVI of Book Two, should remain unchanged, by all means.

Two more general remarks before entering into details. Although war memoirs must naturally deal with military affairs, political problems, political strategy, political battles are even more important, as they determine military operations. I feel therefore that at least 25% of the text should be devoted to political issues. Not only because of their supreme importance, but mainly because you are the only man who can leave the facts on these matters to posterity. Many generals are about to write their memoirs on the various military operations. But in view of the fact that Roosevelt is dead and Stalin will never publish his documents, you are the only man who can reveal the decisive issues of the last war. At the end of Vol. III Book II you devote six chapters to your visit to Washington. These chapters constitute in my opinion the most interesting section of this volume and should be made an example for the handling of the other important meetings, not only with Roosevelt and Stalin but also with the heads of governments of lesser states. I feel that the chapter on the Atlantic Meeting should be extended and that four or five chapters each should be devoted to the Conferences of Teheran, Yalta, etc. narrating events, if possible, hour by hour and printing as many stenographic notes on conversations as possible. I trust that detailed protocols on these meetings are available.

It is in view of the space which has to be reserved for the more important, and politically more interesting events that the revision of Vol. III should be undertaken. Entirely on my own responsibility and without having ever heard of your intentions in this respect, I assume that the work will contain six volumes. In assuming this, I would like to see Vol. III shortened and the narrative carried forward somewhat, so that Vol. IV might end with the surrender of Italy.

I fully realize your reluctance to do this as your visit to Washington is a majestic ending to Vol. III. But if you examine the material of the volumes to come and the space that must be reserved for their proper handling, you may also feel this necessity. Otherwise you may be faced with the alternative of a seventh volume or of a considerably accelerated rhythm in the narrative of the events of 1944 and 1945, both of which, I believe, should be avoided. If you decide against carrying forward the narrative of Vol. III, then the next best solution appears to me to be the reduction of the text to about 200–220,000 words.

My last general remark is that all abbreviations should be avoided and every word should be written out in full. I realize that for you and for your collaborators all these abbreviations come as a matter of fact. But I am certain that already today many Englishmen do not remember the meaning of most of these abbreviations and I fear that in two generations few of them will. In the U.S. almost all corresponding military organizations and terms had other designations and other abbreviations. To the American public, even today, British abbreviations are meaningless. This is even more the case in all the foreign language countries. It is true that at the end of each book a list of the abbreviations with explanations could be printed, but it is rather irritating for a reader to interrupt reading in every second paragraph and turn to another page to find the meaning of an abbreviation. In the interests of fluent reading I would suggest therefore that before final proofing one of your collaborators should mark for the printer the full name of every abbreviation, so that the reader in Chicago and in Zurich (most important people!) should know that when you are writing to the C.I.G.S. you are actually writing to the Chief of the Imperial General Staff.

Emery Reves to Winston S. Churchill [1]

22 August 1949

RE VOLUME IV
(Preliminary)

This volume is superb. I shall remit to you shortly some remarks on the chapters I have read.

Today I would merely take the liberty to make suggestions regarding the titles. "Defeat" and "Success" appear to me too general and not characteristic to these books as we had suffered some defeats also in previous books. I would like to see as titles more of your own expressions used during the war and I would suggest the following titles:

Book I "The End of the Beginning."
Book II "The Beginning of the End."

As for the entire volume, at the moment I like best the title you give to one chapter: "The Torch is lit". But there may be a better one. [2]

E.R.

1. Chap. I. After the dramatic close of Vol. III, this exchange of telegrams with Curtin seems to be a somewhat weak opening of Vol. IV. As these telegrams refer to the turn of the tide in Russia, perhaps it would be appropriate to begin this Volume with the big battles raging in Russia which at that time dominated the scene, followed by the controversy with the Australians. [3]

    I understand that you are telling in this work only the British story of the War. But the great political and military events in America and in Russia cannot be completely ignored. The battles of the Philippines, Midway, Guadalcanal, Moscow, Leningrad, Stalingrad, etc. must, I submit, be mentioned at proper places, so that the reader may have a complete and correct picture of the overall war situation at every moment and in a position to see the unfolding story in proper perspective. I believe one or two pages should be given to each of the major events in the American and Russian war. Perhaps it would be advisable to indicate your method in a short preface to Vol. IV in which events outside the British fronts begin to influence the course of the war.

2. Chapters II and III "The Set-Back in the Desert" and "Retreat in Malaya" do not seem to be completed.

3. Chap. IV ("The Dark Valley") p. 4, line 2. "This I will describe when the time comes". It should be mentioned what you have in mind, otherwise reference meaningless.

4. Chap. V "A Vote of Confidence and its Background". First part most interesting, afterwards too many telegrams without narrative.

5. Chap. VI "The Fall of Singapore". First paragraph is too journalistic. It will be outdated already in a few years. It should either be rewritten or deleted.

6. Same Chapter, last page, "President to Former Naval Person"— reference to "episode in the Channel". What was this episode?[4]

7. Chap. VII "Burma. The End of ABDA".[5] The first part of this Chap. is very interesting. In latter part several detailed telegrams might be deleted.

8. Chap. VIII "U Boat Paradise". p. 4, Why could the damage made to Scharnhorst and Gneisenau not be made public? The enemy knew about it. Please, explain.[6]

9. Same Chapter, p. 4, par. 4, line 1, "the Atlantic East Coast" should read "the Atlantic East Coast of America"—otherwise one thinks of the European coast.

10. Chap. X "The Cripps Mission". This Chap. is excellent and strong. p. 6, par. 1, President on India . . . "I reacted so strongly . . . etc" What did the President say? And what did you answer?[7]

11. Chap. XII "The Arctic Convoys" p. 2, President to F.N.P.,[8] reference to "Bolero". Please give meaning of this code word in parenthesis or footnote. Chapter excellent, but ending somewhat flat.

12. Chap. XII "Madagascar". "Madagascar 1941" Was it not 1942?[9] Several telegrams to different persons express the same thought, i.e. that Madagascar was supposed to be a help and not a hindrance, and that the troops must go on to India. Some of these telegrams might be deleted, merely indicating that similar messages were sent to X, Y, Z . . . On the other hand the operation in Madagascar itself, the arrangements with the local French and the Free French need more detailed description.

13. Chapters XIV, XV, XVI "Second Front Now", "The Molotov Visit", and "Strategic Natural Selection" are superb!

14. Chapter XVII "Rommel Attacks" p. 2, par. 7, reference to Cologne bombing. In my opinion the Bombing of Cologne must be described in detail. Preparation, operation, results.[10]

15. Chapter XVIII "My Second Visit to Washington. Tobruk." An excellent chapter but certain passages should be extended.
    a) Your first meeting with Eisenhower deserves 1–2 pages. Tell your first impressions and perhaps give a short portrait of him.[11]

b) There are many telegrams on Tobruk, but a dramatic description of the Battle of Tobruk and circumstances of the surrender is lacking. Believe that 1–2 pages on that event should be included.

16. Chap. XX "Decision for Torch". Chapter very good, but ending needs something more exciting.

VOLUME IV, BOOK II.

17. Chap. I "My Journey to Cairo". This Chapter needs some polishing off at the end to lead over to the next chapter which begins: "Late that night . . ." What night?

18. Chap. II "Moscow". Excellent!

19. Chap. III "Return to Cairo". A good chapter, but not as finished as the preceding two chapters. The messages need to be bound closer together by narrative. The arrival of Montgomery and your first meeting with him should be described in more detail. Just as when you first met Eisenhower in Washington, a leading actor of acts to come appears for the first time on the scene. He needs proper introduction, a short portait, an appreciation.[12]

20. Chap. IV "The Final Shaping of Torch". Excellent!

21. Chap. V "Suspense and Strain". Last two letters to "Mr. Barrington-Ward" appear to be out of context. Who is he? (The late Editor of The Times?) To what do these two letters answer? Believe they should be deleted, or episode—if important—described.[13]

22. Chap. VI "The Battle of Alamein". I have so often suggested condensations of African events that I may be permitted to say here that this crucial battle needs to be described in greater detail. The chapter should have a special ending, emphasizing the importance of this event. Perhaps you might end this chapter with the words you used the other day in our conversation: "Before Alamein we never had a victory. After Alamein we never had a defeat."

23. Chapter VII "The Torch is Lit."
   a) Gen. Clark's secret mission to Algiers needs to be told in 1–2 pages. Otherwise the later role of Gen. Juin and some events are not clear.[14]
   b) Giraud's escape from France to Gibraltar should be described in about one page.[15]

24. Chapter VIII "The Darlan Episode".[16] This Chapter is very interesting but incomplete. The "Episode" should be told to the end, including Darlan's assassination. Reference to the assassination is made in Ch. XI p. 7, last par., but this is not sufficient. Suggest 3–4 additional pages containing further dealings with Darlan, his assassination and the political situation in Algiers after his death.

25. Chap. X "Russia and the Western Allies" p. 12, "Former Naval Person to President." This should read "Stalin to Prime Minister".

26. Same Chapter. Two references to Stalingrad (Congratulations to Stalin.) In my opinion the Battle of Stalingrad must be described and appreciated in at least 5–6 pages.[17]

27. Chap. XI "Our need to meet." p. 1, line 2, "The End of the Beginning was at hand." If title of Book II is "The Beginning of the End", this phrase should read "'The Beginning of the End' was at hand."

28. Same Chap. p. 2, par 3, ". . . as my following telegram to the President shows." should read ". . . as the following telegram of the President to me shows."

29. Chap. XII "The Casablanca Conference". Excellent!

30. Chap. XIII "Adana and Tripoli" p. 3, par 2, "Admiral Q". It should be explained that this is Pres. Roosevelt. Chapter is very good but ending does not seem to be finished.

Chapters XIV, XV and XVI appear to be unfinished.

I have not seen Chapters "Political Tensions", "The Bay of Bengal", "The Vote of Censure" of Book I.

1.   Churchill noted on this document, "Miss Sturdee. Please make 4 or 5 copies of this in typescript and keep handy." He added, "Not for printer" and "Put by."

2.   Churchill chose "The Hinge of Fate" as the volume's title and called the two books "The Onslaught of Japan" and "Africa Redeemed."

3.   John Curtin was Prime Minister of Australia from 7 October 1941 to 13 July 1945. Churchill decided to keep all the Australian telegrams (twelve pages of telegrams in all) and to make them the central theme of his opening chapter.

4.   Churchill deleted this reference altogether (using omission marks) in the published version of the President's telegram. The episode was the escape of three German warships from Brest through the Channel to the North Sea.

5.   The American, British, Dutch, and Australasian Command in the Far East.

6.   Reves could not know, and Churchill was unable to explain, that the details of the damage made to the two battle cruisers were known to the British only through their clandestine reading of top-secret German naval signals (Ultra).

7.   Churchill had sent Sir Stafford Cripps (formerly the British Ambassador to the Soviet Union) to India, to report on what measures of Indian constitutional reform ought to be considered. In the final version of the chapter, Churchill published his telegram to Roosevelt in which, on 4 March 1942, he explained his position on India.

8.   F.N.P. (Former Naval Person) was the code name Churchill used in his correspondence with President Roosevelt after he left the Admiralty in May 1940 and became Prime Minister (before which, as First Lord of the Admiralty, he was Naval Person).

9.   Churchill deleted the year altogether as it was predominantly 1942, but there was a reference to General de Gaulle's proposal for a Free French operation against Madagascar "as early as December 16, 1941, after the entry of Japan into the war."

10.   Churchill was content with the ten lines devoted to the bombing of Cologne (mostly from his speech to the House of Commons on 2 June 1942).

11.   Churchill first met General Eisenhower in Washington, at the time of the preparation of the Allied landings in North Africa in November 1942, which Eisenhower commanded; they subsequently met many times before and after Eisenhower's appointment as Supreme Commander of the Allied Expeditionary Force, which landed in Normandy in June 1944. Churchill was content with the half page devoted to his first meeting with Eisenhower and Clark. "I was immediately impressed by these remarkable but hitherto unknown men. . . . We had a most agreeable discussion, lasting for over an hour."

12.   General Montgomery (later Field Marshal Viscount Montgomery of Alamein) commanded the 8th Army in North Africa from 1942 to 1943 and during the invasions of Sicily and Italy; he was Commander-in-Chief, Ground Forces, for the Allied landings in Normandy. As Churchill was with his few lines on Eisenhower, he was also content with the two paragraphs he had already written about Montgomery. These contained the report Churchill had been given of "Montgomery's brilliant qualities as a commander in the field."

13.   Churchill took out the two letters he had written to Barrington-Ward.

14.   General Mark Clark was chosen by General Eisenhower to plan the 1942 Allied landings in North Africa (to which end he made a secret visit to Vichy-controlled Algiers); he was subsequently Commander of the Allied forces in Italy. General Alphonse Juin was captured by the Germans in 1940, released in 1941, and made Military Governor of Morocco. He changed sides after the Allied landings in North Africa, helping to defeat the German Afrika Korps.

15.   General Henri Giraud was captured by the Germans in 1940 but escaped, reaching North Africa in 1942, when he joined the Allied cause.

16.   Admiral Jean-Louis-Xavier-François Darlan was Commander-in-Chief of the French Navy, 1939–1940; Minister of the Navy under Vichy, 1940–1941; and commander of the French forces in North Africa, 1942 (when he concluded an armistice with the Allies). He was killed by an anti-Vichy assassin.

17.   Although Churchill did not write as long a section on Stalingrad, he did have twelve references to the battle at different places in the volume.

Winston S. Churchill: engagement cards

29 August 1949   Cap d'Ail

5 p.m.   Mr. Reves.

Winston S. Churchill to Emery Reves

1 September 1949   La Capponcina,[1]
                                                                          Cap d'Ail

My dear Reves,

I am sorry I shall not see you again before I leave. Thank you so much for your invaluable corrections, all of which will be most carefully studied. I am now going to concentrate on Volume III.

I would be glad if you would return the copy of "THE END OF A.B.D.A.", as soon as you have finished with it.

Yours sincerely,
Winston S. Churchill

1.   Lord Beaverbrook's villa in the South of France.

Emery Reves to Winston S. Churchill

6 September 1949   Villefranche sur Mer [1]

Kindly find enclosed the Chapter "The End of A.B.D.A." I like this chapter very much except its title. Very few of your readers will remember what "A.B.D.A." means. I would suggest

"The Japanese conquest of the Dutch East Indies"
"Conquest of the Dutch East Indies"
"Conquest of the Dutch Empire"
"Loss of the Dutch East Indies"
"Defeat in the Far East"

or something like that, expressing the subject of the chapter. [2]

I am leaving for Geneva and shall return to Paris on the 15th (33 Champs Elysées). Perhaps you might send over the remaining political chapters of Vol. IV which I have not yet seen.

Emery Reves

1.   Villefranche is on the French Riviera, five miles from the Cap d'Ail, where Churchill was staying.
2.   Churchill chose the title "The Loss of the Dutch East Indies."

N. S. Sturdee to Emery Reves

20 September 1949   28 Hyde Park Gate

Dear Mr. Reves,

Mr. Churchill received your letter of September 6, for which he thanks you. He agrees with what you say about "A.B.D.A." and is changing the title of the chapter. [1]

I enclose herewith Chapter IV of Volume IV, Book I, A VOTE OF CONFIDENCE and Chapter V of the same book, POLITICAL TENSIONS: CABINET CHANGES, which Mr. Churchill would be glad to have back after you have read them.

Yours sincerely,
N. S. Sturdee
Private Secretary

1.   The title chosen for the chapter on ABDA (American, British, Dutch, Australasian Command in the Far East) was "The Loss of the Dutch East Indies."

Emery Reves to Winston S. Churchill

27 October 1949   Paris

Dear Mr. Churchill,

I have given much thought to the titles of Book I and Book II of
Volume III which for foreign language publications should be changed. The
title of the Volume "THE GRAND ALLIANCE" is, of course, excellent.

These are my thoughts:

1°—DING DONG—I am afraid very few of your foreign readers will
know the poem by Sterne and will grasp the meaning of it. It
seems to me that the translation of the poem is most difficult, and
will not be intelligible to foreign readers without explanation. Also
the imitation of the sound of bells is different in many languages. I
believe in German it is "Bim Bum".

2°—MIGHTY ALLIES—As you know, most foreign language publishers issue each book under separate cover, at different times.
The title page of Book II would therefore read:

THE GRAND ALLIANCE
MIGHTY ALLIES

This is a repetition.

My feeling is that the titles of the Books should not be general or symbolic
but should express the main event of each book, viz. the entrance in the War
of Soviet Russia and of America, which together created "THE GRAND
ALLIANCE", the title of the Volume.

My suggestions for titles are therefore:

Book I —The Invasion of Soviet Russia
         Soviet Russia attacked
         Germany attacks Soviet Russia
         The German-Russian War [1]
Book II—America at War
         Attack on America
         America Attacked
         War comes to America [2]

These are merely suggestions. You will certainly formulate the titles better in
your own language. But the structure of the Volume would be clearer if the
titles would be like this:

THE GRAND ALLIANCE
Book I   Book II
The Invasion of Soviet Russia   America at War

I would be most grateful if you would let me know what you think of those
suggestions which I am making from the point of view of foreign language
publications.

I would also be grateful if you would be good enough to tell me whether you can foresee when Book I may be delivered.

1.   Churchill chose as the title for Book 1 "Germany Drives East."
2.   Churchill chose as the title for Book 2 "War Comes to America."

Winston S. Churchill to Emery Reves: telegram

5 November 1949   Westerham

Distribution of Book Five must await 250 printing stop Hope this will be completed in ten days or so stop I have sent you one copy for your personal convenience only Best wishes

Winston Churchill

Winston S. Churchill to Emery Reves: telegram

7 November 1949   Westerham,
                                                                            Kent

Should be glad to hear your impression of Book Five stop Hope to begin 250 printings by November 15th The Daily Telegraph can no doubt issue them to you in batches as they come through

Winston Churchill

N. S. Sturdee to Emery Reves

25 November 1949   28 Hyde Park Gate
                                                                 London S.W.7.

Dear Mr. Reves,
    Mr. Churchill would like to know what you think of this Preliminary Matter for Volume III. He says you may mark it in any way you like, but he would like it back by next Tuesday.

Yours sincerely,
N. S. Sturdee

Winston S. Churchill to Emery Reves

27 November 1949   28 Hyde Park Gate
Private

My dear Reves,
    Thank you for your letter of [October 27]; I note the suggestions you make for titles.
    I prefer for Book I, "Germany Drives East," and for Book II, "War Comes to America."

The approximate wordage is at present:—

Book I 115,000
Book II 95,000
210,000

There will be about 80,000 words in the Appendices, which are very extensive. I have noticed how popular the Minutes have been with many readers, but in this volume there are also a great many important Directives. The total wordage of the book will therefore be a little under 300,000.

Yours sincerely,
Winston S. Churchill

Winston S. Churchill: engagement cards

30 November 1949 [1]   28 Hyde Park Gate

    12 noon   Mr. Reves.

    1.   Churchill's seventy-fifth birthday.

Winston S. Churchill: engagement cards

2 December 1949   28 Hyde Park Gate

    10 a.m.   Mr. Reves.

Winston S. Churchill: engagement cards

26 December 1949   Chartwell

    1.15 p.m.   Mr. Reves to luncheon.

F. W. Deakin to Emery Reves

2 April 1950   Chartwell
CONFIDENTIAL

My dear Reves,
    As I told you on the telephone on Saturday, I am writing to you about the French Preface. The main point is that Mr. Churchill has received an aggressive and disagreeable letter from M. Pirenne, acting on behalf of King Leopold, and quoting as evidence for complaint the paragraph in the revised Preface for the second French and Belgian editions which refers to the Belgian Army in 1940.

Although Mr. Churchill now realises that this Preface has been used in the French and Belgian Press, he does not want it to appear in any new edition of his Memoirs so long as the present political crisis in Belgium continues.

Would you therefore please ensure that the Preface is withdrawn?

I hope that we can meet in London at the end of the month,

Yours sincerely,
Bill Deakin

Winston S. Churchill to Emery Reves

3 April 1950   Chartwell

My dear Reves,

I have looked through the book you kindly sent me. It surprises me to find so many great mistakes in so small a book entitled GREAT MISTAKES OF THE WAR.

I received the one advance copy of THE GRAND ALLIANCE some days ago. Perhaps the others are on the way. I am so sorry that you have not been able to transmit the corrections with which we have furnished you to the people who are setting up your text. It is not that my corrections came too late for Volume editions but that Houghton Mifflin have published very early indeed and your clients have imitated them.

I am having the latest versions of the contents tables of Volume IV printed and will send you confidentially a copy during this week.

Your paragraph 4. I have not said anything about a delivery of Volume IV earlier than the middle of August. I still think this will be possible.

I note what you say about announcing that the Work will contain six volumes at the moment when Volume IV is published, and I will let you know in plenty of time. I have also noted your paragraphs 6 and 7.

I think it would be a good thing if you came over here for a day or two before you go back to New York. I have not yet finally decided on the title for Volume IV. It might be THE BALANCE TURNS. The proofs are in a very advanced condition and you can read them over here if you like to come.

Yours sincerely,
Winston S. Churchill

Winston S. Churchill: engagement cards

11 May 1950   28 Hyde Park Gate

12 noon   Mr. Reves.

Winston S. Churchill to Emery Reves

20 June 1950   28 Hyde Park Gate,
                                                         London S.W.7

My dear Reves,

Thank you so much for your letter of June 13. I cannot form any opinion about State-Secretary Meissner's Memoirs. I did not know that he was writing his story, and I do not know what they contain.

I have had an agreeable letter from Mr. Laughlin saying that he likes Volume IV and that they propose to publish in November.

Yours vy sincerely,
Winston S. Churchill

G. R. G. Allen [1]: *proposed draft letter to Emery Reves*

24 July 1950

Mr. Churchill has read with interest the letter addressed to you by the Elsevier Publishing Co and the enclosure dealing with the activities of Dutch submarines in the Far East in December 1941.

Mr. Churchill considers that no alteration should be made to his own text in the Book but has no objection to the publication, in the Dutch edition of his Volume III, of an amplifying footnote recording further details of the exploits of Dutch submarines at this time in the Allied cause. He is very sensible of the importance of the part they played both then and later.

It should be clearly understood however that any such addition is issued on the sole responsibility of the publishers and it must be explained in the text that Mr. Churchill cannot accept responsibility for the accuracy of the details given.

To assist in the further elucidation of these matters Mr. Churchill has invited the British Admiralty to comment on the details given in the survey by the Dutch Naval Staff. The accompanying note, prepared by one of Mr. Churchill's staff, draws attention to certain minor differences between the information available in Holland and that at the disposal of the Admiralty. This note may be helpful in drafting the final note for inclusion in the book. The Admiralty have no comment to make on other details in the survey.

Finally, Mr. Churchill would have no objection to the inclusion in the footnote of a statement to the following effect:

Mr. Churchill has added that the gallant part played by the Dutch armed forces in the later fighting in the East Indies will be recorded in his next volume.

1.   Commodore George Roland Gordon Allen. A naval officer since 1911, he had served at the battle of Jutland (1916). In 1942 he had been Officer-in-Charge of the naval landings in Algeria. From 1945 he helped Churchill on the war memoirs, principally on the naval aspects. He died in 1980, at the age of eighty-nine.

Malcolm Muggeridge: diary [1]

23 August 1950

Received unexpected call from Churchill's secretary to go down to Westerham to see him. Drove down in an office car accompanied by character named Emery Reves, who has long acted as Churchill's agent. Churchill has the characteristic 18th-century nobleman's attitude that he should have a Jew to look after his financial affairs, and in this case there is no question but that the choice has turned out well. Driving down Reves explained to me how he had first managed to persuade Churchill to let him look after his interests. He said that Churchill had an insatiable need for money and reckons to spend about £10,000 a year net. His family costs him a lot, and though he doesn't live luxuriously, he lives amply and travels with a great suite, which is very expensive.

1. Malcolm Muggeridge, a popular writer and broadcaster, published this diary extract in *As It Was* (London, 1981), page 408.

Winston S. Churchill: engagement cards

23 August 1950   Chartwell

5 p.m.   Mr. Muggeridge & Mr. Reves.

Winston S. Churchill: engagement cards

1 October 1950   Chartwell

1.15 p.m.   Mr. Emery Reves to luncheon.

Emery Reves to Winston S. Churchill

3 November 1950   Paris
Private

Dear Mr. Churchill,

I have just returned to Paris from a Scandinavian trip. I felt it necessary to discuss personally the question of Volume VI with the publishers of your Memoirs in Amsterdam, Copenhagen, Stockholm and Oslo. In these countries the change from five to six volumes is bound to have disastrous consequences which, unfortunately, I had not anticipated.

You probably know that in Holland, Denmark, Sweden and Norway the publishers have issued your work on a subscription basis. All readers, by signing a subscription contract, pledged themselves to take all the five volumes, and the publishers in turn pledged to deliver "THE SECOND WORLD WAR by Winston S. CHURCHILL" in five volumes, at a price fixed in

advance. They cannot raise the price, nor can they force their subscribers
to accept and pay for a sixth volume without breaking their contracts with
thousands of subscribers.

For three weeks I have been discussing this problem with the Scandinavian
publishers who are quite desperate. They have been your publishers for several decades and would be only too happy to publish each year a new volume
by you for another few decades. But this time, they are in a terrible situation
if they cannot fulfill the contracts with their subscribers.

They are particularly frightened because, some time ago, a great Danish
publishing house tried to change a similar subscription contract in connection with a dictionary they offered in 24 volumes. When they were nearing
the end of the alphabet, they discovered that they needed 27 volumes, and
tried to sell the additional three books. One subscriber took the matter to
Court. The Court decided that the publishers had contracted to deliver the
entire work in 24 volumes and that they either must deliver to the subscribers
the additional three volumes free of charge or take back from the subscribers
the volumes already delivered and refund to all readers their money.

We have had long discussions with lawyers, particularly in Copenhagen in
Mr. Hasselbalch's office. All lawyers say that the publishers cannot risk a lawsuit and that they will have to print and deliver the Sixth Volume free of
charge to all the subscribers. This, of course, means that these publishers
would end the publication of the Memoirs with a considerable loss.

In this connection, I would like to mention that the profits of these publishers have always been extremely small as they have calculated their subscription price on the basis of 5 volumes of 150.000 to 200.000 words each,
as foreseen in the contracts. In view of the fact that each volume was nearly
twice as long, their printing and paper expenses were considerably higher,
owing to the subscription contracts, they could not raise the price accordingly.

During these recent negotiations, I was trying to find a solution. Finally, I
think, I have found one. Anyway, the four publishers in question greeted it as
their salvation and are now praying that you accept it.

I feel that what makes a sixth volume necessary is mainly the need of a
detailed description and analysis of the Conferences of Yalta and Potsdam
and the postwar consequences of the decisions taken at those two Conferences. Examining the draft Tables of Content you gave me for Volumes V
and VI, I believe that you could easily finish the military story of THE SEC-
OND WORLD WAR, up to the capitulation of Germany and your resignation from office, mentioning only briefly, whatever is unavoidable, of the
Yalta meeting. This way you would not deviate from the original contract
and you would complete your story of "THE SECOND WORLD WAR" in
five volumes, as foreseen. The following year, or later, you could then publish
an additional volume on the postwar arrangements and their consequences,

giving all the documents and facts on Yalta and Potsdam in connection with postwar developments.

If you could adopt this plan, all your publishers could truthfully say to their subscribers that they have delivered to them your "MEMOIRS ON THE SECOND WORLD WAR" in five volumes. One year later, they could then issue an extra volume by you, under a different title, the same way as you have published "Aftermath" after "The World Crisis". This extra volume (which would be de facto the sixth volume) could be, of course, a much shorter one. 100.000 – 120.000 words seem quite sufficient and may have a higher value than a volume of 300.000 words.

When this idea was unanimously and enthusiastically welcomed by the publishers, I wondered whether it would appear attractive to you. I believe there are several reasons why this plan may be preferable from your own point of view. Permit me to mention a few:

1) During our last meeting you said that Volume V will not be as good as Volume IV. In the interest of the work such decline must be avoided. Analyzing the draft Tables of Content of the next volume I find, indeed, that the material is somewhat meagre and that there is less "meat" in Volume V than in Volume IV. Military operations in Sicily, the Aegean Islands and Burma are of limited interest today, and this Volume could be as good as any previous one, if you reduced the documentation on these secondary military operations to a minimum, if you gave Teheran, Cairo, Washington and Quebec in all details, Yalta only very briefly, and narrated the military liberation of Europe until the capitulation of Germany and your resignation.

2) During our last conversation, you also mentioned that political conditions in 1952 may require the postponement of the publication of Volume VI containing your story of Yalta and Potsdam. If you dealt with these Conferences in a separate book, you would have complete liberty to decide when that book should be published, without the danger of your MEMOIRS ON THE SECOND WORLD WAR remaining unfinished. As things stand now, it is certain that you will finish and publish Volume V. But in one year, or in 1952, you may be in office, there may be a war, and you may be unable to publish your story on Yalta. If you would plan to publish this story in a separate book, there would be no harm in delay, or even in not publishing at all such a book. But if that story is planned to be the Sixth Volume of your MEMOIRS ON THE SECOND WORLD WAR, there is a danger that this work, which will certainly go down in History as your greatest literary accomplishment, will remain unfinished.

3) The question of payment. I raised this question with several of the most important European newspapers. They all take the same attitude as Life and The New York Times. They categorically refuse to make any additional payment for a sixth series, saying that the contracts clearly state that they have

purchased the serial rights of your War Memoirs at a fixed price and that I am, by contract, obliged to deliver to them the complete work irrespective of the number of volumes. They all say that they will publish a sixth series, if necessary, but that they would not pay anything beyond what they contracted to pay for the entire work. There can be no question that their legal position is sound.

This, of course, does not alter my pledge to pay Lord Camrose for a Sixth Volume. In making your decision, I beg you to disregard my personal problem, and to consider only your own interests and the interest of your Work. I am communicating the reaction of your publishers merely for your information.

I do not know what Life and The New York Times will finally decide. But even if they would make an additional payment, after the attitude they have taken, they would certainly do so only under a moral pressure which would inevitably leave some unpleasant thoughts in their minds.

All this would be avoided if you would not ask for a change of the contracts but would fulfill them to the letter by finishing the military history of The Second World War up to your resignation in five volumes. There can be no doubt, in my opinion, that if we would offer, after the completion of "THE SECOND WORLD WAR", an additional volume, under a separate title, dealing with Yalta, Potsdam and the postwar developments, all publishers and newspapers would be glad to publish it and would accept to pay for it substantial amounts, probably even more than for any of the previous volumes.[1]

For your information, I am enclosing copies of the letters I received from the Attorney of the Publishing House Hasselbalch in Copenhagen, and from the Director of the Publishing House Elsevier in Amsterdam.

Trusting that you will give this problem your serious consideration and that you will be able to make a final decision within 2–3 weeks,

I beg to remain,
Yours very sincerely,
Emery Reves

P.S. I am sending a copy of this letter to Lord Camrose, assuming that you will discuss this matter with him.

ER.

---

1. In the event, both the British and American publishers accepted a sixth volume of the war memoirs. It was published in 1953, on both sides of the Atlantic, as "Triumph and Tragedy."

Winston S. Churchill: engagement cards

21 January 1951

11 a.m.   Mr. Emery Reves.

Winston S. Churchill: engagement cards

2 May 1951

    11.30 a.m.   Mr. Emery Reves.

Winston S. Churchill: engagement cards

4 May 1951

    3 p.m.   Mr. Reves.

Emery Reves to Winston S. Churchill

10 May 1951   Paris

Dear Mr. Churchill,

Before I left London I had an opportunity to see Lord Camrose who promised me to discuss with you the matter of your letter to the Publishers.[1]

I am afraid I have not explained clearly enough the purpose of such a letter. Nobody questions your right to write your War Memoirs in six volumes instead of five, as originally contemplated. Consequently, there is no need to re-state your right which is self-evident.

Some publishers face a serious problem. In order to try to solve this problem, they are anxious that their readers should receive directly from you the information that your War Memoirs will consist of six volumes. There is no question of making an "apology". What is requested is a simple statement of facts. You as the author of this work should inform your various publishers that you have decided to complete your work in six volumes instead of five for such and such reasons. That is all your Publishers ask. This seems to me a simple gesture of courtesy without any legal meaning. It certainly cannot be interpreted as an apology.

I feel that the letter you drafted is very good if you leave out the legal phrase which would give your letter an entirely different character. It would draw the attention of people to a legal question which does not exist and which is precisely our purpose to avoid.

It would be perhaps nice if you would mention in your letter the highlights of Volumes V and VI which would clearly indicate the reasons why you need a sixth volume. I have indicated these subject matters in my original draft which, together with your draft, I left with Lord Camrose.

I would be most grateful if you could let me have your final draft and if your Secretary would also send over to Paris 15–16 sheets of your letterhead. I shall then prepare the letters to the various Publishers and submit them to you for signature.

With all my apologies for this trouble,
Yours very sincerely
Emery Reves

1.   Reves wanted Churchill to write direct to his various publishers about the reason for the increase in the number of volumes.

Winston S. Churchill to Emery Reves

24 May 1951   Chartwell

My dear Reves,

At the time I began to write my book on the Second World War it was impossible to foresee, from the start, how the story would go. I thought that five volumes would probably suffice, but as I got on with my task I found a sixth volume indispensable if the tale is to be told properly. I am sure the story I have to tell could not have been fully expressed in a shorter space.

I should like to hope that my readers everywhere will feel that the story in the sixth and last volume of my War Memoirs will be worth reading as strongly as I feel it is worth telling.

Yours very sincerely,
Winston S. Churchill

Emery Reves to Winston S. Churchill

30 May 1951   Paris

Dear Mr. Churchill,

I just received, at this very moment, your letter of the 24th of May with a clipping from the U.S. WORLD AND NEWS REPORT which I am returning immediately.[1]

I do not know anyone on the Editorial staff of the U.S. World And News Report and I assure you that I have never mentioned to anyone the point raised in this paragraph. I have made it a rule never to divulge anything you tell me in private and I shall never deviate from this rule.

I must tell you that I was startled myself when, a few months ago, some Americans in New York, discussed not only this point, but also the financial problem between The Daily Telegraph and Life–New York Times. (I know one person to whom this was told by a high official of these publications). When I was asked whether I knew about this matter, I answered that I have nothing to do with the arrangements between The Daily Telegraph and the American publications.

Mr. Longwell also must have known about this. Three months ago he told me that he would like to serialize Volumes V and VI together this year, but that you would probably not permit publication of certain parts of Volume VI before the end of 1952. There are so many people involved in this matter in New York that it is hardly possible to keep any "hot news" confidential, once it is discussed in these large editorial offices.

You know that it is my very personal interest to avoid that any information on Volume VI should be published until this problem has been solved by my Publishers and they can inform their public that there will be a sixth Volume. Believe me, dear Mr. Churchill, that this indiscretion is at least as unpleasant to me as it is to you. To prove this to you, I enclose copy of a letter I received today from Mr. Hasselbalch in Copenhagen. It is self-explanatory. The Danish comment is obviously taken from the U.S. World And News Report.

To my mind, there is no problem at all in this respect. Your work is published at a rate of one Volume per year. Volume IV is published everywhere just now. Volume V will be published during the winter 1951–52. Consequently, Volume VI will be published during the winter 1952–53, i.e. after the American Election. It is only normal that Volume VI should appear after the American Election. It would be abnormal to publish it before that event. My feeling is that, at the time we release Volume V next Fall, an official statement should be published through the newspapers and Publishing houses publishing your work, pointing out this fact, without even referring to the misstatements which appeared previously in the Press.

Thank you very much for sending me your letter. I shall do my very best to make the publishers understand that they cannot expect a personal letter from you and that they have to be satisfied with this communication addressed by you to me.

Yours very sincerely,
Emery Reves

1.   On 11 May 1951, *U.S. News and World Report* wrote, in its "Whispers" column, "Winston Churchill is stipulating that the sixth volume of his war memoirs shall not be published until after the 1952 presidential campaign in U.S. Mr Churchill is critical of President Truman for withdrawing U.S. troops from Czechoslovakia to let the Russians take over in 1945 and is critical of General Dwight Eisenhower for not wanting to take Berlin, instead of leaving it to the Russians, when the chance was open in 1945. The wartime British Prime Minister does not want these criticisms to get deeply entangled in U.S. politics."

Emery Reves to Winston S. Churchill

2 August 1951
Château de Madrid,
Moyenne Corniche,
Villefranche-sur-Mer
Alpes Maritime

Dear Mr. Churchill,

During the past few weeks I have been in Brussels, Amsterdam, Copenhagen, Oslo, Cologne, Munich, Zurich, Bern and Milan to discuss with newspapers and publishers the problem of the sixth volume. Last week, coming from Italy, I arrived at my refuge on the Riviera for a short rest, where I am

now awaiting the news from the Daily Telegraph that they have completed
the selection of their series, whereupon I shall come at once to London to
organize the distribution.

Please find enclosed my remarks on Volume V, some of which you may
find useful in making your final corrections. Needless to say, I tried to be as
critical as possible. I was handicapped by the fact that many chapters make
this volume certainly the best of all hitherto published. Of all my suggestions,
three require your immediate attention:

1) The transposition of the first three chapters of Book I;
2) The change of title of Book II;
3) The elimination of the far too many code names in the text and
   their replacement by clear language. I trust that, even in case you do
   not agree with this suggestion in connection with the English and
   American editions, you will not object to it for the foreign-language
   editions.

In view of the fact that the release date for serialization has been fixed for
October 5, I must distribute the series by August 25 at the latest. I do hope
that you will be able to correct the entire volume, or at least the Daily Telegraph series, before that date. If you think that I may be of any help in making the final corrections, you know that my time and movements are at your
disposal.

I hear that Lord Beaverbrook is expected here one of these days. Are you
not coming down too? I am asking this question because I should like to
extend my stay here in case you were coming. Otherwise, I shall leave here
in about a week for Paris, Holland and from thence to London. I should be
most grateful if you could tell me whether you are expecting to be in London
between August 20 and September 15, when I have to be there.

I have much to tell you about the situation in the various countries, which
I prefer to do à vive voix. In the great majority of countries, publications will
go on. Several publishers, of course, have a great financial problem, which
they and I shall have to face together. We hope that it will not be as bad as
the lawyers foresee. In a few countries publications will cease. In the Argen-
tine, the disappearance of La Prensa puts an end to serialization. This was the
biggest newspaper after the New York Times and the Daily Telegraph. As
you know, the former proprietor is in exile in Uruguay, and I prefer not to
offer the serial rights to one of the Fascist papers of Madame Evita.[1]

The Brazilian book publication will probably stop, as it has sold less than
2,000 copies, the publisher losing money. The reason for this is that there are
very few people in Brazil who are interested in such a work and those few
know English and prefer to read you in the original.

In Turkey, both serial and book editions have stopped. The book sold less
than 800 copies and the publisher lost money, which he says he cannot afford
to do any longer.

But the most unexpected situation is in Germany. I thought that the greatest success of your work outside England would be in Germany and that the people there would be anxious to read your story. As a matter of fact, the last volume sold scarcely 5,000 copies, and the newspapers say that serial publication brought them hundreds of letters of protest and caused a serious drop in circulation. This is merely a natural symptom of a general situation. The resurgence of German nationalism is tremendous. They hate everything British and American, just as under the Nazi régime. My publisher friends say that there is a clearly organized boycott in the German book trade against Anglo-American literature and that the sales of the books of Cronin, Bromfield, Faulkner and all the others have dropped to quite insignificant figures.

These are, of course, exceptions and in most countries publishers expect that, by the very nature of their subject matters, Volumes V and VI will have a larger circulation than the previous volumes.

Should you be able to answer this letter before August 10, please send it to the above address at Villefranche-sur-Mer; afterwards to my office in Paris.

with kind regards,
Yours very sincerely,
Emery Reves

1. Evita Perón, the wife of the Argentinian President and dictator Juan Perón, who ruled Argentina from 1945 to 1955, and again from 1973 to 1974 (when he died suddenly of a heart attack).

Emery Reves to Winston S. Churchill

2 August 1951

Remarks by Emery Reves on
Volume V
Book I
"Italy Won"

1) Chapt. I

This chapter is in itself most interesting, but is it interesting enough to open Volume V? I believe it would be much more dramatic to start the volume with Chapter II, "The Conquest of Sicily," as it is. I would therefore suggest to transpose the first three chapters as follows:

I   —The Conquest of Sicily
II —The Fall of Mussolini
III—The Command of the Seas

I feel it is always of great importance to begin a book as strongly as possible, and "The Conquest of Sicily" and "The Fall of Mussolini" appear to me a very exciting opening.[1]

2) Chapt. I; p. 2; par. 1; 1. 3rd from bottom

"The safety of the 'Torch' Convoys . . ." should read, "The safety of the North African Convoys . . ." [2]

This volume contains perhaps even more abbreviations and code names than the previous volumes. There is a general complaint about the many code names, which make the reading very difficult. It must be realized that only a fraction of one percent of the readers knows or remembers what these many code names signify. And in a few years the number of people who will readily know the meaning is bound to be even less. Several publishers have printed in the previous volume in the appendices a long list of the code names, giving their meaning. But this is only theoretical help, as it is most irritating to be forced every second page to look up in the appendices the meaning of the most important words. It is like reading Goethe's "Faust" with a dictionary. It is certainly a greater pleasure to be able to read it without a dictionary.

I strongly feel that it is better to say "North African Convoys" instead of " 'Torch' Convoys," "Quebec Conference" instead of " 'Quadrant' Conference," etc. I shall indicate in the following some of the most irritating code names which should be put in clear language, but it seems to me it would be advisable for someone to go through all the proofs and change in the narrative all the code names into clear language. In the documents, after the code names, their meaning in clear language should be indicated in parentheses.

3) Chapt. I; p. 6; par. 5; 1.3

"This experience of 'Torch' was in our minds" should read, "The experiences of the North African landings were in our minds."

4) Chapt. I; p. 10; par. 4 and footnote

Suggest to delete this quotation, as few books are lesser known by fewer people than Mr. Morison's book. [3]

5) [4] Chapt. II; p. 1; par. 1; 1.6

"In contrast with our experience in 'Torch' . . ." should read, "In contrast with our experience in North Africa . . ."

6) Chapt. II; p. 2; par. 1; 1.8–9

". . . eleven British divisions to four American." On the same page, the following paragraph, lines 8–10, "The preparations of the armies available in July were: British, eight divisions; United States, six." There seems to be a contradiction in these two statements. Obviously, there is a time difference, which should be indicated. [5]

7) Chapt. II; p. 4; par. 3; 1.10–16

Phrase beginning "General Dempsey's . . ." and ending with ". . . on the battlefield." Suggest to delete these seven lines, which are too technical and seem unnecessary.

8) Chapt. II; p. 10; par. 3; 1.17–22 and 24–27

Two phrases from "Their 3rd Infantry . . ." to ". . . towards Messina" and from "Their 3rd Division . . ." to ". . . it had been in reserve." Suggest to delete these two phrases for the same reason. They seem irrelevant details of a purely technical nature.

9) Chapt. II; p. 12; last par.; first 10 lines

Is it necessary to name the numbers of divisions? It seems sufficient to say "American" or "British."

In this chapter there are several passages (as indicated above) which reveal the hand of a military expert.

10) Chapt. II; p. 13; last par.; 1.1

"At the 'Trident' Conference." Which was the "Trident" Conference? Although, in all modesty, I may say that I know more of the political events of the War than the average reader, I must frankly admit that at this moment I am confused and do not remember which was the "Trident" Conference. I shall have to look it up.[6]

11) Chapt. II; p. 14; par. 2; 1.12

Again "'Trident' Conference." The proper name of the Conference should be given.

12) Chapt. III; par. 4; first sentence

". . . Mussolini . . . had raised the Italian people from the Bolshevism into which they were sinking in 1919 to a position in Europe such as Italy had never held before." I am afraid this phrase will be strongly contended and criticised in Italy. There were rather chaotic conditions in Italy in 1919, but there was no "Bolshevism," which means rule by the Communist party; i.e., the opposite of chaotic conditions. The Facta Government, overthrown by Mussolini's march on Rome, was a very weak, but liberal, government. It may be that, without Mussolini's coup d'état, the Communists might have staged their own coup d'état, but this is a hypothesis which most Italians scoff at. It seems to me unnecessary to make a controversial statement and suggest to delete this reference.

13) Chapt. IV; p. 6; second footnote

Was Professor Bernal a Communist? The reader does not know. The case should either be explained in more detail or the footnote deleted.[7]

14) Chapt. V; p. 4; last minute

The code name "Culverin" appears twice in this minute. What is it?[8]

15) Chapt. VII; p. 1, 1.1

"The Conference ended . . ." should read, "The Quebec Conference ended . . ." This amplification seems necessary, as the preceding chapter interrupts the story of the Quebec Conference.

16) Chapt. VII; p. 4; par. 3

The story of the armistice negotiations with Italy is missing: persons, places, conditions, etc. I feel this is an event which should be narrated in at least three or four paragraphs.[9]

17) Chapt. VII; pp. 7–8

This correspondence with General Smuts raises for the first time the question of the Balkan landing. In the light of postwar events, this would certainly have been the correct strategy. It appears to be such an important point that I believe these passages in the two letters should be commented upon and the original text should be printed in italics.[10] I refer to the last five lines of page seven and to the opening phrase of paragraph two of the Prime Minister's letter on page eight.

18) Chapt. VII; pp. 12–14

This very long minute should be transformed into narrative.[11]

19) Chapt. VIII; p. 3, last telegram

"Premier L. V. Stalin to President . . ." What do the initials "L.V." mean? It is probably a printing error, as the initials of Stalin are J.V.

20) Chapt. IX

I wonder whether one should not have the courage to eliminate this chapter entirely.[12] It consists exclusively of extracts from speeches and documents, without any narrative. The long extracts from the speech in the House on September 21 add hardly anything to what was told in the previous chapters. It is a brilliant recapitulation, but the speech—if my memory serves me correctly—has already been published in one of the war speech volumes. My suggestion is either to delete this chapter[13] and to transfer some of the most important documents (perhaps even the House speech) to the appendices or to radically re-write this chapter. As it stands now, it is certainly the weakest point of the volume.[14]

21) Chapt. X; p. 2; last par.

"See St. Matthew, chapter vii, verses 16 and 20." Suggest to quote this passage from the Bible in a footnote.

22) Chapt. X; p. 12; 1.1

". . . we had recognized at 'Quadrant' . . ." should read, ". . . we had recognized at Quebec . . ."

23) Chapt. XI; p. 1; par. 2; 1.8

"King Victor" should read, "King Victor Emmanuel."[15]

24) Chapt. XI; p. 5; second letter

"Prime Minister to President Roosevelt." "I have not answered U.J.'s telegram . . ." "U.J." obviously means "Uncle Joe." In subsequent telegrams this abbreviation appears very often. Sometimes the person meant is obvious, sometimes it is not quite clear, sometimes one might even think of a new submarine type. As this is a nickname, I suggest that in all telegrams "U.J." should be written out "Uncle Joe."[16]

25) Chapt. XII

The title of this chapter, "Rhodes. Leros," seems not expressive enough. Perhaps it may be preferable to say

"Controversy over the Island of Rhodes"
or
"Rhodes, Key to the Balkans"[17]

26) Chapt. XII; p. 2; par. 3; 1.3

"'Quadrant' decisions . . ." should read, "Quebec decisions . . ." [18]

27) Chapt. XIV

The title of this chapter, "The Renewal of the Arctic Convoys," appears to me not strong enough for this excellent chapter. Suggest the following title, with sub-title:

"Soviet-British Frictions"
"The Renewal of the Arctic Convoys" [19]

28) [20] Chapt. XIV; p. 4; par. 1; 1.2

". . . the full J.W.?" What is "J.W."?

29) Chapt. XIV; p. 13; last par.

As the sinking of the Bismarck filled a whole chapter, I feel that the story of the destruction of the Tirpitz should be told, somewhat dramatized, in more detail, perhaps in one or two pages. [21]

30) Chapt. XV; p. 1, last par.; 1.2

". . . to hear again from Bruin . . ." Who is "Bruin"?

31) Chapt. XVII

Title:

"Preparations for the Triple Conference"

Suggest as title:

"Preparations for the Teheran Conference"

32) Chapt. XVII; p. 1; 1.1

". . . my visits to the Citadel . . ." should read either, "Quebec" or "the Citadel of Quebec."

33) Chapt. XVII; p. 5

The telegrams on that page contained five times the abbreviation "U.J.," which should be changed to "Uncle Joe."

34) Chapt. XVII; p. 9; last par.; 1.3

". . . get the Generalissimo to join us . . ." Suggest to add after "Generalissimo" "(Chiang Kai-Shek)" [22] as otherwise one may think of Stalin.

35) Chapt. XVII; p. 12

"Prime Minister to President Roosevelt," paragraph two, line two, "Gib." should read, "Gibraltar."

BOOK II
"THE SUPREME ADVENTURE"

The title of Book II seems to be deviating from the type of titles used for the previous books. While the titles of each of the five volumes have been of a general symbolic character, the titles of each of the books have always been concrete and specific, expressing the dominating event of each book ("Italy Won," "The Onslaught of Japan," "Africa Redeemed," etc.). This rule has proved to be an excellent one and should be followed throughout the entire work. "The Supreme Adventure" may be a good title for a volume; it may be taken into consideration for Volume VI. But for Book II of Volume V, a title should be given which expresses more concretely the subject-matter of this book. In an earlier version, the title of this book was "The Teheran Conference." I suppose that this title was given up because the book contains more than the Teheran Conference. I would suggest, therefore, as title, "Teheran to Normandy." The titles would read, therefore:

"CLOSING THE RING"

Book I

"ITALY WON"

Book II

"TEHERAN TO NORMANDY" [23]

36) Chapt. I; p. 6; last par.; 1.6
   "Quadrant" should read "Quebec." [24]

37) Chapt. I; pp. 4–6 & pp. 8–10
   Perhaps these two long documents could be transformed, at least partially, into narrative. [25]

38) Chapt. I; pp. 11–12
   Is it necessary to include here the Mosley episode? It appears to be out of context and irrelevant. It should be sufficient to mention it in one or two paragraphs without printing six official telegrams, or perhaps delete the episode completely. [26]

39) Chapt. II, III, IV, V
   Although in these pages I have to restrict myself to criticism, I must say that these four chapters on the Teheran Conference are superb and brilliant. My only remark concerns the ending of Chapter V. I feel that the ending of the Conference should be described at least on one or two additional pages. What happened at the last meeting with Roosevelt and Stalin? What were the last words and the farewell greetings? Was there any closing ceremony? What were the departure scenes? Did Stalin accompany you to the airport? [27] I believe a short addition along these lines would put the finishing touch on this great story.

40) Chapt. VI & VII
   These two chapters abound in code names. Overlord, Accolade, Hercules, Pigstick, Avalanche, Anvil, Shingle, Buccaneer, etc., chase each other in almost every paragraph. It is extremely difficult to read the text fluently for anyone who is not a military technician. I think it would be a great improvement to eliminate these puzzling words. For instance, Chapt. VII; p. 8; par. 2; 1.2–6 read:

   "A far greater effort must be made with the Turks, as well as to expedite the operation and the subsequent return of landing-craft for 'Anvil' (the assault on Southern France). To abandon 'Hercules' was to abandon the prize . . ."

Would it not be simpler if this passage read:

"A far greater effort must be made with the Turks, as well as to expedite the operation and the subsequent return of landing-craft for the assault on Southern France. To abandon the Isle of Rhodes was to abandon the prize . . ."?[28]

41) Chapt. VI; p. 6; last par.

Is there any photo showing the Triple Conference among Churchill, Roosevelt and the Sphinx? I would be most anxious to obtain a copy for the publishers.[29]

42) Chapt. VII

The second half of this chapter consists almost exclusively of technical documents. Would it be possible to delete some or to transform some into narrative?

43) Chapt. VIII; p. 2

The telegram from President Roosevelt to the Prime Minister is purely a code telegram. It should be put in plain language.[30]

44) Chapt. VIII; p. 3; 1.2

"Max has just flown in from London." It should read, "Max Beaverbrook has just . . ."

45) Chapt. VIII; p. 16; 1.7–8

Talking of the battleship King George V: "She made her way out of Algeciras Bay wide into the Atlantic, and thence to Plymouth and London." Did the King George V actually dock in London? I presume you must have come from Plymouth to London by train.

46) Chapt. IX

This chapter on Yugoslavia is excellent, but it contains ten proof pages of documents to three and a half pages of narrative. Could this balance be improved (I mean in favour of the narrative?).

47) Chapt. IX; p. 12

Quotes from speech in Parliament. As there are far too many documents printed in small type, quotations from your own speeches in Parliament might easily be bedded organically in the narrative in large type. Footnotes can indicate the date of each speech and the volumes in which they are printed.

48) Chapt. X; pp. 1–2

On both pages there is a footnote, "See map," which should be deleted. Each volume contains many maps, and it is obvious that the reader will look up the maps whenever required. These two footnotes are unnecessary, or similar footnotes will have to be printed on many other pages. Hitherto it has not been done.

49) Chapt. X; pp. 8–10

Regarding this long quote from the House of Commons speech of February 22, 1944, see my remarks under No. 47.

50) Chapt. X; pp. 10–11

The printing of this exchange of telegrams with General Smuts seems unnecessary. Most of their content is already known to the reader, and the few new items could be told in one or two paragraphs.

51) Chapt. X; p. 12; last line

". . . towards the success of 'Overlord'" should read, ". . . towards the success of the Normandy landing."

52) Chapt. XI; p. 3

Regarding the quote from speech, see again No. 47.

53) Chapt. XI; p. 8–9

This long telegram from General Alexander[31] to the Prime Minister should be condensed and put into narrative and the "thank-you telegram" of 21 Mar 44 deleted, being unnecessary.

54) Footnotes "See map" may be eliminated in Chapt. XIV, p. 2; Chapt. XV, p. 1; Chapt. XVI, pp. 1, 2 & 9.

55) Chapt. XVI, "Rome"

A description of the occupation of Rome is missing. The circumstances of this major event should be told on at least one or two pages.

56) Chapt. XVI; pp. 7–8

There are too many congratulatory telegrams. It may be sufficient to mention in a few lines the names of the persons to whom congratulatory telegrams were sent.

1.   Churchill retained his original plan, to open Volume Five with "The Command of the Seas, Guadalcanal and New Guinea."
2.   Churchill agreed to remove the code word "Torch" and refer to North Africa, and to reduce the subsequent use of code names.
3.   Samuel Eliot Morison, the American historian whose work Churchill much admired, was in the process of publishing the fifteen-volume *History of U.S. Naval Operations in World War II* (Boston: Little, Brown, 1947–1962).
4.   Churchill wrote against 5, 6, 10, and 11, "Yes." Against 4, 7, 8, and 9 he wrote, "No."
5.   General Pownall wrote against 6, "I don't think much of this comment. The figures are correct and the time differences plain."
6.   Churchill ticked this and the next comment (number 11). His literary assistant, Denis Kelly, wrote against 10, "Now amended," and on 12, "now amended." At the top of the document he wrote, "All in notes on master copy, DK 7/8/51."
7.   Churchill has ticked this paragraph. A note in the margin states, "Out."
8.   Denis Kelly has written in the margin of this and the next item, "Await reprint." Reves's points had arrived at the very last moment for change before the first printing.
9.   Bill Deakin was asked to do this. When Kelly later noted, "What about query No. 16. The chapter comes back from the printer tonight," Deakin commented,

"Surely all that is needed is a footnote reference to the chapter on the Italian Armistice!"

10.   Jan Christian Smuts, a South African general and political leader, was a member of the Imperial War Cabinet (London) in the First World War and Prime Minister of South Africa, 1919–1924 and 1939–1948. Kelly noted in the margin that the American publisher had wanted to cut out the two Smuts letters altogether. The letters remained, but without the commentary Reves had suggested. Churchill had written in the margin, "No."

11.   Churchill wrote above the word "narrative," "No."

12.   Churchill wrote at this point, "No. It is most important to the British public." The chapter, entitled "A Spell at Home," included large sections of Churchill's speech to the House of Commons on 21 September 1943 and the full text of his memorandum "War—Transition—Peace" of 19 October 1943.

13.   Churchill wrote at this point, "The more is even the better."

14.   Churchill circled the word "weakest" and wrote in the margin, "No—almost the strongest."

15.   Denis Kelly noted in the margin of 21, 22, and 23, "Done."

16.   Churchill noted in the margin, "No."

17.   Churchill contemplated calling the chapter "The Small Back Door." In the end the title chosen was "Island Prizes."

18.   Churchill agreed.

19.   The title chosen was "Arctic Convoys Again."

20.   Denis Kelly noted that this had been amended, as had 30, 32, 33, 34, and 35.

21.   Churchill noted in the margin, "No."

22.   The Chinese Nationalist leader Chiang Kai-Shek and the Soviet Communist leader Joseph Stalin had both accorded themselves the military rank and title of Generalissimo.

23.   Churchill circled "Teheran to Normandy" and noted in the margin, "Yes." The title finally chosen was "Teheran to Rome."

24.   Churchill ticked this suggestion.

25.   Churchill wrote in the margin, "No."

26.   Churchill proposed putting this in an appendix. It was published as Appendix F, "The Release of the Mosleys. Constitutional Issues."

27.   Churchill wrote in the margin at this point, "No," but agreed to add a few extra lines.

28.   Churchill agreed.

29.   Churchill wrote in the margin, "No."

30.   Churchill agreed with this and all Reves's subsequent points, except numbers 50 and 53.

31.   General Alexander (later Field Marshal Earl Alexander of Tunis) was Supreme Allied Commander in the Mediterranean Theater, 1944–1945. He had earlier commanded British troops at Dunkirk, in Burma, and in North Africa. Like Churchill (and like King Hussein of Jordan and Nehru), he had gone to Harrow School.

Emery Reves to Winston S. Churchill

6 August 1951   Paris

Dear Mr. Churchill,

In my letter of August 2, I forgot to mention a rather important point.

All the publishers are anxious to be able to indicate the highlights of

Volume VI at the time they inform their public of the extension of the work from five to six volumes. Knowing your reluctance to let anything be published on a volume on which you are working, I thought you might agree to release the following items as being the highlights of Volume VI.

> The Landing in Normandy—The Pilotless Bombardment—The Landing in the South of France—Mr. Churchill's Visit to Italy—The Final Destruction of Warsaw—The Second Quebec Conference—The Liberation of France and Belgium—Meetings in Moscow in October 1944—In Liberated Paris—The Rundtstedt Offensive—The Rescue of Greece—Mr. Churchill's Christmas Visit to Athens—The Yalta Conference—Crossing the Rhine—The Polish Dispute—Frictions between the USSR and the Western Powers—Death of President Roosevelt—President Truman—Strategic Controversies—The Capitulation of Germany—The Division of Germany into Zones—The Potsdam Conference—The Atomic Bomb—General Elections in Britain—The End of the Account.

I believe that every one of these items is self evident and has to be dealt with in a historical volume covering the period from the Normandy landing until your resignation. This enumeration of the main events contains no revelation whatever, and I see no reason why the publishers should not be able to include these highlights in their release. I very much hope, therefore, that you will not object to the publishers' mentioning these subject-matters in connection with the sixth volume. This is not supposed to be a table of contents, and, consequently, such a release would leave you entire liberty to add anything else you might wish.

I should be most grateful if you would let me have your view on this matter as soon as possible.

Yours very sincerely,
Emery Reves

Emery Reves to Winston S. Churchill

7 August 1951

Château de Madrid
Moyenne Corniche
Villefranche-sur-Mer
Alpes Maritimes

Dear Mr. Churchill,

Very many thanks for your telegram and kind invitation. I trust that you received my message in time, which I telephoned through to you today. I arrived here after a long business trip with considerable "apparatus," with my car, which I drive myself, and with an "ambulant office," as I have to do four or five hours of office work every day. If I had flown to London today, I would have had to fly back here to pack my things and move my caravan northwards. I also have two or three appointments in this region during this week. My plan was to come to London around the 25th of August for a three weeks' stay. I shall now accelerate matters in order to get there during the latter part of next week. Please do let me know by wire in case you intend to leave England, as I would change all my plans and fly to London in order to avoid missing you on my arrival.

As soon as the proofs of the revised chapters are delivered to the Daily Telegraph, I shall receive one copy immediately. I am anxious to read the new proofs, although I am certain that they will now be perfect and ready for printing. In case you have an extra copy, I should be grateful if your secretary could air-express it to me. If it can leave London before Thursday early afternoon, it should be sent to the above address at Villefranche-sur-Mer; afterwards to my Paris office, where I expect to return Monday.

Regarding my suggestions, my feeling is that most of them, particularly those concerning Book I, could be done in two or three days, with the exception of the transposition of the many code names into clear language. But there is no need to reprint the proofs for that reason alone. This is purely an editorial work, which—in case you agree with it—you can certainly entrust to the publishers and translators. Anyway, I am sure that Houghton Mifflin Company have the necessary editorial staff to make these modifications, which is a routine work, if you instruct them. As for the other publishers, we have time. Of course, if you yourself can make these transpositions in all the chapters which are still to be reproofed, this would be a great help.

I look forward with great pleasure to seeing you within a few days.

Yours very sincerely,
Emery Reves

Winston S. Churchill: engagement cards

18 August 1951   Imperial Palace Hotel,
                                                                    Annecy

11 a.m.   Mr. Reves & to stay to luncheon.

Winston S. Churchill: engagement cards

25 September 1951   28 Hyde Park Gate

10 a.m.   Mr. Reves.

～

On 26 October 1951 Churchill became Prime Minister for the second time.

～

Emery Reves to Winston S. Churchill

21 December 1951   Zurich

Dear Mr. Churchill,

Thank you so very much for your thoughtfulness in sending me a Christmas Card with your lovely painting of Cannes.

It reached me in Zurich in the very room where you stayed when you were here four years ago.

I send you my very best wishes, and I hope that 1952 will be the happiest and most successful year of your life.

Affectionately yours
Emery Reves

Emery Reves to Lord Camrose

2 February 1952   Zurich

Dear Lord Camrose,

Several American reviewers of Volume V expressed their doubts as to whether Mr. Churchill will be able to complete his "Memoirs" now that he is back in office. This rumour has spread all over Europe and some of my publishers, particularly those who issued the work on a subscription basis, are rather worried. They have to answer many questions from booksellers, and they have asked me to authorise them to deny this rumour, and to reassure their public that the sixth and last volume is already in an advanced stage, so that it is certain that the work will be completed.

When I last saw Mr. Churchill, just before the elections, he showed me the proofs of Volume VI and told me that it was 60% ready and that he will complete it for publication whether he was returned to office or not.

I should be most grateful if you would kindly let me know whether it is proper for me to authorise European publishers to deny the American press rumours and to reassure the public that the sixth and last volume is already in an advanced stage, and that it is certain that the "Memoirs" will be completed and the last volume published in time.

With all my thanks,
I am,
Yours very sincerely,
Emery Reves

Emery Reves to Winston S. Churchill

30 September 1952   Paris

Dear Mr. Churchill,

Please find enclosed my comments on Volume VI Book 1, some of which you may find useful.[1]

It was a great joy for me to see you again after so many months and to find you in such grand form and good humour.

With my kindest regards,
Yours very sincerely,
Emery Reves

1. A note on this letter stated that Reves's points were studied by Churchill on 19 October 1952. There is also a note by Churchill on 23 December 1952: "Already in."

Emery Reves to Winston S. Churchill

30 September 1952

MEMORANDUM FROM MR. EMERY REVES TO MR. WINSTON CHURCHILL ON VOLUME VI BOOK 1 READ AT CAP D'AIL ON THE 21ST AND 22ND SEPTEMBER 1952.

As expected, this volume is certainly the most interesting of the entire work.

The title of the volume "TRIUMPH AND TRAGEDY" is excellent and harmonises completely with the titles of the previous volumes.

Hitherto the titles of the volumes were symbolic whereas the titles of the books were concrete, conveying clearly the main topic of each book. Consequently the titles of the books of Volume VI should be of the same character. "THE TIDE OF VICTORY" is not of that character, and "YALTA TO BERLIN" appears to me to be too insignificant for the concluding book of the work.[1]

I think an appropriate title for Book 1 would be "THE LIBERATION OF EUROPE". This is the theme of the book and it corresponds to the "TRIUMPH" in the title of the volume.[2]

The title of Book 2 should correspond to the "TRAGEDY" in the volume title. My first suggestions would be "BREAK-UP OF THE GRAND ALLIANCE", "COLLAPSE OF THE GRAND ALLIANCE", "END OF THE GRAND ALLIANCE", or something expressing this idea better, which I think was the "TRAGEDY" meant in the volume title.[3]

(1) Chapter 2, "The Struggle in Normandy" does not appear to be an appropriate title for this chapter which covers not only the struggle in Normandy but also battles in various other parts of France including the liberation of Paris. A more appropriate title might be "Normandy to Paris".[4]

(2) Chapter 3, page 1, paragraph 3, line 1. "Mary was still serving . . ." To avoid confusion this should read "My daughter Mary was still serving . . ."

(3) Chapter 4, "'Dragon' alias 'Anvil'". Code names are most awkward in titles as the overwhelming majority of your readers do not know what they

mean before reading the chapter. I suggest therefore as title for this chapter "The Landing in the South of France".

(4) Chapter 4, page 7 and page 9. Paragraph 13 of Roosevelt's letter as well as paragraphs 7 and 9 of your answer to Roosevelt should be set in italics. These two passages best show the differences of opinion existing between you and Roosevelt, and also how right you were.

(5) Chapter 5, "Our Balkan Perplexities". Perhaps a more expressive title for this chapter would be "Soviet-British Divergencies in the Balkans".[5]

(6) Chapter 5, page 4, last line. "U.J." should be written out "Uncle Joe".

(7) Chapter 6, "My Visit to Italy". This title does not quite convey the importance and interest of the subject matter of this chapter. A more expressive title might be "Meeting Tito and Watching the Landing on the Riviera".[6]

(8) Chapter 6, page 3, paragraph 4. ". . . the new Yugoslav Prime Minister . . ." should read ". . . the new Yugoslav Prime Minister of King Peter's Government in London . . ." otherwise the reader might be confused when on the following page 4, paragraph 4, lines 4 and 5 you say ". . . Dr. Subasic, whom he (Tito) was meeting for the first time . . ."

(9) Chapter 6, page 11, last paragraph. This paragraph of Smuts' letter should be in italics.

(10) Chapter 8, page 2. I suggest deleting the letter to General Smuts. This letter contains nothing new. Everything in it has been told several times before. This repetition is not only superfluous but weakens the argument by repeating it once again.[7]

(11) Chapter 10, page 14, end of the chapter. "I had a long talk with the President about Tube Alloys . . ." Instead of "Tube Alloys" please say "Atomic Bomb" or "atomic research" as 99% of your readers would not know what "Tube Alloys" meant. Further, could you add a few phrases telling as much as possible of what you discussed with Roosevelt on that subject? This is surely a most important point and the reader would be disappointed if you did not say more about it. If, for any reason, you do not want to tell more, then I suggest that you cut this passage out and do not refer to this conversation on the atomic bomb at all.[8]

(12) Chapters 11 and 12, "The Advance in Burma" and "The Defeat of Japan at Sea". These two chapters are the only weak part of the volume. I believe that this weakness is inherent in the subject matter and cannot be remedied by mere rewriting. There have been so many descriptions of battles in previous chapters and previous volumes that they become monotonous, particularly when they refer to unimportant geographical localities in remote places. At this stage of the war and at this stage of your War Memoirs (when your readers have read nearly two million words), the great strategic moves and the vital political struggles are of interest.[9] If such an important battle as that of Caen is not described in detail (and rightly so!) there is no need to describe individual battles in Burma.

Your report on the Burma situation at the Quebec Conference gave a complete picture and appears sufficient. I suggest that you entirely delete Chapter 11, incorporating only one or two paragraphs of it in Chapter 12, making one condensed and more interesting chapter on the Far Eastern war situation at that time, instead of two weak ones.

All the other chapters of this book are so good that this small surgical operation, eliminating the one weak spot, would tremendously improve the book. It would then have no weakness anywhere.

(13) Chapter 13, "The Liberation of France and Belgium". In view of the fact that a great part of this chapter deals with battles in Holland the title should be either "The Liberation of France, Belgium and Holland" or "The Liberation of Western Europe".[10]

At this point I feel obliged to convey to you a widespread resentment felt in Holland that in your Memoirs you have neglected the Dutch, whereas in many places you have recorded the actions of the French, Belgians, Poles, Greeks, Norwegians and other allies. You have no doubt overlooked this point and I believe in this chapter, perhaps in connection with the battle of Arnhem, you should insert one or two paragraphs paying tribute to Dutch resistance and the Dutch contribution to the war. They are very touchy about this and I am convinced that you could correct this impression in Holland by adding a paragraph or two.[11]

(14) Chapter 13, "The Battle of Arnhem". There is a widespread belief in Holland that there was an intelligence leakage and that the Germans were waiting in position for the descending British parachutists, which was one of the reasons, perhaps the main one, for the failure and the massacre of the British soldiers. Is there any truth in this? I feel that you should either confirm or deny this belief.[12]

(15) Chapter 14, "Prelude to a Moscow Visit". This chapter is extremely interesting until your landing in Naples (the middle of page 10). The last two and a half pages of the chapter, describing the Italian battle situation, are completely out of context and disturbing. I suggest that you delete these last two and a half pages and transfer a short condensation of them to a later chapter dealing with the Italian campaign, perhaps chapter 9 of Book 2, "Alexander's Crowning Victory".[13] In any case at this stage, when one's interest is geared to your meeting with Stalin, there should not be an interruption of the main narrative.[14]

(16) Chapter 15, "Our October Meeting in Moscow". This is another superb chapter but I feel that a few short descriptions of the meetings should be added, particularly a description of your last meeting with Stalin of which the reader learns only indirectly through your letter to Roosevelt.[15]

(17) Last chapter, "Christmas at Athens". This chapter, excellent in itself, is not good enough to end the book. There is nothing in it that would conclude the story of the book.

If I remember rightly, in a previous draft of the volume, Book 1 ended with a chapter telling of the preparations for Yalta, whereas Book 2 started with the Yalta Conference. This was a much better structure and I highly recommend you to revert to it.

What your readers are most anxiously waiting to read in Volume VI is the authentic account of the Yalta Conference. I think therefore that you should use as last chapter of Book 1 what is now the first chapter of Book 2, telling of the preparations for the Yalta Conference and ending the book with your departure for this vital meeting. This would be a most dramatic ending for Book 1, leaving the reader in a state of suspense, similar to the great ending of Volume V when the allied Armada left the British coast for Normandy.

Should you decide to end Book 1 with that chapter, I would suggest calling it "Preparations for Yalta" or "Departure for Yalta" and not to use the code name "Argonaut" in the title as it means very much less than Yalta which is known by everybody.[16]

Emery Reves

1.   On Reves's first point, Churchill decided to keep "The Tide of Victory" for Book 1 but to change "Yalta to Berlin" to "The Iron Curtain" for the title of Book 2.

2.   Churchill wrote "Yes" against this suggestion, but Denis Kelly pointed out, "The liberation was NOT completed in Book 1."

3.   Churchill wrote "Yes" in the margin. The title eventually chosen was "The Iron Curtain."

4.   Churchill agreed to this, and also to Reves's points on sections 2, 3, 4, 6, 8, and 9.

5.   Churchill circled "Soviet-British Divergencies in the Balkans" and wrote, "Better." Denis Kelly pointed out that "Balkan Convulsions" had been the original title. The title chosen was "Balkan Convulsions. Russian Victories."

6.   Churchill wrote in the margin, "Consider." The title chosen was "Prelude to a Moscow Visit."

7.   Churchill kept the letter to Smuts.

8.   Churchill deleted all reference to the Quebec Agreement on the Atomic Bomb. For this and other references to the atomic bomb not in Churchill's war memoirs, see Volume 6 of the official Churchill biography, *Road to Victory: Winston S. Churchill, 1941–1945*, pages 415–419, 470–471 (Quebec 1943, including the Articles of Agreement of 19 August 1943), 487, 715, 938, 969–970 (Quebec 1944), 1060, 1222–1223, 1265–1266, and 1302.

9.   Churchill noted in the margin, "pregnant criticism," but Denis Kelly wrote, "I don't agree at all about cutting out Burma. This is forgetting the 14th Army with a vengeance! But there is duplication with the Quebec chapter. I will submit proposals if you wish." General Pownall added, "I heartily disagree with Mr Reves—only a few days ago a senior officer in XIV army told me that he thought that army had been rather curiously treated in Vol 5. I assured him it wd get more in Vol 6. It was the only campaign in which a whole Japanese army was defeated by land/air fighting." The "Advance in Burma" chapter (nine pages) was retained, as was "The Defeat of Japan at Sea," renamed "The Battle of Leyte Gulf" (twelve pages).

10.   Churchill wrote "yes" against "The Liberation of Western Europe" and this became its title.

11.   Churchill agreed to mention the Dutch, adding four words (italicized here) to

his existing account: "No risks daunted the brave men, *including the Dutch Resistance,* who fought for Arnhem."

12.   Churchill neither confirmed nor denied, or discussed, this Dutch belief. "Had we been more fortunate in the weather," he wrote, "which turned against us at critical moments and restricted our mastery in the air, it is probable that we should have succeeded."

13.   Kelly noted in the margin at this point, "Much too late," and suggested moving the section back to an earlier chapter. Churchill noted on this, "Consider," but the section was not moved.

14.   Churchill retained these pages on the battle in Italy.

15.   Churchill did not add any such description, as Reves had suggested, but he did end the chapter with a telegram he had sent to Stalin after the conference: "Eden and I have come away from the Soviet Union refreshed and fortified by the discussions which we had with you, Marshal Stalin, and with your colleagues. This memorable meeting in Moscow has shown that there are no matters that cannot be adjusted between us when we meet together in frank and intimate discussion. Russian hospitality, which is renowned, excelled itself on the occasion of our visit. Both in Moscow and in the Crimea, where we spent some enjoyable hours, there was the highest consideration for the comfort of myself and our mission. I am most grateful to you and to all those who were responsible for these arrangements. May we soon meet again."

16.   Churchill noted in the margin, "Yes," and the chapter (which in the event became the first chapter of Book 2), was entitled, "Preparations for a New Conference."

Emery Reves to Denis Kelly

15 October 1952   Paris

Dear Kelly,

Please forgive my answering your letter with such delay. As you know, I did go down to the Riviera and have read carefully Book 11. I have sent a memorandum containing my comments to Miss Gilliatt[1] at 10 Downing Street. I wonder whether you have seen it. I have sent the paper in duplicate, so please read one copy and tell me what you think of it.

I am going to send, also through Miss Gilliatt, a few clippings from the Figaro containing a series of articles on the intelligence leakage which supposedly caused the massacre of Arnhem. The articles are written by Col. Oreste Pinto. This confirms my remarks on the description of the Battle of Arnhem.

I am sorry to hear that you have a problem regarding your future. I always thought that your intention was to practice law and that your helping Mr. C. was merely an excursion in strange territory. Nothing is more difficult than to give advice in such matters as one should always be guided by one's own inclinations and aspirations, no matter how difficult the road appears. At least this has been my experience.[2]

I must tell you that my own future appears to me also somewhat uncertain. My international newspaper syndicate I have built up during the prewar years does not very well fit into postwar conditions, and it may be that the Churchill Memoirs are my swan song in this profession. It may be that after publication of Volume VI I shall decide to write another book on a predominantly British subject in which case I may ask you to help me doing some research work in London, if you will have time. We shall talk about this when I am next in London.

With kindest regards,
Yours sincerely,
Emery Reves

1.   Elizabeth Gilliatt, who was Churchill's principal personal secretary (in succession to Kathleen Hill) from 1946 until his retirement in 1955.
2.   Denis Kelly remained in Churchill's employ to help with the revisions of *A History of the English-Speaking Peoples,* before returning to the law and becoming a barrister.

Emery Reves to Winston S. Churchill

11 December 1952   Claridge's Hotel,
                                                    Brook Street,
                                                    London W.1.

Dear Mr. Churchill,
    You are no doubt aware that President Truman is planning to write his Memoirs after leaving the White House. As he has no experience of writing, there is a danger that he may follow the advice of some people close to him with even less literary experience and judgment, so that he may produce a rather insignificant book like "Mr. President". This would be a great pity as he is the only man who could write the authentic history of 1945 to 1952 with authority comparable to yours in writing the history of 1939 to 1945. I am sure no comparison will be possible from a literary point of view, but undoubtedly he is the man who made the great decisions in that period (use of the atomic bomb, Berlin airlift, Korea, etc.). Your story ends at Potsdam, and it is precisely there that Truman enters the scene. So I would like to persuade him to write not a general biography beginning with his childhood, but a serious, documented historical work, starting with Roosevelt's death and Truman's inauguration, narrating all major events up to his retirement.
    I know several close family friends of Mr. Truman very well, so I expect to meet him soon after my arrival in America. But this is not sufficient, as it would be most awkward for me to tell him about my experiences in this field so that he should listen to me. You are the only man who can help me in this respect as you have honoured me with your confidence in literary matters for nearly seventeen years. So may I ask you whether you feel that you could give me an introductory letter—or introduce me in some other way—to President Truman, so that he may seriously consider my suggestions. Naturally I would not only like to advise him on his Memoirs, but also to acquire or handle the publication rights, at least outside the U.S.A.

Needless to say, I would only accept your help if your personal relationship with Truman makes it possible, and if this would not cause you the slightest inconvenience. I shall understand it perfectly if you prefer not to assist me in this endeavour.

No matter what you decide, I thank you for having read this letter to the end.[1]

Yours very sincerely,
Emery Reves

1. One of Churchill's secretaries added on this letter, "Mr C spoke to Mr Reves when he saw him (Regret) 20.12.52."

Emery Reves to Winston S. Churchill

15 December 1952   Claridge's Hotel,
Brook Street,
London W.1.

Dear Mr. Churchill,

Before sailing I should like to express my gratitude for the confidence you have shown me in permitting me to read Book 12. I fully appreciate your problem so please rest assured that nothing will be said by me to anybody, not even the fact that I had the privilege of reading it.

As to the title "Triumph and Tragedy" I never thought of any other interpretation except that "Triumph" meant the victory of the Grand Alliance over Nazi Germany, and the "Tragedy" meant that this victory did not bring peace, but the breakdown of the Alliance, the Iron Curtain and the new war situation. I am certain that nobody can interpret the title in any other way, and you may easily underline this in the Preface. To make this meaning even more clear perhaps Book 2 should be entitled "The Iron Curtain". This way no misunderstanding is possible, with "Triumph" meaning "The Tide of Victory" and "Tragedy" meaning "The Iron Curtain".[1]

During the next five to six weeks I shall be at the Plaza, Fifth Avenue at 59th Street in New York. Of course I shall return at once any time the volume is completed.

With my very best wishes for a restful and sunny Christmas holiday I beg to remain,

Yours very sincerely,
Emery Reves

1. Churchill wrote in the margin of the first paragraph, "Yes," and put a tick against "The Iron Curtain." He also noted on the letter, "Keep with book things, WSC 17.12.52."

Emery Reves to Winston S. Churchill

15 December 1952

MEMORANDUM FROM MR. EMERY REVES TO MR. WINSTON
CHURCHILL ON VOLUME VI, BOOK 12, READ IN LONDON ON THE 12TH
AND 13TH DECEMBER 1952.

This book will certainly come up to, if not surpass, all expectations. The titles (volume and book titles) appear to me to be as good as any of the previous volumes, if not better. I trust that you are also satisfied. I am more and more convinced that "Triumph and Tragedy" is a great title, reminding one of "Crime and Punishment" and other classics.

(1) Chapter 1. "Preparations for a New Conference".

I feel obliged to begin with the same suggestion I made at the end of my memorandum on Book 11. This chapter should definitely be the last chapter of Book 11. It would be a superb ending to that book, which does not seem properly finished with the chapter on Greece. For the English and American editions, printing the entire volume under one cover, this may be of secondary importance. But in most of the translations the books are issued under separate covers at certain intervals. From the point of view of such presentation I feel that this is perhaps one of the most important suggestions I have been permitted to make during the entire work. This transfer would not require any additional work, not one word needs to be changed, merely the chapter transferred. By this small operation not only Book 11 would have a magnificent ending, but Book 12 would have a much stronger opening.

I see that the title has been changed from "Preparations for Argonaut" to "Preparations for a New Conference". Yalta is the magic word, so I suggest as a title of the last chapter of Book 11 "Preparations for Yalta".

(2) The three chapters on the Yalta Conference are extremely interesting. Two events seem to me to have been dealt with in a somewhat summary manner. The end of the Yalta Conference and your last meeting with Stalin [1] (Chapter 4, page 4, para 3), and your last meeting with Roosevelt on the Quincy in Alexandria (Chapter 4, page 6, para 5). These two highlights of the story should be dramatised and commented on in somewhat more detail in your own literary style. [2] Your impressions of how Roosevelt looked when you last saw him are particularly missing.

(3) Chapter 6, "The Polish Dispute".

The footnote "Not printed here" is disturbing. One automatically asks: why? I suggest deleting this footnote.

(4) Chapter 10, "President Truman".

This would be a very good title for a chapter, but unfortunately it does not fit this chapter which deals exclusively with the Polish question. Unless this chapter is amended and some passages are included on President Truman, the title should be changed in order to reflect the subject of the chapter, which is the eternal Polish question.

(5) Chapter 11, "The Final Advance".

As this chapter deals with the discussions on the occupational zones, which is a most important subject, I suggest that its title should be "Occupational Zones".

One crucial point is left without a mention in this chapter. How was it that the Allies agreed that, whereas Berlin and Vienna were each cut into four zones, both of the capitals were submerged in the Russian zone without corridors being provided between the Western zones of Berlin and Vienna and the Western zones of Germany and Austria, through which we could communicate without Russian interference and control. The fact that British, Americans and French can only go to the British, American and French zones of Berlin and Vienna by passing through Russian controls has led to many dangerous and costly conflicts, such as the Berlin airlift.

Was this probability never raised? And how did these peculiar arrangements come about? I feel that some explanation of this vital question should be given.

(6) Chapter 17, "A Fateful Decision", page 6, last para. "Now it is Britain and Western Europe who are urged . . ." "Now" is disturbing. It should read "A few years later it was Britain and Western Europe . . ."

(7) Chapter 19, "Potsdam: the Atomic Bomb", page 7.

The scene describing Truman telling Stalin of the atomic bomb. This is a most exciting episode, but Stalin's strange attitude needs explanation. Did not his silence and rather sarcastic attitude show that he was not surprised and knew quite a lot about the atomic bomb, as the British, Canadian and American spy trials later revealed? You may, perhaps, add one or two paragraphs, whether you agree with this supposition, or whether you think his reactions have some other explanation.[3]

(8) Chapter 20, "Terminal: The Polish Frontiers."

I suggest to revert to the first version and use "Potsdam" in the title and not "Terminal".

This chapter needs a tailpiece.[4]

I am greatly relieved to find how few changes are necessary in view of the new situation in America. There are less than a dozen telegrams in two or three chapters which you may have to reconsider. I have given a great deal of thought to this problem and wonder whether their elimination is the best solution. It has to be borne in mind that

(a) the world and posterity expect you not only to tell the truth but all the truth.

(b) there is nothing new to the Americans in these telegrams. Every American knows what they contain, but these mistakes have already been forgiven as the results of the elections show.

(c) every public statement of Eisenhower and Truman made during the past three to four years prove that they realise the mistakes they have made and that today they completely share your views on the Russian problem.

(d) the misconceptions of the American leaders in 1944–45 were unfortunately the misconceptions of the American people at large, and were merely reflected in the policies of their leaders.

In view of all these points I wonder whether, instead of eliminating the documents, it would not be preferable to leave them in the book, adding, wherever necessary, a few lines of comment expressing understanding of the mistakes the American leaders made, who had to take into consideration the mood of American public opinion which, in its vast majority, trusted the Russians, ignored every political problem of Europe, and looked upon war as an exclusively military problem without any political implications.

I venture to submit these thoughts for whatever they may be worth.

Book 12 is so good and so advanced that I feel after a fortnight's work it could go to the printers. It would be most important if you could finish it around January 20th, so that the 150 copies might be ready by February 1st. This is the latest date which would permit serialisation before the Coronation. Serialisation must start by the end of March to be finished by May 15th, after which date the Daily Telegraph will have to reserve space for Coronation stories. July and August are most unsuitable months everywhere for the serialisation of such an important work so, unless we can distribute the series at the beginning of February, publication will probably have to be postponed until September next. I do not believe that these dates will trouble you, as I am confident that you can comfortably complete the volume by the end of January.

1.   Churchill noted at this point, "See Potsdam."
2.   Churchill wrote across this sentence, "No."
3.   Churchill ticked this paragraph, but in his text he did not speculate on the matter at all or refer to the controversy.
4.   Churchill rejected this advice. The chapter ends with the text of the Joint Communiqué on Poland and no further commentary.

On 17 September 1953, following his recovery from a stroke, Churchill went to the South of France for a two-week holiday. He stayed at La Capponcina, Lord Beaverbrook's villa at the Cap d'Ail. It was during this visit that Emery Reves invited Churchill to lunch with him at La Pausa, at Roquebrune, five miles from La Capponcina, where Reves was living with Wendy Russell. The villa had been built in 1927 for Coco Chanel by Churchill's friend

Bendor, second Duke of Westminster. It was there that Churchill met Wendy Russell for the second time (they had met earlier, briefly, in Jamaica, in 1947).

Following his lunch at La Pausa, Churchill invited Reves and Wendy Russell to lunch with him at La Capponcina on the next afternoon.

On 30 September 1953 Churchill returned to Britain and resumed his duties as Prime Minister.

Emery Reves to Sir Winston Churchill[1]

31 March 1954   Paris

Dear Sir Winston,

At the end of our last meeting in London, in November, you suggested that I write to you in a few months on the question of the HISTORY OF THE ENGLISH-SPEAKING PEOPLES.[2]

Many rumours are being published in the world press on your next work (including a mysterious midnight sortie of Luce[3] from No. 10 with a big batch of proofs under his arms . . .), and I am receiving so many enquiries that I would be grateful if you could give me some information on the following points.

1) Do you feel inclined to talk on this subject with me at this time? If not, please disregard all the following points and forgive this letter.

2) I understand that you control all serial and book rights except the British and American book publication rights. If this is correct, would you be willing, in principle, to discuss with me the sale of all foreign-language publication rights either on a royalty basis or in the form of an outright sale?

3) I believe that, wherever possible, this work should be published by the same publishers who published your War Memoirs. Have you any commitments anywhere which would necessitate a change in this plan?

4) Are you planning the publication of this work volume by volume, like the War Memoirs, or do you intend to hold back the publication until the entire work is completed?

Thank you ever so much for any information you might give me, so that I may be in a position to answer in some concrete manner the enquiries reaching me.

It is a great joy for me to realize from the Parliamentary debates in what grand form you are.[4] I feel lucky not to be a Labour M.P.

                                        Yours very sincerely,
                                        Emery Reves

1.   Churchill had been made a Knight of the Garter in April 1953: henceforth he was Sir Winston Churchill.

2.   Entitled *A History of the English-Speaking Peoples,* this book was virtually completed by Churchill before the outbreak of war. It was being revised and was subsequently published, in four volumes, as Churchill's last book.

3.   Henry Luce, the owner of *Time, Life,* and *Fortune* magazines. Before publishing Churchill's memoirs in *Life,* and in order to stake his claim to them, Luce had bought and published Churchill's *Secret Session Speeches* as—he told the Editor of *Life,* Daniel Longwell—a "pig in a poke."

4.   Following his stroke in June 1953, which had been kept secret, Churchill had not spoken again in public until October, first at the Conservative Party Conference at Margate and then at question time in the Commons. On 2 March 1954 he made an important speech in the Commons on the hydrogen bomb. Four weeks later, on 30 March, in answer to Labour criticisms, he told the House that the British government was "not prepared to make any action which might impede American progress in building up their overwhelming strength in nuclear weapons, which provided the greatest possible deterrent against the outbreak of a third world war."

Jane Portal[1] *to Anthony Moir*[2]

7 April 1954   10 Downing Street

Dear Mr. Moir,

Sir Winston has asked me to send you the enclosed letter he has today received from Mr. Emery Reves. He says he would like to have a talk to you about it in the near future, so I will get in touch with you as soon as possible—probably when the House rises for Easter next week.

Yours sincerely,
J.P.

1.   Jane Portal, one of Churchill's secretaries from 1949 to 1951, during work on the war memoirs, and throughout his second premiership.

2.   Anthony Moir, of the London solicitors Fladgate and Company, Churchill's solicitor and adviser on legal matters.

Sir Winston Churchill to Emery Reves

18 April 1954   10 Downing Street

My dear Reves,

Thank you for your letter of March 31.

I have for some time been thinking about THE HISTORY OF THE ENGLISH-SPEAKING PEOPLES as I told you at our last meeting, and have discussed it with Luce. There is however no question of a plan taking any shape until next year as I am not committed to anything until the fall of 1955. You must understand that while I am here I can do nothing, but I would be very glad to discuss it with you early next year and we will try and work something out together. In the meantime I would prefer that it did not get about.

With kind regards,
Yours sincerely,
Winston S. Churchill

Elizabeth Gilliatt to Miss Foote[1]

18 April 1954   10 Downing Street

Dear Miss Foote,

At long last the books have been signed.[2] I have written (by air mail!) to tell Mr. Reves, but I thought I had better let you know also, in case you want to come and collect them. They are in the hall here addressed to Mr. Reves. If you can't get here for them, let me know.

Yours sincerely,
E.G.

1.   Private Secretary to Emery Reves.
2.   The Spanish edition of *The Grand Alliance* volume of Churchill's war memoirs.

Elizabeth Gilliatt to Emery Reves

18 April 1954   10 Downing Street

Dear Mr. Reves,

I can't tell you how happy I am to be able to inform you that the books have been signed at last. You will see that I think of them all the time, even on Easter Sunday!

Your cri de coeur made my heart bleed, and I deeply regret it should have been necessary.

With every good wish,
Yours sincerely,
E.G.

Elizabeth Gilliatt to Sir Winston Churchill

27 April 1954   10 Downing Street

PRIME MINISTER

Mr. Reves' Secretary is exceedingly sorry but by mistake they asked you to sign two copies of Book II of the Spanish edition of THE GRAND ALLI-ANCE. Would it be possible for you to sign a copy of Book I, please?

E.G.

Elizabeth Gilliatt to Miss Foote

10 October 1954   10 Downing Street

Dear Miss Foote,
   I now send you herewith the signed copy of Book I of the Spanish edition of THE GRAND ALLIANCE. I am sorry this has been so long, but Sir Winston was very happy to do it.

                                                      Yours sincerely,
                                                      E.G.

Emery Reves to Sir Winston Churchill

6 November 1954   Paris

My dear Sir Winston,
   I am sending you these 80 Magnums of your beloved golden liquid— hoping that it will fortify and prepare you to withstand victoriously the concentrated assault the world will launch against you on the 30th of November.
   On that great day I shall open a bottle myself and drink to your health.[1]

                                                      As ever,
                                                      Yours
                                                      Emery Reves

   1.   Churchill, for whose eightieth birthday Reves had sent the champagne, told Elizabeth Gilliatt (as she noted on Reves's letter), "I must write, WSC, 10/11/54."

Sir Winston Churchill to Emery Reves: telegram

10 November 1954   10 Downing Street

   Thank you so much. Writing.[1]

                                                      Winston Churchill

   1.   It appears that no letter did in fact follow the telegram. On 28 December 1954 Churchill told Elizabeth Gilliatt, "It's all settled."

Sir Winston Churchill to Henry Luce: telegram

21 November 1954   10 Downing Street

ENGLISH-SPEAKING PEOPLES

   I know you must have been very busy lately but have you seen my Solicitor's letter to Heiskell[1] of October 26 STOP I don't want to sell the foreign language serial rights and would like to have them handled by Emery Reves who has made a wonderful success abroad of the War Memoirs and who has worked with me since the ante-Hitler days before the War STOP Although

I have made no personal profit by sale of the War Memoirs abroad it is a great pleasure to me to feel that these books are translated into 26 different languages and I am sure no one could have done it except Reves who buzzed around the world for nearly a year making contacts STOP I had never realized that our arrangement could possibly be understood to extend beyond the serial rights other than English and Eire in the English language STOP It may well be that this is also your view STOP Kindest regards.

Winston Churchill.

1.   Andrew Heiskell, of Time Inc., the Publisher of *Life,* and in 1947 one of the two negotiators for Churchill's war memoirs in the United States (the other being General Julius Ochs Adler, General Manager of the *New York Times*).

~

Churchill resigned as Prime Minister on 5 April 1955. Immediately after his resignation he went on holiday to Sicily.

~

Alberto Mondadori[1] *to Emery Reves*

16 April 1955   Milan

Dear Emery,

I'm following up the cable addressed you on even date, as soon as the paper brought me the news of the meeting between Sir Winston Churchill and Mr. Luce, meeting during which, as the Press informs, an agreement has been signed for the bringing out of Sir Winston's new work.

First of all I must say that I was rather surprised by the news given so suddenly by the Press, since it was agreed, by mutual consent, that the news had to remain confidential.

But the main purpose of this letter of mine concerns the title of the work. HISTORY OF THE ENGLISH SPEAKING PEOPLES is a rather solemn title, suggesting books written for historians and for specialists in history. Now, as far as I know, I think that this is neither the form nor the intent of the book, which is an interpretation of the most important historical events and characters, given by a personage of quite exceptional historical importance.

This applies of course for the bringing out in volume form, but even more for the serialization and I beg you to note that I'm making this remark not only as Publisher, but also in the name of EPOCA and of the Press.

Therefore I'm applying to your kindness, asking you to interpose your good offices so that Sir Winston may, at least for Italy, change the originally chosen title in a more agile and inviting one, so to appeal to our readers: in the work of a great politician as Sir Winston Churchill the Italian readers seek that immediate contact between a man of action of men of action, which can give rise to a new and personal vision.

Looking forward to hear from you I remain, with my very best regards. [2]

Most sincerely yours,
Alberto Mondadori

1.   The owner of Arnaldo Mondadori Editore, one of Italy's leading publishers.
2.   Reves received similar letters from the Swedish publisher Skoglunds Bokförlag and from the Swiss publisher Alfred Scherz. The titles eventually chosen were *Storia* (Italian), *Historia* (Swedish), and *Geschichte* (German).

Emery Reves to Sir Winston Churchill

20 May 1955   Roquebrune[1]

I have just arrived in Roquebrune from New York, where I spent three months. I was sorry indeed to hear that you had such bad weather in Sicily, while here there have been seven weeks of uninterrupted sunshine. The more one sees of this earth, the more one realizes that no place can be compared with this bit of paradise.

I am preparing a short memorandum on the first volume, which I shall send you, or bring to London myself, shortly after the elections. The purpose of this letter is to enquire whether you have yet decided upon a final title, as I see in the draft contracts the work called "tentatively entitled: 'History of the English Speaking Peoples.'" I am happy indeed that you do not consider the present title final, which most of your publishers, including myself, feel not up to the importance and interest of this work.

Above all, this title is too long and sounds schoolbookish. Further, it does not correctly cover the subject. It is too broad, inasmuch as the work is not a complete history of the English speaking peoples but covers only certain highlights of that history. And it is too narrow, as the work contains many interesting passages covering non-English speaking peoples, as, for instance, the chapter on the French Revolution. Also, I understand, there already exists a work entitled, "History of the English Speaking Peoples," by R. B. Mowat and P. Slosson.

The great value of this work is that it contains your very personal views on certain events and certain personalities of history, and the title should express just that.[2]

How would you like as a title GREAT MOMENTS OF HISTORY—?[3] Until now I have not been able to find anything better, but I feel this is the kind of title the work should have. So I venture to suggest it, being certain that you will coin a more immortal phrase.

It would be of great help if you could decide upon a final title now, so that it may be included in the contracts. There is a great deal of publicity on this work in the world press, referring to it as "History of the English Speaking Peoples," and it would be advantageous for the book to be mentioned by its final title as soon as possible.

With my kindest regards and very best wishes,
Yours very sincerely,
Emery Reves

    1.   In 1953 Reves purchased La Pausa, a villa in the hills above Roquebrune. The villa having been deserted for many years, Reves spent fifteen months restoring it. It then became his home. Roger Berthoud has written, "Reves was a passionate and discriminating collector, not just of Impressionist paintings (nine Renoirs, four Cézannes, three Degas etc.—all of high quality) but also, with his wife, of furniture, carpets, porcelain, old glass and Renaissance jewellery. Few museums have one sixteenth century rug as good as the eight or nine at La Pausa." ("The Idealist Who Sold Churchill to the World," *Times* [London], 7 September 1981).

    2.   Against this paragraph Churchill wrote, "No."

    3.   Against this query Churchill wrote, "No."

Sir Winston Churchill to Emery Reves

25 May 1955

My dear Reves,

    Your letter of May 20. Let me know when you will be coming over here. After the Election is over, in the first week of June, would be quite convenient to me, and we have important business to settle.

    I am sorry you do not like the title "The History of the English Speaking Peoples". This is the character of the work as I have viewed it for more than twenty years, and in regard to which the original contracts with Cassell were made. I am advised that the fact that there is a text book of that name constitutes no legal obstacle. Quite a lot of books have been published by different people under the title of the "History of England". As to the length of the title, "The Decline and Fall of the Roman Empire" was considered short enough by Gibbon, whose work I have always admired.

    I am afraid we do not agree at all on the idea that the 'great value' of the work is personal to myself. I hope and believe that it has some merits of its own.

    I hope you will reconcile yourself to the title, for I am not considering any other.

    I am pondering over the question of subtitles for the four volumes, in addition to the subtitles already assigned to the books in each.

    Please let me and Mr. Moir know as soon as possible when you will come.

With kind regards,
Yrs sincerely
Winston S. Churchill

Sir Winston Churchill to Emery Reves

[May 1955]

To Emery Reves Esq.

With reference to the contract under which the foreign language book rights in "The History of the English-Speaking Peoples" were vested in you, we confirm that there will be no objection to your publishing this work under any title which you may select provided it is clearly stated in each volume that the work is the same as that published in England under the title of "The History of the English-Speaking Peoples".

Emery Reves to Sir Winston Churchill

14 June 1955   Paris

My dear Sir Winston,

I am terribly sorry that my letter regarding the title of your forthcoming work was not clear enough and made such a bad impression. Naturally, everybody will abide by your final decision but I feel it is my duty to submit for consideration the almost unanimous opinion of your foreign publishers.

Please find enclosed copies of letters I have received from your French, German, Italian and Swedish publishers. I share their views as the term "English Speaking Peoples" is untranslatable and nothing can be found in the other languages which could be used as a title resembling the original.

The only possible French translation is "Histoire des Peuples de Langue Anglaise" which means retranslated "History of the Peoples of the English Language". It sounds just as bad in Italian and in Spanish. The German translation "Geschichte der English Sprechenden Voelker" is closer to the original but the German and Scandinavian publishers say that it is a most artificial sounding title which they could not use. As you will see from the enclosed letters several publishers feel that the present title indicates a "manuel d'histoire", a "schoolbook".

You are no doubt aware how unhappy Henry Laughlin is that he could not get the American book rights, and he is making great efforts to buy the American rights from Dodd Mead. He would pay almost any amount to be the American publisher of your work. Although I do not believe that he will succeed we had long talks and I recall him saying that if he could acquire the rights, the first thing he would do would be to suggest changing the title. So it seems to me that even for America and England the title is not as great as the work demands.

Permit me to say, after having read Volume I, that I am overwhelmed by its beauty. I am convinced that this is going to be considered your greatest literary work. One cannot stop reading it, the narrative is more dramatic than any fiction and the language sometimes evokes great paintings, sometimes lovely music. I have never so clearly visualized Roman Legionaries,

Vikings and Normans, and no poet has ever given a more perfect character-ization of Richard II and Joan of Arc. Reading the description of events one would swear that you had been a war correspondent at the time of Julius Caesar.

The book is so fabulous that with any title it will become one of the top ranking works of world literature. But it deserves a title as stirring as its content.

I entirely share your admiration for Gibbon, but "Decline and Fall of the Roman Empire" is a tremendous, ringing title. Gibbon says "Decline and Fall" and not "History" and he says "Roman Empire" and not "Latin Speak-ing Peoples". As you end your narrative with the death of Queen Victoria, a gibbonesque title might be "The Birth and Rise of the British Empire".

There is no question of changing the character of the work as you have viewed it for more than twenty years. It would be simple, however, to explain in the preface that, as you have been progressing, the work outgrew your original conception. It became more universal in character as many of the events and personalities treated in the work are part of world history. And that you did not attempt to give a complete history of the English Speaking Peoples but dealt merely with events and personalities which appeared to you of lasting and general interest. This evolution of the work required another title, more appropriate to the finished product.

Please forgive this long letter. I shall not raise the question again if you feel that the arguments of your foreign publishers do not deserve consideration.

with kindest regards,
yours sincerely,
Emery Reves

P.S.—I have difficulties in obtaining passage (the railroad strike fills all the airplanes) and accommodation in a London hotel. I have reservation at Clar-idge's for Monday the 20th. Should I be able to arrive this week I shall send you a telegram.

Sir Winston Churchill: engagement cards

16 June 1955   28 Hyde Park Gate

   12.30 p.m.   Mr. Emery Reves.

Alan Hodge[1] *to Sir Winston Churchill*

22 June 1955   History Today

Dear Sir Winston,

I return Mr. Reves' letter, which Kelly and I have discussed. We both agree that the difficulties of translating the title of your work into French and German are no reason for changing it. It is surely up to foreign publishers to suggest to you a title suitable in their own languages. English-Speaking Peoples is a phrase well understood in all countries stemming from these islands. If it cannot be turned into, say Swedish or Portuguese, it is up to the Swedes and Portuguese to propose alternatives.

Yours sincerely,
Alan Hodge

1. Alan Hodge, the editor of the magazine *History Today* and, from August 1953, Churchill's principal assistant on *A History of the English-Speaking Peoples*.

Sir Winston Churchill: engagement cards

23 June 1955   Chartwell

1.15 p.m.   Mr. Emery Reves to luncheon.[1]

1. The other guests were John Colville, Churchill's former Principal Private Secretary, and Anthony Moir, his solicitor.

Sir Winston Churchill: engagement cards

13 August 1955   Chartwell

1 p.m.   Mr. Emery Reves for luncheon.

Emery Reves to Sir Winston Churchill

18 August 1955   Claridge's Hotel
London

My dear Sir Winston,

Here is the typescript of Mr. Truman's first volume (Books 1 and 2), which you asked me to send you. Please forgive the delay, but I wanted to attach a detailed table of contents, chapter titles and sub-headings so as to make it easier for you to find the passages you want.

I am sure you will appreciate it if I ask you kindly to keep this confidential, as I am not supposed to show the manuscript to anybody before its publication in October.

On the other hand, should you find that certain passages concerning you are not correct, I should be grateful if you would let me know. I shall then draw Mr. Truman's attention to them, naturally without mentioning you, as if I had discovered them myself.

Kindly return this typescript, after perusal, to my London office in the Daily Telegraph building and let me have your comments, if any, at my usual Paris address (33 Champs-Elysées), where I expect to return tomorrow.

Thank you very much for your kind invitation last Saturday. As always, it was a great pleasure to spend a few hours with you. I am greatly looking forward to seeing you again in Cap d'Ail in the middle of September, by which time I shall have carefully read the proofs of your first volume.

with kindest regards,
yours very sincerely,
Emery Reves

P.S. This is an uncorrected copy, a number of corrections are on the way.

E.R.

Sir Winston Churchill to Emery Reves

31 August 1955   Chartwell

My dear Reves,

Thank you so much for letting me see the proofs, about which I shall, of course, observe all discretion. I have returned them to your London office as you ask.

Yours sincerely,
Winston S. Churchill

Sir Winston Churchill: engagement cards

27 September 1955   Cap d'Ail [1]

    8.30 p.m.   Mr. Reves to dinner.

   1.   Churchill had gone to stay at Lord Beaverbrook's villa, La Capponcina, at the Cap d'Ail on 15 September 1955 and stayed there until 14 November 1955, writing his memoirs and painting. Among those who came out to help him with his memoirs were Denis Kelly, Alan Hodge, and Bill Deakin. Also with Churchill for some of the time were his Private Secretary, Anthony Montague Browne, and Montague Browne's wife, Nonie.

Doreen Pugh [1] to Emery Reves

30 September 1955

Dear Mr. Reves,

Sir Winston has received a fairly late edition of the Second Volume. The chapters on Good Queen Bess and The Invincible Armada are being reprinted, but will be out shortly. However, Sir Winston thinks you will get a very good impression from the text he encloses. The whole of this volume is under revise, but none the less he thinks it would be worth reading.

Please let Sir Winston have these back at your convenience.

Yours sincerely,
DP
Private Secretary

   1.   Doreen Pugh, Churchill's secretary for the last decade of his life.

Sir Winston Churchill: engagement cards

8 October 1955   Cap d'Ail

   1.30 p.m.   Lunch Mr. Reves.

Sir Winston Churchill to Emery Reves

9 October 1955   La Capponcina,
                                                                  Cap d'Ail
                                                         Alpes Maritimes[1]

My dear Reves,
   I confirm that, in exercising the foreign language book rights of "The History of the English-Speaking Peoples", there will be no objection to your publishing this work under any title which you may select, provided it is clearly stated in each volume that the work is the same as that published in England under the title of "The History of the English-Speaking Peoples".
                                                      Yours very sincerely
                                                      Winston S. Churchill

   1.   Churchill was staying with Lord Beaverbrook, whose villa, La Capponcina, was less than five miles from Reves's villa, La Pausa.

Sir Winston Churchill: engagement cards

24 October 1955   Cap d'Ail

   Lunch with Mr. Reves.

Sir Winston Churchill to Clementine S. Churchill

26 October 1955   Cap d'Ail

EXTRACT

   I am bidden tomorrow to lunch with Reves and Madame R. at the St. Pol Restaurant.

Sir Winston Churchill: engagement cards

27 October 1955   Cap d'Ail

   Luncheon with Mr. Reves.

Sir Winston Churchill: engagement cards

31 October 1955   Cap d'Ail

   Luncheon. Reves.

Sir Winston Churchill: engagement cards

3 November 1955   Cap d'Ail

6.15 p.m.   Emery Reves.

Sir Winston Churchill to Alan Hodge

10 November 1955   La Capponcina
                                                                      Cap d'Ail

Reves has given me back the amended text which I proposed of the Preface. He has had lengthy telephonings with French, German, Italian and Scandinavian publishers, showing what they want for their editions. I am quite willing to cut out 'of the English-speaking peoples' at the bottom of the first page in the foreign editions.

Sarah Churchill[1] to Wendy Russell and Emery Reves

[20] November 1955   Chartwell

Dear Wendy & Emery,
    A small belated note to you & Emery to tell you how much fun we had with you—and to thank you for all your kindness.
    It was quite hard to come to Earth—and I have little to say about English weather in November!
    He is very well—and I went with him & Mummie the day he received the Freedom of Harrow and then to his old school where they have Sing Songs—great fun—and then a sherry party and then Mummie and I collapsed at home but he went roaring on to a dinner at one of his clubs! So you see he is well and beats us all.

    1. Sarah, Churchill's second daughter, was born shortly after the outbreak of war in 1914.

Denis Kelly to Sir Winston Churchill

8 December 1955

SIR WINSTON
    May these[1] please be sent to the Daily Telegraph and to Reves? Mr. Moir says this is urgent. You scrutinised another copy of this with Hodge and myself. He and I have been through it again, and it is in order.
                                                                            DK

    1. The proof sheets for the first *Daily Telegraph* serialization of *A History of the English-Speaking Peoples*.

Doreen Pugh to Emery Reves

9 December 1955

Dear Mr. Reves,

Sir Winston has just received from LIFE their selections from Volume I for serialisation, and has asked me to send you the enclosed copy. He has already gone through this with Mr. Hodge and Mr. Kelly, and approved it.

Yours sincerely,
DP
Private Secretary

Sir Winston Churchill to Emery Reves

9 December 1955   Chartwell

My dear Reves,

Thank you so much for your letter of December 2.[1] Lady Churchill was much impressed by it. We should be very glad to accept your kind invitation to stay at La Pausa, and I should like to come out for the latter half of January and all February, provided that you will let me pay for the housekeeping. Lady Churchill has some obligations over here and will come out later. During this period I shall hope to arrange something permanent in the neighbourhood, either by rent or purchase. Purchase from a French proprietor will be very difficult on account of the Treasury regulations.

We are greatly obliged to you for your proposal.

My regards to Wendy,
yours vy sincerely,
Winston S. Churchill

1.   Not found (but inviting Lady Churchill to La Pausa).

Emery Reves to Sir Winston Churchill

29 December 1955   La Pausa,
Roquebrune,
Alpes Maritimes

My dear Sir Winston,

I cannot tell you how happy we are that you are coming to La Pausa. We only regret that Lady Churchill cannot come with you. In a separate letter we are trying to persuade her, as it would be lovely if you could enjoy the sunshine together.

I understand that you will arrive on January 11th. I would be grateful if you would let me know 3–4 days ahead the exact time of your arrival so that I may be at the airport and have everything prepared.

I would also like to know who is coming with you and whether I should make reservations in a hotel in Monte Carlo (10 minutes by car) or in Roquebrune (5 minutes by car) for your Secretary and the others who will come with you. As I have told you, I have accommodation in the villa besides you and Lady Churchill for one of your children or Anthony and for Kirkwood.[1]

We are returning from Paris to Roquebrune tonight and you can always reach me by telephone at Roquebrune 29064. Please do not hesitate to let me know if there is anything particular I should do to prepare your arrival.

Looking forward with greatest joy to see you soon, and wishing you a very happy new year, I am

Yours very sincerely,
Emery Reves

1. Anthony Montague Browne, a wartime pilot who had been awarded the Distinguished Flying Cross, had been seconded from the Foreign Office to Churchill's Private Office during the second premiership. After Churchill's retirement in 1955, he remained as Churchill's Private Secretary and confidant for the next decade.

Kirkwood was Churchill's valet. One who remembers him well commented to me (on 30 May 1996), "He was rather a military sort of gent. You wouldn't want to take advantage of him. He didn't last very long. I rather think he left under a cloud."

Emery Reves to Sir Winston Churchill: telegram

31 December 1955   Monte Carlo

Weather report number one today brilliant sunshine blue skies birds singing bees buzzing mimosas budding happy new year a bientot

Emery

BUSINESS AND FRIENDSHIP

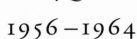

1956–1964

Churchill spent his first holiday at La Pausa in January 1956. He returned there many times in the following four years. While at La Pausa he completed his last book, A History of the English-Speaking Peoples, *the first volume of which was published in May 1956, the fourth volume in March 1958.*

Sir Winston Churchill to Emery Reves: telegram

25 February 1956   Westerham
2.05 p.m.

Have decided postpone departure till Monday 5th. Hope I can bring Diana[1] and Montague Browne then.

Churchill

    1.   Diana, Churchill's first child and eldest daughter, born in 1909.

Sir Winston Churchill to Emery Reves: telegram

25 February 1956   Westerham
4.15 p.m.

In view postponed return would you please send back all proofs, also package addressed Hodge, by air freight. Will collect from London airport.

Churchill

Lord Moran: diary[1]

11 April 1956

When I asked him how he had been in France he answered: 'I'm all right, I think. I look like living on, getting more and more useless.' When I put my finger on his pulse he said cheerfully: 'I don't think it will cause you anxiety.'

I asked Miss Pugh, who had been with him in France, if he was in good form. 'My goodness, yes. For the last three weeks he seemed twenty years younger, and now he is as happy as a child to be home again at Chartwell.'

The office sometimes finds Winston better than in fact he is. They are led astray by the uplift in his spirits when he visits the Reves' house at Roquebrune. A few days in London, perhaps one troublesome speech, and we are back in gloom.

1. Lord Moran (formerly Sir Charles Wilson) had been Churchill's doctor since 1940. His diary was published in 1966, a year after Churchill's death, as *Winston Churchill: The Struggle for Survival, 1940–1965* (London: Constable, 1966).

Wendy Russell and Emery Reves to Sir Winston Churchill: telegram

14 April 1956   Roquebrune,
                                                   Cap Martin

Sunshine gone with your departure Thinking of you and missing you Have a happy happy family reunion love to all

                                                   Wendy Emery

Anthony Montague Browne to Emery Reves and others[1]

19 April 1956

Sir Winston Churchill has asked me to write to you concerning the date of delivery of the second volume of "A History of the English-Speaking Peoples". He has arranged with Cassell & Co. Limited to send to you on or about the 1st of May next the printed proofs of the volume to which you are entitled and thus the formal date of delivery will be the 1st of June.

Owing to a printing strike, work on earlier proofs has been seriously delayed, and consequently the proofs which you will receive in May will be subject to final correction. The further corrections and additions will not materially alter the volume and need not, for instance, delay the selection of material for serialisation, or preliminary work in connection with volume publication.

As soon as the final corrections are made, which it is hoped will be not later than about the 20th of July, copies will be made available to you. Perhaps you will let me know how many of these you will require.

Sir Winston Churchill is sorry that the proofs which will be despatched to you next month will not be in final form, but the printing strike has caused unavoidable delay.

A. A. D. Montague Browne

1.   Andrew L. Heiskell, Time, Inc.; Michael Berry, *Daily Telegraph* (later Lord Hartwell); Edward Dodd, Jr., Dodd, Mead and Company, Inc.; and J. G. McClelland, McClelland and Steward Ltd., of Toronto.

Sir Winston Churchill to Wendy Russell and Emery Reves

30 April 1956 Chartwell

My dear Wendy & Emery,

Let me thank you once more for your kindness and hospitality to me during my ten weeks with you. You certainly made up for the weather. <u>Indeed</u> I passed a peaceful and happy time under the shelter of your palatial roof.

With regard to your further attractive invitation, Lady Churchill is going to stay with a friend in Paris for a week beginning 24 May, and would like very much to come to stay with you for a few days after that. I will myself come over on Monday 28 or Tuesday 29 May, if that will suit you, and should like to stay until about the middle of the month, if you will keep me so long, when I must go home to take part in the Garter celebrations and racing engagements. Let me know if this is all right.

Yours vy sincerely,
Winston S. Churchill

Wendy Russell and Emery Reves to Sir Winston Churchill: telegram

8 May 1956

Overjoyed your return to us end May. Shall telephone you Monday next to discuss details. Fly fast and well to Germany.[1]

Wendy and Emery

1.   On 9 May 1956 Churchill flew from London to Aachen, where he was presented with the Charlemagne Prize. From Aachen he went to Bonn, where he saw Chancellor Adenauer, before spending three days with British troops on the Rhine.

At the end of May 1956, Churchill returned to the South of France to spend two weeks with Emery Reves and Wendy Russell at La Pausa.

Sir Winston Churchill and Sarah Churchill to Wendy Russell
and Emery Reves: telegram

14 June 1956   London

Arrived safely armed with memories of another delightful visit to Pausaland. Thank you both so much.

Winston and Sarah

Sir Winston Churchill to Wendy Russell

22 June 1956   28 Hyde Park Gate

Dear Wendy,

I have now been home a week, and it has passed so slowly because of the many things we had to do that it might have been a fortnight. My horse, First Light, did not distinguish himself at Ascot, and my other horse, Le Pretendant, runs on Saturday, when, alas, I have to be in my Constituency. Mr. Truman is coming to luncheon on Sunday—a family gathering, plus Max.

Although we had a wonderful reception when we arrived, and gleaming sunlight gilded the scene, we only just got home before there was a thundershower. Since then the weather has been beneath contempt for this time of year; two or three hours of sunshine in the early morning, and cloud and rain storms for the rest of the day. I am now going down to Chartwell under grey skies.

I wonder what luck you and Emery have had. It certainly has been a very disappointing year for weather.

I have made no plans as yet for the future, but I will write to you as soon as I do.

I have been asked many questions about the princely couple[1] who entertained us to their first official luncheon, and have replied giving them both a good character.

Give Emery my regards. I hope the proofs are reaching him punctually. I am toiling at them and I hope to make an end of the Second Volume by the weekend.

Thank you both once more for your delightful hospitality. The warmth of your welcome and your kindness made my stay most memorable. I am so grateful to you for all the trouble you took—not least in preparing for me such a beautiful and sunny room.

Yours ever
Winston S. Churchill

1. Prince Rainier of Monaco and Princess Grace (formerly the actress Grace Kelly).

Sir Winston Churchill: engagement cards

26 July 1956   Chartwell

   1.15 p.m.   Mr. Reves to luncheon.

Sir Winston Churchill to Wendy Russell

16 August 1956   Chartwell

My dear Wendy,
    I was very sorry you could not visit this country with Emery. It would
have been very jolly to see you again. Emery will have told you about my
present plans, which remain to visit you about the middle of September. I
hope that the Egyptian situation will not develop in a way to delay or prevent
it.[1] I don't see why it should. I look forward to coming back to Pausaland
again, and will do the same thing about the motorcar and Mario if that can
be arranged.
    I have been toiling at the book, but have not made the progress I expected. I
hope, however, that it will all be finished by the end of January. Five months.
    I am sorry that the Princess[2] did not reply to your flowers. Did you make
it clear that they came from you and not from me? She wrote a very nice letter in answer to mine. She may be tripping over the irregularity. It makes it
difficult for people in formal surroundings.
    Clemmie has gone to St. Moritz. She had a painful fall before leaving. She
thought it was only bruises, but knee and ankle have been afflicted by a torn
muscle, and she is unable at present to walk. She is coming back here on
Thursday next.
    The weather is disappointing. When June failed, I hoped for July. When
July disgraced itself, my thoughts turned to August. We have had the most
curious changes of weather. Sometimes the most beautiful day without a
cloud in the sky, but nearly always succeeded by periods of rain and gales.
I wonder what sort of weather you are having and whether the lavender has
fulfilled your courageous hopes?
    Christopher's official work takes him up to London a great deal, & Mary
has her brood,[3] but I can live a solitary life without great discomfort.
                                                Yours very sincerely,
                                                       Winston

    1.   Following the nationalization of the Suez Canal in July 1956 by President Nas-
ser of Egypt, the British government had at first sought negotiations and then, in
August, after holding secret discussions near Paris with French and Israeli leaders, decided to use force. In November, British troops landed at Port Said and advanced
several miles along the canal. Following American economic threats, however, Prime
Minister Eden was forced to accept a cease-fire. The crisis precipitated Eden's resignation in January 1957.
    2.   Princess Grace of Monaco.

3.   Christopher Soames, his wife, Mary (Churchill's youngest daughter), and their children Nicholas (aged 8), Emma (7), Jeremy (4), and Charlotte (2). Their fifth child, Rupert, was born in 1959.

Sir Winston Churchill to Emery Reves

24 August 1956   Chartwell

My dear Emery,
    I enclose you a letter from Moir which speaks for itself.[1]
    We are having characteristically anti-harvest weather here. I suppose you are having sunshine in Pausaland?
    Looking forward to seeing you both soon,

I remain,
Yours very sincerely,
Winston S. Churchill

1.   The letter from Moir has not been found.

Sir Winston Churchill: engagement cards

17 September 1956   Chartwell

    Reves to Chartwell.

∽

On 17 September 1956, Churchill returned to La Pausa for his third visit that year. While he was there he suffered a stroke, and eight days later, on October 28, he flew back to Britain.

∽

Sir Winston Churchill: engagement cards

17 November 1956   Chartwell

    Mr. Reves to luncheon and to stay the weekend.

Sir Winston Churchill: engagement cards

21 November 1956   Chartwell

    1.15 p.m.   Mr. Reves to luncheon.[1]

1.   The other lunch guests that day were Baron and Baroness de Rothschild and Anthony and Nonie Montague Browne.

Sir Winston Churchill: engagement cards

28 November 1956   28 Hyde Park Gate

Mr. Reves to luncheon.[1]

    1.   The other lunch guest that day was Lady Diana Cooper.

Sir Winston Churchill to Wendy Russell

29 November 1956

My dear Wendy,
    Emery leaves by the Q.E. tomorrow afternoon. He has been most companionable to us during his short stay in London. He visited us at Chartwell for a weekend, and I think he enjoyed himself.
    I am looking forward very much to coming out in January to Pausaland. I gathered from what Emery said that you very likely would not be able to receive me before, perhaps, the 15th. If this should be so, let me know in good time. Otherwise, expect me about the 3rd, and may I bring Anthony Montague Browne with me? We have had a stirring fortnight between England and America, but I think it is all calming down now. At any rate, I do not think that these great affairs will interfere with the pleasant company we keep.
    Let me know if you ever got the letter I sent to you for your voyage. I thought I was so clever, but it appears that we did not address it right.
    I am looking forward very much to our meeting again.

Sir Winston Churchill to Emery Reves: telegram [1]

14 December 1956   London

    Subject to my final approval of an agreement you have sole option to negotiate sale of television and cinematograph rights of history until January 1 on minimum basis of figure mentioned on telephone

                                                            Winston Churchill

    1.   Reves had gone to New York, where he was staying at the St. Regis Hotel.

Sir Winston Churchill to Emery Reves: telegram

28 December 1956   London

    BIOW[1] has option on same terms as yours until end of February stop Letter from Moir follows Please send BIOWs address

                                                            Winston Churchill

    1.   I have been unable to identify BIOW.

Sir Winston Churchill to Emery Reves: telegram

4 January 1957   Westerham

Tentative discussions which Henry Salamon[1] had in London refer to purchase of television rights on final chapter only of History stop This is not
connected with option you have which refers to sale of television and cine-
matograph rights of the whole History

Winston Churchill

1.   I have been unable to identify Henry Salamon.

*Churchill returned to La Pausa early in January 1957, for six weeks. While
he was there, he completed work on the final volume of his final book,* A
History of the English-Speaking Peoples.

Mary Soames: recollection[1]

[1960]   [La Pausa]

Clementine did not enjoy herself there. She found life at La Pausa claus-
trophobic. Not having a car, it always meant hiring one specially; and to take
a walk outside the villa grounds was difficult, as the mountainside was very
steep. Winston worked all morning in bed, and after luncheon painted or
rested; in the evenings he liked to play cards for a while; he loved her being
there, but he was not companionable. Emery and Wendy were full of care
for Winston, and solicitous for all their guests' pleasure, but Clementine
found she was really the prisoner of kindness and of other people's plans.
And although it was mostly smiles and pleasantness on the surface, there was
very little she and her hosts had in common.

1.   Mary Soames, *Clementine Churchill* (London: Cassell, 1979), p. 462.

Emery Reves to Sir Winston Churchill

29 January 1957   La Pausa
Confidential

I understand that with the final reading of one more chapter and the pref-
aces your work on Volumes III and IV is completed. Another reading of the
proofs for spelling and punctuation seems unnecessary as this is the responsibility of the publishers. However, Mr. Wood[1] can no doubt do this job without your spending any time on it.

This gives us 17 days until February 15th, 17 long days to write a Preface to the abridged edition of the War Memoirs your publishers desire. In this respect I would like to say the following:

1) For the world rights of a Preface of approximately 10.000 words I can offer you £20.000.-- (Twenty Thousand Pounds). I believe this is the highest amount ever paid for a manuscript—£2.- per word.

2) I have consulted Mr. Moir who confirmed to me that this amount could come under the new arrangements and would not be taxable.

3) I have discussed the matter with the other publishers who are my partners in this offer. To simplify matters, one short 1-page contract with me would be sufficient. I would then re-transfer the various rights to Cassells, Houghton Mifflin, etc. without any trouble for you or Mr. Moir.

4) I would remit the amount any time fixed by you and Mr. Moir.

5) With Hodge, Kelly and Anthony[2] being around, they could submit you a draft of this Preface within 2–3 days. I think that in 8–10 days it could be completed.

Emery Reves

1.   Charles Carlisle Wood, a publisher's proofreader, who had been proofreading Churchill's books for a quarter of a century. At Chartwell, proofreading was known as "wooding."

2.   Alan Hodge, Denis Kelly, and Anthony Montague Browne.

∽

On 13 February 1957 Churchill returned briefly to London.

∽

Sir Winston Churchill: engagement cards

16 February 1957

Return to La Pausa (until March 22).

Sir Winston Churchill to Emery Reves

20 February 1957   La Pausa

Dear Mr. Reves,

I understand that, in your contract with the Daily Telegraph Ltd. relating to the WAR MEMOIRS, there is a provision that no abridgement of that Work shall be made without my approval.

I am well aware that you are planning to bring out an abridged edition and, as I have now retired from my literary profession, I am writing formally to let you know that I hereby waive my rights to approve it. In doing this, I know I can rely upon you to ensure that the abridged edition for which you will be responsible will be of the same high standard as that of the six-volume edition.

Yours sincerely,
Winston S. Churchill

Sir Winston Churchill and Sarah Churchill to Emery Reves
and Wendy Russell: telegram

22 March 1957   London

Arrived safely lovely journey all well

Winston and Sarah

Sir Winston Churchill to Emery Reves

27 March 1957   Chartwell

My dear Emery,

I got back here all right as I told you, and found everything in good order. You will be glad to hear that three cygnets have been born to the black swans, and so far are all alive and thriving. They are very beautiful, and I am very glad to have them.

I must thank you for my very pleasant visit and for all your hospitality. I am afraid I have been a great burden to you.

With all good wishes,
Yours very sincerely,
Winston S. Churchill

Emery Reves to Sir Winston Churchill

1 April 1957   Paris

My dear Sir Winston,

Upon arrival in Paris I found your letter of 28 March including a copy of Mr. Moir's letter of 27 March.[1] I have studied carefully the observations made by Mr. Moir and I am glad to say that in the meantime all the questions raised by Mr. Moir have been solved.

1) When calculating my offer I was naturally thinking to make the payment the way in which 99% of the payments from Switzerland to England are made. I deposit the amount in Swiss Francs at my Bank in Geneva and

the Bank issues an official check drawn on their Swiss account in London. Approval of such payments from Switzerland is automatic. In drafting the first application by your Bankers a different method was indicated and this led to a minor complication. However, Mr. Moir informed me that the Bank of England accepted the payment as suggested by my Bankers in Geneva. So this problem is solved.

2) I thought that you were selling to Cassell's, Dodd Mead, etc. your contracts for a lump sum and took it for granted that I am supposed to purchase your Time contract for a lump sum. I never realized that Mr. Moir merely wanted to sell me "the right to receive the outstanding instalments." Being convinced that I am purchasing your contract in the same manner the others do, I have accordingly written to Andrew Heiskell. I asked him whether Time Inc. would agree that you assign to me their contract, which means that I would take over all your rights and all your obligations deriving from that contract. I have also asked him whether they would subsequently agree to make the total payment to me in the near future and not in three instalments in 1957, 1958 and 1959. To this letter Heiskell cabled me as follows:

IN ANSWER TO YOUR LETTER OF MARCH 21 WE ARE WILLING TO DO ANYTHING IN THE CIRCUMSTANCES WHICH WOULD HELP AUTHOR OR YOU WITH TAX PROBLEM INCLUDING PAYMENT FULL AMOUNT DUE.

Life is therefore in full agreement that the contract should be assigned to me.

Mr. Moir's remark that although you have fulfilled your main obligations under the contract "Life still has the benefit of the stipulations into which you entered and under which you may not permit publication of any volume before certain specified times . . ." this has been surpassed by recent events. Under the 1955 contracts simultaneous publication was stipulated all over the world. In England, France and elsewhere we could start serial publications on the same dates Life published their first instalment. Under these circumstances they were naturally anxious to be protected against copyright infringement in case a European magazine starts publications 1 or 2 days ahead of Life. Last year Life asked me to advance publication dates considerably. The English and Continental magazines could not accept Life's proposed time table but I succeeded in persuading them to let the American edition of Life publish whenever they wanted. So Life is going to serialize Volumes III and IV 6 to 8 months before anybody else can start publications. The clause raised by Mr. Moir is therefore completely outdated and has no more meaning for Life. Anyway, if Time Inc. agrees to the assignment of the contract which would automatically relieve you from these minor and hypothetical obligations, why would you insist to retain personal responsibilities after your retirement without being requested to do so?

I sincerely hope that this clarifies the situation and that Mr. Moir will be satisfied that there is no objection as far as Time Inc. is concerned to the assignment of the contract to me. This would be the simplest and easiest solution. If I purchase the contract, I know exactly where I stand as I can act as principal. My tax problem is clear. I could remit the amount due to you immediately upon signature of the assignment. And I am confident that Life will remit to me the total amount due within 3–4 weeks. So in a month after our final agreement the contract will be consummated and may be filed in the archives.

On the other hand if I merely purchase "the right to receive the three out-standing instalments due from Life" I see a serious tax problem. I may be considered merely a collecting agent and the American Internal Revenue people are extremely suspicious in such situations. They may suspect that ulti-mately the money will go to England where the proprietor resides. My lawyer advises me that if I do not become unquestionably the proprietor of the U.S. serial rights, sold to Time Inc., I should submit the case to the tax authorities in New York and ask for a ruling. Probably—not certainly—the ruling will be favourable, but it may take one or two months.

I am sending a copy of this letter to Mr. Moir so that he may submit to you his remarks without delay.

Enclosed please find a letter from Dodd Mead received at Pausaland just before our departure. We arrived in Paris yesterday and shall write to you about other matters in 2–3 days. Many thanks for your private letter. Please, please eliminate from your vocabulary the word "burden". It has nothing to do with facts.

As ever,
Yours
Emery

1.   These letters have not been found.

On 18 May 1957 Churchill returned to La Pausa for his sixth visit in just over a year. His daughter Sarah was with him. They returned to England in the second week of June.

Sir Winston Churchill and Sarah Churchill to Emery Reves and
Wendy Russell: telegram

[ ] June 1957   London

Safely home thank you for a lovely time

Winston and Sarah

Sir Winston Churchill: engagement cards

16 July 1957   Chartwell

Mr. and Mrs. Reves[1] to luncheon.

1.   Emery Reves and Wendy Russell were not married until 1964. They had met in New York in 1945 and had lived together since 1949.

Sir Winston Churchill: engagement cards

20 July 1957

Reves to Chartwell (until 22 July).
4.30 p.m.   Mr. and Mrs. Reves to stay.[1]

1.   Churchill's other guests at Chartwell that weekend were his daughter Sarah and his nephew Peregrine.

Emery Reves to Sir Winston Churchill

26 August 1957   La Pausa

My dear Sir Winston,
    We returned to Pausaland last week after a restful holiday in Switzerland. Wendy's mother arrived from New York and is going to stay here until the beginning of October.
    This gives me an opportunity to carry out a number of business engagements in several countries, and I shall be away most of the month of September. But I shall stay all October in Roquebrune and am greatly looking forward to new battles of bezique, inspired by fire and music. Of course, Wendy and her mother will be at La Pausa all the time.
    My next departure will be for Barcelona on the 2nd or 3rd September. I would be delighted to meet you at the airport and take you to Capponcina in my car, if this suits you. So unless I hear from you to the contrary I shall be waiting for you at the airport. The weather is magnificent here!
    Bon Voyage and—à bientôt!
    With all my respects to Lady Churchill.

                                                                                            Yours ever
                                                                                            Emery

Sir Winston Churchill: engagement cards

1 September 1957   Cap d'Ail

Mr. & Mrs. Reves to dinner.

Sir Winston Churchill: engagement cards

10 September 1957

    1.15 p.m.   To luncheon at La Pausa.

Emery Reves to Sir Winston Churchill: telegram

13 September 1957   Milan

Belated but heartfelt congratulations on yesterday's anniversary.[1]

                                          Emery

    1.   Churchill and his wife celebrated their forty-ninth wedding anniversary on 12 September 1957.

Sir Winston Churchill to Emery Reves: telegram

14 September 1957   La Capponcina,
                                                Cap d'Ail

Thank you so much for your kind message

                                    Winston Churchill

Emery Reves to Sir Winston Churchill

30 October 1957   Paris

My dear Sir Winston,

    I was glad to learn that you had a nice trip back, and we see from the newspapers what a busy life you have been leading since your return home.[1] We are greatly looking forward to hearing how Lady Churchill and the family found you and your last paintings.

    The weather here continues to be absolutely heavenly. Since your departure, there has been not one cloud, but only warm sunshine all day. The only thing that has interfered with the deep blue of the sky has been the "Spoutnik," which flew over Monte Carlo and Pausaland twice this past week.

    We arrived in Paris today, so if you think of us, please address your letter to me here.

    I learned from American friends that about a week ago one of the great television networks in the U.S.A. televised a full hour show on your life. I understand it was a most dignified and excellent performance, but as it was commercially sponsored, I wonder whether you knew about it and whether this does not prejudice other plans.

                                        with all the best,
                                        yours ever,
                                        Emery

    1.   Since returning from La Pausa, Churchill's one public engagement had been
his annual visit to Harrow School on October 25, for the school songs, where he had
spoken briefly to the boys.

Sir Winston Churchill: engagement cards

10 November 1957   Chartwell

    Mr. Reves to lunch and dine.

Sir Winston Churchill: engagement cards

13 November 1957   28 Hyde Park Gate

    8 p.m.   Mr. Reves to dinner.

Emery Reves to Sir Winston Churchill

14 November 1957   London

    As we shall not be here on the 30th November,[1] Wendy and I send you
this little box in which you may carry your golliwags. (Please correct the
spelling).[2]
    Wishing you a very happy birthday and many more of it.
    A très bientôt.[3]

                                                                       Yours
                                                                       Emery

    1.   Churchill was eighty-three years old on 30 November 1957.
    2.   "Golliwags" was one of Churchill's made-up words.
    3.   On 4 December 1957 Churchill declined an invitation from Lord Beaverbrook
to stay at La Capponcina, telling Beaverbrook, "I am however engaged to go in January
and February to La Pausa and I fear I should upset the Reves if I changed."

Sir Winston Churchill to Wendy Russell and Emery Reves

22 November 1957

My dear Wendy and Emery,
    How very kind of you to send me such a beautiful, original and useful
Birthday present. I shall treasure it with its charming inscription, and will
certainly make use of it for the "golliwogs" as you suggest. I am touched
by your thought of me, which you have expressed in this kind and most
attractive way.
    I have had a letter from Mr. Onassis containing an invitation to go on

a cruise on the "Christina" some time this winter. He said that he had had news of me from you.

Clemmie joins me in sending you her best wishes, and we look forward to seeing you on your return.

Yours vy sincerely,
Winston S. Churchill

Sir Winston Churchill to Emery Reves: telegram[1]

29 December 1957   Westerham

Regret Capitals Look proposal on pictures not acceptable as occasion non-commercial[2] stop Glad to hear about preface and look forward to seeing you both Warm regards

Winston Churchill

1. Reves was in New York, staying at the St. Regis Hotel.
2. Some of Churchill's paintings were being exhibited in Kansas City, under the auspices of Joyce Hall of Hallmark Cards. It was the first exhibition devoted solely to Churchill's paintings. Hall later established a small permanent exhibition of Churchill's paintings in Kansas City ("the largest collection of Churchill paintings west of the Mississippi").

Emery Reves to Sir Winston Churchill: telegram

3 January 1958   New York

Writing from boat calling from Paris trust you withhold decision until letter arrives Regards

Emery

Sir Winston Churchill to Emery Reves: telegram

3 January 1958   New York

Magazine in question is being allowed to reproduce two pictures to illustrate review of exhibition. No charge is being made and the rights are not repeat not exclusive. I am allowing newspapers to reproduce up to four pictures two of which may be in colour if they are covering exhibition. No charge is being made.[1]

Winston Churchill

1. Anthony Montague Browne noted on this telegram, "Cleared with Mr Moir. Approved by Sir Winston."

Emery Reves to Sir Winston Churchill

8 January 1958   Cunard Line
                                                          R.M.S. *Queen Mary*

My dear Sir Winston,

Many thanks for your cable which I received just before sailing and for your radiogram. I am terribly sorry for having caused this perhaps unnecessary incident, but I feel that it prevented a series of events contrary to your intentions. Your radiogram was a great surprise to me as the information you received is in contradiction to the facts as I found them in New York.

When I made arrangements with LOOK for the publication of your Preface, they asked me whether I could arrange for them to reproduce in colour 6–8 of your paintings. They wanted to publish them the week the exhibition opened in the Metropolitan Museum and offered you for the permission an amount of $10,000.-. I thought this was an interesting suggestion for various reasons. LOOK and LIFE are the only weekly magazines in America producing fine colour reproductions. Only these two magazines, among the weeklies, can reproduce properly paintings in colour. In view of the strange attitude of LIFE (I shall tell you the whole story personally), and the profound admiration of Gardner Cowles (owner of LOOK) for you, I thought that LOOK is the ideal medium for colour reproductions. Further, since they have absorbed Collier's, LOOK has made tremendous progress and has reached a circulation of 5,5 million, the circulation of LIFE.

Having communicated LOOK your first two cables, they perfectly understood your position. They offered the money for a charity you or Mr. Hall designate and they were happy to learn from your cable that "no rival will be given facilities either".

At the request of LOOK, I telephoned to Mr. Hall to let him know LOOK's proposal and to find out what his plans were. Hall told me that this matter is entirely in the hands of a Mr. Robert Breen in New York. He arranged for him to see me.

Mr. Breen represents a New York advertising agency called "Carl Byoir & Associates", who have been charged by Mr. Hall to handle the publicity of the exhibition. Answering my question about his plans, Mr. Breen proudly told me that he has made a deal with THIS WEEK magazine, giving them the <u>exclusive</u> rights to reproduce in colour four of your paintings. (THIS WEEK later reduced the number to two pictures: Venice and the Orchids). He added that he was in negotiations with other magazines for further prints.

Permit me to interject that THIS WEEK is a "give-away" publication, not sold independently, but distributed freely as a Sunday supplement by some 25–30 newspapers in a circulation of about 12 million. It is a big, commercial advertising business, but a low class magazine with very poor printing.

To my question, whether Sir Winston approved of this exclusive arrangement, Breen replied somewhat embarrassed that he had received authority from Mr. Hall to get the paintings reproduced. I told him about LOOK and tried to arrive at a compromise. As he already made his deal with THIS WEEK, I suggested that this should stand, provided that THIS WEEK would co-ordinate publication with LOOK. I would then try to persuade LOOK to select some of the remaining paintings and publish simultaneously with THIS WEEK. Mr. Breen was very happy and left to discuss the matter with THIS WEEK. An hour later he telephoned, telling me that he could not change anything as THIS WEEK was publishing the pictures in their February 9th issue which was already in the presses.

LOOK was rather unhappy about this fait accompli, particularly as it was in such contradiction to your cable saying that "no rival will be given facilities either". However, I was able to persuade them to disregard THIS WEEK and reproduce a few pictures in their March 4th issue which coincides with the opening of the show in the Metropolitan in New York. They maintained their offer to give a certain amount to a charity you designate. I called again Mr. Hall to find out whether all the paintings had been photographed in colour. To my greatest surprise he knew nothing of the deal Mr. Breen had made with THIS WEEK.

This happened the day of my departure from New York, so everything has been left in abeyance. Permit me a few remarks regarding the information you sent me by radiogram.

You say: "Magazine in question is being allowed to reproduce two pictures to illustrate review of exhibition". I am afraid this is not what I have learned from an Editor of THIS WEEK. They are not "reviewing" the exhibition as they print the issue 4 weeks before the opening of the exhibition. According to my information they have obtained from Odhams permission to reproduce a section from "Painting as a Pastime" [1] and will print it in the form of an article under the title "WHY I PAINT AND WHY YOU SHOULD—by WINSTON S. CHURCHILL" illustrated by the two paintings. Naturally, at the bottom of a page, or somewhere, they will mention in small characters that this was taken from your book, but the mass of the readers will get the impression that this is a special article written by you for THIS WEEK.

The fact that THIS WEEK does not pay for the reproduction of the pictures does not prove that this was not a commercial deal. For an advertising agency to be able to grant such favours to their clients as to enable them to reproduce your paintings at such an important occasion, is very much of a commercial deal—in favour of the advertising agency. Magazines like THIS WEEK, LIFE, LOOK, etc. are commercial enterprises accustomed to payment for what they publish. The proper way to make such an event noncommercial is not to let these giant business enterprises have something valuable for nothing, but to make them pay appropriate amounts to a charity or to a cause.

Naturally, daily newspapers are different. They will review the exhibition and will reproduce 2–3 pictures in black and white. It is self-evident that this service must be free of any charge. Only colour reproductions present a problem, as this procedure takes 6–8 weeks and no magazine can undertake it without previous arrangement.

All this is not too important, and most probably Carl Byoir & Associates will make no more such deals. I am only sorry that the only magazine which had the great desire to reproduce, as a portfolio, in an artistic and dignified manner some of your paintings, the magazine that most deserved it and was willing to make a great effort for it, now will probably be excluded. The deadline for the March 4 issue of LOOK is January 15th. So there is still time, if you so desire, to instruct Hall to allow LOOK to select 6 or 8 paintings for colour reproduction and to reserve for them exclusive colour reproduction rights until after publication date.

To sum up, it does not seem to be right that a magazine of the class of THIS WEEK, which has never published any of your writings, should have the privilege of being not only the first (which cannot be changed anymore), but also the only magazine in America to reproduce your paintings in colour.

We had a ghastly crossing. Old Queen Mary just kept on rolling four days and four nights. Baggage and furniture were flying around in the cabin, the soup ran away from the plate and it was impossible to stay in bed, even for a minute, without acrobatic exertions.

I shall call you from Paris. Greatly looking forward to your approaching visit to Pausaland

and à très bientôt
as ever
yours
Emery

1.   The British company Odhams had published (with Ernest Benn) Churchill's book *Painting as a Pastime* in London in 1948. The book contained two essays ("Hobbies" and "Painting as a Pastime") previously published in book form, in 1932 in Churchill's volume of essays *Thoughts and Adventures*.

Sir Winston Churchill to Emery Reves

10 January 1958

My dear Emery,

Thank you for writing so fully to me about the Exhibition. There may possibly have been a misunderstanding between Mr. Hall and his agents, but I think the position is now clear. I enclose a copy of the telegram I sent him on the Press arrangements by which he will abide. I am afraid that I cannot give LOOK the exclusive rights for which you ask. On the other hand, they are welcome to reproduce four of the pictures, two of which can be in colour, in the same way as the other newspapers.

I much look forward to seeing you both at Pausaland on the 15th.

Yours vy sincerely,
Winston S. Churchill

∽

*While at La Pausa on 17 February 1958, Churchill was taken ill with bronchial pneumonia. He was eighty-three years old. "*SIR WINSTON ILL*" was the banner headline across all eight front-page columns in the* Daily Mail *on the following morning.*

∽

Lord Moran: diary

19 February 1958

Last night Dr. Roberts telephoned from France: Sir Winston was feverish and coughing. This morning I flew to Nice, and when I examined Winston's chest found that he had bronchopneumonia.

The day before his illness began, Winston had lunched with Onassis on his yacht. About three o'clock Winston expressed a wish to go to the Rooms at Monte Carlo to have a little gamble. Reves suggested that they might play chemin-de-fer on the yacht instead. They played for high stakes and drank more alcohol than usual. Winston got very excited. As the afternoon wore on it was noticed that he was very white and tired. About seven o'clock Reves ventured to remind him that they had been invited for lunch. Was it not time to go home? Winston grumbled that Reves was breaking up the party. When they got home, Winston seemed 'all in.'

∽

When Churchill recovered, the Prime Minister, Harold Macmillan, with the leader of the opposition, Hugh Gaitskell, telegraphed (on 27 February 1958): "At Question Time today whole House asked that a message of congratulations should be sent to you on your recovery, conveying the warm good wishes of us all." Churchill flew back to London on 7 March 1958.

∽

Wendy Russell and Emery Reves to Sir Winston Churchill: telegram

7 April 1958   Monte Carlo

Happy Easter to all

Wendy Emery

Sir Winston Churchill to Wendy Russell and Emery Reves: telegram

8 April 1958

The same to you both and many of them

Winston Churchill

Emery Reves to Sir Winston Churchill

12 April 1958   La Pausa

My dear Sir Winston,

We are leaving for Paris today. So kindly address all communications to my above office. We are staying at the Bristol Hotel, 112 Fbg. St. Honoré. (Telephone: Elysées 23-15).

Just before leaving I would like to mention two "business" matters:

The day after your departure the van left early in the morning and did not take the 12 bottles of champagne Madame Pol Roger sent you. I cannot ship them to London as the exportation of wine requires a special license in France. So I can either ask Mme. Pol Roger to send them to you, or keep them until your next visit. Please tell me what to do.

I received through Andrew Heiskell, of Life, a rather unusual proposal for you. A number of aircraft companies, shipyards and steel companies in America are worried by the very great emphasis that is being placed on missiles as against carrier-based air-forces. These companies are attempting to put together an eight-page illustrated article which would appear as a paid announcement in one or more major publications. They would like the article to be both a brief summary of the part that navies and, particularly, carriers have played in recent times, and a review of their importance today and in the near future. They hope that you could be induced to write such an article of 3–4000 words for which they offer $100,000.-.

I know that you could not write such an article, but I do not feel authorized to decline such a proposal in your name without submitting it to you. So kindly let me know how should I formulate my reply.

Since your departure the weather here has been almost as bad as in England. Cold, rain, even snow in the mountains.

I shall write more from Paris.

with much love to all,
yours,
Emery

Anthony Montague Browne to Emery Reves

14 April 1958

Sir Winston has asked me to thank you very much for your letter. He is not very well at the moment, as you will have gathered from his letter to Wendy,[1] so he hopes that you will excuse him from signing this personally.

He would be very glad that the champagne should remain at La Pausa, and hopes that you will make use of it yourselves in the interim.

You were quite correct in assuming that he could not undertake what Mr. Heiskell asks. Will you let him know, or shall I?

1. Several of Churchill's letters to Wendy Russell were published in Volume 8 of the Churchill biography (*Never Despair*).

Emery Reves to Sir Winston Churchill

19 June 1958   Paris

My dear Sir Winston,

As you are no doubt aware we are arriving at Claridge's Sunday evening. This morning we received Lady Churchill's invitation and it is with the greatest pleasure that we shall come for lunch on Thursday next.

I am rather anxious to discuss with you a business matter at your earliest convenience.[1]

Will you be in London next Monday or Tuesday? I would be most grateful if you could reserve for me a short half hour and if you would ask your secretary to leave a message for me at Claridge's.

Looking greatly forward to the pleasure of seeing you again,

Yours ever
Emery

1. Reves had been approached by the Italian publisher Mondadori with a view to entering into a comprehensive arrangement with regard to *A History of the English-Speaking Peoples.* Reves was also involved at this time in a project to publish complete minutes exchanged between Churchill and Anthony Eden during the Second World War. Nothing came of either scheme.

Sir Winston Churchill: engagement cards

24 June 1958

5.30 p.m.   Mr. Reves.

Sir Winston Churchill: engagement cards

26 June 1958

   1.15 p.m.   Mr. & Mrs. Reves to luncheon.

Sir Winston Churchill: engagement cards

5 July 1958   Chartwell

   Mr. & Mrs. Reves for week end.[1]

   1.   The other guests that weekend were Churchill's daughter Diana and Field Marshal Viscount Montgomery of Alamein (who was also sometimes a guest at La Pausa).

*Sir Winston Churchill and Sarah Churchill to Emery Reves
and Wendy Russell: telegram*

[ ] August 1958   London

   Safely home thank you for a lovely time[1]

                                                      Winston and Sarah

   1.   On 8 August 1958, while staying at La Capponcina as Lord Beaverbrook's guest,
Churchill had gone to La Pausa for lunch.

Emery Reves to Sir Winston Churchill

20 November 1958   Paris

My dear Sir Winston,
   I am sending you herewith last week's Paris-Match publishing on two
pages a photograph of you while painting at Pausaland.
   I understand that the photograph has been reproduced in many other
publications, probably also in some English newspapers and magazines.
   I have made some investigation and found out that this and several other
pictures were taken by a special photographer of Paris-Match who must have
been informed that you were painting on that particular spot. They brought
a ladder and climbed over the wall which at that particular spot is over ten
feet high.
   The pictures were taken partly from the top of our water tank (about
30–40 feet from where you were painting), partly at an even closer range.
   I feel more and more that such violation of privacy by certain newspapers
and magazines has to be stopped, otherwise private life will become just as
intolerable as in a communist dictatorship.
   I have consulted this morning one of the leading French lawyers who said

that the existing French law in this respect is categoric and that no newspaper or photographer has the right to take shots within a private property and publish them without the explicit consent of the persons involved.

I am considering a symbolic law suit against Paris-Match for damages of one Franc. This may help to stop certain organs of the Press from destroying the privacy and the liberties of the individual.

We are sailing to-morrow morning. For the next three–four weeks I shall be staying at the St. Regis Hotel, Fifth Avenue at 55th Street in New York.

I would like to take this opportunity to tell you once more how happy we would be if you would spend the winter months again at La Pausa. The villa is entirely at your disposal.

I am sure that you do not doubt that this "invitation" is sincere and comes from our heart. I would only ask you to be kind enough to let me know your plans, so that we may adjust ours accordingly.

Wendy is writing today a separate letter.

With all my love to Lady Churchill and the Family,
Yours ever,
Emery

Sir Winston Churchill to Emery Reves

25 November 1958   Chartwell

My dear Emery,

Thank you for your letter of November 20. For myself I do not think that a law suit would be worthwhile.

I hope you have had an agreeable crossing and enjoy your stay in New York.

Yours very sincerely,
Winston S. Churchill

Emery Reves to Sir Winston Churchill

25 November 1958   St. Regis Hotel,
Fifth Avenue at 55th Street
New York 22, N.Y.

My dear Sir Winston,

Here is your portrait by Leo Michelson which Wendy and I would like to give you as a birthday present, believing that you like it.

In commissioning this painting, I was trying to get an artistic interpretation of you, as you are today. But tastes are different and we would not like to impose such a picture on you if Lady Churchill or your children feel that it is not good enough. So, for the time being, please consider it as a "condi-

tional" birthday gift, exchangeable for an adequate quantity of champagne or
brandy, if your family feel that it should not hang at Chartwell. I would suggest a three months' option.

We send you our warmest wishes for a gay and sunny birthday. On that
day we shall drink a bottle of champagne to your health and shall be with
you in our thoughts.

All our love,
Wendy and Emery

Sir Winston Churchill to Wendy Russell and Emery Reves: telegram

29 November 1958   Chartwell

We are much excited by the picture and have hung it in the dining room
at Hyde Park Gate. It is charming of you both to have thought of this gift for
my birthday

Winston Churchill

Emery Reves to Sir Winston Churchill

26 December 1958   St. Regis Hotel
Fifth Avenue at 55th Street
New York 22, N.Y.

My dear Sir Winston,

We were delighted to receive your letter and to learn about your plans for
the winter. I do not think it is necessary for me to tell you how thrilled we
are that we shall all be together again at Pausaland. We only regret that this
year you will arrive so late. However, this may not be final, I assume. If Marrakech does not come up to your expectations, or if you get bored among so
many Arabs, please do not hesitate to let us know and come sooner.

Michelson agrees entirely with you that the hand is not good enough. He
says that he knows exactly what has to be done and is anxious to repair it as
soon as possible. At the moment he is in New York where he is preparing
an exhibition for March. Immediately after this exhibition, he will return
to Paris and that will be the best time for him to do the work. We shall see
where you will be at that time and which place will be most convenient for
you. He can just as well do it at Pausaland or in London.

The McFall statue created a real tempest in America.[1] It was reproduced
and commented upon by hundreds of newspapers. It was unanimously, even
violently condemned. I am enclosing two typical clippings. What a pity! I
wonder how you feel about the statue and what is going to happen?

We are living in a strange world. If somebody produces a poor, even bad,
work of art like Sutherland or, it seems, McFall, it is reproduced everywhere

and the artist becomes a world-famous celebrity. But if somebody creates a good, even great, work of art, like Nemon or perhaps Michelson, this is unnoticed and the artist remains unknown. This is not a very cheerful Christmas thought and I see no Saviour arising to change mankind in this respect.

When are you leaving for Marrakech?[2]

Wendy is writing you a separate letter.

Please, give my love and respects to Lady Churchill and convey my very best wishes for the new year to all the Family, including Toby.[3]

as ever,

yours

Emery

1.   David McFall, who created a statue of Churchill, was pilloried in some American papers for his "Libel in Sculpture" (*New York Daily News,* 6 December 1958). "To us," the paper wrote, "this piece of work looks like a statue of a moronic—indeed, an apelike—lug dug out of a Limehouse flophouse and dressed up by some prankster in an old suit of clothes a couple of sizes too big for him."

2.   Churchill and his wife flew to Marrakech on 7 January 1959 and stayed there for just over five weeks.

3.   Churchill's budgerigar.

Sir Winston Churchill: engagement cards

20 June 1959   Chartwell

Mr. Reves.[1]

1.   Churchill's daughter Diana was the only other visitor at Chartwell that day.

On the last day of August 1959, Emery Reves suffered a heart attack, two weeks before his fifty-fifth birthday.

Emery Reves to Sir Winston Churchill

24 September 1959   La Pausa

My dear Sir Winston,

It is the 25th day of my prison term in bed. I cannot tell you how sorry I was that this happened the day before your return and that you could not come back.[1] I was meeting a Spanish publisher at the Hôtel du Paris when I felt a general 'malaise' and slight pain in my chest. I drove home myself and went straight to bed. Fortunately, my New York doctor was in Paris and when I gave him the symptoms over the telephone, he advised to take an electrocardiogram at once. This showed a 'complete left bundle branch block', in other words coronary thrombosis. For a man who never had any illness except flu, this was a severe diagnosis.

However, I feel very comfortable, the pain disappeared after a few hours and never came back, my temperature dropped to normal on the fifth day and has been normal ever since. All the tests show that I am getting better.

But this is a very slow process. I must remain virtually immobile until the middle of October. Then, for another 3 weeks I shall have to stay in bed most of the time and sit a little while each day. If there is no sign of a relapse, only then can I start walking a little and gradually resume normal life.

All this is very much against my temperament—but I am determined to follow the example of Eisenhower and not that of Alex Korda.[2]

My only target is complete recovery, so that during the winter we may have some fun together at Pausaland.

With all my love to you, Lady Churchill and the Family.

As ever,
Emery

1.   As a result of Reves's heart attack, Churchill was unable to return to La Pausa. Following an invitation from the Greek shipowner Aristotle Onassis to cruise on his yacht *Christina,* Churchill embarked on the first of more than six long cruises, in the Mediterranean and to the Caribbean.

2.   President Eisenhower had suffered a heart attack in September 1955. For six weeks he recuperated at Denver, Colorado, before returning to the White House. Alexander Korda, like Reves, was Hungarian-born and Jewish. He died, following a heart attack, in 1956, aged sixty-three, having decided to go on working despite his condition. He was a distinguished film maker, and one of his films, *Lady Hamilton,* was Churchill's favorite. In 1946 Korda paid Churchill the equivalent of more than a million pounds for the film rights of *A History of the English-Speaking Peoples.* The film was never made.

Sir Winston Churchill to Emery Reves

29 September 1959   Chartwell

My dear Emery,

I was so glad to see your handwriting again. Thank you very much for your letter which we have all read with the greatest interest and sympathy. We are thankful that at any rate you have been spared too much pain, but the immobility must be very hard to bear. I am glad you intend to emulate the President.

Here we are much engaged with the Election. I am making some speeches in my Constituency. I am conducting my campaign from Chartwell where we are still having the most beautiful weather.

With very good wishes to you. I hope that your progress, though it must be slow, will be steady.

Yours ever,
Winston S. Churchill

Sir Winston Churchill to Emery Reves

30 September 1959   Chartwell

My dear Emery,

You and Wendy are much in my thoughts, and I do hope that you are continuing to make good progress.

Here the Election is approaching its climax and I am gradually drawn into it more and more. I think however, on the whole, that our chances are still good, though not so good as they ought to be. However, in another week we shall know for certain. Indeed you may not get this letter before the results come in. I have had two charming letters from Wendy and hope the rest she has taken amid her anxieties will do her lasting good.

It was a great disappointment to me not to come out again to Pausaland. We have, however, had enchanting weather here and not a day on which the sun has not shone brightly.

With all good wishes for your complete recovery, believe me

Yours ever,
W

Emery Reves to Sir Winston Churchill

9 October 1959   La Pausa

My dear Sir Winston,

It was a pleasure to follow over the radio your great victory. Congratulations![1]

I am also nearing the end of my fight and hope to win. Monday I shall start sitting in a chair half an hour, raising it gradually to 3–4 hours a day. If all goes well, the following week I shall begin to walk in the room for a few minutes. In short, I have to learn all over again everything I learned when I was one year old.

Although I shall not be able to leave my bedroom for another fortnight, at the earliest, I am dictating my mail in bed and using the telephone with moderation.

The first thing I want to do is pay all my debts. Life has made an arrangement with the BBC for the production of a gramophone record reproducing excerpts from your War speeches. The illustrated abridged edition of your War Memoirs, together with this record, will be ready towards the end of

November. So please find enclosed a cheque for £2,500, according to our agreement, in payment of the use of some of your war speeches.

I read in the papers how beautiful the weather is in England. In fact, several times you had higher temperatures and more sunshine than here. But, I am afraid, the tide is about to turn and for the next few months I would bet on the Riviera.

Wendy is not in a very good shape. She is extremely weak and nervous. I think I frightened her too much and now she is reacting to it. Dr. Roberts is giving her all sorts of iron and vitamin shots to pep her up. However, I am confident that both of us will be in good shape by the beginning of November.

Have you made any plans for the near future? The coming 3–4 weeks will be crucial for me and decisive for the remaining part of my life. So I do not dare to make any plans until I know that I am fit again.

With all my love to the Family

Yours ever
Emery

1.   In the general election held on 8 October 1959, the Conservatives were returned to power (with 365 seats, as against 258 for Labour and 6 for the Liberals). Churchill himself was reelected for his Woodford and Epping constituency, which he had represented since the end of 1924.

Sir Winston Churchill to Emery Reves

14 October 1959   Chartwell

My dear Emery,

It gave me pleasure to receive a letter from you and to know that you are making satisfactory progress. You must certainly take every care not to do too much too quickly. You are very wise to take all precautions.

Thank you also for sending me the cheque. I trust the recordings will be a success.

The Election has gone very well and I think we can look forward to a period of stability at home.

I look forward to seeing you again.

Yours ever,
W

Sir Winston Churchill to Wendy Russell and Emery Reves

3 March 1960   28 Hyde Park Gate
London S.W.7.

My dear Wendy and Emery,

After many plans and counter-plans, we have now arranged to go to the West Indies on the CHRISTINA, so I shall not be coming back to Monte

Carlo for the time being. We sail from Gibraltar on March 8, and I shall probably fly back in time for General de Gaulle's visit here in early April. Charles Moran [1] and his Wife are coming with us, and I hope that we shall find some sun.

I do hope that all goes well with you and that Emery's health continues to improve. Do let me have news of you.

Yours ever,
W

1. Lord Moran had been Churchill's doctor since 1940.

Wendy Russell and Emery Reves were upset by Churchill's decision to spend his next holiday as a guest of Aristotle Onassis on a cruise to the West Indies. They had felt for some time that Churchill had deliberately been avoiding visiting La Pausa. They were even more offended when they discovered that Onassis had been asked not to invite them on the cruise. They became convinced that some of those close to Churchill had decided that it would be better for him not to return to La Pausa.

In the second week of August 1960, Churchill telegraphed to them suggesting that he return to La Pausa on 6 September 1960, to stay there for a while.

Emery Reves to Sir Winston Churchill

21 August 1960   La Pausa

My dear Sir Winston,

Your telegram suggesting to come to Pausaland on the 6th September was a great surprise for us. Since last winter when you declined our repeated and even persistent invitation and went to the Hôtel de Paris, we have been convinced that you had decided not to come back to us. We could understand that cruises had a greater attraction to you than our villa, but we could not interpret your decision to stay at a hotel rather than at Pausaland in any other way than that we had done something, or behaved in a manner which prevented you from returning to us.

This was a sad conclusion we had to draw but, no matter how painful, "facts are better than dreams". Our, perhaps foolish, dream was that during the years 1956, 1957 and 1958, when you spent about a third of each year at Pausaland, we had become friends. Both Wendy and I are devoted and dedicated to the ideal of friendship which is for us the only real joy in life.

You cannot imagine how shocked we were when two years ago we suddenly remarked that all kinds of intrigues started destroying this friendship and a few months later we realized that these forces had succeeded in destroying what was a happy and lovely companionship.

It is not possible for me to describe the humiliations and sufferings we had to endure which left deep marks both in Wendy and in me. During the past two years Wendy has suffered deeply and dangerously with mental depressions. There is a certain way of disregarding other people's feelings which drives sensitive human beings to the border of insanity. I am fully aware that all of this was not intended, and that you were a victim, perhaps even more than we were.

During my long life I developed the capacity to end a big cry in laughter and today I can only smile at the past two years. How childish and unnecessary all those intrigues were, how easy it would have been to maintain our beautiful relationship and to add to it anything that might have attracted you. But Wendy is not yet capable to master a deep emotional stress and her wounds are still open. She is a different woman, disillusioned and unbelieving. The doctors warned me most seriously to let her live a quiet life and to protect her from any possible emotional stress.

You must believe me that all this makes me heartbroken and terribly unhappy. I pray that the "Pausaland atmosphere" will return, that all this nightmare will one day be forgotten and that you will enjoy again, together with us, the peace and privacy of Pausaland. But this can only return gradually, and I am very much afraid that if we precipitate matters, you may be disappointed. I want you to find here, when you return, the old and happy atmosphere and not a strained and unhappy one.

I sincerely hope that this will be possible. Should we not be able to defeat the intrigues that so unnecessarily separated us, then I am anxious to preserve the memories of our association during the years 1955–58. After all, what does one keep in life as time passes? A certain number of memories . . . I do not know what memories you have of those years, but mine are unforgettable. It was a tremendous happiness for me to be able to put at your disposal a home, a garden, a piece of sunny sky, a fireplace, Wendy's devotion—which contributed so much to your recovery after your illness and retirement. And for all this you repaid me bountifully with your incomparable company. This memory I cherish more than anything and I shall not permit anyone to destroy it.

Please forgive me for pouring out my heart to you. Probably it is a mistake. But only sincerity and frankness may dissipate all the clouds of misunderstanding and bring back the pleasures of our old friendship.

Wendy must undergo medical examinations in Paris between the 4th and 12th September. This date was fixed last June. We may have to stay longer there but, if all goes well, we shall return to Roquebrune the middle of the month. In October we are planning to go to New York. So this year, unfortunately, I cannot invite you, but I hope that if you will spend the months of

September–October at Capponcina, or some other place on the Riviera, you
will come to Pausaland as frequently as possible. And . . . And I do hope that
after this we shall be able to arrange a new reunion at Pausaland during the
Winter.

I am longing to see you and trust that we shall soon meet on the Côte
d'Azur. Should you not come down in September, I would come to London,
if you will allow me to pay you a visit.

with my very best wishes,

as ever,

yours

Emery

P.S. I have typed this letter <u>myself</u> to facilitate your reading. E.

Clementine Churchill to Wendy Russell

23 September 1960   Chartwell

I write to let you know that Winston and I and Anthony [1] will be coming
to stay at the Hôtel de Paris next Wednesday for two or three weeks.

Winston showed me Emery's letter, which had grieved him. He was surprised and sorry that you should feel the way you do. I do not think that any
good purpose would be served by debating what Emery said, but I do want
you to know that as far as we are concerned there are no intrigues; and we are
all deeply grateful for the hospitality we have enjoyed with you.

We hope that you will come to luncheon with us one day at the Hôtel
de Paris.

    1.   Anthony Montague Browne.

Sir Winston Churchill: engagement cards

28 November 1960   Chartwell

    5 p.m.   Mr. Reves.

Sir Winston Churchill to Emery Reves: telegram [1]

1 December 1960   Knightsbridge

Thank you so much for the beautiful bezique set and the fine orchids I am
so grateful to you

Winston

    1.   Reves was in London, staying at Claridge's Hotel.

Sir Winston Churchill: engagement cards

26 August 1961   La Capponcina,
                                                                      Cap d'Ail

Mr. and Mrs. Reves to dine.

Sir Winston Churchill: engagement cards

28 March 1962   28 Hyde Park Gate

Mr. and Mrs. Reves to luncheon.

Wendy Russell and Emery Reves to Sir Winston Churchill: telegram [1]

8 July 1962   Roquebrune

Our thoughts are always with you. We are sending you all our love and
heartfelt wishes for another triumphant victory.

Wendy and Emery

1.   Churchill was in the Middlesex Hospital, London, having broken his hip in a
fall at the Hôtel de Paris, Monte Carlo, on 28 June 1962, and been flown back to
London on the following day. He left the hospital for Hyde Park Gate in the third
week of August.

Sir Winston Churchill to Emery Reves and Wendy Russell: telegram

12 July 1962   London

Thank you both so much for your sympathetic message.

Winston S. Churchill

Doreen Pugh to Emery Reves

4 September 1962   28 Hyde Park Gate

Dear Mr. Reves,

So sorry to bother you, but can you tell us if Professor Eneas Camargo
of Brazil translated the HISTORY OF THE ENGLISH-SPEAKING
PEOPLES vol. 2 from English into Portuguese? He says he did and asks for
an autograph, and if he really did we think he probably deserves it. But we
thought we should check with you first.

I do hope you and Wendy are well.

Sir Winston is doing tremendously well, and has even walked, with assistance, down the steps into the garden here. He is delighted with his new
bedroom.[1]

1.   Churchill's new bedroom at Hyde Park Gate was on the ground floor.

Emery Reves to Doreen Pugh

7 September 1962   La Pausa

Dear Miss Pugh,

Thank you very much for your letter of the 4th September.

Indeed the second volume of the Brazilian edition of The History has
been translated by Mr. Eneas Camargo, the other volumes by other
translators.

This is rather an unimportant edition of the work and Sir Winston never
signed copies for his translators. I remember that he refused to do this for the
French, German and other translators of his War Memoirs who were more
important people. During the publication of the War Memoirs when I
received a great number of requests for autographed copies, he made it a rule
to sign one single copy only for each of the publishers, and nothing more.

When I saw, after a few years, how he sincerely disliked signing copies,
I stopped even that so that very few of the publishers of The History have
received a signed copy. I wonder whether a signed copy for Mr. Camargo
would not encourage others to make similar requests.

However, I must leave this entirely to you.

We are delighted to hear that Sir Winston is doing "tremendously well"
as you say, and we do hope that he will soon be fully recovered and that
unfortunate accident forgotten.

With kindest regards,
Yours very sincerely,
Emery Reves

Sir Winston Churchill: engagement cards

21 April 1963   Hôtel de Paris,
                                                        Monte Carlo

Mr. and Mrs. Reves to luncheon.

Emery Reves to Sir Winston Churchill

21 August 1963   La Pausa

My dear Sir Winston,

The other day Mrs. Rose Kennedy (the President's mother) came to
dinner, together with several of the closest personal friends of President
Kennedy.

During the conversation I learned how much the President is longing
to have a painting by you. There is nothing he would cherish more and, in
redecorating the White House, they often remarked how lovely it would be
to hang one of your paintings. But he is a very shy man in such matters and
would never ask you directly or even indirectly through one of your friends.

You know that he is one of your truly great admirers and is particularly proud for having signed the act of your Honorary Citizenship.[1]

I thought that you may like to know about this, so I am conveying to you in all confidence the gist of a table conversation.

Wendy joins me in sending you all our love and very best wishes.

Yours ever,
Emery

1.   Churchill had been made an Honorary Citizen of the United States on 8 April 1963, making him the first foreigner to be so honored since the Marquis de Lafayette in 1782 (after Lafayette had fought as a major-general throughout the American Revolutionary War).

Sir Winston Churchill to Emery Reves

24 August 1963   Chartwell

My dear Emery,

Thank you for your letter. I was glad to have news of you, and I will reflect on what you say.[1]

With good wishes to you both.

Yours very sincerely,
W S Churchill

1.   Before any decision was made about giving a Churchill painting to President Kennedy, he was assassinated (22 November 1963).

Sir Winston Churchill: engagement cards

7 December 1963   Chartwell

6 p.m.   Mr. Reves.

Sir Winston Churchill: engagement cards

19 June 1964   Chartwell

5 p.m.   Mr. Reves.

❧

Winston Churchill died in London on 24 January 1965, at the age of ninety. Emery Reves died in Switzerland on 5 September 1981, eleven days before his seventy-seventh birthday.

❧

BIOGRAPHICAL INDEX

COMPILED BY MARTIN GILBERT

Ulmanis (Latvian Prime Minister), 29
Unden (Swedish diplomat), 29
Urey, Harold Clayton, 254
Usbore, Rear-Admiral Cecil Vivian, 181, 190

Vansittart, Sir Robert (later Lord), 192, 280
Vayo, Alvarez del, 29
Victor Emmanuel III, King (of Italy), 322
Voroshilov, Marshal Klimenti, 5, 145

Wall, Miss (at Home Office), 236
Wallace, De Witt, 260, 262
Warburg, James P., 29
Ward, Dr. Stephen, 289 n.1

Watson, Arthur E., 109, 123, 143
Westminster, Second Duke of, 340–341
Weygand, General Maxime, 293
Wilde, Oscar, 90–91
Wilhelm II, Kaiser (of Germany), 77
Wilhelmina, Queen (of the Netherlands), 244
Winchell, Walter, 256
Wirth, Karl Joseph, 4
Wolf, Councillor (of German Foreign Office), 5, 6
Wood, Charles Carlisle, 363
Wycliffe, John, 82

Young, Owen D., 29

DATE DUE